SIMULATION AND EVENT MODELING
FOR GAME DEVELOPERS

JOHN P. FLYNT
BEN VINSON

THOMSON

COURSE TECHNOLOGY

Professional ■ Technical ■ Reference

ISBN: 1-59200-848-8
Library of Congress Catalog Card Number: 2005927435
Printed in Canada

05 06 07 08 09 WC 10 9 8 7 6 5 4 3 2 1

Publisher and General Manager, Thomson Course Technology PTR:
Stacy L. Hiquet

Associate Director of Marketing:
Sarah O'Donnell

Manager of Editorial Services:
Heather Talbot

Marketing Manager:
Heather Hurley

Senior Acquisitions Editor:
Emi Smith

Senior Editor:
Mark Garvey

Marketing Coordinator:
Jordan Casey

Project Editor:
Jenny Davidson

Technical Reviewer:
John Hollis

Thomson Course Technology PTR Editorial Services Coordinator:
Elizabeth Furbish

Interior Layout:
Jill Flores

Cover Designer:
Mike Tanamachi

Indexer:
Kelly Talbot

Proofreader:
Sara Gullion

THOMSON

COURSE TECHNOLOGY

Professional ■ Technical ■ Reference

Thomson Course Technology PTR,
a division of Thomson Course Technology
25 Thomson Place
Boston, MA 02210
http://www.courseptr.com

JF—This book is dedicated to its readers.

BV—This book is dedicated to my friends, family, and pals.

ACKNOWLEDGMENTS

JF and BV

Our gratitude goes to John Hollis for being smart, wise, and understanding as a technical reader and in so many other ways. To Paul Whitehead, who helped with the creation of the meshes. Likewise, to Adrian Flynt, who developed some of the art for the book. To Emi Smith and Stacy Hiquet for arranging for the publication. To Jenny Davidson for watching over the schedule.

BV

Thanks to John for having faith in me and allowing me to assist with the creation of this book.

Thanks to my friends and family for tolerating me during great times of stress and sleep deprivation. You were always able to put me in a better mood when I wasn't feeling so well.

Also, thanks to André LaMothe for creating all of his wonderful books. You are the one who got me started with game programming after all!

JF

Thanks to Bob Aaron at DeVry for support and encouragement. Thanks to Josephine Leong and others at the Savannah College of Art and Design for the opportunity to present Chapter 12 and discuss game development generally. Also, thanks to Patricia Helbig and others at SCAD for help in many ways. Thanks to Kristin Viera, Jennifer Labossiere, Drew Strawbridge, John Malone, and others from Thomson Course Technology who worked with SCAD to put together the GDX conference in Atlanta. Again, thank you Emi

Smith and Stacy Hiquet. Also, Julianne Petersen and Rajiv Malkan at the TCCTA in Austin and to Margaretha "Mary" Johnson at Kingwood College. Thanks to Nancy Birkenheuer for help and advice. To Mike Busch for being there. To Rob Johnson, Anne Halsey, and Beth Walker for advice on writing. To Charlie Allbee for mentoring.

At Front Range Community College (Larimer campus), thanks to Victoria Eisele and Phyllis Abt. At SmartDraw, thanks to Christine La Grange. At Phoenix College, thanks to Shar Halford. At Quovadx/Rouge Wave, thanks to Nicole Willson, Kevin Claver, Tim Szekely, Keith Hoaglin, Nick Gunn, Rakhi Uttamani, Raleigh Gould, Dave Noi, Boris Meltreger, Leonid Meltreger, Michelle White, Tom Troy, Keen Butterworth, Martin Sebor, Liviu Nicoara, Courtney Lane, Ravi Inampudi, Alessandro Perucchini, Jessica LeBeck, Jeremy Dean, Andrew Black, Brian Bender, Damon Zuetell, Marcia Steele, Unmesh Churi, Vikas Mehta, Giai Truong, Mohan Seripalli, Harvey Wagner, Cory Isaacson, Scott Lasica, Patrick Leonard, Chelsea Wittenbaugh, Patty Tate, Amit Jindal, Tim Adams, Nowell Outlaw, Robert Pincus, Erin Foley, and Dave Goossen.

Thanks, Ben, for being a great partner.

Thank you Marcia for your faith, love, trust, guidance, and support. Amy, thank you for everything.

ABOUT THE AUTHORS

JOHN P. FLYNT works in the software development industry and has developed requirements and design specifications for software that addresses financial and other types of simulations. He has taught at colleges and universities and has authored courses and curricula for several college-level game development programs. Among his works is *Software Engineering for Game Developers* (Thomson Course Technology, 2004). John lives in the foothills near Boulder, Colorado. He works as a software engineer for Quovadx/Rogue Wave.

BEN VINSON is a game developer and software engineer with extensive experience in development of games for multiple platforms. He has programmed many commercially successful games that have incorporated sophisticated simulation scenarios. In other respects, Ben has created training resources for teachers and students interested in simulation, and he worked with John Flynt to develop *Ankh,* the game used as the central teaching tool of *Software Engineering for Game Developers* (Thomson, 2004). Ben works for Electronic Arts and lives in Redwood City, California.

CONTENTS

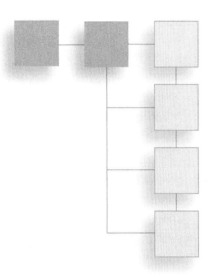

INTRODUCTION

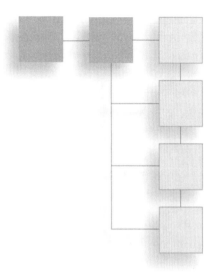

This book provides you with a starting point for understanding simulation and event modeling as a game designer, a programmer, or someone who has ambitions in both directions. The design focus of the book is on how to understand simulation and event modeling as they relate to software development for games and other types of software. The programming focus is on how to use C++ and DirectX to build applications that incorporate simulated components or draw from formally structured event models.

One of the great problems you face when you decide that you have an interest in simulation is that the books on the market tend to be either heavily laden with highly theoretical, rigorously mathematical discussions or focus on the use of simulation software that addresses very specific phenomena. While such books possess great value for experts, academics, and specialists, they often prove difficult if you are looking for a starting point for developing simulations.

This book provides a basic, technical approach to the topic that allows you to read some theory, do a little math, write code, and generally have a hands-on starter experience with simulation and event modeling. The projects the book contains can be compiled using Microsoft Visual Studio .NET (2002 and later). DirectX is used as the basis of the graphical presentations, so you can learn quite a bit about how to set up 2D and 3D applications.

This book provides you with a total of 48 separate projects that are discussed in detail and that you can use for your own starter efforts. All chapters except the first two offer accompanying software projects. Along with the code samples, you can find extensive, detailed discussions of the basic ideas behind simulation, event modeling, entity creation, world creation, and simulation testing. Lists of supplementary texts appear when applicable, but the emphasis is on keeping the tasks and topics as basic as possible so that you can master them on your own terms.

Developing software based on simulations involves embracing a philosophical perspective that in many ways marks a tremendously important transformation in how people develop and use software. As sociologist Pierre Lévy and designer Suguru Ishizaki have pointed out, the age of spectacle and static presentation is coming to an end and the age of participation has begun. Simulation and event modeling are activities that address software that is capable of regenerating itself based on information it obtains from user interactions. For this reason, the study of simulation and event modeling provides the best possible inroad to understanding how to design, program, and test such software.

The simulations the book provides tend to focus on games, so you will find several starter games you can develop with or without focusing on the lessons the book offers on simulation and event modeling. Chapter 8, "AI and Physics for Simulation," provides you with a 3D pong game that you can develop in any direction you want. Chapter 9, "Environments of Simulation," provides you with a game called *Gold Finder*, which incorporates controls, collision detection, and animated meshes. If you need a starter 3D game that you can learn how to develop, go to Chapter 9.

The first two chapters, Chapter 1, "What Is Simulation?," and Chapter 2, "Specifying Events," offer no code but provide you with a foundation for understanding the goals and priorities of simulation development. The themes these chapters provide receive attention and are expanded throughout the book. One theme that receives close attention concerns the somewhat limited definition many people give to simulation. Many people think of simulation as an activity of creating software that simply reproduces events you see out in the world. This is true enough, but simulation involves much more. Among other things, simulation allows people to participate in experiences that extend their understanding of the world far beyond anything they have encountered through direct experience.

If you have an interest in examining the technical foundations of a program or application for simulations, Chapter 3, "Designing an Application Framework," and Chapter 4, "Implementing the Framework," provide you with a solid introduction to developing applications using C++, the Win32 API, and DirectX. In the process, you also receive an introduction to the Open Dynamics Engine, which you can use for developing applications that incorporate realistic physics.

Chapter 5, "Design for Entities," and Chapter 6, "Implementing Entities," help you learn how to use DirectX to control an animated mesh. Different meshes are provided, and you see how to control their basic features. In addition to controlling the meshes, you learn about lighting and other DirectX features that enhance the display of a mesh.

Chapter 7, "Creating a World," shows you how to associate entities with events and how to place entities and events in a world. After learning how entities, worlds, and events work together to form the basis of games and simulations, you then build the framework for a 3D game.

As mentioned before, Chapter 8, "AI and Physics for Simulation," provides you with a complete game. The game is a form of pong that uses bouncing blocks and platforms placed at different levels. You implement a scoreboard and other features that add to the game's appeal. The game incorporates functions from the Open Dynamics Engine, so when entities collide as a part of the game, you are able to apply things like gravity and torque to them.

The game you develop in Chapter 9, which receives the title of *Gold Finder*, allows you to fully explore a complete game architecture. You work with an animated mesh that you can navigate using arrow keys. Collision detection allows you to impede the movements of the character and change the animations you associate with it. Anyone who knows an early version of *DOOM* will enjoy tinkering with this game.

In Chapter 10, "Simulation of Physical Systems," you create a simulation of a forest fire. The simulation code is simple enough that you can easily adapt it for other purposes. Working with a simulation of this type allows you to understand the tasks at hand without being overwhelmed by mathematical or scientific details. Given a starter project like the forest fire model, however, you can build in details that reflect your depth of involvement in your subject of study and your level of mathematical expertise.

What Chapter 10 does for a model that relates to the physical environment, Chapter 11 does for a social and economic environment. A scenario familiar to many people features a large store that moves into a community and runs many of its small stores out of business. Using this phenomenon, you create a model of a small economic and social system. By adjusting the data you submit to the model, you change the behavior of the system.

In Chapter 12, "Testing Simulations and Event Models," you have a chance to investigate in detail how to test an application using a cognitive model. Toward this end, this book provides you with an application called *Inspect*. You employ *Inspect* to examine data you generate from sessions of play involving *Gold Finder*, the game you develop in Chapter 9. The chapter includes discussions of cognitive science, hermeneutics, and systems theory as applied to understanding how simulations and games engage their audiences. The concept of "cognitive saturation" is dealt with in detail. *Inspect* is programmed with C#. The project and all the source code are included, and you can easily adapt it to explore its algorithms and alter them for your own purposes.

This book will not turn you into a world-class simulation developer, but by the time you finish working through it, you will be able to understand the primary objectives of simulation as applied to games and other software applications, and you will have at hand a substantial amount of code that you can experiment with as you develop simulations on your own.

Obtaining the Code for the Book

It is essential that you obtain the code for the book if you want to fully benefit from the chapters that discuss code. To obtain the code, access www.courseptr.com/downloads and enter the title of the book.

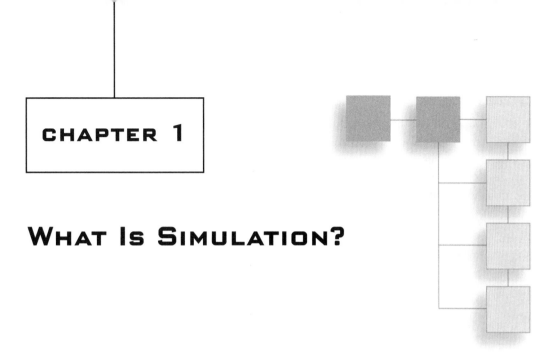

CHAPTER 1

WHAT IS SIMULATION?

Most people understand simulation as an activity of making one thing look or act like another. Simulation developers are viewed as people who closely study real-world events and then create programs that imitate them. While this notion about simulation proves true and pervasive, it remains that simulation holds much greater potentials as a medium for *regenerating experience*. Regeneration of experience involves equipping people to extend and broaden experience, often without reference to imitated or original events.

Successful simulation involves event modeling. Understanding event modeling requires that you investigate a wide variety of topics that extend from philosophy to specific topics of the hard sciences. A topic closely related to event modeling is event mapping. Many maps might stem from a single model. When you create a map of events, you concentrate on different types of events. You can regard some as objective. Others you can regard as subjective. The discussion eventually extends to the notion of how you narrate events. One topic of interest is plotless narration. The topics unfold almost endlessly. Here are a few that this chapter explores:

- What simulations are used for
- Subjective and objective simulation models
- What makes a good simulation
- The pragmatics of communication
- Creating event models
- Storytelling and persuasion
- The importance of interaction
- Cognitive saturation

Groundwork

If you think of simulation as creating an "artificial experience" that imitates a "real experience," then your view corresponds to the most generally accepted notions about what simulation involves. A flight simulator, for example, creates an experience on a desktop that resembles what you might experience if you were in the cockpit of a plane. You vicariously practice flying.

The scope of a simulation can extend so far as to be almost incomprehensible. In the version of flight simulation Microsoft developers created, for example, you can practice taking off and landing at practically any airport on Earth.

Flight simulation encompasses but one of a multitude of pathways simulation software has followed. Here is a short list:

- **Training.** Training needs address almost all academic and professional areas. The purpose of such applications often involves allowing students to perform repetitive or rote tasks that enable them to solidify their understanding of different bodies of knowledge.

- **Entertainment.** Simulations provide visual spectacles for movies and computer games. The success of games depends on progressively more realistic simulations. At the same time, the effect simulation has had on action films has been extraordinary. Such simulation often follows an *as if* scenario. Rather than imitation of the known universe, the developers seek to model a universe that exists in an imaginary (*as if*) context.

- **Industrial testing.** Simulations for testing provide an invaluable service to industries of all types. Developers transfer the characteristics of chemicals, metals, people, animals, plastics and almost anything you might imagine to software models. Using the models, they can view the behaviors of their products in a wide variety of contexts without having to go to the expense of using actual or live specimens or of repeatedly setting up different laboratory configurations. While laboratories still provide empirical confirmation of the simulations, software significantly decreases the overall expense of operations.

- **Therapy.** Simulations provide rich potentials to aid psychologists, cognitive scientists, neurologists, psychiatrists, and many other health and medical researchers and practitioners as they explore ways to better human life. Among many other applications, computer simulation can aid people with disabilities and illnesses in a vast number of ways.

- **Experimentation and research.** Scientists develop simulations to conduct experiments and further research. The models they create can incorporate a vast number of variables. While an experiment might involve the performance of a physical operation, the computer simulation of the experiment allows the scientist to explain how a large number of factors play into the observable result.

- **Commerce.** Businesses develop simulations for a variety of purposes. Such simulations can be used to develop models of customer behaviors and needs. They can serve as tools for refining sales and service techniques. They can serve to enhance the understanding managers have of business organizations.

The simulation industry represents enormous revenues and millions of participants. So pervasive has the role of simulation software become that almost everyone who lives in an industrialized nation has had direct experience with it in one way or another.

Expanding the View

To say that simulation creates an "artificial experience" that imitates a "real experience" is only part of the story. Generally, a successful simulation has its own life, and many people who participate in simulations have little or no concern with whether the experience the simulation provides anticipates another "real" experience. In this respect, simulation involves, rather than anticipation or imitation, *participation*.

It is possible to go so far as to say that a successful simulation ultimately depends less on its capacity to imitate than its capacity to fulfill. Developers of simulations seek to immerse you in an environment, imaginary or imitative, and the result of this immersion is an experience that fully satisfies your expectations in the context of events the simulation provides.

Effective simulations allow you to develop the capacity to create and extend experience for yourself. Your experience goes beyond imitation. It provides you with capabilities to immerse yourself in, extend, construct, and create the world that the simulation allows you to enter.

Object and Subject

Software simulations that seek to immerse you in an experience provide *subjective* simulation experiences. Software simulations that allow you to understand a phenomenon as an observer provide *objective* simulation experiences. Whether a simulation emerges as subjective or objective depends to a great extent on whether you apply some rather arbitrary terms to your analysis of the simulation you have elected to study. In the end, you can probably find that any given simulation possesses both objective and subjective factors. However, it does not hurt to establish some fairly definitive categories at the start of a discussion of simulation to make it possible to distinguish the varying ends developers seek as they construct simulations.

Figure 1.1 illustrates associations that might be established among a few of the terms that surface in discussions of simulation. These terms receive extensive discussion throughout this book.

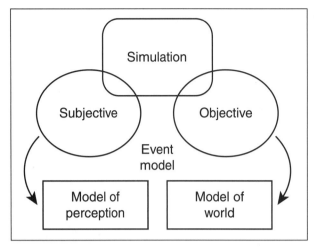

Figure 1.1 Simple terms begin the discussion.

When a simulation falls into the subjective category, it extends what might be considered a primarily personal and arbitrary experience. When a simulation falls into the objective category, it extends what might be viewed as a public and experimentally verifiable experience.

Both subjective and objective simulations draw upon event models. You can view an event model as the collection of events that those who create a simulation decide constitutes the domain of the model. A domain is something akin to a playing field of possibilities. Consider, for example, the event model for a rat in a maze. As Figure 1.2 illustrates, you can reduce the experiential dimensions of the rat's interactions with the maze to a set of turns that correspond to the cardinal directions of the compass. The event model for this world, then, consists of the pathways the maze provides and the set of events that transpire as the mouse moves through the maze.

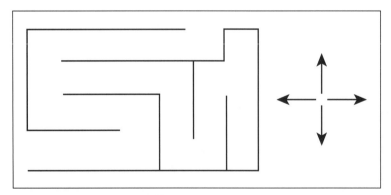

Figure 1.2 An event model limits interactions.

An event model collects events that you consider legitimate, realistic, ethical, or in some other way appropriate within the setting, experience, or phenomenon the event model addresses. In the context of systems theory, an event model consists of the rules and actions that constitute the system. This topic receives much more discussion in Chapter 2, "Specifying Events."

Models Drawn from Perception

An event model originates with your perceptions of the world. Specific aspects of your perceptions might include such qualities as heightened color sensitivity, acute hearing, sensitivity to light, a refined sense of touch, color blindness, extremely acute perceptions of detail, blindness, myopia, or dyslexia. All such conditions are relative to your ways of perceiving and are so varied and numerous that they prove impossible to definitively name. For some people perceptions underlie artistic creativity; for others, they constitute troublesome obstacles to psychological health.

If you can look at a row of trees along a river or road and discern the genus and species of each tree, your perceptions differ from those of someone who looks at the trees as a mass of undifferentiated greenery. If a person lacks the knowledge that field botany provides, such ignorance probably proves relative, however. An artist who paints a picture that features the trees and brings their images into an aesthetically rich vision might not know the names of the trees but can still appreciate them in a deeply rewarding way.

A simulation can address perception because it allows you to engage in an experience that ultimately defies confinement to a strictly defined set of objectives or goals. Imagine a simulation that involves looking at trees. What end could you assign to this activity? Obviously, you might address the activity of either the painter or the botanist. You might address many other perspectives as well.

Perception might be viewed along the lines Aristotle once presented when he tried to explain how vision works. He described vision as a kind of projection, somewhat along the lines of a flashlight. As wrong as this explanation might be in terms of optics, it remains that it retains some virtue as an explanation of how it is that what people see acquires meaning. What people perceive depends on understanding and sensitivity. As another philosopher put it, what you see depends on what you can see.

Models Drawn from the World

Models of the world, like the rat's maze, provide you with a set of actions and events that limit or shape what you perceive. Models allow you to account for some type of phenomena. When game designers design games, they usually work from a model. The model establishes the sequence of events that leads from the beginning to the end of the proposed game. The sequence of events might comprise a large set of alternative courses of events, but it remains that the model accounts for them all.

When scientists want to study almost any natural event, be it the growth of a cancer cell or the eruption of a volcano, they create an objective model. Such a model consists of a collection of explicitly defined, experimentally verifiable events. Among many other things, these events might be chemical formulas, chemical reactions, or mathematical equations. The model allows the scientists to relate these events to each other so that they can explain a complex phenomenon.

The objective universe provides countless occasions for modeling. When you model phenomena objectively, your approach differs from that of someone seeking a purely subjective, perceptual approach to experience. Certainly, what you are up to still involves perception, and ultimately everything is probably subjective, but when you seek to model the world in objective terms, you do so with an eye to public discourse and public channels of examination, experimentation, and verification.

An artist painting a row of trees does not have an obligation to explain his or her techniques of painting to those who view the painting. The artist does not create the painting as an object that he or she expects others to be able to precisely re-create. The situation differs with a scientist endeavoring to explain some event in nature. He or she must specify the precise conditions under which an experiment is performed and provide others with the information they require to repeat the experiment for themselves.

Criteria for Simulation

You mode events to create a simulation, and a simulation provides you with a way to construct and extend experiences. You construct and extend experience subjectively or objectively. When you extend experience subjectively, you can view your adventure as something like a rich dream that lingers with you as you arise from a deep sleep. While the dream's meaning might be largely beyond the capacities of others to comprehend, it remains that you can draw upon the memories you have of the dream to interpret your waking thoughts. The psychologist Jung contended that the interpretation of dreams constitutes an essential aspect of psychological health.

In contrast, when you extend experience objectively, you do so using an explicit model that you can explain in great detail to others, allowing them to re-create the same experience you have had.

Even with the differences between these two general divisions of simulation, it remains that a large number of common factors characterize them. Consider the following, among others:

- **Realism.** Realism consists of the quality of resembling everyday experience. If a game realistically simulates climbing a mountain, then at points you expect to see great precipices, glaciers, crevasses, and other features of a mountain familiar to climbers or those who have watched climbing films. On the other hand, realism does not concern only what a mountain looks like. It concerns the psychological aspects of the experience of climbing. An effective simulation induces the feeling of immediate involvement, facing a challenge, feeling fear or confidence, happiness or sadness, being lost in a blinding snowstorm, or sensing the weariness of a long climb up a face. Climbing a mountain presents a vastly complex experience that ultimately reaches into every aspect of your psyche.

- **Fulfillment.** Simulation can create experiences that are not possible through direct experience. Consider, for example, being in the depths of space. Such an experience lies beyond the means of almost everyone living. Using images from the Hubble telescope, however, you can simulate such an experience. You can, among other things, look deep into space at distant galaxies or more locally at a planet in the solar system. The experience you derive from the visions you see provides you with a sense of fulfillment that far exceeds anything you can hope to achieve through direct means.

- **Cognitive complexity.** Both objective and subjective simulations accommodate and foster cognitive complexity. When you create a vastly complex model to map weather patterns, the number of variables and functions you include to manipulate your model might easily number in the tens of thousands. When you create a vastly complex model of a social system, you can vividly consolidate into one massive model a thousand aspects of the human condition (suffering, joy, starvation, satiation, fear, anger, and so on) that are beyond the lone capacity of almost any individual to know. The model provides a framework in which to structure complexity. The work of the model is to simulate the event the complexity generates.

- **Interactivity.** One of the greatest potentials simulations offer involves allowing their users to interact with them. Among other possibilities, interaction can consist of being entertained or being able to exert control over events. With respect to entertainment, for example, a simulation might be said to offer greater interactive potentials because it can be extended to controls that allow you to dynamically alter its cinematography and plot, among other features. You can control the angle of the camera, the events that unfold in front of the camera, the lighting, the dialogue, the perspective—everything that the domain of the simulation comprises. Interactivity allows you to participate in the experience the simulation fosters in an instrumental way.

Pragmatics

When you interact with a simulation, how you interact shapes and defines your perspective. When you play a computer game that simulates basketball, the play absorbs your attention and at moments seems to totally immerse you in the perspective of the player. You can see the opponents on the floor. You prepare to take a shot. A guard comes directly at you, obstructing your shot. But you remain limited in many ways from completely entering into the world of the player.

Games tend to incorporate a variety of perspectives. You select shots from tables. You select team plays using diagrams. You can organize teams, configure players, set plays, and manage public relations. The instructions you receive direct you to manipulate data or select options. You are not yet in a position of entering into a matrix-like framework where the camera, as such, resides in your mind.

One realization that might arise from this situation involves the pragmatics of communication. The basic idea behind pragmatics involves how people interact with each other. Generally, from a pragmatic perspective, the individual subject is both autonomous and dependent. An autonomous person can make decisions independently of the influence of others. On the other hand, the individual's decisions usually occur in a context that others create and to a great extent depend on the influence of others. See Figure 1.3.

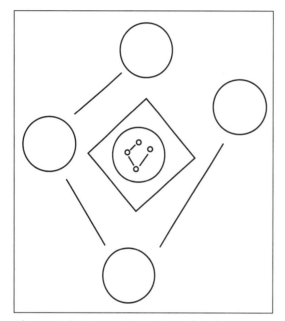

Figure 1.3 Communication is mediated.

The event model you create for a simulation ultimately involves an experiment in the pragmatics of communication. The experiment is one that resembles that of someone who communicates with others and then, at some point, decides to draw back and assess the meaning of the communications. Isolated, the meaning of the communications seems to differ from what existed as the communications were taking place.

What arises from this situation is analogous to the Heisenberg Uncertainty Principle. According to this principle, named after Werner Heisenberg, when you are trying to determine the precise position of a subatomic particle, the more precisely you determine the particle's position, the less precisely you will be able to determine the particle's momentum.

This notion can be transferred to a general systems context if you consider that whenever you study or in any way interact with a system, you change it. In this respect, then, it is not possible to participate in a system in any purely objective way because you cannot stand outside the system. Likewise, in the context of communications, when you draw back and consider in isolation something that emerged in a context of dialogue, you discover different meanings.

When you communicate an idea, your actions tend not to be defined solely by performance. See Figure 1.4. You do not stand upon a stage, isolated from others. Instead, the act of communication shapes the message communicated. In fact, the act of communicating shapes the speaker.

The pragmatics of communications provides an approach to understanding why simulation can fail. A computer simulation provides potentials for both complementing and stifling communications. When you interact, if you change what you interact with, then you participate in a system. But then, if you interact with a system, the system also changes you.

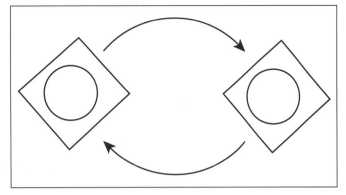

Figure 1.4 To shape is to be shaped.

Applying Models Objectives

As much as it might be said that all simulations possess strongly subjective characteristics, it remains that ostensibly objective simulation accounts for the vast majority of simulation exercises performed each day using software. Objective simulations put the participant outside the immediate context of simulation. Even in this situation, the simulation has vast pragmatic potentials. It can serve as a tool that allows the developer of a model to interactively perfect the model by repeatedly testing it through the simulation.

Economists, biologists, medical researchers, sociologists, physicists, environmental scientists, systems theorists, disease control experts, military planners, and a multitude of other experts develop simulation software to test models of events. In many cases, the goals these modelers set for themselves entail creating models that can account for or generate data sets that precisely correspond to what they observe in nature.

Such simulations have enormous value because they constitute a primary way that people involved in scientific exploration can test and refine their theories. A theory is a model, and simulation offers an interactive, self-critical approach to developing a model. When model builders translate their models into simulations, the simulations generate data that allows the model builders to become critical of their models in particularly fruitful ways.

The more easily you can generate data to test your model, the more information you have to evaluate and improve your model. Repeated exploration of a model through simulation puts you in a position to progressively adjust the parameters of your model until the data it generates precisely mirrors the data you gather from naturally occurring phenomena. If the data generated by your model resembles what you observe in nature, you are not therefore guaranteed that you have correctly reconstructed a process occurring in nature; however, the correspondence of your data set to the one that nature provides certainly does not constitute an undesirable outcome.

Focal Points

Objective simulation puts the participant outside the simulation but at the same time serves the same role as subjective simulation, for it extends experience. After all, a model represents experience, even if the experience modeled has been formalized. Given the pervasiveness with which simulation can complement and extend experience, one particularly widespread use of simulation is training.

Professionals involved with rescue, military, medical, and other activities characterized by high-intensity, one-time operations use simulators to allow trainees to practice critical tasks in a cyclic, self-critical way. Repetition constitutes a key element in such simulators. Human trainers can lead people through exercises and provide close, intensive coaching. In fact, they work best as coaches. But when people who are in training require repeated experiences to solidify their understanding or tone their performances, simulators often provide a preferable alternative to human trainers. While the repetitive, rote exercises that a simulator easily handles often exhausts human trainers, such repetitive, rote exercises may be precisely what trainees require to become proficient at the tasks that their jobs entail.

Simulations automate a large number of activities that human trainers engaged with many trainees can handle in only a marginal way. Sometimes the activities seem almost insignificant but nevertheless prove essential to successful training efforts. Almost everyone has had the experience of watching a coach stand at the edge of a field with a clipboard recording times. Such activity characterizes almost any type of training, whether it is of athletes, pilots, soldiers, nurses, doctors, or bank tellers. Trainers gauge the suitability of candidates on the basis of performance data. Practice sessions amount to simulations.

Simulation software coupled with the appropriate interactive equipment can easily and accurately collect performance data. Using this data, trainers can fine-tune their individualized training sessions so that trainees receive maximum benefits.

With respect to computer games, consider what the simulated driving sessions in *Grand Theft Auto* do for you as a player. When you are able to again and again practice making sharp turns or avoiding collisions, your skills as a player improve, and with this your capacity to successfully overcome the obstacles the game presents. Most successful, enduring games have incorporated tutorials that involve simulations. One interesting aspect of such training is that while some of the simulations incorporate extremely realistic physics, others pursue an equally interesting project of training you to work with the *unreality* the game offers.

Regardless of the directions they take as vehicles for training, simulations tend to provide fruitful results because they can furnish continuously changing scenarios into the training context. Changing scenarios constitute one of the most valuable aspects of simulation.

Simulation and Complexity

Both objective and subjective simulations tend to be selective in the phenomena they explore. A game might ultimately offer only a very limited set of events. This course of events can still remain highly absorbing for the player, however. The reason this occurs rests with the center of attention that the game sustains. The center of attention the player adopts proves successful when it can change to reflect the goals, interests, and skills of the player.

The key to success in this respect requires a development effort that seeks the opposite of what might result if you were to pursue simulation only as a project involving the addition of realistic details. Instead, success hinges on selectively hiding details and in some ways undermining or subverting realism.

Successful computer applications selectively hide complexity. They hide complexity that does not relate to the work (or play) users of the application engage in during their sessions with the application. Consider, for example, an application that aids designers of airplanes to develop wings and other features of aircraft. The developers of such an application are likely to conceal complexity that relates to generating graphical images or storing specifications. On the other hand, they are likely to fully expose users to ways of using mathematics to purse objectives related to the development of aerodynamically sound components. Table 1.1 profiles in a simple way a few application development contexts.

Architecture, Exposure, Concealment

A simulation is like any other computer application. It hides complexity relative to the user's needs and preferences. When an application hides complexity, it narrows the way you interact with the constituent processes and data the application presents. In Table 1.1, for example, the professional photo developer seeks ends that differ from those of the home photo developer. The ends the professional pursues relate to the core knowledge the professional developer possesses. This person may be trained in graphical design or graphics arts and might use photographs as a starting place for the development of ads. The home user, in contrast, seeks the photo as an end in itself. Standard formats and easy-to-apply procedures constitute this home user's primary concerns.

To narrow the ways users interact with applications, developers of computer applications have tended to standardize their approaches to understanding the architecture of applications. If you read almost any publication that addresses the software development community, you find after a time that developers have reduced application components to a few categories. Figure 1.5 illustrates a selection of these categories.

Table 1.1 Application Priorities

User	Discussion
Operating room doctors	An application monitors heart rates during operations. It is highly unlikely that a doctor would want to interact with the application in any way other than to see the heart rate information displayed in a clearly visible real-time manner.
Auto mechanics	An application assesses cylinder combustion pressures. It is not likely that the mechanics want to struggle with interpreting numerical output. They want to see high, low, and acceptable categories. But on the other hand, they want to adjust the application to indicate the type of engine being tested.
General authors	An application allows them to create mathematical formulas and then to easily insert them into texts. They do not need to generate results using the formulas, but they want to easily and accurately depict and transfer the formulas.
Auto racing game	Players drive a car along various types of race courses, most of them modeled on famous races around the world. The player is interested in the realism of the scenery but does not want lessons in geography.
Authors of math books	An application allows authors to set up mathematical formulas and then apply the formulas to problems. They want to work the formulas they write, and they want to be able to incorporate the results of their work in problems in texts they are writing.
A home photo processor	An application allows users to transfer photos from a digital camera to a computer and then to size and print the photos. Users want standard photos suitable for albums.
Professional photo developer	An application that allows users to transfer photos from a digital camera to a computer and then to process the photos in a variety of ways to achieve both standard formatting ends and artistic effects. Users want to create all sorts of effects for commercial uses.

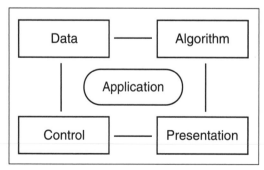

Figure 1.5 Encapsulated services conceal the complexity of the application you use.

Information the application uses usually falls under the rubric of data. The information your application uses can vary in enormous ways. You might use flat files containing ASCII text data. You might use binary files containing graphical images. You might make use of voice recordings, meshes, sprite images, or music. The extent of the resources you use can become enormous, encompassing gigabytes of data for a single game or simulation.

Included with the data is the ability to determine whether the data is valid. Along with concerns for correctness, you also face issues of speed and security of access. Do you have to search for a specific file name, with the assumption that you know what the file contains? Or do you ask for the information you want, without ever having to worry about what the names of the files that contain the information might be? What if you are developing a multi-tier online application that caters to users with different access permissions? How do you control such data? The questions go on.

The algorithms that process the information the application uses embody the intelligence of the application. Most applications combine a multitude of tasks that range from filtering data to generating graphical images, but it remains that you can design an application so that it accords in look and feel to the type of processing that is most central to it. Consider a word processor. On the other hand, consider collision detection in a game. With the word processor, correcting grammar or spelling might be fully exposed to the user. With the game, collision detection might be completely concealed.

Information must be represented to be meaningful. The representation or display of information has to do with the level of interpretation you apply to it and what you want to do with it. Consider, for example, the data contained in a table. Microsoft Excel provides you with a large number of charting options. Each depicts the data in the table differently. Each such representation conveys the meaning of the data in a different way, one that can be understood in a different mode of logic. Such views ensure both that the same person can see the data in different ways and that different audiences, with different ways of reasoning and different priorities, have access to the data in a way that for them proves meaningful. This primary feature of all representation often creates a nemesis for both simulation and game developers. Choosing the wrong medium for representing data can create havoc or alienate players.

A final point involves the use of controls. Controls guide your activity as you use an application. They are your inroad to participation. Studies of how to make an application accessible to its users fall under the heading of Human Computer Interaction, and an enormous amount of literature has developed on this topic. Studying how and why computer applications follow the conventions that they currently follow involves investigating a long and twisted history that reaches back to the first days of computer history. However, the fact remains that a subtle set of restrictions apply to what you can and cannot do with an application.

If you can draw a general lesson from considering the architectural features of an application, it might be that exposing complexity tends to be a subtle undertaking, one that requires both science and art. In many respects, every chapter in this book investigates the hazards and advantages of developing one or another architectural feature. Ultimately, every implementation involves a balancing of exposure and concealment.

Tradeoffs

The general perspective on hiding complexity leads to the problem of how to effectively model events. Ultimately, when people negotiate their day-to-day lives, they do so through implicit event models. Such models might lack precise logic or rationally established objectives, but they nevertheless represent some of the most stable and universal faces of human existence. People get through life by learning how to ignore most of what is happening in the world and concentrating on what is close at hand.

Some anthropologists contend that most people function in a semi-conscious, trance-like state. A trance in this respect consists of a restricted field of understanding that allows you to see as sensible, perceptible, and important only what corresponds to the goals and priorities that you have set in your own life.

Such an understanding of human consciousness reflects the general perspective maintained by phenomenology. As is pointed out in greater detail in Chapter 2, "Specifying Events," the perspective sustained by phenomenology stipulates that all experience is *mediated*. Understanding mediates experience. Understanding is, in fact, the capacity an individual possesses to create meaningful experience.

As abstract as this discussion might seem, it still does much to explain why games and simulation applications fail. When people who invest in a computer application find that its features do not address their interests, they often want their money back. People pay for an application that allows them to extend their experience, and this activity begins with the understanding that people bring to the applications they purchase. They use what they know to explore what they do not know. The application is a means to this end.

Heuristics

Hiding complexity involves creating an application that centers on the user of the application rather than any of the architectural features of a computer application. When you interact with an application on your own terms, you derive the benefits offered by what the sociologist Pierre Levy has characterized as a "collective" intelligence. Collective in this context applies to the way that a computer application brings knowledge into view for the individual user *on the user's own terms*. It filters data according to the needs of the user. Levy makes the following observation:

> Rather than distributing a message to recipients who are outside the process of creation and invited to give meaning to a work of art belatedly, the artist now attempts to construct an environment, a system of communication and production, a collective event that implies its recipients, transforms interpreters into actors, enables interpretation to enter the loop with collective action.
>
> Pierre Levy, *Collective Intelligence* (Perseus Books: Cambridge, MA, 1997, p. 123).

New interactions can occasion frustration. This is especially so when the developers of an application you might be interacting with have designed it in a way, to use Levy's expression, that leaves you "outside the process of creation." The frustration results from having to go outside the normal structure of your experience. You must learn according to patterns the developers of the application have established, not according to patterns that extend your own understanding in a consonant way.

When you consider what to hide as you develop a simulation, you should first establish an understanding of what your users expect. This topic has already received some discussion previously in this chapter, but it is important to emphasize that application users, like application developers, want to concentrate on what they do best. Within the realm of what they do best, they establish practices that allow them to easily move from the familiar to the strange. Analysts refer to this as a *heuristic*. Every activity has at hand a heuristic. Successful simulation involves keeping this notion at the center of the development effort.

When an application associates familiar contexts of activity with irritatingly strange heuristics, it destroys its own potentials, for it does not effectively extend experience through experience. One way to picture this might be to consider a scenario involving someone engaged in a simulation that features a ship on a sea. Where you sail in the ship might be endless, extending to every ocean or waterway on earth. To sail the ship, you manipulate the sails. Your skills improve. You sail to different places. The heuristic becomes a means to navigating into strange places and learning new things. But suppose that at some point, after mastering the knowledge and skills of seamanship, you are suddenly forced to abandon the ship and take to some other means of transportation? The result could be that the entire undertaking becomes thrown out of context. From learning through skills, you suddenly find yourself learning only skills.

Simulation and Plotless Interaction

Heuristics relates to story telling. A story teller uses techniques—patterns of telling. As much as simulations imply heuristics and heuristics implies patterns, it is likely that critics of game aesthetics will eventually decide that simulation subverts classical story telling. In this respect, it might be that the kind of thinking you do as you contemplate simulation ultimately presents the potential to subvert a good deal of the current wisdom regarding how to design and construct computer games.

This remains to be seen, but even if you dismiss the more radical perspectives respecting the potentials simulation offers, you can still benefit if you pause to consider that a difference exists between classical forms of story telling and what happens when you create a simulation. A simulation does not tell a story. Instead, it creates the capacity to create, find, or explore stories.

For the most part, computer game designers have inherited much of what they profess to know about story telling from the film industry. The film industry has inherited what it knows about story telling from the theater and cinematography.

What arises from this history is that you hear much about games as interactive films. Designers who present this perspective often talk about choices, challenges, and destinations. The talk is relative to a plot. (See Figure 1.6.)

Figure 1.6 Simulation subverts current assumptions about story telling and interactive films.

Computer game developers have adopted almost every imaginable technique they can from the film industry. A central aspect of this adoption of techniques involves the role of the plot. A plot consists of a carefully planned, carefully implemented course of events that guides the game player or film spectator through the story the game or film offers. Along the way, the heuristics through which the adventure takes place are implicit in the way the film is directed, filmed, and embodied in the performances of the actors. Generally, this approach to experience might be viewed as *plotted interaction*.

When you view games as interactive films, you can easily miss the significance of simulation. Simulation is actually a wholly different undertaking. It involves, among other things, what might be viewed as plotless interaction.

Rhetoric and Persuasion

Plotless interaction takes a little explaining. One approach to understanding why simulation involves more than following a plot stems from notions that artists, speakers, entertainers, and others have developed over the centuries stemming at least since the time of Socrates. The notions constitute what is generally known as the study of *rhetoric,* which is the art or science of *persuasion.*

The first significant treatise on rhetoric resulted from the teachings of Aristotle. Since Aristotle left it to his students to record his lectures, his surviving works consist of notes his students took down and transformed into books. One such book is referred to as the *Rhetoric*. In this work, Aristotle explains that the art of persuasion can be a powerful, even dangerous practice. It can be dangerous because it allows an effective speaker to lead large groups of people to accept falsehoods. On the other hand, it is necessary for the good of the state, for philosophers, judges, statesmen, and stateswomen must be in a position to effectively define *beliefs*.

At the heart of what Aristotle discussed is the notion that your task as an orator (one who practices rhetoric) is to persuade people to accept some type of belief. You can view belief as something akin to a structure of understanding or a way of interpreting things. When an orator persuades you to believe that things happen in a given way, then you begin to understand what you hear according to this belief. (See Figure 1.7.)

If you study the history of film, you can find without much trouble that the vast majority of film directors and producers who lived during the twentieth century embraced the ideas Aristotle proposed. At the heart of a successful mainstream film is whether it induces its viewers to

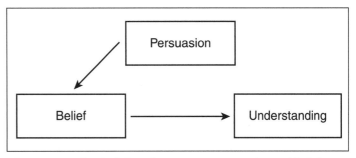

Figure 1.7 Classical rhetoric centers on persuasion and belief.

embrace a belief or set of beliefs. The belief or set of beliefs allows you to suspend your own beliefs, whatever they might be, so that at least temporarily you can surrender yourself to the plotting or mapping of events the film offers.

Interpretation and Simulation

Games have tended, like films, to follow the path Aristotle charted. The texts now beginning to emerge on theory and criticism of computer game aesthetics tend to accept without question that a game is primarily a means of persuasion. It remains, however, that other approaches are at hand to explain games.

As Figure 1.8 illustrates, at the heart of this alternative perspective is the notion that meaning arises as much from *participation* as from belief. Participation can be viewed as almost the opposite of persuasion. When you gain understanding through participation rather than beginning with belief, you begin with what amounts to plotless interaction.

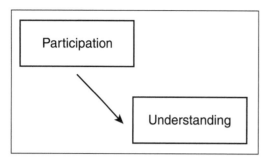

Figure 1.8 Simulation centers on participation and exploration.

What you derive from the experience of plotless interaction depends, not on the application of belief but on the exercise of heuristic exploration and *interpretation*. Your explorations render you a multitude of meanings, and the meanings you derive from the explorations allow you to find significance in what you do, not because it reinforces belief, but because you find in the experience a pure medium for extending experience.

Applied Event Modeling

If the discussion of how persuasion and participation differ from each other proves a little too abstract to easily assimilate without huge questions, a closer view of the practical aspects of creating a simulation based on participation rather than persuasion tends to do much to clear things up.

If you begin with the assumption that your goal as a designer or developer is to create contexts of participation, then you are in an excellent position to derive a great deal from working with simulations.

Whether from the objective or the subjective view point, you can understand a simulation as an experience that creates and extends experience. Rather than trying to persuade an audience, you face the task of inducing an audience to begin to involve itself in what amounts to a wholly open (plotless) system of interaction. You are, in essence, asking your audience to create their own story. The central activity simulation supports is interaction. Toward this end, the next few sections discuss some of the primary activities involved in planning interaction. Here are the central notions:

- Establishes goals
- Sets out maps
- Stages events to mark the map
- Provides incentives
- Induces learning

Figure 1.9 provides an overview of the sections that follow.

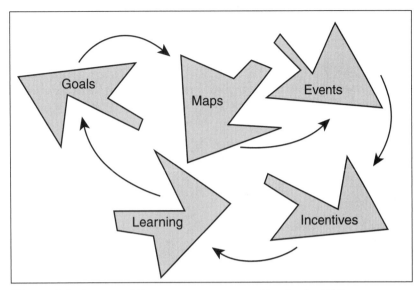

Figure 1.9 Event modeling encompasses several involved activities.

Goal Discovery

It is easy to forget that a visual experience depends on the viewer as much as the techniques and technology that create the visual experience. This is especially easy to forget if you have worked endless hours trying to create a multitude of fascinating visual effects. DirectX and other 3D libraries embody enormous capabilities. You can begin to believe that the use of these capabilities alone guarantees a successful application. If you follow this path, it is not very likely that you will arrive at a satisfying end. The reason is simple. The experience a computer application offers begins with the person who interacts with it, and the goals this person sustains almost always define the type of experience that results. Goals shape perceptions because people see what has meaning relative to their goals. (See Figure 1.10.)

Some sociologists, psychologists, and anthropologists go so far as to contend that goals guide all human perception, and perception guides behavior. A goal can he viewed as a center of gravity, point of curiosity, a way of questioning, or anything that in some way leads you to search for new information in a given way. A goal usually leads you to establish a set of assumptions or a general disposition that guides your behavior. You usually decide, in light of a goal, to confine your activities to a restricted context that the goal allows you to acquire information in what you regard as a fruitful way.

When you confine your activities to a context that a goal defines, you usually explain your actions and offer interpretations in terms of your goal. You likewise explain your goal in terms of the specific activities you perform as you seek the goal.

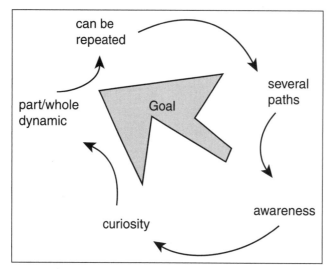

Figure 1.10 Goals provide inducements to chart paths.

Goal-shaped behavior tends to take on its own logic, so that it gains in coherence and meaning the longer you sustain it. You find ways to perfect activities you find meaningful in the light of a goal. The goal justifies adopting routines (heuristics). For this reason, people who have cognitive perspectives on thinking and acting often emphasize the importance of goals in shaping cognition.

In other respects, goal-shaped activities possess an ethical dimension. People set goals so that they can do things in what they regard as the best possible way. When you seek the best way to do things, one implication of your goal is that you compare your goal with the goals of others. You consider what you do in a generalized context.

It remains, however, that a goal need not extend to a universal framework of activity. After all, it might be that people engage in an activity because it is, for them, something deeply personal. Such a goal might be viewed as characterizing an activity itself rather than an objective lying beyond the activity.

Map Making

A map is a formalized way of assessing the awareness that can arise given the assumption of a goal. If you assume, for example, that you set a goal for yourself and then engage in a set of experiments to discover the best path to your goal, tracking the possible paths involves creating maps. When you create a map, you generalize and summarize. A map is not the path itself; rather, it is a way to understand, remember, and reconstruct the path. (See Figure 1.11.)

Maps offer you a way to understand that different paths lead to different goals. It might be the case that you decide that a given goal brings with it no one best path of reaching the goal. It might be that you find that you can enhance the satisfaction you feel about attaining a given goal if you diversify the ways you reach the goal. A map allows you to trace all such situations.

Consider a basketball player who can make a lay-up, shoot from inside, shoot from outside, or make a trick shot. Each specific path brings satisfaction with the game. The paths together, however, provide a wider, more encompassing understanding of satisfaction. A map reminds the player of the multitude of paths that any given goal affords.

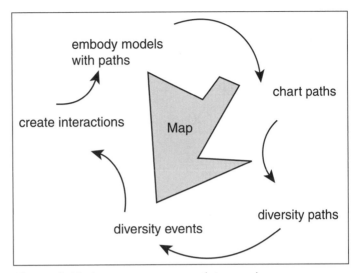

Figure 1.11 A map represents a path to a goal.

Some people set a goal of finding diverse paths to a goal. This endeavor involves discovering events that might lie along two or more of the same paths. Each path might be viewed as constituting a way to interpret the event—an event that allows you to see a convergence of different paths (see Figure 1.15). When you map paths, you map interactions, and when you map interactions, you create contexts of interaction.

When you create maps, you also create the basis of a model. A model formalizes a map in the same way that a map formalizes paths. A model, however, also takes into consideration that the events that characterize your activities constitute a *system*. When you create a model, you have a formal way to refine your understanding of a map of events so that you can view the events as a system.

Event Exploration

Simulations create events that themselves allow you to create events. Drawing from a statement the philosopher Wittgenstein once made, when you know how to do something, you can "go on with it." Working from this notion, a simulation proves effective when it allows you to engage in an activity that you can extend beyond the basic context the simulation provides. (See Figure 1.12.)

An event in the context of simulation allows you to express emotion and thought; it also embodies emotion and thought. When you establish a goal, for example, and you discern paths of interaction that give expression to the goal you have established, the world that opens up for you consists of a multitude of events. An event is basically anything that makes sense or that you can perceive as significant in light of your understanding of the world.

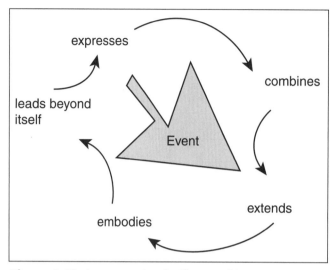

Figure 1.12 An event gains significance with a map.

With respect to the development of a simulation program, when you add a control such as a button to the user interface, you equip the user of the application with the ability to evoke an event. An event brings a mapping to life. Events combine with other events and meaningful experiences result.

A significant, meaningful, or valuable event tends to extend a path. Another way to look at this is to say that meaningful events both exercise and result from heuristics.

Developing Incentives

An incentive is an activity that induces someone to extend experience. An incentive differs from a goal in the same way that an intersection between two roads differs from the beginning or end of a journey. An incentive provides a context of experience that creates features of maps. As you extend a map, you enhance your ability to recognize the significance of specific events. The more you understand the significance of specific events, the more you have with which to sense the significance of the goal that guides you as you experience new events. (See Figure 1.13.)

Incentives increase the significance of events. As your map grows, so does the capacity to see the significance of any given event. When you create a map that embodies your own understanding, you create a basis for claiming ownership of an event. Ownership is not in this context something along the lines of a purchased commodity. Instead, ownership implies that a given event is significant for you, in a way that you can relate using your own pathways of understanding, your own maps, your own complex of events.

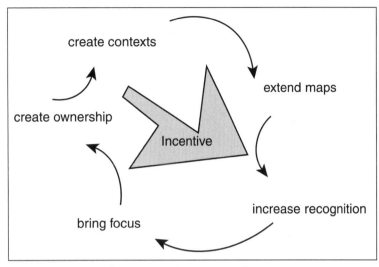

Figure 1.13 Significance contributes to significance.

Learning

Ultimately, simulation is about learning. Learning corresponds to an enhanced capacity to interact with the world. Learning implies that you own a map. In addition, however, successful learning means that you can extend the map for yourself. (See Figure 1.14.)

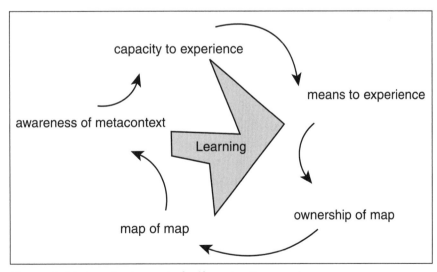

Figure 1.14 Learning is a sort of self-constructive mapping.

In this respect, simulation brings with it a way to increase the capacity to have experience. It invites you to become involved in a given type of experience, and then, through the experience it provides, it equips you with sensitivities, understanding, and skills that enable you to extend the experience on your own terms and according to your own mappings, models, and goals.

Learning also has the peculiar quality of being an activity that creates a map that maps itself. In the language of communications theory, learning provides a *metacontext*. It allows you to regard one map as a means to other maps.

Regeneration

When a simulation invites participants to map experience for themselves, its success depends on its capacity to endlessly regenerate experience. Mapping events involves creating a context in which those who become involved in a set of events can emerge from their experience with new ways of understanding.

To gain a sense of how a heuristic fostered by simulation might offer you a world characterized by plotless interaction, you can explore an image that seemingly represents either a duck or a rabbit (see Figure 1.15). The value of this image for simulation designers and developers cannot be underestimated. The value lies in the extent to which the image embodies a key characteristic of simulation as this book discusses it. When you examine Figure 1.15, for example, you can continuously cause your attention to find either a duck or a rabbit. Along the same lines, you can trace the map on the left to discover different paths and events. A goal in this respect offers only an occasion for collecting information.

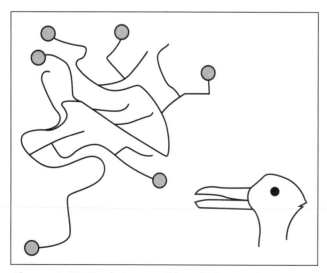

Figure 1.15 Simulations provide multiple mappings.

Modes of Understanding

You can also consider the implications of the illustrations in Figure 1.15 in terms of *multi-modal logic*. As is discussed in greater detail in Chapter 2, the richness of a simulation depends on the extent to which it both embodies different paths of understanding and yet sustains as a goal the mapping of paths. This dynamic seems to present a paradox. How is it that you can both instill an application with endless paths of exploration and at the same time structure it so that regardless of the path the user follows, he can align his activities with a goal? How can you effectively integrate the part and the whole?

Inductive and Iconic Logic

Iconic logic constitutes an expression developed in detail in different contexts throughout this book. Use of the expression is intended to pose an understanding of meaning that contrasts with what arises when you evaluate the significance of a system using a logic that is external to the system. (This is the usual approach you find to plotted narratives.)

An iconic approach to interpreting meaning involves asserting that the meaning of a given experience can be known only through the experience itself, not through a summary assertion you make about the experience. On the other hand, experience, generally, can be viewed as a whole, and any event that takes place in the context of a given experience can be viewed as a part of this whole. The whole determines part, and the part determines the whole.

Significance

A further notion that plays a part in the development of designs for simulation involves *significance*. You can gauge the significance of the events a given system of interaction generates if you evaluate the system in terms of the complexity of the interactions the system fosters. Contrast this point of view with what you might hear in a traditional context involving someone discussing the "significance of an event relative to the plot."

What happens when you do away with the plot? Generally, as subsequent chapters explore in a number of ways, the capacity of a simulation to create significant experience depends on its capacity to fully involve its user. The difficulty successful simulations pose to developers in this respect presents yet another contrast with the work of creating games that follow a plot or seek a specific objective. Significance in the context of simulation designates what can be called cognitive saturation.

Saturation

Cognitive saturation has to do with the extent to which a context of participation—a system—brings into play all the possibilities that apply to the experiential framework of the participant. Saturation becomes cognitive when it relates to the types of thinking, problem solving, questioning, or other activities you engage in as you are involved with the system.

Conclusion

The discussion this chapter initiates continues on during the remainder of the book. If one theme prevails, it is that simulation does not involve only making things look real or imitating real-world events. Instead, simulation involves creating the capacity to create experience.

In the chapters that follow, much of the effort involves attending to the details of using C++ and DirectX to create some basic tools you can use to develop simulation programs. Often, the discussion centers on programming. On the other hand, whenever possible, an effort is made to reintroduce and elaborate the notions this chapter presents.

As you read the subsequent chapters and undertake the programming projects they propose, keep in mind that the potentials for simulation development are enormous. The future is likely to present opportunities for simulation developers that today remain largely unexplored.

One particularly promising area of simulation in the entertainment industry involves plotless games. If you take time to understand the basic work involved in this type of development, you are in an excellent position both to pursue currently established simulation projects and to plan and undertake projects that go in wholly different directions. The applications in this book provide you with a simple set of functionality that you can use to initiate your own simulation projects. Each chapter provides aesthetic, theoretical, and technical frameworks for the activities they discuss.

The following books provide further insights into the topics this chapter presents:

Daniel C. Dennett, *Consciousness Explained* (Boston: Little, Brown and Company, 1991).

Dedre Gentner, Keith J. Holyoak, and Boicho N. Kokinov, *The Analogical Mind: Perspectives from Cognitive Science* (Cambridge, Massachusetts: MIT Press, 2001).

Ian Haywood and Barry Sandywell, *Interpreting Visual Culture: Explorations in the Hermeneutics of the Visual* (London: Routledge, 1999).

Suguru Ishizaki. *Improvisational Design: Continuous, Responsive Digital Communication* (Cambridge, Massachusetts: The MIT Press, 2003).

George Lakoff, *Women, Fire, and Dangerous Things: What Categories Reveal about the Mind* (Chicago: University of Chicago Press, 1987).

Pierre Lévy. Trans. Robert Bononno, *Collective Intelligence: Mankind's Emerging World in Cyberspace.* (Cambridge, Massachusetts: Perseus, 1997).

Lev Manovich. *The Language of New Media.* (Cambridge, Massachusetts, The MIT Press, 2001).

Sun-Joo Shin. *The Iconic Logic of Peirce's Graphs.* (Cambridge, Massachusetts, The MIT Press, 2002).

CHAPTER 2

SPECIFYING EVENTS

When you model an event or design a simulation program, it is useful to consider the context of your simulation. Contexts of simulation can be identified using such elements as data, events, devices, and models. In addition, such notions as duration, tension, motion, and emotional impact come into play. Drawing from your understanding of these elements, you can picture games and simulations as cybernetic systems. If you combine this perspective with a few insights from cognitive psychology, you can then investigate how user competencies impact the way you map events in games and simulations. Competencies concern what users seek in the rules and logic that relate to games and simulations. From this foundation, it then becomes useful to investigate a more practical issue, one that involves putting use cases to work to draw together the elements involved in models and simulations so that you can effectively plan your work. Although this chapter offers many ideas, a short list still provides a good summary of what it presents:

- Contexts of event modeling and simulation
- Elements to consider when developing event models
- Understanding how prototypes extend simulations
- Experiential and objective perspectives
- Prototyping and repetition in simulation
- Tools and techniques for modeling
- Approaches to analysis
- Repetition and learning

Contexts of Simulation

When you consider what development of a simulation program requires, the context of the simulation arises as one of your first priorities. A context is a setting, a psychological space in which a simulation occurs. The two main components of the context are the simulation you want to create and the model you use as the basis of your simulation. To determine what comprises the context of a simulation, first consider that when you create a simulation, you usually start in one of two ways. You might start *experientially*, which implies that your personal experiences form the basis of your simulation. You might also start *objectively*, which implies that you adopt a hypothesis or formal model as the basis of your simulation.

Even if these two approaches to simulation do not cover all possibilities, they provide two general categories that you might find you can use to account for most simulations. More importantly, however, when you start with these two perspectives, you have a convenient approach to viewing how simulations developed for games often differ from simulations developed for others purposes.

note

Consider the terms *realism* and *idealism*. Realists assert the world exists without dependencies on human perception; idealists assert that the world exists only because it is mediated by human perception. Consider, likewise, what happens if you add *surrealism* to the mixture. Surrealists assert that realism and idealism are secondary; instead, the sense of duration takes priority.

A philosopher of the nineteenth century, Immanuel Kant (1724-1804), contended that a structure of understanding mediates our interactions with the universe. (See Figure 2.1.) During the twentieth century, other philosophers applied the term *phenomenology* to this approach to describing understanding and experience. This way of approaching understanding provides a good point of departure for describing contexts of simulation.

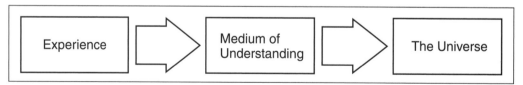

Figure 2.1 Experience depends on mediation.

From the perspective given by phenomenology, those who investigate how understanding happens can investigate the medium of understanding from three vantage points. The first concerns everything "out there" in the universe. The second is everything "in here" in your thoughts, which is also called experience. And third is the understanding that turns what is out there into experience. Another way to put this is that understanding *mediates* the transformation of undifferentiated phenomena into experience. Consider the following points:

- **Experience.** Think of experience as the result rather than a starting point. When you experience something, you are not experiencing anything directly. Instead, your experience results from information that understanding filters or mediates. Experience might be viewed as data or information that has significance *for someone*. Experience is data or information imbued with meaning.

- **Understanding.** Think of understanding as a program that allows you to filter information and generate output. The output is experience. Understanding might be viewed as the application of an event model. An event is any occasion that creates meaning or significance. The model forms what might be viewed as the *static* basis of understanding. Understanding is a *dynamic* activity that transforms undifferentiated data or information and shapes it into experience. Understanding in any given setting might differ from person to person. It is the filter that shapes information into experience.

- **Phenomena.** Phenomena can be viewed as a kind of undifferentiated source material that your understanding filters to create the experiences that you consciously recognize as experiences. It also provides a way to avoid declaring that the universe is just this or just that. The universe, as a phenomenological realm, exists for those who perceive it as a manifestation of the tools of understanding they apply to it.

Phenomenology serves as a good starting place for discussions of simulation because it provides a way to understand that a simulation is not simply a *presentation* or *representation* of reality. Instead, a simulation is a context (you might call it a *manifold*) in which possibilities of understanding combine to offer a participant in the simulation the opportunity to generate new experience.

Experiential Simulation

Different approaches characterize how you can depict what might be viewed as the sources of simulation. You might view one approach as *experiential simulation*. Experientially, for example, you begin the work of creating a simulation program by revisiting an event drawn from your past. As you revisit the past, your understanding of the past begins to take shape according to a vast collection of sensitivities that characterize your own psyche. You use your understanding to gather and refine your memories. You can filter and reshape the past to eliminate things that prove confusing. You concentrate on details that give events added significance. You are not making up the past. Rather, you are finding in the past information—data—that allows you to emphasize some things while leaving aside others. What you then view as experiences is not something immediate or direct but something mediated through your understanding (see Figure 2.2).

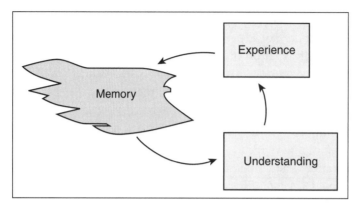

Figure 2.2 When you re-create an event experientially, you select information according to a personalized perspective on the significance of your experience.

Art might be viewed as experiential simulation. Simulation is an event in which understanding, in whatever form, is applied to some body of information, and experience results. Artists at work might be viewed as people who seek to construct a simulation. The simulation induces those who participate in it to create experiences for themselves through the work of art. The work of art is something dynamic. It induces those who view it to reorganize and filter sensory data so that new experience results. The artist's job involves, not creating experience, but rather making the work of art a medium of understanding through which the participant in the work of art (the viewer) creates experience.

Objective Simulation

From an approach that might be called *objective simulation*, you do not so much begin with memory as you begin with a hypothesis about something you think will happen in a given way. In many instances, the context of your simulation involves a world that you consider as existing apart from how it impacts the feelings of those who experience it. Consider, for example, the scientists who work at the US National Oceanic and Atmospheric Administration (NOAA). These scientists create sophisticated computerized simulations of weather events. While exciting implications might result from their simulations, the scientists are not seeking only excitement. Instead, the results of the simulations contribute to understanding of the behavior of weather and, as importantly, confirmation of the validity of a *hypothesis*.

A hypothesis provides a conditional statement that scientists can test for validity. When you use simulation as an objective undertaking intended to test a hypothesis, you create a set of experiments that produce a body of information that enables you to confirm a given type of understanding. Scientists creating a simulation resemble artists at work, but in the scientific endeavor, the understanding that mediates sensory data and translates it into experience is highly formalized.

The objective approach requires that you first formulate the hypothesis and then set up experiments that gather information. If the hypothesis and the experiments comprise what might be viewed as understanding, then precisely how you articulate your hypothesis and the experiments that go with it becomes particularly important. As the primary media of understanding, the hypothesis and the experiments generate data and experience. Further, the data and experience that result cannot be one-time occurrences. At the basis of scientific activities lies the requirement that you be able to tell others how to repeat the experiments you have performed and generate the same data you have generated. You must take care as you plan your activities that others can repeat the work you perform. (See Figure 2.3.)

n o t e

An experiment is a formalized way to recognize information and create experience. It is also a formalized way to test a hypothesis. A simulation can be an experiment, and an experiment can be a simulation.

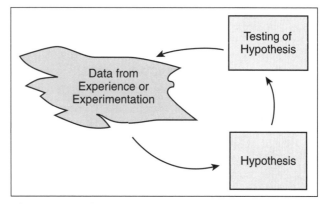

Figure 2.3 When you re-create an event objectively, you work from a hypothesis.

Event Models and Mediation

An event is an occasion for the creation of meaning. With both the reconstruction of a remembered event and the construction of experiments to test a hypothesis (a formal event), your activity usually involves having an *event model* in place to guide your activities. An event model is a practical device that allows you to determine how to recognize, limit, translate, transform, and present data. It is more or a less a guide you use to move from the undifferentiated realm of data, through understanding, and at last to experience.

The creation of an event model might begin with a central image you sustain as a result of a personal vision. You seek to elaborate this image until you can see its full significance in many different ways. The means you use to achieve this end involves simulation. Along other lines, the creation of an event model might begin with an equation you want to exercise for purposes of teaching or learning. To reach this goal, you create an event model that guides you as you construct the context in which the experience you seek can be generated.

The discussions concerning experiential and objective simulation can be reduced to a consideration of what event model you establish as the basis of your simulation. The event model for experiential mediation might be the vision or inspiration of an artist during a moment of artistic activity. The model for objective mediation might be a vast array of equations put together by atmospheric scientists. In either case, the event model helps you establish just how it is that a meaningful occasion arose and can be limited for purposes of exploration, interpretation, and simulation.

Every event model serves first as a way to help you understand the scope of your undertaking. Scope establishes boundaries. It helps you understand, for instance, what kinds of data you want to use and what kinds of experiences you want to generate. If you are involved in a project that concerns creating bizarre sounds, then the model you develop might exclude visual data. If the model you are working on concerns only line graphs, then the scope might dictate the exclusion of all but a few colors and styles of lines.

The event model helps you understand the complexity of the mediation you want to embody in your simulation. The context of a simulation serves to engender a collection of potentials for creating experience you want to provide to the user of your game or your simulation program. For this reason, you face the need to refine your understanding of precisely what it is that you want to achieve. You can view your work developing a model as that of creating a framework of experimentation or exploration. You might also view it as the creation of a workshop or studio that allows you to sustain a certain type of activity that leads to a certain type of experience.

An event model both *abstracts* and *filters* information. An event model abstracts and filters information because it filters (or normalizes) data according to given forms of presentation. As an abstraction, the event model serves as a kind of template. It guides you as you subordinate the data you use to the realm of experience you want to address. Samuel L. Clemens once remarked that if you are a hammer, then the world becomes a nail. This notion applies to the use of event models. An event model filters information because it provides you with an explicit set of criteria for determining what information to use and how you treat this information. (See Figure 2.4.)

Dangerous Things

When you mediate data using an event model, the data you work with ultimately becomes the content of someone's experience. Every model, to some extent, implicitly filters data. It creates a *bias*. In some cases, it alters the data so that it can be used effectively. In other instances, it distorts it so that it becomes deceptive or confusing. Dangers accompany mediation. Good modelers consider the dangers from the start and try to consider fully whether the tools they have chosen for their work mitigate the risks mediation poses. Among some of the more obvious risks are the following:

- **Reduction.** The model so distorts the data that the data loses its integrity. Imagine, for instance, that you adopt a tool that takes all shades of blue and reduces them to one. Cultural and linguistic elements play heavily in such considerations. The Inuit have dozens of names for snow that allow them to precisely describe aspects of the world they live in. If someone were to translate the speech of an Inuit that included mention of many "shades" of snow, much of the speaker's meaning would be lost.

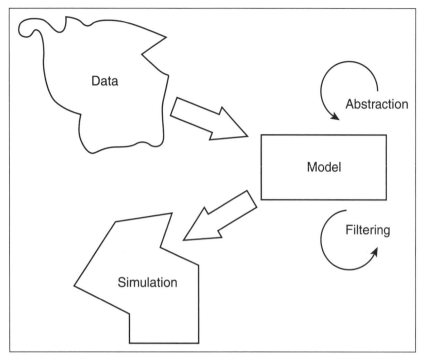

Figure 2.4 An event model abstracts and filters experience.

- **Exclusion.** The model excludes data that centrally contributes to a full presentation. For example, consider a model of ocean currents that does not show the depths of oceans. In one sense, if the model seeks specifically to show currents as surface phenomena, then the modeler can probably safely argue that no danger exists if the model does not account for ocean depths. Danger arises only if the modeler makes an assumption that since currents can be modeled without consideration of ocean depths, ocean depths have no bearing on currents.

- **Symmetry.** The cultural anthropologist Edward Hall told a story of a man from the American Midwest who was invited to dinner while residing in Japan. At the dinner, he made certain that he finished every item on his plate to show his appreciation to his hosts. His host, however, kept filling his plate every time he finished his food. This was symmetrical bind. Both parties were being polite, but an empty plate communicated a request for more to the host while it showed satiation on the part of the guest. The man gorged himself and left unhappy. Models pose dangers of combing information in a way that leads to what the anthropologist Gregory Bateson referred to as schizophrenic modes of understanding. Every translation of data creates a possibility that symmetrical binds can result.

▪ **Reification.** The model abstracts an event through analysis and ends up confusing the abstraction for the event. The technical term for this is *reification*. Bertrand Russell, the renowned philosopher, characterized this as confusing the map with the territory mapped. Models used as analogies often lead to reification. For example, some people create models of nation states based on traditional family structures. Others think of atoms as onions, where electron layers can be peeled off. While an analogy serves to allow people to discuss complex ideas in simple terms, when the analogy distorts the event under discussion to the point that everyone begins to talk in terms of the analogy, then the model becomes counterproductive as a medium of understanding.

As an extension of the points just summarized, consider another term that might be applied to faulty models or uses of models: *stereotyping*. Computer games incorporating simulations can become vehicles of racism, sexism, hate psychology, class bigotry, and jingoistic nationalism. Mediation of information, of data, gives rise to an occasion for understanding. Understanding is a filter, and a filter can distort.

Promising Potentials

If your goal involves re-creating a personal experience, memory and imagination often work in automatic ways, and this becomes the basis of both rich artistic visions and psychological illness. When you are working toward an artist vision or a scientific discovery, risks are necessary and justified.

Consider, for example, the writings of Marcel Proust (1871-1922). This writer's prose model led him to write at extraordinary length on incidents that took but a moment to transpire. For him the briefest memory held implications that he felt could be shown to be woven throughout the whole of life. In contrast, as psychologists have shown, some people encounter extremely painful events and find that they cannot remember what they have experienced even though, on a day-to-day basis, they are plagued by neurotic tendencies that express the unconscious influences of their suppressed memories.

The psychologist C.G. Jung said that full assimilation of both dreams and waking experiences characterizes psychological health, and in at least one sense, this observation about psychological health also applies to creating event models. If you want to accent or emphasize the significance of a given event through simulation, then you must approach the event in a holistic way, acknowledging that both conscious and unconscious forces are at play. Comprehending why an event possesses significance and how you want to emphasize its significance involves using many different tools to construct event models. Among these tools are those of psychology, linguistics, anthropology, optics, phonics, physics, graphical arts, and software design, to name but a few. Hardly any realm of art, technology, or science can be excluded. Such knowledge allows you to consider exactly why you have chosen each element of your model and why you have presented it in a given way. (See Figure 2.5.)

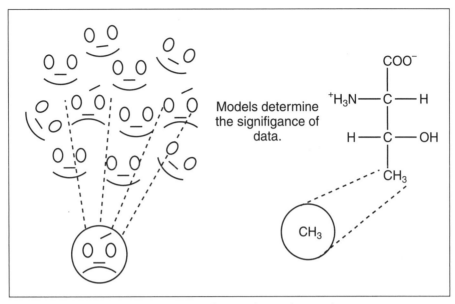

Figure 2.5 Event models impact how data can be used in simulation.

Event Model Fundamentals

Whether the event you want to model originates with reconstructed experience or arises as you develop experimentation to test a hypothesis, you usually face a burdensome problem when you determine how you want to isolate and define the data that is relevant to the event you are modeling. In scientific realms, data usually takes the form of measured quantities, rates of change, or durations. In experiential settings, data takes the form of psychological states and feelings. When you create a good model to abstract and filter the data, you accomplish a great deal. Sometimes, however, knowing that you have arrived at a way to isolate and record data can be rather painful, for you realize that for every item you have learned how to include in your model, you have excluded what amounts to an infinite set of other items.

You cannot replay reality to create a simulation. Even if you could replay reality, such a replay would not constitute an effective simulation, for an effective simulation is effective because the model behind the simulation incorporates a limited body of data that you present in a way that emphasizes given themes. The themes shape the data so that its audience derives from it a specific potential for experience.

To derive a sense of what happens as you move from an event to a model of an event, imagine that you have spent a year or two colleting flowers from plants in a given ecological zone. After a time the data you have collected reveals that flowers tend to bloom from spring to fall. You decide you want to create an exhibition for the county fair to show what you have discovered to others.

A simple simulation seems to be a good approach to the project. The simulation will create a context in which others can view the data you have collected and experience for themselves the discovery that flowers bloom continuously throughout the growing season.

The event is the activity of discovery. The event model is the collection of data you have amassed over months of botanical exploration, combined with the sense of effort, discovery, and reward that you felt when you at last arrived at your discovery. Consider the following components of an event model:

- **Collection of data during successive months.** There is a sense of duration in this activity. You went into the field repeatedly. You photographed flowers. You recorded data in a notebook.

- **The growth of awareness.** With each passing week, you saw new flowers coming into bloom. The sight of the new flowers brought pleasure while at the same time contributing data to your notebook and leading you to more confidently arrive at a generalized statement about how flowers bloom.

- **Duration of effort.** Patience and persistence characterized your effort. On some days rain fell. On other days the sun blazed.

To create an event model, you both identify the data you want to use and also consider how each type of data can be brought into play in a way that places it in the appropriate context. For instance, duration of effort in this context implies a content in which you felt great satisfaction with your work. Duration in this context is not that of someone locked in a lab and working in a bored, stifled way through a box of dead specimens. It is something characterized by invigorating effort.

To set up a context for the simulation, imagine that the people who run the county fair have told you that you can use only a poster. The poster provides a static medium. To create a context for a dynamic experience, you must induce the viewer of your poster to perform acts that result, not in detached observations, but in actions that in some way mirror those that you undertook during the months you worked in the field. Figure 2.6 shows the layout of the poster.

The poster creates a context for a dynamic event. The viewer must look first at the top, examine the flowers displayed there, and then examine each lower row sequentially. The simulation emerges from the experience of seeing the different rows of flowers, reading the month labels, and then drawing from the experience a sense of discovering when flowers bloom during different parts of the year. The event model allows you to mediate experience in the form of photographs, tables containing data recorded over the months of observation, memories of walks across fields, the sense of time's passing during the term of discovery, and emotions conveying the satisfaction of discovery. Consider in slightly closer detail the way the event model allows data to be mediated:

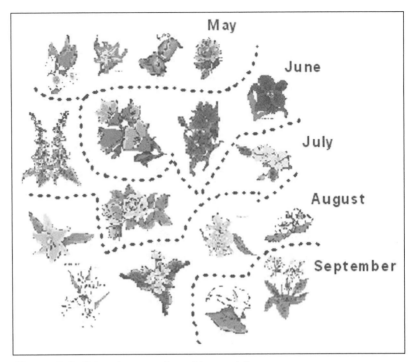

Figure 2.6 Cultural assumptions drive models.

- The viewer takes a few moments to assess the information that is spread out over the poster. At first the meaning of the poster might not be evident. Moving your eyes around the poster becomes a kind of localized field work.

- The lines separate the flowers into rows, but the lines are uneven and just a little difficult to untangle. The lack of strict linear presentation creates a moment of tension even if the viewer can understand that the lines represent divisions. Once the divisions become clear, however, the viewer of the poster experiences what it is to gather data into coherent groupings.

- The placement of the names of the months to the right side of the poster proves a ready way for the viewers to reconstruct and understand the significance of the divisions, but by setting the words to the side, you force the viewer to take a moment to draw together the different elements of meaning the poster presents and arrive at formal summaries. The month names serve to confirm the effort the viewer makes to connect the fairly self-evident display of the flower with the explicit naming the words provide.

A simulation induces the participant in the simulation to experience the emergence of awareness. A simulation does not tell its viewers its message, nor does it show its viewers its message. Rather, it provides a way that the viewers can re-create for themselves an experience from which they can derive meaning. The event model sets the state for this activity. If you have taken time to carefully construct an event model, you can substantially enrich the potentials the simulation offers.

Translating Event Models to Simulations

When you create an event model, you establish a starting place for mediating data so that it is accessible to the participant in the simulation. To mediate data, you do so through a set of devices. Here is a short list of the devices the flower poster puts to work:

- **Devices that create a sense of duration.** The poster, simple as it might be, contains enough information that a certain amount of time passes before the viewer of the poster fully explores its content. Duration (or time) might be a wholly relative medium, but for human beings, it is still fundamental to the unfolding of consciousness.

- **Devices that mediate movement.** The poster sorts flowers into rows arranged from top to bottom, so that the meaning of the poster arises only after the viewer takes a moment to assess the significance of the spatial arrangement of the flowers. To accomplish this task, the viewer goes on a short journey of sorts, examining the flowers as they are spread out over the poster.

- **Devices that foster emotional tensions.** The lines, the names of the months, and the number of flowers, in addition to the top-to-bottom sorting of the flowers, creates a moment of tension that the viewer of the exhibition endures while viewing the exhibition. The moment of tension results from participation. Participation brings both confirmation and internalization of the events the model and the simulation introduce.

- **Devices that invite participation in a moment of satisfaction.** Moving your eyes or head is not necessarily an event that results in life-long memories, but for the poster, which provides its viewer with inducements to investigate a body of data, the viewer's efforts to look first at the top and then lower down, at each row, serve to simulate the activity of observing flowers for a number of months and discovering their differences through successive observations rather than all at once.

When you create a simulation, you begin with a source collection of data, impose order on the data through an event model, and move from the model to some type of mediation. Just as event models are enriched by drawing analytical tools from many fields of study, so the mediation is enriched if you incorporate a wide variety of devices. For the poster, the devices listed are fairly abstract and appeal largely to psychological categories.

In later chapters in the book, devices relating to DirectX are dealt with in extensive detail. In the creation of a basic application for simulation, such devices give you much greater power over event mediation than a simple device. With the creation of games, you use devices drawn from a multitude of sources. Among these are those of music, cinematography, 3D rendering, and gaming etiquette and logic. Ultimately, you find that as you work with event mediation, you need to be prepared to draw devices from almost every area of applied knowledge.

To select a device, you determine what best conveys your data. A number of factors come into play at this point. One of the most significant is your prospective audience. The importance of audience considerations is dealt with at length a little further on, but for now the main point respecting audiences is that devices tend to bring with them potentials for impacting on different audiences in different ways.

In the broadest terms, you should choose the devices that are appropriate for the audience your simulation addresses. Later in this chapter, the audience cognitive competence is presented as one way to evaluate audiences. For now, it is important to emphasize that audience expectations create a context for experience, even if devices make possible the experiences. The impact of a message depends to a great extent on the receptiveness of your audience to the message you are communicating. (See Figure 2.7.)

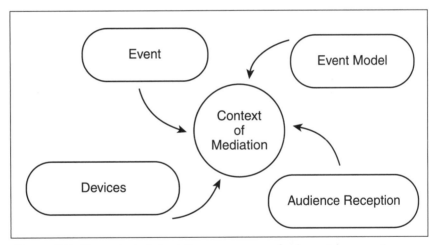

Figure 2.7 The context of simulation encompasses fundamental perspectives.

Unfortunately, no easy path exists to successful mediation of an event model, but if you gain a sense of the complete context of mediation, you stand a good chance of success. Consider, for example, what might be called the perspectives that constitute the context of mediation. Table 2.1 summarizes these perspectives.

Table 2.1 Perspectives Involved in Simulation

Perspective	Discussion
Event Data	The event data shape constitutes what you consider as you contemplate creating a simulation. More generically, data can be referred to as *information*, but the term information can be tricky to use, for it does not imply, as does data, that you have derived it or selected according to a conscious, purposeful motive. A successful simulation begins with a rich set of source data for the simulation. As you assemble a data set, you face two major risks. On one hand, you can allow your predispositions to lead you to prematurely exclude data from consideration. On the other hand, you can fail to realize that some of the data you gather might not or does not contribute beneficially to the simulation. A good event model is the surest way to mitigate such risks.
Event Model	The event model establishes how you intend to filter the data you consider as the source of your simulation. Event models have many forms, and you can find that scientists, artists, and others have developed them for almost every imaginable event. An event model is a way to understand something. A religious fanatic might view an earthquake catastrophe as an act of a demon. A scientist might view a natural catastrophe as manifestation of the friction of tectonic plates. Each individual has a model for organizing and filtering the data to be used in defense of his point of view. When you model an event, you implicitly or explicitly filter your source data. Fear can be an implicit part of an event model. The results conform to your view of the essential meaning of the event.
Devices	The psychological categories, techniques for interpreting data, techniques of art, software components, or any other means you employ to translate data from the event model to the presentation ultimately allows you to enrich the context of mediation. If you have a weak or poorly employed set of tools, even if you have an interesting model and solid set of data to work from, you are likely to fall short of success. The notion that devices of presentation dictate the media you can work with helps you overcome the limitations that arise when you assume that simulation of an event involves making it "look like real." Reality varies according to the devices performers employ to render reality.
Audience	The psychological state of the participant in the simulation you have created determines the effect of the simulation. A simulation addresses someone. It has no reality apart from how its audience perceives it. For this reason, for a simulation to succeed, you might find that you must first closely evaluate your audience and find collections of devices that the audience finds easy to use. In other instances, you might teach your audience how to recognize and use devices.
Context	The overall phenomenological interplay of event, model, devices, and audience determines the success of your simulation work. Failure to afford attention to any one of these areas usually results in a defective or ineffective product.

Formalizing Tools and Thematic Objectives

As emphasized previously, contexts involve creating models, and models serve to mediate the data you ultimately make part of your simulation. Ultimately, mediation entails arriving at what might be called a "thematic focus" for your simulation. Everyone who sets about mediating the content of an event model intentionally or otherwise forms a thematic objective.

Thematic objectives originate in thematically shaped experiences. In other words, people usually see what they can see or want to see. They are predisposed to see some things as significant, other things as not significant. This is generally the perspective phenomenology affords. The medium of perception you employ to view a given event shapes the event you view, and the outcome is that the event you view tells you more about your medium of perception—your way of seeing—than about the event itself. Generally, the results of art and science can be characterized as *ways of seeing*.

Hermes and Interpretation

The usual term applied to the activity of creating a theme is *interpretation*. Philologists, philosophers, and archaeologists sometimes use the term *hermeneutics* to refer to the activity of creating themes. A theme is a way of seeing. A way of seeing allows you to interpret data and substantiate a given form of understanding.

A historical perspective can be added to the work of creating themes if you consider the ancient Greek god Hermes. Among other things, Hermes was responsible for promoting commerce and carrying messages from the gods to mortals. A brief examination of the work Hermes performed provides a convenient way to investigate some of the implications of creating themes.

Consider, for example, what happens when a commercial transaction takes place in an open market. Two people encounter each other. One has something to sell. The other desires what is for sale. The creation of both the product for sale and the desire for the product involve long and involved histories. The chance of the transaction might be viewed as arising in a spontaneous way, but if you investigate the histories of the two people involved in the transaction, you might find fairly involved sets of events leading to the transaction. The ancient Greeks found such coincidences so interesting that they attributed them to the work of Hermes. The transaction manifests itself in a theme. The theme is the way that the buyer and seller interact to find meaning in the exchange of goods. (See Figure 2.8.)

Hermes also brought themes to occasions other than those characterized by commercial transactions. For poets, artists, legislators, judges, religious oracles, commanders of armies, and anyone seeking to bring together a diverse set of facts, figures, and impressions into a coherent understanding of a difficult situation, Hermes offered aid. He brought to mortals ways to understand complex collections of events. He brought themes. The moment of thematic unification amounted to a vision or message sent by the gods.

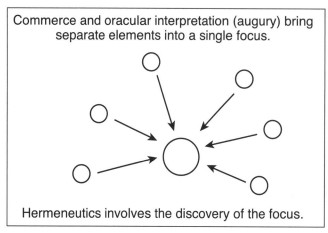

Figure 2.8 The god Hermes oversaw commerce and messages from the gods.

Hermeneutics, a branch of philology and philosophy derived from the lore of Hermes, arose as a formalized discipline a few hundred years ago, when linguists in Europe were seeking to translate the writings of the ancient Greek, Sumerian, Hebrew, Egyptian, and Roman authors (among others) into modern languages. Determining meanings often depended on establishing contexts of understanding. This activity became a science insofar as the translator had to carefully amass a collection of items (words, phrases, symbol, images) that would create a context from which understanding of the entire collection might emerge. The whole could give meaning to the part; but the parts gave meaning to the whole. Still, the whole had to be considered something more than the sum of the parts. This became known as "the hermeneutic circle." To make translations of ancient texts possible, it was necessary to find ways to thematically unify words, phrases, archeological artifacts, or other items into wholes from which the meaning of parts could then be known.

In more recent times, detective novels and films illustrate the work of Hermes (hermeneutics) in excellent form. The detective story provides you with a set of apparently disconnected clues which the resolution of the plot allows you to see as associated in a perfectly coherent way.

Event Analysis and Requirements

You can analyze data drawn from an event model in terms of explicitly stated requirements for mediation. The requirements identify the thematic objective you want to achieve through mediation. The thematic objective helps you establish criteria you can use to determine which devices to use.

Thematic objectives are both essential to your efforts to create simulations and at the same time possible sources of risk. The risk is that the thematic objective can turn the mediation into a narrow, uninteresting performance that represents a sales session or a courtroom argument. In other words, everything that happens tends to be used as evidence for the theme rather than as a source of experience guided by the theme.

When you create requirements, you increase the chances that you will avoid the risk of asserting a theme too harshly. The reason for this is that when you develop requirements, you have a chance to thoroughly investigate the scope of your undertaking and to give extensive consideration to the mixture of devices you can use as you create your simulation. Narrowly asserted thematic objectives usually represent hastily assembled simulations.

Consider a scenario in which you design a simulation of an avatar in a mountain scene. (See Figure 2.9.) Your event model might take any number of forms, but assume that the first theme in your model is one of having the avatar climb a mountain, overcoming as he goes a number of obstacles that include dead-end caves and cliffs that top out and force the avatar to climb back down. To establish the initial thematic objective, you focus on finding actions and paths that carry the avatar to the top of the mountain.

The danger is that you can make climbing the mountain an obsessive activity. You stray into obsession when you do not take time to implement features that make climbing the mountain an interesting, adventurous ordeal that includes varied, captivating experiences. A requirements effort might allow you to assemble a number of possibilities along the following lines:

- A sheer vertical surface with a few nubbins and hand and finger holes.
- Ice fields that are slippery and steep.
- Thin ledges along high precipices that can be traversed only by facing outward and inching along.
- Creatures and foes that guard narrow passages. You must fight them or find ways around them.
- Moments when you enter caves that might lead in relatively easy spirals to a place higher up or instead terminate in deep, dark dungeons.
- The necessity of jumping again and again to find a way to reach a hand hold.
- Views of a sheer, towering cliff that must be climbed.
- Spectacular views of distant peaks topped by cragged masses of ice and snow.
- Gaping crevice that you must leap across.
- Easy passages make it possible for you to rest and perhaps gain a spectacular view.

Creating requirements for devices to mediate events ultimately provides an excellent way to refine your event model. In the instance of the avatar that climbs the mountain, the prevailing theme is one of ascent, of attempting to follow one path after another and finding in the end the path that leads to the top. But given the list above, it can also involve effects and devices that bring to the event model an extended set of opportunities for making new and effective uses of the basic data used to communicate the avatar's ascent. Using data in different ways contributes to the experiences the participant in the simulation can enjoy. (See Figure 2.9.)

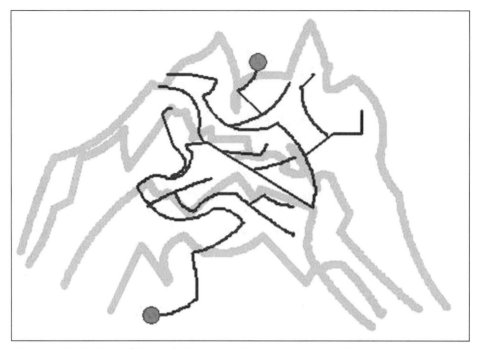

Figure 2.9 Analysis of themes helps you enrich the ways you mediate the event model.

Climbing a mountain is one of the most common themes in game development. As Figure 2.9 shows, such a thematic objective can easily overwhelm every other aspect of the simulation. But then analysis of the primary theme opens up opportunities for bringing other themes into play. Consider what happens when you start with climbing but then extend this basic theme into other activities:

- The primary theme involves finding alternative paths to the top.
- Successive challenges offer risks of being led into dead ends or falling to death.
- The psychological landscape can change if increasingly grand vistas and more harrowing cliffs appear as the climber climbs higher.
- Ice spots and other obstacles present close-range, involved problems that contrast with larger elements.
- Beasts or villains guard the passages and each has unique characteristics.
- Falling water enhances the beauty of given scenes.
- An avalanche provides a moment of awe.
- Camera angles continuously accent heights, depths, and distances.
- Briefly following the image of a soaring condor shows dynamic vistas.

- The moons rays on the castle at the top accentuate the passage of time and the grandeur of the setting.
- Movements, such as jumping, leaping, walking, inching along, battling, and diving for cover, increase the attention the avatar receives.
- The primary emotions the play fosters can be those of struggling to ascend, fearing to fall, contemplating or puzzling over alternate paths, estimating the risks foes pose, feeling disappointment at a dead end, or feeing delight at a path that continues on.

Game designers work diligently to ensure that players find rich, involved, varied challenges and occasions for thrill without at the same time having to endure domineering themes. Devices employed to achieve these ends foster graphical richness and complexity of play. Edging along a narrow shelf becomes more interesting and challenging if the camera angle shifts so that the player looks over a high precipice. On the other hand, a high precipice becomes more visually appealing if it includes a view of a lush river valley accentuated by waterfalls and streams of mist. If the perilous shelf is in a cave inside the mountain, then boiling lava far beneath adds to the effects that induce fear. (See Figure 2.10).

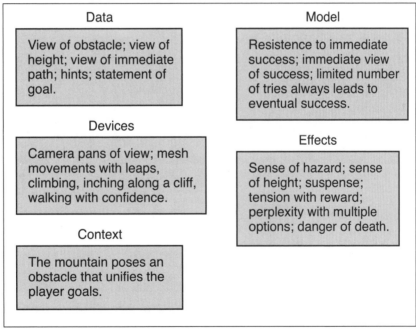

Figure 2.10 Requirements bring elements of the simulation into focus.

Requirements allow you to establish priorities relating to the model, the data, the devices, the effects, and the general context of mediation. The complex of elements that a requirements-gathering effort can allow you to bring into play enables you to refine the ways you mediate the event model. That requirements enhance your efforts in this way forms one of the strongest justifications for developing them.

Prototyping

Prototyping has exerted an enormous influence on the way software and other products are designed. Prototyping is an approach to software development that involves building a product incrementally. When you build a product incrementally, you work closely with those who use the product to determine what they consider important and how they want to use the product. Design and development efforts benefit from prototyping because developers and software users interact with the product as it is developed. The information they exchange makes it possible for the product to be developed with much greater sensitivity to how it will be used and what features it should possess.

In addition, however, prototyping can also be discussed purely in terms of design. In other words, people who design products frequently like to work in an incremental, iterative way. Their approach may be to come up with a basic design and then rework it in several ways to see how the product changes as they rework it. At one time, such an approach to design would have been too costly to follow, for drawing designs or filling in paper spreadsheets was extremely time-consuming. With computer automation, however, the picture changes. Designers can afford to change product designs repeatedly. Software does all the detail work, eliminating costs and delays.

Prototyping and simulation resemble each other in many ways. The difference is that prototyping is usually associated with development efforts, whereas simulation is usually associated with playing out scenarios. People who possess experience as designers, for example, prototype products as part of their development efforts. On the other hand, pilots, soldiers, and others work with simulations as a part of their training efforts.

This simple division becomes untenable after a certain point, however. For example, scientists often develop a simulation as a way to explore phenomena or test a hypothesis, but as a part of their effort to develop a simulation, they engage in continuous prototyping. In fact, the effort of prototyping might not come to an end. Instead, the scientists working on a given simulation might view their work as one of continuously tuning the design of their simulation so that it can generate increasingly accurate predictions.

Computer applications for simulation and prototyping perform the work of Hermes. They both draw together data, devices, models, and effects in a context in which their users can arrive at new forms of understanding. To draw things together, computer-aided design (CAD) tools usually include a large set of features that allow designers to easily explore both different views of products being designed and differed approaches to design. The key to being able to improve designs or products is to be able to change them so that opportunities for improvement become evident. Making subtle differences in design visible to designers might be said to be the central feature of prototyping as an approach to design.

The same general notion applies to simulation in situations in which people are trying to learn things or explore nature. Being able to see how things change enriches experience. Such enrichment helps those who participate in simulations gain a much deeper understanding of events than would otherwise be possible. In some cases, it helps them become aware that they possess an understanding of the experience.

One other observation is that prototyping and simulation tools differ from simple design tools. A simple design tool allows you to create a specification for a product. It is something akin to a device for recording complex ideas. It has a multitude of features built into it that make it easier for you to store, retrieve, and present information, and it is designed to help you finalize the presentation of your design. In contrast, a prototyping makes it as easy to challenge, change, and transform your design. (See Figure 2.11.)

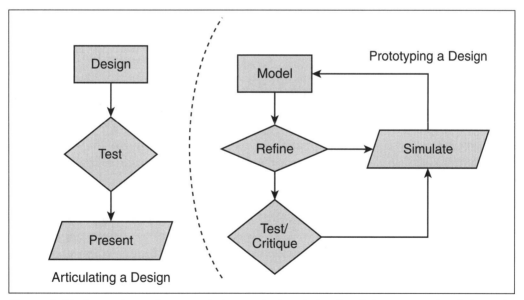

Figure 2.11 Prototyping tools support designers who iteratively refine their concepts using design tools.

Prototyping involves changing a design to see how to perfect a design. Simulation involves changing a context of understanding so that experience is enriched. Consider once again what experience is from a phenomenological perspective. Understanding mediates experience. If you can develop tools or applications that change your way of seeing along with what you see, you can perform both prototyping and simulation.

Remediation and Synthesis

To extend the discussion of prototyping and design a little, note that approaches to design sometimes arise from the way that the design effort pursues innovation. Historically, innovation in engineering has stemmed more from the evolution of designs than from the development of wholly unprecedented designs. It is for this reason that histories of technology feature genealogies of tools. Such a genealogy shows how, for instance, a hammer starts as a rounded rock, evolves to an elongated head with planed ends, and goes on from there to acquire a handle and the many modifications that eventually lead to a hammer in one or another current manifestations. (See Figure 2.12.)

Figure 2.12 A genealogy of the hammer showed design evolution.

The non-prototyping perspective emphasizes careful conceptualization of the product to be designed before the activity of rendering or presenting the design begins. Into this picture the designer might fold information about the previous version of the product under design. For example, in the engineering history of bridges, information about design failures has often been among the most important information bridge designers can use. In addition to information about how designs have failed, information valuable to designers includes items such as construction materials that weigh less and have greater strengths than materials previously available. Possessing a traditional view of how to design, the designer folds such information into what amounts to a standard concept. Creating a design, then, is largely a matter of enhancing a design.

In this world, techniques for extending or modifying existing designs help the designer assess criticisms of previous designs and introduce innovations that address these criticisms. The process of design tends to be conservative and directed toward *remediation*. (See Figure 2.13.)

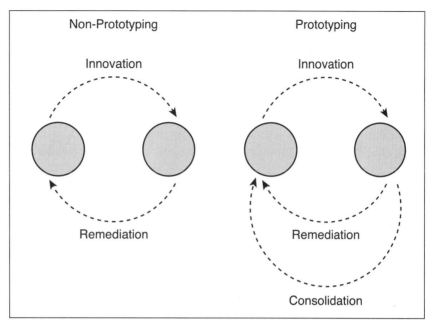

Figure 2.13 Approaches to design can emphasize remediation or synthesis.

In contrast, prototyping emphasizes what might be viewed as *synthesizing*. Synthesizing solutions entails creating contexts of product evaluation in which two important activities take place. The first is that the application places a significant number of components in proximity to each other. The second is that those involved in the development of the application can combine these components.

Each combination of components presents the designer with a different view of how the product might be designed. Some of the combinations are from the first impracticable or even ridiculous, but generally, the process of being able to recombine or synthesize design elements in different ways accentuates features of the design that might not otherwise be visible. From this process arises an approach to creating the product design that encourages continuous innovation. Further, the designer enjoys freedom from design as remediation, for the goal becomes one, not of extending an existing design, but of discovering entirely new ones.

The history of science abounds with examples of prototyping and synthesis. For example, in the history of biology, Francis Crick and James Watson used a synthetic approach to discover the DNA molecule. The two scientists faced the problem of figuring out how to picture a molecule that could arrange combinations of adenine, thymine, cytosine, and guanine. According to the account Watson gives in *The Double Helix*, this work involved first amassing a large set of criteria for candidate molecules. Keeping all the criteria in mind as they did so, the two scientists then set about cycling again and again through design possibilities until they found the one that fit.

This description of the discovery (or creation) of the DNA molecule overly simplifies the factors involved, but it remains that many scientific and technological developments have arisen from this type of synthesis. Other stories that reveal such patterns arise with Charles Darwin and his development of the theory of evolution and Albert Einstein and his development of the theory of relativity. Each scientist gathered information and then set about putting it together in different ways until he had arrived at a synthesis.

In addition to addressing what works, prototyping and synthesis also address what does not work. The fact that prototyping often creates solutions that do not work is in many ways as important as the fact that it addresses solutions that do work. As the record of fossils shows, enormous power lies in the development of prototypes that do not work. Bizarre prototypes often create properties of design that become enormously successful when placed in the right context.

note

While developing a prototype that does not work flies in the face of common sense, it remains, as Albert Einstein once reflected, that common sense is often one of the leading obstacles to innovation precisely because it impels people to prematurely dismiss ideas that ultimately prove the most valuable.

Simulation as Work and Craft

One of the leading problems with innovation in design is that when designers pursue the development of designs that are outside of existing categories, those who must finance such work tend to voice objections. Wholly new approaches to design create liabilities. To an extent, iterative approaches to design can reduce the liabilities. While they do not ensure that more innovative designs will be successful, they do afford a way to examine designs in ways that allow them to be understood from different perspectives. By inspecting designs from a number of perspectives, those who are asked to finance such ventures have a way to be more confident that the designs will be successful.

Mitigation of risk establishes the primary reason that computer-aided design became the dominant instrument of technical progress during the twentieth century. Computer simulation provides a way to remove most of the expense from the effort involved in creating innovative designs. It also removes the need to regard design as primarily reme-dial. Prototyping requires, however, a strong sense of the *craft* of a given product. Craft begins with tradition, and tradition in this sense is the awareness of the *patterns of design* that are most appropriate for a given type of product.

To gain a sense of what craft implies, consider the history of furniture. Everyone knows, generally, the features of a table, but if you are involved in the craft of making furniture, you know that hundreds of approaches to finishing, embellishing, and joining can be applied to any given effort of building a table. Each of these approaches is a pattern. An experienced craftsperson knows these patterns.

When you bring craft to a given development effort, you bring with you an approach to your work that is fundamentally *heuristic.* A heuristic approach to development involves continuously cycling between drawing in new patterns, making changes, and testing the result. Throughout, you maintain a holistic sense of the complexity of the product, and every aspect of your work is governed by a sense of symmetry of design. Again, such a sense of symmetry can be sustained only if you possess an understanding of the craft you are engaged in, which encompasses both a knowledge of how to make changes as well as what is amenable to change. (See Figure 2.14.)

Cybernetics and Systems

Prototyping and synthesis allow designers to investigate the features of their designs so that they can discern ways to improve or refine their designs. Such an approach to design can be characterized as *playful* because it takes place in a context, not of what is and must be but of what *might be.* Work becomes play when the process of developing a design is no longer a linear activity of first formulating a design and then displaying it.

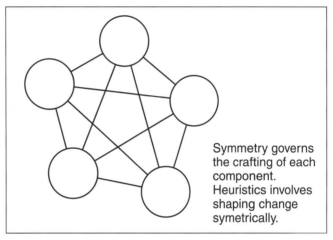

Symmetry governs the crafting of each component. Heuristics involves shaping change symetrically.

Figure 2.14 Craft encompasses heuristic approaches to design.

To gain an understanding on a more formal level some aspects of how work can be viewed as play, you can draw upon a few concepts introduced by *cybernetics.* Cybernetics, simply put, is the study of systems of information. A game can be viewed as a self-sustaining system of information.

A cybernetic system is a system in which all the actions within the system relate directly or indirectly to all other actions within the system through a set of rules. The classical example of a cybernetic system depicts a thermostat. According to this picture of things, the thermostat, representing the central set of rules governing the system, responds to the temperature of the house. If the temperature is low, then a coil in the thermostat expands to induce the furnace to ignite and begin heating the house. If the temperature becomes high, then the coil in the thermostat contracts and shuts down the furnace. (See Figure 2.15.)

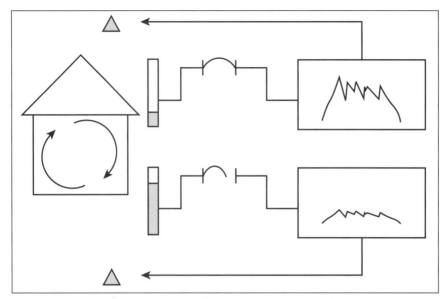

Figure 2.15 A cybernetic system unifies the actions of a thermostatic, the work of a furnace, and the changes in the temperature of a house.

The temperature of the house is information. Information is the primary data of the system. It is the primary data of the system because it is the information that is meaningful to the system. The rules of the system are designed to process this information. When information is processed using rules, *communication* takes place. Other information, on the other hand, might be referred to as *noise*. Noise is information that the rules of the system are not designed to process.

A party might be going on in the house, and a number of people might be assembled around a piano singing as someone plays. While this activity might create pleasant sounds and a certain amount of emotional warmth among the revelers, the information relevant to the rules—which, again, the thermostat embodies—does not encompass sounds of music or positive feelings among singers. The primary communication within this system consists of the information the heat conveys as processed through the rules the thermostat embodies. (See Figure 2.16.)

Communication in the context of cybernetics, then, involves information that is relevant to the actions the system is designed to perform. When information is channeled so that it effects changes predicted by the rules that govern the system, then it is said to be communication. Given this perspective, it is useful to investigate a few generalizations relative to the study of cybernetic systems (see Table 2.2).

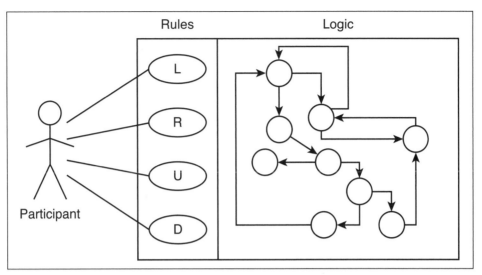

Figure 2.16 Communication can be considered to be information that rules render meaningful.

Table 2.2 Terms from Cybernetics and Systems Theory

Concept	Discussion
Information	Information is data. Information might be viewed as either possessing meaning or not possessing meaning. Information that possesses no meaning might be referred to as noise, but noise tends to possess meaning, if only as a background to what does possess meaning.
Communication	Information that a system can find meaningful is said to constitute communication. An act of communication involves transferring information using rules. The rules are those that define the system. When information and rules combine successfully, communication results.
System	A system, like a hermeneutic whole, might be regarded as a collection of functional elements that together form a whole that constitutes something greater than the sum of the parts. A system can be regarded as a collection of activity that can achieve what is known as a *steady-state*. This means only that the system is self-sustaining. Clearly, however, systems come and go. For this reason, systems are said to experience *escalation, decay*, and *stagnation*. Within a system's context, elements do not exist in isolation from each other. Elements are not *atomistic*. You find the meaning of the activity of any given element of the system by relating it to the activity of the other elements of the system.
Closed systems	Ervin Laszlo, one of the most recognized writers on systems theory, contended that ultimately such discoveries as the second law of thermodynamics make it impossible for any system in the known universe to be closed. However, it remains that for purposes of research, forensics, and other practical pursuits, people often do assume that a system can be closed. You can characterize a

continued

closed system as one in which you can account for all of its possibilities (information) in the system by applying a limited set of rules you have concluded defines the system. Day-to-day life is, in fact, largely accounted for by assumptions that systems are closed. When you deposit money in the bank, you assume, for example, that the bank will account for every penny. In the case of a murder trial in which an individual on trial faces death if convicted, the court and jury work with the evidence and arguments stated by the defense and prosecution attorneys as a closed system. The logic of the system predicts the ways the information can be meaningful. For purpose of experimentation, it is often necessary to follow similar assumptions. Scientists attempt to account for every variable that might affect the results of an experiment. (The dangers of hastily "closing" systems emerge continuously, however. Consider the spate of murder-conviction reversals that have resulted from the "opening" that DNA analysis of crime-scene evidence has made of earlier systems of forensic science.)

Open systems

If a system can be influenced by information other than what the standard definition of valid communication within the system prescribes, then the system is said to be an open system. Ervin Laszlo contends that ultimately all systems must be viewed as open. However, it remains that this does not throw the universe immediately into chaos. It means only that in time every system is subject to failure or success. This is not all that devastating a consideration. Consider, for example, that over ninety percent of the species that have existed on Earth over the past 4.5 billion years have gone extinct. A species is a system regulated by genetic rules. From a different perspective, consider a computer program as a system. It consists of a set of rules that govern the flow of information. After a time, the users of the computer system gain an awareness of the system that enables them to exert external pressures (through modifications of the software) to change the system. Ecologists generally contend, among other scientists, that within the Earth's system, no isolated closed systems exist. In other areas, consider, for instance, someone arguing for freedom of will. If humans possess free will, then how can every possible factor in their lives and the decisions they make about living be accounted for through a closed system?

Holarchies

This term refers to a collection of systems. A collection of systems can consist of, for example, mechanical, biological, and computational systems. A collection of systems can consist of different social groups organized according to different governmental, cultural, or religious grounds. If they combine to create a synthetic outcome that you cannot readily categorize as a type of system characteristic of any of the constituent systems, then you are probably looking at a *holarchy*. A holarchy is not a hierarchy. A hierarchy implies that the larger collection of things is organized successively in tiers or levels, so that each successive tier or level subordinates those beneath it. A holarchy can be viewed as a complex in which a multitude of systems combine in a mutually influential way.

Games and Systems

Applications that help designers prototype designs or that allow learners to learn through simulations can be understood as systems. They can also be understood as games. If there is a way to distinguish a system from a game, the terms *logic* and theme might offer the best initial points of discussion. A game is a system in which the participant encounters a set of rules that regulates his or her activities. The game player, then, agrees to communicate according to the game for the duration of the game. Communication in this sense involves rendering information meaningful, and the work of the game in this respect might be viewed as one of helping the player process information according to a given logic or theme.

A game creates a comfortable psychological landscape characterized by consistent communications. The consistency of communication arises from the sense that the game offers a bounded arena of activity governed by a theme or logic that allows for interpretation of meaning to take place during the play of the game. It is, in fact, this type of consistency that creates player satisfaction, for this is how the game, as a matrix or vortex of meaningful activity emerges. (See Figure 2.17.)

When you bring into play a concept from communications theory (which is the study, specifically, of communications within systems), you can begin formulating some notions about how meaning and inter-pretation relate to transforma-tional systems (see Table 2.2, "Terms from Cybernetics and Systems Theory"). Systems basically describe what happens when people learn, for learning involves taking a given set of rules and information and in some way changing it.

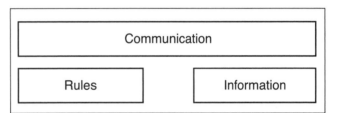

Figure 2.17 A game is a cybernetic system characterized by rules and logic.

Two important concepts in this respect are those of *context* and *meta-context*. A context is a loose term for the psychological or environmental setting in which a given game unfolds. Theme and logic usually relate to context, for a context can be said to be a setting that allows you to explore a given theme or a given logic. Consider, for example, the commutative postulate of addition. Figure 2.18 shows a context of exploration for the commutative postulate. Within this context, participants can explore the concept of commutation by examining the postulate (which might be viewed as a rule) at the top and then engage in the use of information in the examples listed below.

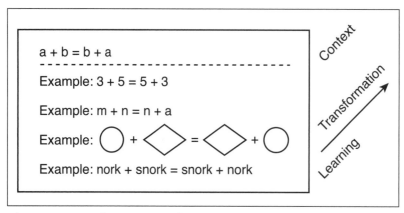

Figure 2.18 Exploring contexts furnishes participants with information to transform rules.

A context can be viewed as a setting in which participants in a game can explore a given body of information according to a given set of rules. What arises from the exploration is an awareness of the way that the rules apply to the information. The ability to take this awareness and extend it in a multitude of ways is evidence of learning. Transformation of the information in the system from information to communication involves grasping the working of the logic or theme the context provides.

A further extension of the notion of a context is that of a *meta-context*. A meta-context is a context that includes other contexts. Generally, as you progress through different levels of education, one context leads to anther, and after a while, you find that as you go, you discover that one context might include many others. (See Figure 2.19.)

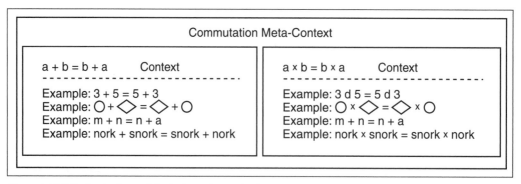

Figure 2.19 Contexts contribute to meta-contexts.

An important notion underlying the ability of the participant in a context of play (or learning) is *feedback*. Feedback occurs when you participate in the system so that you learn how to effectively communicate in the context the system provides. In almost every imaginable system involving information, *positive feedback* is feedback that induces you to transform the context of your activity. Transformation involves becoming aware of how to subordinate a continuously expanding body of information to the rules the system establishes. It also involves, after a time, realizing that the context of play you are engaged in can be viewed as but one of many possible contexts. At this point, you go from context to meta-context. (See Figure 2.20.)

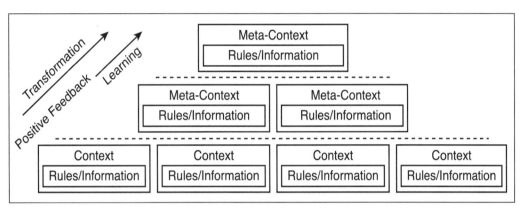

Figure 2.20 Feedback fuels contextual transformation and learning.

Games that fail to provide feedback tend to fail. On the other hand, feedback affects those who encounter it in different ways. Note the following:

- **Positive feedback.** Positive feedback encourages those who participate in a given context of play to transform the information by using the rules that apply to the context. It allows them to perceive the rules. It allows them to understand how the organization of the information confirms the rules and how the rules confirm the organization of the information. This interaction forms the basis of *participation.*

- **Negative feedback.** Negative feedback bar those who participate in a given context of play from transforming the information so that it becomes, for them, communication. This can happen in any number of ways, but a starting point is to view the obverse of positive feedback. Those dealing with such a system find it extremely difficult to learn how the rules confirm the information or the information confirms the rules. Psychological warfare experts tend to specialize in creating systems' negative feedback.

As a game, a simulation unfolds successfully if it creates an experience that provides its participants with memories that are unified according to a specific theme. As the discussion of climbing a mountain showed, the theme can take the form of a collection of devices or modes of behavior the participant encounters while playing a game. For example, the avatar of the mountain game jumps, edges along cliffs, encounters open and closed passages, and, among others things, battles and defeats foes. Each device in this context can be a form of positive feedback governed by the game's model of play—its logic, or theme.

The game unfolds as a cybernetic system—which can be understood as a context of play. If this context of play gradually allows its participants to grasp how rules relate to information, they become effective in using the communication patterns the game sustains. The more they communicate, in the different contexts the game provides, the more they become aware of meta-contexts. If designed effectively, the game can provide a large variety of successive meta-contexts. With each successive transformation of the information the game offers, the participant in the game experiences a moment of satisfaction.

Interface Design and Cognitive Psychology

The participant in a simulation interacts with the simulation through an *interface*. An interface can be viewed as the collection of devices that allows a participant to communicate with the simulation as a system. Interface design amounts to an undertaking that has for a long while been a topic of cognitive psychology. For the development of computer applications, the application of the findings of cognitive psychology often fall under the heading of Human-Computer Interaction (HCI) design. In more recent times, the study of HCI has tended to migrate into areas other than cognitive studies alone. The reason for this is that those who study how humans interact with computers have become interested in the settings or environments that characterize computer use in addition to the psychologically oriented concerns of cognition or psychology.

The result of broadening the work of HCI has been that significant changes have been made in how interaction (also called interface) designers design computer applications. It might be said that they have gone from designing interfaces to designing contexts of experience. A key factor in this change has been the use of prototyping. Prototyping allows interface designers to interact directly with application users as they create their interface designs. The insights gained from such interactions would not be possible if designs were created in isolation from the users. A major factor in this type of design is that the user enters the context of interaction more from the perspective of one seeking and using information than from one seeking and applying rules. (See Figure 2.21.)

Designers almost always face a problem encountered by anyone trying to teach someone else how to do something. They usually approach a given body of information from a clear (or established) view of the context, the rules, and the information involved, and their disposition is to begin communicating from this vantage point rather than that of the user, who may have no comprehension at all of the rules or the relevant information.

Effective design of an application such as a spreadsheet or a word processor involves making it as easy as possible for users to go from the set of information they possess to the set of rules that allows them to transform the information into tables or memos (to name two products of such applications).

On the other hand, while creation of a game that involves simulation cannot be reduced to making it as simple as possible for the user to move from information to rules, it remains that something along the lines of transforming information needs to take place. Play involves an *opening out* of contexts, one to another. Players gain satisfaction from being allowed to discover different facets of the logic or theme behind the game. The game needs to grow more interesting and sophisticated the longer the player plays the game. The game must, in this respect, allow them to use the information they have to find contexts for its application and elaboration. (See Figure 2.22.)

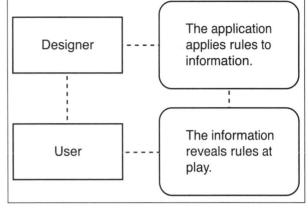

Figure 2.21 Prototyping allows designers to directly interact with users.

Mappings and Selection

Ways in which a simulation program can allow its users to interact with it on an increasingly more involved basis depends on *mappings* of the application. From the perspective afforded by HCI studies, a mapping is a way to interact with the application. Some applications provide the user an almost endless set of mappings. Others provide very few. The number of mappings depends on the users the designers anticipate.

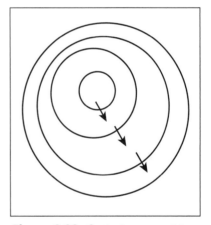

Figure 2.22 Contexts open out to contexts; contexts to meta-contexts.

A mapping is not simply the touch of a key or the positioning of a cursor on a control. A mapping is a pathway to interacting with the game so that a context of play can be explored. The event model allows you to design the contexts, and it also allows you to design the mappings you can apply to the contexts. Mappings create the pathways through which understanding of the system the game sustains can emerge.

In some cases, game designers limit the number of mappings to a minimum. In other instances, game designers seek to make mappings as numerous and as complex as possible. HCI analysts usually refer to this activity, collectively, as the *scope of selection*. (See Figure 2.23.)

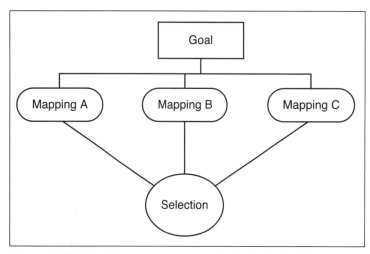

Figure 2.23 Multiple mappings create the basis of selection.

The scope of selection is high or large when you provide many mappings. The scope of selection is low or small when you provide only a few mappings. Large selection scope throws open the possibility that the users of the software will be able to explore the event you have modeled in a number of ways. In such situations, the experience for the user might be extremely rich. On the other hand, large selection might create a situation in which users are continuously engaged in contradictory or self-defeating actions that result in frustration. Along the same lines, low selection scope might restrict player options to a bare minimum and provide pathways that enable players to accomplish actions almost without effort. While immediate gratification might be pleasing to some, it might prove boring to others.

Constraints

A constraint applies to the scope of selection, and it serves largely as the specific way that you either enlarge or decrease scope. A game might provide a realistic simulation of geographical features of a given part of the Earth. Different constants govern how the game will be mapped and how the mappings will convey the event model. For example, consider a small set of different constraints that might apply to different types of games:

- The game makes use of only two buttons on a controller that offers eight.
- The game makes it so that each challenge can be overcome in a unique way.
- The game provides attractive graphical representations of the mountain ranges, rivers, seas, national boundaries, and other data. It also provides population figures, heights of mountains, lengths of rivers, and other such information. The player is invited to follow different approaches to gaining information.
- A "vacation simulator" provides a context for laying out a prolonged travel venture in which different themes can be explored.
- A "fact finder" provides a search capability for isolated queries about geography.

Figure 2.24 illustrates a few of the possibilities that emerge as you apply constraints. Constraints bear on the ways a user of an application interacts with its event model and becomes aware of the context of interaction it provides. How you introduce constraints shapes the user's experience.

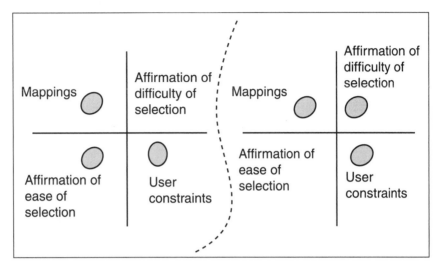

Figure 2.24 Constraints govern the profiles of mappings and selection.

A number of hypothetical arguments might be presented to justify different types of selection. Consider the following:

- **Fewer mappings.** The marketing group has determined that the audience of a given game wants to experience a type of play that rewards easy-to-learn actions with immediate, definitive rewards. In this case, the game is designed to teach math skills to elementary school students.

- **More mappings.** The marketing group has established that the audience for the game consists largely of users who seek a large number of ways to achieve a given goal but at the same time a large number of possibilities that the ways they choose to follow will lead to failure. They enjoy both difficult play tasks and facing the possibility that the course they have decided to take might not lead to the goal.

- **Fewer mappings and less selection.** The game addresses training needs for the military, and the requirements for the game have been strictly specified to emphasize that players of the game should become thoroughly familiar with one specific set of actions meant to accomplish a given task.

- **Fewer mappings and more selection.** The players of the game seek largely the end result of the play rather than prolonged interaction and intricate mapping details, but at the same time, they want to have a number of ways available to them of triggering events.

Competency Analysis

Determining how to approach selection and mapping can be accomplished in part by assessing player *competency*. Competency in this context refers to the general character of the way a player of a game or the user of an application wants to perform tasks. Generally, competency can be modeled in three basic ways, as Table 2.3 shows.

Table 2.3 Competency Models

Concept	Discussion
Skill-based competency	A roulette wheel provides a good model of this type of competency. The player wants to see very few options, only those that enable him or her to immediately interact with a familiar model of play. Such forms of interaction are usually regarded as appealing to skill-based behavior (SBB). Such a player might be said to be one who wants to become good at winning the game, not playing it.
Rule-based competency	A Dungeons-and-Dragons game draws largely from an elaborate set of rules that govern the powers of avatars as they encounter each other. Games that are heavily dependent on data and require players to develop skills in using this data in the context of an elaborate set of rules tend to call for a great number of mappings but a low level of selectivity. Such forms of interaction are usually regarded as appealing to rule-based behavior (RBB).
Knowledge-based competency	The most complex form of interaction involves high selectivity and multiple mappings. The player or user possesses a high degree of sophistication in the area of knowledge that the application or game involves and also wants to reshape the game itself. Software used for design applications tends to characterize such games. Games that require players to select and customize avatars, set up entire scenarios of play, and customize world characteristics fall into this category of interaction. Such forms of interaction are usually regarded as appealing to knowledge-based behavior (KBB).

Use Cases with Modeling

Up to this point, most of the discussion in this chapter has concerned fairly theoretical concerns. This section addresses the practical concern of using specific tools of analysis to identify material you can use to create simulations and event models.

The use case is a software engineering tool that you can employ as you develop features of simulations and games relevant to every topic this book presents. A use case can be a narrative or a diagram, depending on what best serves your needs. Use cases usually provide you with a way to easily capture a sequence of actions that you anticipate the software you are constructing will perform.

With respect to analyzing a model, one approach is to try to reduce the most fundamental aspects of the rules and logic of the model to a set of use cases. You can then use this basic set of use cases to create a hierarchy of interaction contexts.

When you work with use cases, it is beneficial to keep in mind that a use case is a description of a sequence of actions that produces a result for the user of the product you are developing. A use case provides a way to track results that someone who is going to play a game or participate in a simulation will find significant. If you develop use cases with this perspective in mind, you can prevent situations from arising in which you ultimately fail to establish effective feedback mechanisms.

Use case analysis of an event can begin with a use case diagram. Figure 2.25 provides an example of a use case diagram.

A use case diagram graphically depicts how the player or user experiences a set of events. A set of events can be single actions, as Figure 2.18 shows, or other use cases. Note the following features of Figure 2.25:

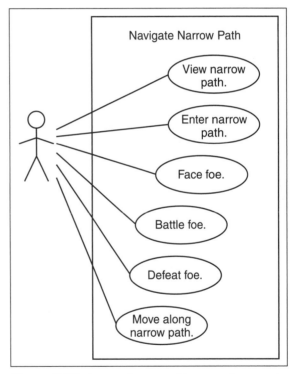

- **Actor.** The stick figure is generically called an *actor* and represents the player of the game or the participant in the simulation.

- **Events.** The ellipses each represents either an event that is part of the current use case or a set of events that can be viewed as a separate use case.

- **Interactions.** Analysis of isolated moments of action together with how these moments connect with the user or with each other is the starting point of your effort to

Figure 2.25 An actor interacts with a scenario or events.

create an event model. The lines show interactions. In Figure 2.18, the interactions are limited to those that occur between the actor and the events. In more complex representations, events can relate to each other (as when one event automatically triggers others).

- **Contexts and names.** The box around the ellipses represents the context of the sequence or collections of events you are investigating. Inside the box, you can place a use case diagram name, which appears inside the box. Practices concerning use case diagram names differ. You obviously don't need to name a use case diagram if you are experimenting—even then, however, it helps.

Deriving Rules and Information

The use case diagram provides an excellent tool for analysis of event models because its three basic components equip you in effective ways to explore what makes a given context of play interesting. Regardless of which of the phenomenological approaches you use as you develop your event model, when you examine every event model as a set of states (events) that are linked by actions (interactions) you have a way to initially create a context for your system and a way to investigate how one event can lead to another. (See Figure 2.26.)

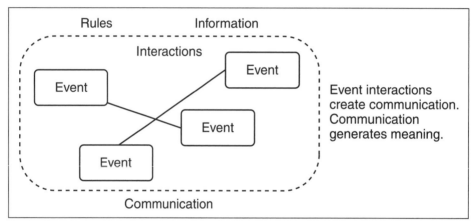

Figure 2.26 Events and interactions create a context of communication.

To draw from the discussion presented previously, communication in a systems context emerges as information passes in a meaningful way through the logic the system provides. A use case helps you identify sequences of activity that provide you with an understanding of how the logic of the system emerges. For instance, experientially, if you find that your memories are associated in a given way, then the association is a feature of the logic that characterizes your event model. Consider, for example, the path up the mountain discussed above. The path provides a basic logic for the overall game. The prevailing theme might be one of moving along the path toward the castle at the summit of the mountain. This is a starting point for analysis of the event model. For example, as shown in Figure 2.27, when your avatar overcomes an obstacle, then the logic of the game probably dictates that he should move higher along the path, not lower.

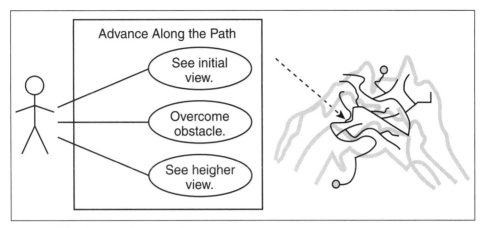

Figure 2.27 Expose the logic with use cases.

Use Cases Using Tables

Analysts work with different forms of use case tables, as mentioned previously. In Figure 2.28, for example, you see a narrative use case. The narrative begins with what is known as a trigger event, and the best way to determine this is to just determine the event that marks the beginning of a meaningful sequence of events. In Figure 2.28, for example, the trigger event might be that the avatar sees the initial view, which is of the path up the mountain. This then leads to a second action, which is of an obstacle that blocks the path. The series of events continues as the avatar overcomes the obstacle and advances to a higher view.

The tabular use case shown in Figure 2.28 has been created with SmartDraw. How you create your tables is up to you. (You might use Microsoft Word, for example.) Following is a brief review of the features of the use case shown in Figure 2.28:

- **Use case name.** This is the context name or the name of the sequence of events you want to explore. Notice, also, that a number has been assigned to the use case. This proves helpful with use case storyboards.

- **Requirements explored.** This cell will be discussed at greater length in Chapter 3, "Designing an Application Framework," where the framework for the simulation application used in this book is developed. The basic story is that as you create a software application, you can number the elements you explore in relation to a set of goals you establish at the start of your project. These goals are called requirements. If you number the list of requirements, you then have a convenient way to track your work.

- **Context.** As discussed previously, almost everything you do as you develop an event model or a simulation can be examined in terms of contexts. Contexts allow you to identify events and the interactions of events, and after you establish a context, you are in a position to confirm the logic or theme of your game.

Use Case Name: (UC 3) Avatar advances along the path

Requirement(s) Explored: 1

Player (Actor) Context: Avatar learns path of advance

Precondition(s): (UC 2) Player is advancing the avatar on the path up the mountain and has gained powers to confront obstacles.

Trigger(s): Player sees a view of the path and a way to advance that requires overcoming an obstacle.

Main Course of Action: The player moves the avatar along the path. The player can see a panorama that reveals the avatar's place on the mountain. The path shows a way to advance. An obstacle appears in the path. In this case the obstacle is a relatively harmless spirit foe that must be vanquished with a charm. The player applies the charm. The avatar advances. The next view is of a panorama that looks back over the passage just covered.

Alternate Course(s) of Action: The player views the obstacle. The player evaluates the obstacle and sees it is a spirit that must be combatted using a charm. The player sees the avatar has no charm. The player backs the avatar down the path.

Exceptional Course(s) of Action: The player does not know what to do.

Figure 2.28 Use case can be developed with narratives, in an informal way.

- **Preconditions.** Preconditions refer to any data or other items that need to be in place before the event you are investigating can take place. When you name pre-conditions, you can name other use cases, or you can state a specific condition.

- **Trigger.** The trigger is almost always that the player or participant wants to accomplish a given task. It is what allows you to enter into a given context of play. Most of the time triggers are an interaction between the player and the game. In some cases, however, you might want to investigate an event that the game triggers.

- **Main course of action.** The main course of action is the sequence of events and interactions that occur as the use case unfolds. The main course of action occurs after the trigger action and continues on until a goal is reached. Basically, with a main course of action, you are documenting what has been referred to as the "mapping" of the logic of your action.

- **Alternate course of action.** This topic is extremely important if you want to designate different mappings of the same action. To do this, you can simply name the use cases that contain information about the alternate courses of action.

- **Exceptional course of action.** This is where you can say what you think might happen if the main course or alternate course of action is interrupted. You can view exceptions as software errors or problems of design. Note in Figure 2.28, for example, that the issue mentioned concerns the design of the game.

Mapping Meta-Contexts

Use cases can be used as cards in a storyboard, which in turn can be used to map meta-contexts. Meta-contexts, as discussed above, provide a way to understand the overall logic or theme of a game or simulation. A use case table adds to a storyboard card a more exacting demand for details. Although no standard approach to either storyboarding or using use cases with storyboards exists, the approach usually involves employing an application like SmartDraw to organize use cases into sequences and contexts. (See Figure 2.29.)

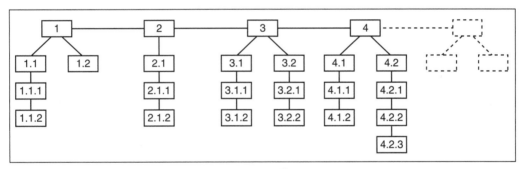

Figure 2.29 Use cases employed with storyboards effectively map contexts.

Repetition and Learning

As a final topic in this chapter, it is worthwhile to mention that almost all teaching and learning takes place in contexts that afford tolerance for repetition. To repeat a message in different ways brings two primary advantages to those who teach or learn. From one perspective, someone who hears something explained in two or more ways often understands the item explained much better than if it were explained in only one way. From another perspective, for a given set of students, it is likely that the students will possess distinct ways of understanding things. A teacher who explains a single idea in different ways, for this reason, is likely to reach more students than one who explains things in only one way.

What applies to teachers applies to games and simulation software. Players of games and participants in simulations benefit if the software supports repetition. When you create opportunities for repetition you use constraints to guide the users of your software through mappings that provide similar contexts and similar paths of communication but lead to the same objective.

Teachers might be characterized as people who are good at structuring and presenting information in different ways based on perceived audience needs. The same applies to software. For this reason, you almost never find a prototyping tool that does not allow its user to view the results of his or her work in different ways. In difference lies the chance that the user will see possibilities for change and refinement. The same applies to games. In every scenario of play, the player finds the experience less frustrating and more enriching if the setting provides different mapping and different views of how to use the mappings. As problem solvers tend to say, if you cannot see how to solve a problem, then change the way you look at your problem.

What applies to teachers and players also applies to those who create games or simulation software. When you are developing an application, try to create it in a way that allows you to continuously view it in different ways. Use cases and storyboards provide you with tools that allow you to closely analyze events you wish to model.

Conclusion

This chapter presents discussions of some of the primary design features involved in simulation and event modeling. Among these factors is how event modeling underlies most simulation work, for a simulation draws its viewer or participant into a context of activity that the event model structures. The event model can structure activities in a number of ways. Two primary forms of such structuring involve experiential modeling and objective modeling. Experiential modeling begins with the experiences of an individual who wants to re-create the significant aspects of an experience. Objective modeling involves asserting the premises laid down in a formal hypothesis. In both cases, the event model allows the developer of a simulation to create an experience that incorporates devices, events, and data that induce the participant in the simulation to understand the experiences or hypothetical issues that the simulation involves in clearer, simpler terms than what might otherwise be the case. Event models and simulation necessarily reduce things to simpler terms.

Event models and simulations have the power to create relations within sets of data or bodies of information that allow the participants in simulations to gain a much deeper and more original understanding of the data or information than would otherwise be possible. For this reason, when you design event models or create simulations, it is important to closely consider the objectives you wish to reach through a simulation. A simulation is a way to help people reconstruct experience with thematic intent.

Reconstructing experience with thematic intent involves movements in several directions. One of the most important directions is that of prototyping in design efforts. Simulations find their most frequent application as a way of reducing the financial risks associated with developing scenarios for doing business or developing products. In light of the enormous potentials that lie with reducing the risk of prototyping scenarios and designs comes the importance of considering the different competencies that characterize the users of simulations. Addressing the selectivity users desire forms an essential aspect of good user interface design for simulation software. Beyond this, one final point to be considered is that simulations are ideal as instruments of teaching, and at the heart of most effective teaching efforts is creative repetition.

Here is a short list of books you might find useful if you want to extend your readings on the topics presented in this chapter:

Virginia Anderson and Lauren Johnson, *Systems Thinking Basics: From Concepts to Causal Loops* (Pegasus Communications, 1997).

Richard Bandler and John Grinder, *The Structure of Magic I: A Book About Language and Therapy* (Palo Alto, California: Science and Behavior Books, 1975).

Richard Bandler and John Grinder, *The Structure of Magic II: A Book About Communication and Change* (Palo Alto, California: Science and Behavior Books, 1976).

Gregory Bateson, *Steps to an Ecology of Mind* (Chicago: University of Chicago Press, 2000).

Ludwig von Bertalanffy, *General System Theory: Foundations, Development, Applications* (Revised Edition: George Braziller, 1976).

John D. Bransford, Ann L. Brown, Rodney R. Cocking, John B. Bransford, *How People Learn: Brain, Mind, Experience, and School* (Expanded Edition: National Academy Press, 1999).

F. E. Emery, Editor, *Systems Thinking: Selected Readings* (New York: Penguin Books, 1978).

Fernando Flores and Terry Winograd, *Understanding Computers and Cognition: A New Foundation for Design* (Addison-Wesley, 1995).

John P. Flynt, with Omar Salem, *Software Engineering for Game Developers* (Boston, MA: Thomson, 2004).

Hans-Georg Gadamer, *Philosophical Hermeneutics* (Trans. David E. Linge. Berkeley: University of California Press, 1976).

James Paul Gee, *What Video Games Have to Teach Us About Learning and Literacy* (Palgrave MacMillan, 2003).

Jamshid Gharajedaghi, *Systems Thinking: Managing Chaos and Complexity : A Platform for Designing Business Architecture* (Butterworth-Heinemann, 1999).

Jurgen Habermas, *Communication and the Evolution of Society* (Trans. Thomas McCarthy. Boston: Beacon Press, 1979).

Neal Hallford with Jana Hallford, *Swords and Circuitry: A Designer's Guide to Computer Role-Playing Games* (Roseville, California: Prima Publishing, 2001).

Ervin Laslo, *Introduction to Systems Philosophy: Toward a New Paradigm of Contemporary Thought* (New York: Harper & Row Publishers, 1972).

Ervin Laslo, *The Systems View of the World: A Holistic Vision for Our Time (Advances in Systems Theory, Complexity, and the Human Sciences)* (Hampton Press, 1996).

Quentin Lauer, *Phenomenology: Its Genesis and Prospect* (New York: Fordham University Press, 1958).

Pierre Levy, *Collective Intelligence: Mankind's Emerging World in Cyberspace* (Plenum, 1997).

Marc Prensky, *Digital Game-Based Learning* (New York: McGraw-Hill, 2000).

Lee Sheldon, *Character Development and Storytelling for Games* (Boston: Thomson Course Technology PTR, 2004).

Sim Van Der Ryn and Stuart Cowan, *Ecological Design* (Island Press, 1995).

Tyler Volk, *Metapatterns: Across Space, Time, and Mind* (Columbia University Press, 1996).

Paul Watslawick, Janel Helmick Beavin, and Don D. Jackson, *Pragmatics of Human Communication: A Study of Interactional Patterns, Pathologies, and Paradoxes* (New York: W. W. Norton, 1967).

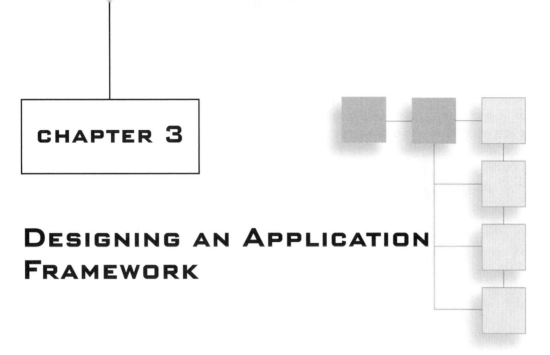

DESIGNING AN APPLICATION FRAMEWORK

I
n this chapter you begin to develop a framework for software simulation. The framework you develop in this chapter appears in all the remaining chapters of this book. In subsequent chapters, you add features to the framework that enable you to implement specific applications for things like sound effects and physics modeling, but the starting framework remains fairly simple. After a consideration of requirements and design strategies, you investigate the potentials software libraries offer. Following this discussion, you turn to implementation of a basic starter application. The starter application involves you in work with Win32 and a number of C++ and object-oriented development strategies. Here are a few of the topics covered:

- The general layout of a framework
- Employing use cases to establish the scope of a framework
- Software architectural views of the framework
- Evaluating the need for supplemental libraries
- Setting up the project and creating basic program files
- Creating a basic window using Win32 components
- Setting up message processing capabilities

Extensible Frameworks

In Chapter 2, "Specifying Events," much of the discussion concerned viewing events as emerging from contexts. A framework is a preliminary context of activity. Its purpose is to provide you with the set of devices that allows you to create contexts. If you wish to support a high degree of graphical verisimilitude in your application, then you should expect to invest a substantial effort in your simulation framework. If the event model your simulation world addresses involves high levels of mathematics, then, again, you should anticipate putting a great deal of effort into developing your framework. A model developed to accommodate econometric equations might require you to develop a graphics engine similar to what accompanies most commercial games, but you might face still more months of work turning the equations you incorporate into such a model so that they allow you to reach the predictive thresholds you have set for yourself.

Your framework possesses both actual and potential qualities. The actual qualities consist of the capabilities you program into your framework from the start. The potential qualities consist of the capabilities you anticipate you might want to develop as time passes. In software engineering parlance, you should try as much as possible to make your framework *extensible*. An effective framework is one that you can build on as you go, adding to it tools and components you might not fully anticipate at first.

Exploring Requirements

While this book does not present an extended discussion of requirements exploration for the simulation framework, it is still important to state clearly that if you intend to develop a software application for creating simulations, then you should extensively explore the requirements for the application prior to development. You can specifically document these requirements using a list, a set of use cases, or both a list and a set of use cases. In a situation in which you are creating a simulation for training purposes, your work on requirements should encompass exploration of the technology you are emulating and profiles of the users of your application.

The importance of requirements development for simulation software cannot be emphasized too strongly. Ultimately, a simulation can be effective only to the point that it simulates an event that captures someone's interpretation of the world. Whether this interpretation of the world is viewed as an artistic rendering of imagined events or a engineered rendering of scientifically recorded events, if you do not comprehensively communicate the event model through a set of requirements that stipulates the creation of the devices and interactive potentials that give full expression to the event, then the application ultimately falls short of its primary purpose.

Refining Requirements

Requirements begin with exploration of the event model and the expectations of the software user. Fully understanding the event model, as was pointed out in Chapter 2, involves examining the subject of your simulation in terms of its context. Starting with a context allows you to understand the event as a system of interacting functions that you can analyze during a requirements development effort.

When you assess your expectations for simulation and event modeling, you might find that your thoughts go in many directions. However, if you formalize your efforts, you find after a time that you can begin to shape your expectations into a fairly limited number of statements. You can present such statements as formal requirements. A list of a few of the requirements that results from an assessment of the topics introduced in Chapter 2 might appear as follows:

- <0001> The user shall support events.
- <0002> The framework shall support controls.
- <0003> The framework shall support entities.
- <0004> The framework shall support modular application development.
- <0005> The framework shall support world creation.
- <0006> The framework shall support complex physics.
- <0007> The framework shall support application development for Windows.
- <0008> The user shall be able to add behaviors to an application on a modular basis.
- <0009> The user shall be able to add animations to an application on a modular basis.
- <0010> The user shall be able to add control sets to an application on a modular basis.

You can refine the requirements the list shows, and such refinement might lead to the elimination of some of them. Regardless of how elementary, however, a simple list of the features you would like to see supported by your framework helps you begin to establish the scope of your development effort. To refine your understanding of your requirements, you can employ use cases. Use cases allow you to establish how implementation of requirements results in features that you, as a user, can visualize. If you cannot visualize how you are to implement a requirement, you should probably consider dropping the requirement.

Exploring requirements helps you refine your understanding of how to implement your framework. It also helps you establish the general architectural goals of your project. Consider, for example, what even the brief list of requirements just shown can help you establish. As the use case depicted in Figure 3.1 shows, one of the first contextual tensions to arise from the exploration of requirements for a simulation framework involves functional relations among a user, an entity subject to control, and events that mediate control.

Use Case Name: User explores the graphical user interface
Requirement(s) Explored: ( )
Player (Actor) Context: User interacting with application
Precondition(s): The application is running, and application has access to different images for display.
Trigger(s): Player moves mouse to show the images.
Main Course of Action: The user sees a set of images. The user sees a set of controls. Using the controls, the user explores how each control is attached to a different image. The user goes back and forth in the exploration of images and learns how to use the controls. When finished, the player closes the session.
Alternate Course(s) of Action: The user selects controls other than those that pertain to graphical images, selecting, instead, a control for a text field. The user interacts with this control and then closes the session.
Exceptional Course(s) of Action: The user exits the session without interacting with its components.

Figure 3.1 A use case provides a starting point for development of the framework.

Examining Tensions

You can employ use cases to explicitly express the interactions among the user, the control, and the entity controlled so that you can view these interactions as events. An event takes place in a world. The framework basically establishes a functional scope that encompasses events and the world in which the events occur. Figure 3.2 illustrates an abstraction of a systems context involving a simulation event similar to what the use case in Figure 3.1 depicts. The analysis concerns how the event under study emerges from the functional potentials that characterize a system user's use of controls to manipulate an entity the system creates. This is the primary context of the event, and it is the context that the event model anticipates.

Successful systems address multiple specific contexts of use. Use cases enable you to explore multitudes of possible scenarios of use, and from examination of these scenarios arises an understanding of how use of the system translates into different mappings. (See the discussion of mappings in Chapter 2.) Figure 3.3 shows how a simple scenario involving the manipulation of a set of two images using a set of two controls provides the user with a mapping of the system's event model.

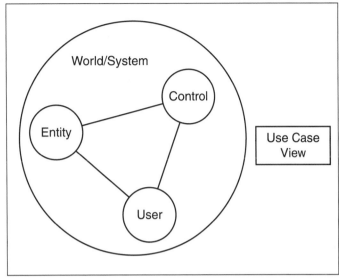

Figure 3.2 An event unfolds as the system establishes the context in which the user uses a control to manipulate an entity.

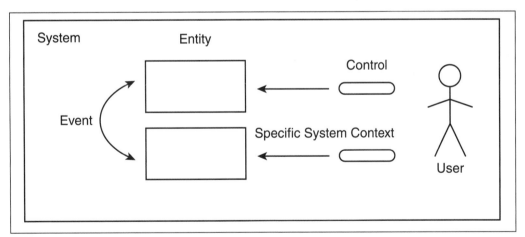

Figure 3.3 The event model emerges from specific contexts of system use.

If you draw from a sizeable collection of use cases similar to the one shown in Figure 3.1, you arrive at an understanding of what an application suitable for simulation might involve. At a high level of assessment, such a system must accommodate a variety of entities, events, and controls. To bring these elements together, the system must be able to maintain a set of world configurations.

A Framework Using Frameworks

Creating a software design or architecture involves analyzing a set of requirements. The requirements state specifically what you want your application to do. As mentioned previously, determining what you want your simulation system to do involves investigating specific contexts of simulation through use cases and drawing from them specific requirements for software functionality. After a time and given enough specific contexts of exploration, you arrive at a set of requirements that is large enough to enable you to understand the scope of your simulation system.

What emerges from an investigation of specific contexts of simulation is that an application suitable for simulation and event modeling needs to be flexible, and one of the best approaches to flexibility in software development is the use of a framework. A framework can be a set of C++ classes used to create a given type of application. A framework for creating simulations and modeling events can also make use of other frameworks.

The frameworks that serve most readily to accommodate the needs of this book are the Win32 components, DirectX, and the Open Dynamics Engine (ODE). Win32 supports developers who program with C/C++ and who seek to develop applications for Windows. DirectX helps developers create applications that interact with the hardware of the personal computer (PC) to produce high-intensity graphical and audio effects. Still another open-source framework is ODE, and among other things, this embodies an extensive set of mathematical and algorithmic capabilities that enables developers to implement collision detection.

The simulation framework this chapter discusses extends these three frameworks into a practical set of classes you can use to develop simulations. The following requirements guide the development of the framework:

- The framework shall allow for the incorporation of a variety of assets, including sound, 2D, and 3D representations.
- The framework shall address different types of data, including simple flat files containing strings and databases containing streamed objects.
- The framework shall offer a flexible set of graphical use interface (GUI) controls to enable developers to interact with events and entities.
- The framework shall allow developers to easily develop mini-applications for demonstration purposes and anticipate the development of several types of event models.
- The framework shall support such activities as collision detection.
- The framework shall be extensible and componential through the use of Win32, Open Dynamics Engine (ODE), and DirectX.

- The controls and the staging area shall enable users to study readily how to implement event models and model mappings.

Software Design

Even with the use of a set of frameworks to achieve your goals, to proceed immediately
from developing requirements to implementing functionality is not the best approach to
software development. Prior to implementation, you should consider *how* you might
approach implementation. In software engineering terms, when you consider how to
implement functionality, you consider the *architecture* or *design* of your framework.

The design tells you how you can develop the components that furnish functionality.
Figure 3.4 provides a first view of the architecture of the framework developed for this
book. The framework consists of six components. These components address data, rules,
graphical user interface (GUI), assets, DirectX, and the Open Dynamics Engine.

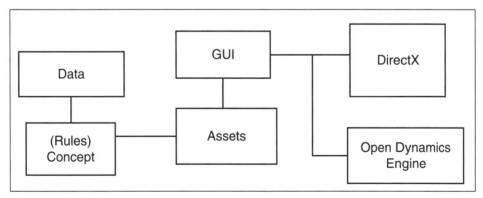

Figure 3.4 The framework reduces to six components.

As the discussion proceeds, each of these components receives extended treatment. At
this point, it is important to emphasize that while Win32, DirectX, and ODE provide
components needed to implement roughly 80 percent of the functionality of any given

simulation, the remaining 20 percent can involve a great deal of work. Also, at this point, no framework of data storage and retrieval has been named. In many cases, database activities constitute a major aspect of simulation development.

note

Use the software framework described in this chapter as a starting point for the work shown in subsequent chapters. You can find the projects that contain the code on the book's download site (see the introduction for how to obtain the code). The projects that contain the code are numbered sequentially and identified according to development stripe (Listing03_01, Listing03_02, and so on).

Assessing Design

As was discussed in Chapter 2, simulation involves attending to data, models, devices, audience needs, and contexts. The requirements stated previously address these concerns. Figure 3.4 provides a design that serves as a starting place for implementing the functionality the requirements stipulate. Table 3.1 assesses the components of the framework.

Table 3.1 Perspectives Involved in Design

Component	Discussion
Data	The data you gather depends to a great extent on the model you develop. Data falls into simple and abstract categories. It must be translated into a digital form and then stored. How you store data can vary according to the sophistication of your data development strategy. The simplest strategy might involve translating the information you use into strings and then using flat files to store these strings. More complex approaches involve using a database, such as SQL Server, mySQL, Sybase, or DB2 and storing and retrieving data objects using streams. The technologies and techniques you use vary depending on such factors as your level of skill, available funds, and desired complexity. Generally, if you embed your data in database technologies that are difficult to use, then you make it difficult, generally, to develop simulations that use such data.
Rules	One goal guiding development of the framework is that you be able to implement complex features without altering the existing components of the framework. The key to accomplishing this task involves avoiding coupling event handling and GUI class elements with the information you communicate. Further, when you implement rules, you should be able to do so in a way that allows them to be clearly identifiable with what you see (view) and how you manipulate (control) activities. Basically, a view is anything that displays something. A controller is a device, such as a button or a dialog, that allows you to interact with your application. Rules govern the events of your application. An architecture based on the MVC (model, view, controller) pattern brings these features together in a coherent way.

GUI	The graphical user interface (GUI) provides the components with which to address the needs of the application user to interact with the events designated for simulation. The Win32 and DirectX components furnish a broad set of controls that you can use for standard user inactions. The controls presented initially in the framework are restricted in scope. With the development of specific simulations, however, you can augment this basic set.
Assets	An asset might be viewed as a type of data, but it differs from what has been referred to as data because, from a purely technical standpoint, it usually starts as a complete file characterized by a given binary file type. Among the most conspicuous assets are those dealing with 2D, 3D, and sound objects. Storage of such assets sometimes involves using compression programs to control their size and using a database to control selection of them. Databases become a decisive factor when the number and scope of your assets become large.
Pipeline	A computer application that depends on a high volume graphical pipeline must employ software capable of communicating directly with the graphical hardware. DirectX is the premier set of such software used for personal computers using the Windows operating system. OpenGL provides a set of software components that can be used in both Windows and Unix environments. In the PC world, however, DirectX has become a preferred tool, but it remains that OpenGL serves the needs of many developers, especially those who want to port applications to Unix. Still, Microsoft has developed DirectX so that it now incorporates more capabilities than OpenGL. This was certainly not true a few years ago.
Algorithms	Pixel manipulation produces every effect you see on a computer monitor. The world of 3D is an optical illusion. How this world unfolds depends on a sophisticated body of algorithms many highly skilled developers have contributed to over several decades. Some of these involve selection and sorting. Others involve mathematical operations. The Open Dynamics Engine (ODE) provides an excellent collection of algorithms you can use to develop simulations..

Configuration and Getting Started

A few topics emerge as soon as you begin implementing applications that involve using DirectX and Win32. The first concern is your Integrated Development Environment (IDE) settings for Microsoft Visual Studio .NET. These can be a problem. The best approach to dealing with such problems is to try to avoid them. For this reason, the code this book provides has been developed in a series of self-contained Microsoft Visual Studio .NET projects. Here is a procedure that should free you from most configuration difficulties:

- Create a folder on your computer called SEMGDCode.

- Download the folders from the website. Instructions for accessing the website are in the introduction of this book.

- Unzip the contents of each chapter into separate directories under SEMGDCode.

The following few sections discuss the directories and projects in greater detail.

Directories and Projects

At this point, I am assuming you have downloaded and unzipped the folder for Chapter03 in a directory called SEMGDCode. Figure 3.5 illustrates the directory structure and where you can find the solution (*.sln) files. Remember that SEMGDCode is a directory you have created.

```
SSEMG DCode
    Chapter03
            bin (resources for the Chapter03 listings)
                (also contains the *.exes for the Chapter03 listing)
            DX Util
            Simulation Include
            Simulation Lib
            Simulation Src
                Listing03_01
                    (contains the *.sln file)
                    Debug (not used)
                Listing03_02
                    (contains the *.sln file)
                    Debug ((not used))
                Listing03_03
                    Debug (not used)
```

Figure 3.5 Access the *.sln file to start the project.

Notice in Figure 3.5 that the executables for all the listings in the chapter appear in the bin directory. The reason for this is that all the executables in this chapter share the resources, so it is easier to do things this way than to have the executable appear in the Debug directory of each project (which may be your normal mode of operation when you are with .NET). Generally, in the exercises in this book, the Debug folder does not receive mention, but it is left in its default location so you don't begin wondering where it went.

The structure of files Figure 3.5 illustrates represents only one approach to organizing projects. As becomes clearer in later chapters, the bin directory receives a great deal of use. Among other uses, it becomes the primary repository for your simulation *assets*. An asset can be a sound file, a bitmap, or a mesh. The bin directory also houses resources used for artificial intelligence. While you can easily follow a different approach to asset storage, one important factor remains: Assets usually proliferate, so when you store them, do so in a way that allows you to keep track of them.

Opening a Project

You have downloaded the Chapter03 /Listing03_01 folder and placed it on your disk drive according to the procedures mentioned previously. To build and compile the listing for this folder, first access the SimulationSrc folder, and then in this folder, access the Listing03_01 folder. In the Listing 03_01 folder, find the Listing03_01.sln file. This is a Microsoft "solution" file. Open this file and build and compile the project.

Figure 3.6 shows the Microsoft Visual Studio project for this Listing03_01. This project contains three working files, CApplication.cpp, CApplication.h, and Main.cpp, which are stored in the SimulationSrc directory. As this chapter progresses, other files and folders are added. Likewise, a few sub-directories are added to SimulationSrc and the other directories currently shown. These are explained as they are added.

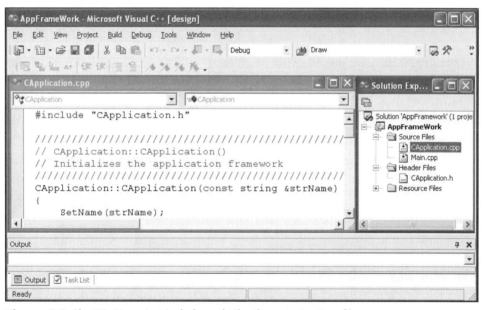

Figure 3.6 The Win32 project includes only the three starter C++ files.

If you have not done so, press F5 to build and compile Listing03_01. The code included in this listing creates the message box that Figure 3.7 illustrates.

Figure 3.7 The code in Listing03_01 creates a message box that displays a classical message.

WinMain Fundamentals

The project shown in Figure 3.6 includes the code you need to start building the framework that you expand on and use throughout this book. As mentioned previously, the project consists for now of three files. One of the files, shown in Example 3.1, contains the code for the WinMain() function. The other two files, shown in Examples 3.2 and 3.3, contain the code that provides the functionality the WinMain() function implements. (That code will be explained shortly.)

note

This book explains as much as can be explained given its mission of being an "intermediate" programming book, but still some things have been left aside. At the end of the chapter, you can find a list of supplemental books. See Peter Walsh's *The Zen of Direct3D Game Programming for Win32* in the context of game development, and see Charles Petzold's *Programming Windows* for a thorough grounding in Win32 programming.

In Example 3.1, notice that the WinMain() function for Listing03_01 appears in Main.cpp. The WinMain() function provides you with what amounts to a C++ main() function designed for Windows applications. Of the four parameter types the WinMain() function features, the most important for the purposes of this chapter is of the HINSTANCE type.

In Windows programming, types such as HINSTANCE result from #define or typedef statements contained by a large file named windef.h. (To view the windef.h file, highlight HINSTANCE, press the right mouse key, and select "Go To Declaration.") Capitalized data type names that begin with an "H" are called *handles*. Such data types are almost exclusively integers. Table 3.2 provides discussion of a few topics that relate to type identification and other aspects of Win32 programming.

WinMain() and the Application

After the #include directive for CApplication.h, at the top of Main.cpp (see Example 3.1), notice that a pointer instance of the class CApplication has been declared. You assign a NULL value to this pointer to conform to good programming practices.

```
CApplication *g_pApp = NULL;
```

The "g_ p" prefix indicates that the identifier is a pointer declared in global space. The identifier is declared in global space so that it can be accessed as needed within the scope of the WinMain() function and in other places.

Table 3.2 Win32 Programming Topics

Topic	Discussion
Win32 Header Files	windef.h provides basic definitions. winnt.h furnishes support for Unicode (wchart_t and so on). winbase.h supplies the kernel functions for the whole Windows system. winuser.h provides convenient services such as message boxes. wingdi.h provides graphical device interface capabilities (these are the Windows graphical capabilities, not those provided by DirectX). Spending a few days of study with the files benefits beginning Win32 programmers in enormous ways.
windows.h	Always include windows.h for basic WinMain programs. This header file provides #include statements for such header files as windef.h.
STL strings	Beginning in roughly 2003, the company that provides the Microsoft C++ compiler (Dinkum) arrived at complete conformity to the ANSI/ISO Standard C++ Library, which is mirrored in the ISO/IEC IS 14882 (approved in 1998 and updated in 2003). Related to this were changes Microsoft made in the string types you find in its Win32 development environment. The result is that STL strings provide a wonderful and safe way to work with Win32 programs.
64-bit programming	As Windows migrates the 64-bit processors, you do not need to worry. Win32 has already been ported to "Win64." The writers at Microsoft use the expression "64-Bit Windows."
WINAPI	In Example 3.1, APIENTRY works as a kind of macro to ensure that the integer value WinMain() is read in left-to-right order. APIENTRY is a redefinition of a general filter called WINAPI, which might have been used in its place. (Go to windef.h for further information.) Generally, you find many such filters in Windows programs. They are all used in roughly the same way, to the left of the function for which they filter the return value.
HINSTANCE	This integer value applies to the specific instance of the application being created. It is a "handle" in the sense that it provides you with a way to access the address of the application if you want to use it for specific purposes. Usually, an "h" is prefixed to the parameter name of the HINSTANCE (hInstance).

note

Such attribute identifiers as "g_p" reflect the "Hungarian" coding convention, which remains one of the most prevalent coding conventions. You can find a table of Hungarian notations at http://www4.ncsu.edu:8030/~moriedl/projects/hungarian/.

Within the scope of WinMain(), the g_App identifier appears once again. In fact, it is the central player in the two statements in the WinMain() function. The first statement uses the C++ operator new to allocate memory for an instance of the CApplication class, and then this memory is assigned to g_pApp. As becomes evident in the discussion of CApplication, the overloaded CApplication constructor provides a string parameter you can use to assign a name to your application. In this instance, the string constant "Application Framework" is inserted as the parameter value. The second statement of WinMain() invokes the C++ delete operator. The memory appropriated for the instance of the application is in this way restored to the operating system.

Example 3.1 (Listing03_01/Main.cpp)

The first move involves instantiating an instance of the application.

```
#include "CApplication.h"
//The global application pointer
CApplication *g_pApp = NULL;
/////////////////////////////////////////////////////////////////////
//WinMain(...)
//WinMain is the entry point for the whole application. This is
//where you create your application framework and start your message
//loop, etc.
/////////////////////////////////////////////////////////////////////
int APIENTRY WinMain(HINSTANCE hInstance,
                     HINSTANCE hPrevInstance,
                     LPSTR     lpCmdLine,
                     int       inCmdShow)
{
    //String parameter allows the name to be assigned.
      g_pApp = new CApplication("Application Framework");
    delete(g_pApp);
}
```

Encapsulation

As Example 3.1 shows, Main.cpp opens with an #include statement for CApplication.h, which contains the header file (or declaration) of the class CApplication. (Example 3.2 shows you the contents of CApplication.h.) If you examine CApplication.h, you see that it begins with an #include statement for windows.h. As Table 3.2 notes, windows.h contains directives to the basic Win32 components you require to build a Win32 application. Following the windows.h #include directive, CApplication.h features an #include directive for the standard template library (STL) string class (again, see Table 3.2 for details). To make use of the STL string class, it is necessary to use the STL namespace, so the C++ using namespace directive follows. The statement accordingly addresses the stl namespace.

n o t e

Note the use of `#pragma once` at the top of the file shown in Example 3.2. This preprocessor directive is part of the C++ programming language and tells the compiler that you want to invoke the resident compiler and that this file is to be open only once during your build. It designates the starting point of your application.

To review a few points of C++ and object-oriented terminology, as you examine Example 3.2 notice that a "C" (for class) begins the name of the class. All classes in this book receive the same treatment unless they represent libraries that developers have not developed using Hungarian notation.

The declaration of `CApplication` features one *attribute*, which is of the STL `string` type (`m_strName`). C++ programmers sometimes refer to an attribute as a class *data member*, and if you use Hungarian notation, you designate data members using a prefixed "m" (for example, `m_data`). After the declaration of this attribute, the class provides a *constructor* that takes a constant reference to an STL `string` as its sole parameter. Following the constructor is a *destructor*. You use destructors to clean up memory when you discontinue using an object (or when the object falls out of scope).

An *initializer* function follows the destructor. The initializer function receives use later on, when you bring some sprites and other objects into the program. Allocating memory for resources constitutes an enormously important activity, and the initializer allows you to keep such activity under control. Following the initializer function, a clean-up function appears, and this can work in conjunction with the destructor to take care of removing dynamically allocated items. When your program dynamically allocates an object, of course, it does so after it has begun running. Two *accessor* operations finish things up. Accessors allow you to set and extract information from class attributes. Functions that change values are sometimes called *mutators*.

In this and subsequent chapters, almost all class declarations occur separately from their definitions. You *declare* a class by naming the class and providing the prototypes (or signature lines) of the functions that comprise the class. You *implement* a class when you expand the prototype to include the code that provides the functionality the function designates. (Example 3.2 illustrates the declaration of `CApplication`; Example 3.3 illustrates the definition of `CApplication`.)

The declaration of `CApplication` appears in a file named CApplication.h. The definition of `CApplication` appears in CApplication.cpp. Generally, programmers use this two-file approach throughout the world of C++ programming. One exception to this divided approach to development occurs when you create *inline* functions. In such instances, you merge declaration and definition activities. Inline declarations can increase compilation time.

Example 3.2 (Listing03_01/Application.h)

Declaration of `CApplication` offers common C++ features.

```
//CApplication.h
//This class wraps up a Windows application so that
//it is possible to write useful code much more quickly
/////////////////////////////////////////////////////////////////////
#pragma once          //compile this once
#include <windows.h>   //the main include for the Windows API
#include <string>      //the STL string class
using namespace std;   //needed for the standard template library
//Here is the declaration of the application framework class
class CApplication
{
protected:
    // The name of the application
    string m_strName; //attribute
public:
    // Initialize the application class--constructor
    CApplication(const string &strName);
    // Destroy the application class--destructor
    ~CApplication();
    // Initializes the application--initializer--reserved for later on
    // when some sprites and other objects will be intialized
    virtual void Initialize();
    // Destroy the application and free all memory
    virtual void Cleanup();
    // Accessors  /////////////////////////////////////
    const string &GetName();
    void SetName(const string &strName);
};
```

Implementation of CApplication

Implementation of the `CApplication` class involves few complexities. Example 3.3 shows you the implementation of `CApplication`. The constructor calls the `SetName()` function. The `SetName()` function assigns the name taken from the constructor's string reference parameter to the class attribute that holds the name. The assignment makes it so that the `CApplication` object (`g_pApp`) can obtain the name using the accessor (`GetName()`). As mentioned previously, in addition to accessor functions, `CApplication` has a destructor. The destructor calls the `Cleanup()` function, which at this point doesn't do anything.

The main feature of the class construction activities occurs in the Initialize() function, which contains a solitary line of code:

```
MessageBox(NULL, "Hello World!", "From CApplication::Initialize", MB_OK);
```

This line of code calls a Win32 function named MessageBox(). The function provides you with four parameters, and its purpose is to allow you to easily create a stand-alone dialog. (Figure 3.7 illustrates the dialog.)

Notice that the first parameter in MessageBox() is set to NULL. The type for the parameter is HWND, which is a handle to a window. You can use this parameter to assign the dialog to a given instance of an application window. Since no application window appears here, NULL suffices for the window instance. The next two parameters are pointers to constant strings (for Win32, the type is PCSTR--"pointer to a constant string"). The first string is the message displayed in the dialog caption, and the second is the message displayed in dialog title bar.

The final parameter, MB_OK, is one of the many values that establish the style of the message box. MB_OK instructs the message box to display an OK button. It is defined in winuser.h and represents a long hexadecimal value (see the discussion in Table 3.2). You can supply other values if you want to change the appearance of the message box. Among these values are MB_OKCANCEL, MB_YESNO, and MB_ICONQUESTION. (Substitute one of these values for MB_OK to see the difference. If you want to try still other values, see the list in winuser.h. To accomplish this, right-click MB_OK and select "Go to Definition.")

Starting a project with a message box constitutes creating a "sanity check." If you are new to Win32 programming or any type of programming that involves a complex file structure, the best approach to a happy beginning involves, above all, reducing to a minimum the complexity of the initial program. This is the intention of the approach used in the development of the CApplication class and the WinMain() function.

Example 3.3 (Listing03_01/Application.cpp)

```
CApplication encapsulates a Win32 dialog box.
#include "CApplication.h"
////////////////////////////////////////////////////////////////
// CApplication::CApplication()
// Initializes the application framework
////////////////////////////////////////////////////////////////
CApplication::CApplication(const string &strName)
{
    SetName(strName);
    Initialize();
}
```

```
////////////////////////////////////////////////////////////////
// CApplication::~CApplication()
// Free the memory associated with the application
////////////////////////////////////////////////////////////////
CApplication::~CApplication()
{
     Cleanup();
}
////////////////////////////////////////////////////////////////
// CApplication::Initialize()
// Initialize the application
////////////////////////////////////////////////////////////////
void CApplication::Initialize()
{
     MessageBox(NULL,"Hello World!","From CApplication::Initialize",MB_OK);
}
////////////////////////////////////////////////////////////////
// CApplication::Cleanup()
// Called when the application terminates to clean up memory, etc
////////////////////////////////////////////////////////////////
void CApplication::Cleanup()
{

}
////////////////////////////////////////////////////////////////
// CApplication::GetName()
// Returns the name of the application
////////////////////////////////////////////////////////////////
const string &CApplication::GetName()
{
     return(m_strName);
}
////////////////////////////////////////////////////////////////
// CApplication::SetName(...)
// Sets the name of the application
////////////////////////////////////////////////////////////////
void CApplication::SetName(const string &strName)
{
     m_strName = strName;
}
```

Comments and Space

At this point, it might not hurt to mention that the code in Example 3.3 and elsewhere uses comments to identify and explain each feature. The code samples that accompany this book all feature a similar number of comments.

It is also the case that in many of the discussions that follow, you will find that the comments are missing. This measure becomes necessary because the book offers a limited amount of space for displaying code samples. Given this situation, keep in mind that you will be able to find comments in the electronic version of the code. Such comments comprehensively supplement the discussion the pages of this book provide.

Finally, if you inspect the examples the book displays against the code in the files, you might notice that the examples in the book possess far fewer blank lines and as a result appear much more crowded. Space limitations in the book necessitate condensing the code. Compilers and disks don't care about white space. On the other hand, discussing code without showing the code makes for boring reading. A compromise becomes necessary.

Generally, most programmers contend that white space is good, and studies have shown that white space contributes to readability. In light of this history, please keep in mind that the occasionally crowded code of the book is not intended as a stylistic norm for programming in C++. For a good online style sheet for C++, see http://geosoft.no/development/cppstyle.html.

Windows and Message Loops

Having set up `CApplication` and a `WinMain()` function, it is now possible to set up a real window (rather than a message box). In addition, given a window, you might as well set up a message loop to process messages for the window. To see where this activity leads, locate Listing03_02 in the Chapter03 directory and open the AppFramework.sln file. After the project opens, press F5 to compile the program. Figure 3.8 illustrates the window.

Adding Message Processing to WinMain

Before turning to the task of creating a window, consider that a window uses messages to control its own behavior (such as closing). A *message* loop provides the means by which a window receives messages. To add a message loop to a window, you make a few changes to both the `WinMain()` function and the `CApplication` class. The changes in the `WinMain()` function occur in the Main.cpp file. Other changes in Main.cpp consist of additional values you feed to the constructor for `CApplication`, a call to the `MessageLoop()` function, and the use of a Win32 function called `WindowProc()`.

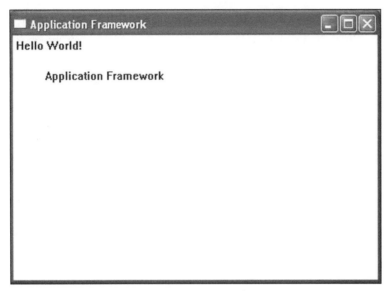

Figure 3.8 The code in Listing03_02 extends CApplication to create a window.

To accommodate the changes you see in WinMain, consider first the change to the call you make to the constructor (see Example 3.4). The change to the constructor involves a second value that makes use of the HINSTANCE parameter of the WinMain() function (which you see as hInstance). Additionally, you see two values that establish the horizontal (640) and vertical (480) dimensions of the window to be created.

An additional element is the CApplication::MessageLoop() function, which the CApplication object (g_pApp) calls right after it is constructed. This function runs continuously and waits for messages you send to it. Later on, you will see in much greater detail that this function caters to messages that pertain to your application message loop rather than the window message loop.

Example 3.4 (Listing03_02/Main.cpp)

Parameters augment the constructor for CApplication, and MessageLoop() is called.

```
// Create the application and run the message loop
    g_pApp = new CApplication("Application Framework",
                              hInstance, 640, 480);
    g_pApp->MessageLoop();
    delete(g_pApp);
//…lines deleted
```

A Win32 function called WindowProc() performs the work of processing windows messages. This function supplements your WinMain() function (see Example 3.5) and makes use of the pointer to the instance of CApplication. WindowProc() returns a value of the type LRESULT CALLBACK, which is a long integer. The parameters of the WindowProc() function establish, first, the instance of the window to which the message loop applies (hWnd). The type of this parameter is HWND, which is a windows handle. The second parameter is an integer that uniquely identifies messages (msg). The last two parameters are long integers that you can use to refine messages (wparam, lparam). To implement the message loop, you use the DefWindowProc() function, which processes the parameters of WindowProc().

Example 3.5 (Listing03_02/Main.cpp)

The WindowProc() function allows you to begin processing messages.

```
//…lines deleted
LRESULT CALLBACK WindowProc(HWND hWnd, unsigned int msg,
                            WPARAM wParam, LPARAM lParam)
{
    // Pass the event into the application's window proc
    if(g_pApp)
     {
         g_pApp->ProcessMessage(hWnd, msg, wParam, lParam);
     }
      return DefWindowProc(hWnd,msg,wParam,lParam);
}
```

Augmenting CApplication for a Window

As Example 3.6 shows, to streamline the process of implementing a window that can process messages, you augment the attributes and functions of the CApplication class. Notice that the attributes for CApplication include a Boolean attribute that you use to check if the application is running, class attributes you use to identify the instance of the application (HINSTANCE) or the instance of the window (HWND), and integer attributes that store the width and height of the window.

One of the most important functions in CApplication is InitWindow(). This function attends to the construction of your window. To accomplish this, InitWindow() performs two primary activities. One activity involves defining a large Win32 struct of the type WINCLASSEX. The second activity involves calling the Win32 RegisterClassEx() function. (These activities will be explored in detail a little later on in this chapter.)

Moving Around

The discussion in this text jumps around quite a bit. To follow the conversation, keep your project Solution Explorer open (press Alt+V+P). To navigate, double-click on the names of files in the Solution Explorer. To find specific member functions, remember the two fields at the top of the Edit window. For other items use the search utility (Control+F). When you use the utility, click first in the file you want to search. (See Figure 3.9.)

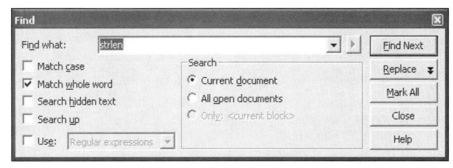

Figure 3.9 Click in the file and press Control+F to use the Find window.

After a while, you might find that you'll have most of the project file open. You can continue to use the Solution Explorer to bring a file to the foreground, or you can press Alt+W, and then a number designating the window you want to view. See Figure 3.10.

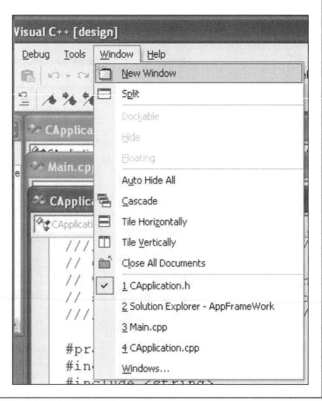

Figure 3.10 Press Alt+W, and the number corresponding to the file.

One other major addition is made to CApplication. This addition consists of the ProcessMessage() function, which as mentioned previously processes the messages for your window. This function makes use of a few new utility functions, notably IsRunning() and SetRunning(). ProcessMessage() wraps the functionality of the WindowProc() function. To run the message loop that ProcessMessage() facilitates, still another function, MessageLoop(), appears. Example 3.6 shows you the declarations of the functions.

Example 3.6 (Listing03_02/CApplication.h)

New functions implement display and message capabilities.

```
//…lines deleted. . . new attributes
     string m_strName; // The name of the application
     bool m_bRunning; // Is the application currently running
     HWND m_hWnd; // Handle to the application's window
     HINSTANCE m_hInstance;   // The instance
     int m_iWidth; // Width of the window
     int m_iHeight;       // Height of the window
// a function to create the window for the application
     virtual void InitWindow();
//…lines deleted … an updated constructor
     CApplication(const string &strName,HINSTANCE hInstance,
                          int iWidth,int iHeight);
//…lines deleted
     // Called when a windows message is generated
     virtual void ProcessMessage(HWND hWnd, unsigned int msg,
                     WPARAM wParam, LPARAM lParam);
     virtual void MessageLoop();  // Run the message loop
     // Accessors
     const string &GetName();  //Get the application name
     void SetName(const string &strName);  //Change name
          bool IsRunning();    //Establish that the application is active
     void SetRunning(bool bRunning);  // Set running to true
          HWND GetHwnd();       //Get the instance of the window
          HINSTANCE GetInstance();  //Get the instance of the application
//…lines deleted
```

Defining WNDCLASSEX

As Example 3.7 shows, most of the work of implementing a window in the CApplication class involves populating the values of a struct of the type WNDCLASSEX. The CApplication::InitWindow() function encapsulates this work. Populating the WNDCLASSEX struct allows you to define several significant features of your window, and such features range from its size, to the color of its client area, to what sort of border it displays. The name assigned to the struct in Example 3.7 is wc. After you populate the struct, you then register it with the operating system (Windows). The following list names and describes the elements of the WNDCLASSEX struct (refer to Example 3.7 as you go):

- **Background color.** The element is named hrbBackground color. To set the color, you use a Win32 function called GetStrockObject() and then supply any of a set of defined values (WHITE_BRUSH, among others).

- **The memory size of the window.** The element is named cbSize, and you can use the sizeof() function with WNDCLASSEX to obtain the needed value.

- **The cursor to use for the application.** The element you use to establish this value is hCursor, and you use the LoadCursor() function to provide the value.

- **The icon for the application.** You can accomplish this using the element hIcon, and you can set the value using the LoadIcon() function with the parameters set to 0 and IDI_APPLICATION.

- **The icon for the reduced size.** The element size is hIconSm, and you can use the LoadIcon() function with the parameters set to 0 and IDI_APPLICATION.

- **The application instance to which the window is applied.** The element is named hInstance, and you can use the value taken from WinMain, which has been transferred to the class attribute m_hInstance.

- **The message process with which the window is to be associated.** To accomplish this, associate the name of the process function (WindowProc()) with the lpfnWndProc element.

- **The string bearing the class name.** You can use the STL string attribute from the CApplication class and append the c_str() function to convert it to a string constant suitable for the lpszClassName element.

- **A menu can be appended.** In this case, a menu is not used, but if you create a menu, you can use the lpszMenuName element to attach it to your window.

- **The window style.** The window style establishes any of a multitude of properties the window can possess, such as whether it has a task bar, whether it has a double border, and whether and how it uses scrollbars. The element for this is named style. A common setting is CS_OWNDC.

As you can see in Example 3.7, after you have populated the WINCLASSEX struct with the appropriate values, you register a reference to the struct. The function you use to register the struct is RegisterClassEx(). To register the struct, you pass a reference (&wc) to the RegisterClassEx() function.

Example 3.7 (Listing03_02/CApplication.cpp)

The constructor and `InitWindow()` set up the basic window.

```cpp
CApplication::CApplication(const string &strName,HINSTANCE hInstance,int iWidth,int
iHeight)
{
    SetName(strName);
    m_iWidth = iWidth;
    m_iHeight = iHeight;
    Initialize();
    InitWindow();
}
//…lines deleted
// Creates the window for the app
void CApplication::InitWindow()
{
    // Set up the style for a windowed application
    DWORD style = WS_OVERLAPPEDWINDOW|WS_VISIBLE;
    WNDCLASSEX wc;      // Set up our window and create it
    wc.cbClsExtra = 0;
    wc.cbWndExtra = 0;
    wc.cbSize = sizeof(WNDCLASSEX);
     // Set the background color to white
    wc.hbrBackground = (HBRUSH)GetStockObject(WHITE_BRUSH);
    // Load the default cursor and application icons
    wc.hCursor = LoadCursor(0, IDC_ARROW);
    wc.hIcon = LoadIcon(0, IDI_APPLICATION);
    wc.hIconSm = LoadIcon(0, IDI_APPLICATION);
    // Set the instance to the one we grab from the WinMain function
    wc.hInstance = m_hInstance;
    // Set the pointer to our window proc function
    wc.lpfnWndProc = WindowProc;
    // Set the class name (just the name of our app)
    wc.lpszClassName = m_strName.c_str();
    // We have no menu currently
    wc.lpszMenuName = 0;
    wc.style = CS_OWNDC;
    // Register the class
    RegisterClassEx(&wc);
    // After setting all of this up, you can create the window
```

```
    m_hWnd = CreateWindowEx( 0, m_strName.c_str(), m_strName.c_str(),
                            style, CW_USEDEFAULT, CW_USEDEFAULT,
                            m_iWidth, m_iHeight, 0, 0, m_hInstance, 0);
}
```

Using CreateWindowEx()

Still working in the CApplication::InitWindow() function, after you set everything up for the window struct (as Example 3.7 shows), you call the Win32 CreateWindowEx() function. When you call CreateWindowEx(), you assign an instance of the window to the handle you have declared to hold the instance of the window. The handle in this case is stored in a class attribute of CApplication (m_hwnd), and its data type is HWND. The CreateWindowEx() function is the last item in the InitWindow() function shown in Example 3.7. Here is a prototype of the function:

```
HWND m_hWnd = CreateWindowEx(DWORD dwExStyle,
                             LPCTSTR lpszClassName,
                             LPCTSTR lpszWindowName,
                             DWORD dwStyle,
                             int x, int y,
                             int intWidth, int intHeight,
                             HWND hwndParent,
                             HMENU hmenu,
                             HINSTANCE hInstance,
                             LPVOID lpvParam)
```

The parameters of CreateWindowEx() could lead to an extensive discussion. Here's a brief summary of some of the main features:

- **m_hWnd** is a handle to a window. The data type is HWND.
- **dwExStyle** is the extended window style. This is assigned 0 in the program because extended windows features are not needed.
- **lpszClassName** is the name of the window class. In Example 3.7, this value is populated using the class attribute for the class name and the string::c_str() function to return a constant. The data type is LPCSTR.
- **lpszWindowName** is the name of the window. In Example 3.7, this value is populated using the class attribute for the class name and the string::c_str() function to return a constant. The data type is LPCSTR.
- **dwStyle** is the window style. The value used to populate this field is WS_OVERLAPPEDWINDOW | WS_VISIBLE, which is one of the many defined values that might be used. The data type of these values is DWORD.

- **int x** and **int y** are the x and y coordinates that identify the position of the upper left corner of the window when it is displayed on your monitor. The data type is DWORD.

- **int intWidth** and **int intHeight** establish the size of the window extending from the upper-left corner to the right border and from the upper-left corner to the bottom border.

- **hwndParent** identifies the parent window. In this case, the value isn't needed, but in many applications windows can be parents or children. The data type is HWND.

- **hmenu** is the menu you attach to the window. The data type is HMENU.

- **hInstance** is the application space for the window. The data type is HINSTANCE.

- **lpvParam** allows you to pass data to the window when it is created. In this case, nothing is passed to the window upon initiation, so the value is not needed. The data type is LPVOID.

Message Processing

If you glance back at the discussion of the WinMain() and WindowProc() functions in Example 3.5, you'll see that in the WinMain() a function called MessageLoop() initiates a continuous cycle of activity that more or less serves as the heartbeat of your application. On the other hand, following the WinMain() function is the WindowProc() function, which serves to detect and process messages generated for the window during the life of the application. To perform specific tasks, within the scope of WindowProc() is the ProcessMessage() function.

You define the ProcessMessage() function in CApplication (see Example 3.8). This function takes the same four parameters as the WindowProc() function. (They were explained previously, in "Adding Message Processing to WinMain.") To process these parameters, you can set up an extended switch structure and then use pre-defined message identifiers for the cases of the switch structure. The identifiers are always integers.

If you take a look at Example 3.8, you notice that the first message in the switch structure is WM_DESTROY, which is issued from the window when you click on the control for closing the window. Processing this message involves using the PostQuitMessage() function, which is a Windows function, and the SetRunning() function, one of the custom functions supplied by the CApplication class. PostQuitMessage() tells Windows to terminate your application. SetRunning() receives a parameter value of false (bool bRunning) and allows you to terminate the message loop.

As Example 3.8 shows, a second case statement in the switch structure processes the WM_PAINT message using a call to the ProcessMessage() function. The window you are working in issues WM_PAINT messages and enables you, among other things, to paint text to the client area of the window. A Windows function, TextOut() allows you to perform this work easily. To paint the text in the client area, you provide `TextOut()` with a handle to the window, the x and y coordinates that establish where you want to position the text in the client area, the text to be painted, and the character length of the text.

note

> To show you that the STL string class works easily with the Win32 objects, note that while the first use of `TextOut()` in Example 3.8 employs a C string and C library functions, the second use of `TextOut()` employs calls to `CApplication::GetName()` to return an STL string. The STL string is then converted to a constant using the `STL string::c_str()` function, and the size of the string is obtained using the `STL string::size()` function.

Example 3.8 (Listing03_02/CApplication.cpp)

`ProcessMessage()` and `MessageLoop` take care of messages.

```
//…lines deleted
void CApplication::ProcessMessage(HWND hWnd,
                                  unsigned int msg,
                                  WPARAM wParam, LPARAM lParam)
{
    // Determine what to do based on the message
    switch (msg)
    {
        case WM_DESTROY:
            PostQuitMessage(0);
            SetRunning(false);
            break;
        case WM_PAINT:
            // Output some text message
            TextOut(GetDC(m_hWnd),4,4,
                "Hello World!", strlen("Hello World!"));
            TextOut(GetDC(m_hWnd),50, 50, GetName().c_str(),
            GetName().size());
    }
}

//…lines deleted
// Runs the application's message loop until termination
void CApplication::MessageLoop()
{
    MSG msg;       // The message to process
```

```
        SetRunning(true);    // Start out running
        // Handle all messages at once (loop while one is available)
        while (IsRunning())
        {
            if(PeekMessage(&msg, 0, 0, 0, PM_REMOVE))
            {
                // If a quit message, return false to signal quit
                if (msg.message == WM_QUIT)
                    SetRunning(false);
                // Translate and dispatch the message
                TranslateMessage(&msg);
                DispatchMessage(&msg);
            }
        }
}


// Returns the name of the application
const string &CApplication::GetName()
{
        return(m_strName);
}
// Sets the name of the application
void CApplication::SetName(const string &strName)
{
        m_strName = strName;
}
// Is the game currently running?
bool CApplication::IsRunning()
{
        return(m_bRunning);
}
// Sets the running flag to the given value
void CApplication::SetRunning(bool bRunning)
{
        m_bRunning = bRunning;
}
// Returns a handle to the application's window
HWND CApplication::GetHwnd()
{
        return m_hWnd;
}
```

```
// Returns a handle to the application's instance
HINSTANCE CApplication::GetInstance()
{
    return m_hInstance;
}
```

Conclusion

This chapter has taken you a long way toward setting up tools you can employ to experiment with simulation and event modeling. Toward this objective, the topics you have
examined began with considerations of what a framework for simulation should
accomplish. By the end of the chapter, you had a working window with message loops
for your window and the simulation events you can implement later on.

Among the leading considerations in the development of a framework is that it should be
extensible. In other words, it should allow you to add features to it as your development
efforts broaden and encompass different tasks. Conducting formalized requirements
analysis for a framework helps you establish the requirements your framework should
address. You can use tools from software engineering, such as use cases, to help you
develop requirements for your framework. Other UML tools, such as component
diagrams, help you visualize the software architecture of your simulation framework.

Including libraries constitutes a key element in the success of development frameworks. If
you use libraries, you make use of the specialized work of others while cutting enormous
amounts of time from your development efforts. In this chapter, you put to work library
components drawn from Win32, DirectX, and the Open Dynamics Engine (ODE).
Assembling documents that help you understand how to use these libraries comprises
part of the work of setting up a framework.

In this chapter, implementation of the framework encompasses creating a basic window
using the WinMain() and WindowProc() functions. To set up the window, you used the
WINCLASSEX struct and the RegisterClassEx() and CreateWindowEx() functions. You encapsulated much of the work of the Win32 functions in a class called CApplication.

Processing messages starts with the WindowProc() function, but to process the messages
specific to your simulation events, you set up a second message processing capability. The
ProcessMessage() and MessageLoop() functions of the CApplication class embody this
capability.

Here are a few books that provide more information on the topics touched on in this
chapter:

> Alistair Cockburn, *Writing Effective Use Cases* (Indianapolis, Indiana: Addison-
> Wesley, 2001).

John P. Flynt, with Omar Salem, *Software Engineering for Game Developers* (Boston, Massachusetts: Thomson, 2004).

Charles Petzold, *Programming Windows, Fifth Edition* (Richmond, Washington: Microsoft Press, 1999).

Peter Walsh, *The Zen of Direct3D Game Programming* (Roseville, California: Prima Publishing, 2001).

Richard J. Simon, *Microsoft Windows 200 API SuperBible.* (Indianapolis, Indiana: Macmillan, 2000).

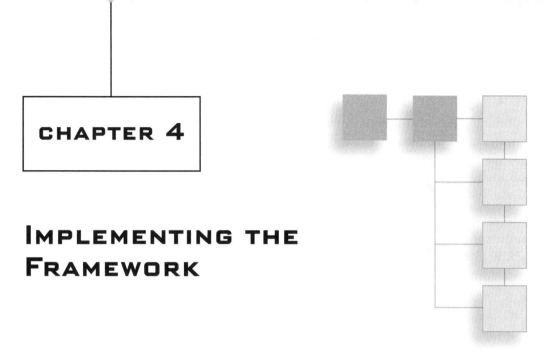

CHAPTER 4

IMPLEMENTING THE FRAMEWORK

This chapter continues with the development of the framework. In Chapter 3, "Designing an Application Framework," you investigated principles of design and then set about creating a basic windows application. In this chapter, you extend that work to encompass adding the ability to deal with DirectX surfaces to your application. To accomplish this, you investigate the basic objects DirectX provides you, and you implement classes that accommodate sprites, which are 2D entities you can use for any number of purposes. In addition to sprites, you create controls for the sprites. Likewise, you learn how to obtain some vital statistics on your application, such as the frames per second it displays. To add features to the framework, you make use of a set of classes Microsoft provides. The code is adopted directly from Microsoft and set up in its own directories. You examine it only when knowledge of its features has direct bearing on development of the framework. In this way, like Open Dynamics Engine and the Win32 components, it becomes a library resource. The specific topics presented in this chapter are wide ranging, but they can be captured under a few general headings:

- Creating a DirectX device to process graphics
- Creating DirectX controls
- Connecting to the Open Dynamics Engine
- Creating sprite entities
- Processing messages created by DirectX controls
- Simplifying application development using a derived application class

Adding Graphics

In this chapter, you proceed to expand the framework so that it accommodates a sprite. A sprite is a 2D entity that comes in handy for many applications. For example, if you want to implement a simple scrolling game, you can use sprites to represent objects. This is an excellent approach to learning how to develop simple games.

When you implement an entity, you also need to control it. Controlling an entity can involve you in any number of activities. One approach is to use visible controls, such as buttons and sliders. In this chapter, you can follow this path fairly easily if you make use of a large library of code Microsoft provides. This library allows you to easily implement the controls that come with DirectX.

To begin the work of implementing sprites and controls, open Listing04_01 and compile the project. Figure 4.1 illustrates the result. The only significant feature you might note is that the client of the window area is now colored. This is a bit of a disappointment, perhaps, in light of the promises of this section's heading, "Adding Graphics," but be assured, you are on your way to pleasant visions even with this humble beginning.

Figure 4.1 The code in project Listing04_01 provides basic DirectX Graphics capabilities.

Implementing functionality that allows you to render graphical images involves making use of DirectX objects. Remembering the libraries to include, the names of the objects to declare, and the order in which you create objects comprises what might be considered the hardest tasks involved in implementing DirectX 3D objects. Despite complexities, things can be simplified if you take time to set up classes to encapsulate the DirectX activities.

Most of the activities involved in supplying the framework with DirectX capabilities occur in the CGraphics class. As with the previous classes, you declare CGraphics in a header file (CGraphics.h) and define it in an implementation file (CGraphics.cpp). Subsequent sections of this chapter discuss this and other code in detail.

Preliminary Additions to CApplication

If you examine the code in CApplication.h in Listing04_01, you'll notice that three high-level changes occur to accommodate graphical objects. In the attributes section of the CApplication class declaration, for example, you'll notice the addition of the following line:

```
class CGraphics *m_pGraphics;
```

This is a declaration of a pointer instance of CGraphics. The use of the keyword class is called a *predeclaration*, and it serves to ensure that the compiler recognizes the class type without having to perform a large number of operations to do so. The pointer holds an instance of the CGraphics object.

note

Predeclarations are also known as "forward declarations," and in general, programmers place them at the beginning of a file just after the #include statements. In this position, you usually see them as nothing more than the declaration of a class: class CGraphics;. Positioning forward declarations at the beginning of the file makes them easier to find if a need arises to change them to an #include (as when you change a pointer to a stack object and thus need to include the actual header for the class). It also prevents you from having to shift the class keyword around if you want to add a statement that references the type of class. Although you can use the class keyword everywhere, you don't need it beyond the first forward declaration.

(Discussion courtesy of John Hollis.)

You create the instance of the CGraphics object in the InitWindow() function of CApplication. You can find the statement that accomplishes this in CApplication.cpp at the end of the InitWindow() function. It occurs just after the line that calls the CreateWindowEx() function:

```
m_pGraphics = new CGraphics(this);
```

For now, it is enough to note that the this keyword used in the CGraphics constructor points to the address of the current instance of the class CApplication. You can find the declaration of the CGraphics constructor in CGraphics.h:

```
// Constructor for the CGraphics class
CGraphics(class CApplication *pApp);
```

Returning to the CApplication class (in CApplication.cpp), notice that a call to the CGraphics::SetGFXMode() function follows the call to the CGraphics constructor.

```
m_pGraphics->SetGFXMode(iWidth, iHeight);
```

The CGraphics::SetGFXMode() function does most of the work of determining characteristics of the display area and defining the DirectX device you need to create in order to render graphical images to your monitor. (The SetGFXMode() function receives much more discussion later on in this chapter.)

In addition to the pointer to a CGraphics object, also notice that the declaration of CApplication features two new functions, UpdateScene() and Render(). These two functions perform important graphical rendering activities. The first function is a timer. The second, Render(), clears the client area of anything that has been painted to it.

Adding DirectX

To understand how you add DirectX capabilities to your application, begin by looking at the CApplication::Render() function in close detail. You'll find the definition of the function in CApplication.cpp:

```
void CApplication::Render()
{
    m_pGraphics->Clear(D3DCOLOR_XRGB(200, 120, 80));
}
```

As you might have surmised, the D3DCOLOR_XRGB() macro creates an RGB (red-green-blue) value to define the background color of the client area. This is one of the two primary macros for defining colors in DirectX. (Another is D3DCOLOR_ARGB(), which takes four parameters.) Permissible values for the D3DCOLOR_XRGB() range from 0 to 255 for each color parameter. The values must be integers. Black results if you use all 0s; white results if you use all 255s.

note

If you're a close student of the code, you might notice that the values assigned here (in the book) to the D3DCOLOR_XRGB() macro differ from those the code assigns (in CApplication.cpp in the project). Use this as an opportunity to experiment a little. Change the values and recompile your application. You'll notice that the color of the client changes.

DirectX, COM, and Devices

Rendering colors such as those you see when you substitute values into the Clear() function involves making use of two fundamental objects from DirectX. The first is the IDirect3D9 COM object (m_pD3D), which you see declared in CGraphics.h. This object is an interface to the Direct3D common object model (COM) object that forms the starting point for the DirectX operations you use as you render a simulation.

Obtaining DirectX Information

When you install the DirectX Software Development Kit (SDK), the installation includes a set of examples and a large body of documentation.

To find the DirectX Help utility, select Start, All Programs, and then find the DirectX Microsoft DirectX menu item. Then, from the pop-up dialog, select DirectX Documentation for C++. See Figure 4.2.

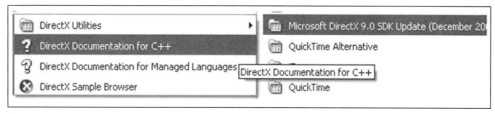

Figure 4.2 Select the documentation for C++.

To look up parameters for functions, use data types and function names as search words in the DirectX C++ documentation window. If you want to know the parameters of a given function, type the object name, the scope operator (::), and the function name (IDirect3DDevice9::Clear). As Figure 4.3 illustrates, a comprehensive discussion of parameters usually results.

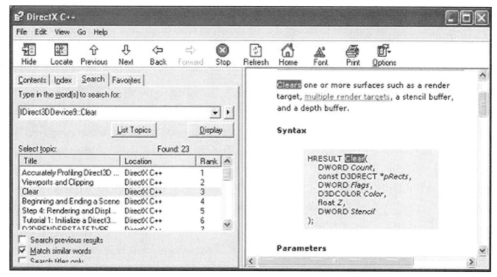

Figure 4.3 Use the DirectX C++ Help utility to obtain parameter information.

An interface provides you with a set of functions that you can use to perform a given group of tasks. You obtain the IDirect3D9 interface by calling the Direct3DCreate9() function. (This is discussed more extensively in the section that covers CGraphics::SetGFXMode().)

You also see a *device* declared in CGraphics.h. A device is also an interface. It is a set of functions that allows you to perform a given group of tasks. The IDirect3DDevice9 interface allows you to perform tasks such as rendering, creating resources, and communicating with system-level variables. It enables you to implement color palettes and create shaders. Here's the code in CGraphics.h that provides you with your IDirect3D9 and IDirect3DDevice9 interfaces:

```
//The D3D Object
IDirect3D9 *m_pD3D;
//The D3D Device
IDirect3DDevice9 *m_pDevice;
```

The IDirect3DDevice9 interface provides you with the function that is, for now, the power behind the CGraphics::Render() function. This is the IDirect3DDevice9::Clear() function. A step is necessary before you reach the IDirect3DDevice9::Clear() function, however. The step is one of encapsulation. The CGraphics::Clear() function calls the IDirect3DDevice9::Clear() function. You can find this bit of work in the CGraphics.cpp file:

```
void CGraphics::Clear(D3DCOLOR color)
{
    m_pDevice->Clear(0, NULL, D3DCLEAR_ZBUFFER |
                     D3DCLEAR_TARGET, color, 1.0f, 0);
}
```

The reason you encapsulate the IDirect3DDevice9::Clear() function is fairly simple. You are protecting yourself from its misuse. By encapsulating it in a CGraphics, you make it possible to use it when you need it, without the risk of messing up your IDirect3DDevice9 object.

The Clear() function is part of the IDirect3DDevice9 interface. The m_pDevice object is of the type IDirect3DDevice9 and calls the Clear() function. The Clear() function erases the content of your rendering target, which in this case consists of the surface you are painting to. What results is the colored window you see depicted in Figure 4.1. The CGraphics::Render() function passes the color value to the IDirect3DDevice9::Clear() function, which clears the visible surface using the color.

The IDirect3DDevice9 device provides around 120 functions, and it is best to look at the DirectX documentation to review them. Still, a few general observations might be made concerning the services the functions provide. As you encounter more and more of the IDirect3DDevice9 functions, you might find the summary groupings in Table 4.1 useful.

Table 4.1 The IDirect3DDevice9 Interface (Selective)

Service Area	Functions
Buffers	`Present()`, `CreateIndexBuffer()`,`CreateOffscreenPlainSurface()`, `GetFrontBufferData()`
Clipping planes	`GetClipPlane()`, `GetClipStatus()`, `SetClipPlane()`
Devices	`GetDeviceCaps()`, `CreateStateBlock()`, `EndStateBlock()`, `EvictManagedResources()`, `GetCreationParameters()`, `GetRenderState()`, `GetRenderTarget()`, `GetRenderTargetData()`, `SetRenderState()`, `SetSoftwareVertexProcessing()`, `ValidateDevice()`
Direct3D	`GetDirect3D()`
Display	`GetDisplayMode()`
Indexes	`GetIndices()`, `SetIndices()`
Lighting	`GetLight()`, `GetLightEnable()`, `GetMaterial()`, `LightEnable()` `SetLight()`, `SetMaterial()`
Pixel Shaders	`CreatePixelShader()`, `GetPixelShader()` `GetPixelShaderConstantB()`, `SetPixelShader()`
Primitives	`DrawIndexedPrimitiveUP()`, `DrawPrimitive()`, `DrawPrimitiveUP()`, `DrawRectPatch()`, `DrawTriPatch()`
Rasterization	`GetRasterStatus()`
Scenes	`BeginScene()`, `EndScene()`
Stencils	`CreateDepthStencilSurface()`, `GetDepthStencilSurface()`, `SetDepthStencilSurface()`
Surfaces	`Clear()`, `Reset()`, `CreateAdditionalSwapChain()`, `CreateRenderTarget()`, `GetBackBuffer()`, `GetGammaRamp()`, `GetNumberOfSwapChains()`, `UpdateSurface()`
Textures	`CreateTexture()`, `GetTexture()`, `GetTextureStageState()`, `CreateCubeTexture()`, `CreateVolumeTexture()`, `GetAvailableTextureMem()`, `GetCurrentTexturePalette()`, `SetTexture()`, `UpdateTexture()`
Transformation	`GetTransform()`, `SetTransform()`
Vertex and Vertex Shader	`CreateVertexBuffer()`, `CreateVertexShader()`, `GetFVF`, `CreateVertexDeclaration()`, `GetSoftwareVertexProcessing()`, `GetStreamSource()`, `GetVertexDeclaration()`, `GetVertexShader()`, `ProcessVertices()`, `SetVertexShader()`, `CreateVertexShader`
Viewports	`GetViewport()`, `SetViewport()`

Device Parameters and Capabilities

In the attributes section of CGraphics.h, just after the declaration of the `IDirect3D9` and its `IDirect3DDevice9` interfaces, notice that the program declares two more attributes. One is a `D3DPRESENT_PARAMETERS` struct; the other is a `D3DCAPS9` struct. The discussion of the `CGraphics::SetGFXMode()` function provides more details about these structs. For now it is important to emphasize that they hold information that defines the behavior of the `IDirect3DDevice9` device. Here's a bit of code from CGraphics.h:

```
//The presentation parameters
D3DPRESENT_PARAMETERS m_d3dpp;
//Stores our D3D device capabilities
D3DCAPS9 m_d3dCaps;
```

The `D3DPRESENT_PARAMETERS` struct defines buffers that regulate the data transferred to your monitor. It also stores information about the size of the window you are working with. The `D3DCAPS9` struct is an entity that in its DirectX9 implementation holds 70 values that establish the *capabilities* that characterize things like how vertexes are treated, textures are displayed, and shading occurs. Figure 4.4 provides a summary of how these structs work with the objects DirectX interfaces to allow you to begin rendering.

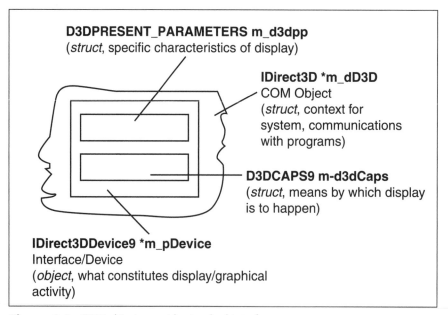

Figure 4.4   COM objects provide standard interfaces.

SetGFXMode

The CGraphics class is your main means to rendering graphical entities. If you refer to the CGraphics.cpp file, you'll see that most of the work of creating the CGraphics class centers on the SetGFXMode() function, and most of the activity this function encapsulates encompasses the following:

- Sizing and positioning the window
- Setting up the IDirect3D9 (object) interface
- Assigning the IDirect3DDevice9 device (interface) to the IDirect3D9 object
- Setting the parameters of the IDirect3DDevice9 device
- Assigning capabilities to the IDirect3DDevice9 device
- Establishing how vertexes are to be processed

The discussion that follows covers these activities as they unfold in the implementation of the CGraphics::SetGFXMode() function. You can follow the code in CGraphics.cpp. To save space, the code that appears in the book leaves out some of the details.

Sizing the Window and Creating a Device Pointer

The CGraphics::SetGFXMode() function sizes your window and positions it in the center of the screen. It requires only two parameters. One is for the height, and the other is for the width of the window you want to create. The first few statements of the SetGFXMode() function assign the parameter values to class attributes (m_iWidth, m_iHeight) so that they can be used where needed in all CGraphics functions. Here's the code from CGraphics::SetGFXMode():

```
bool CGraphics::SetGFXMode(int iWidth,int iHeight)
{
    // Save the width and height
    m_iWidth = iWidth;
    m_iHeight = iHeight;

    // Create the Direct3D9 interface
    m_pD3D = Direct3DCreate9(D3D_SDK_VERSION);
    if(!m_pD3D)
    {
        MessageBox(NULL,
            "Couldn't create Direct3D interface!",
            "Error!", MB_OK);
        return false;
    }
    // Pass the width and height of the actual window. Calculations
```

```
//set the client rect correctly to the adjusted area.
RECT rc;
GetClientRect(m_pApp->GetHwnd(),&rc);
int iActualWidth = rc.right - rc.left;
int iActualHeight = rc.bottom - rc.top;

int iNewWidth = (iWidth-iActualWidth)+iWidth;
int iNewHeight = (iHeight-iActualHeight)+iHeight;

// Get the current resolution of the screen
int iPhysicalWidth = GetSystemMetrics(SM_CXSCREEN);
int iPhysicalHeight = GetSystemMetrics(SM_CYSCREEN);
// Center the window on the screen
int iXPos = (iPhysicalWidth-iWidth)/2;
int iYPos = (iPhysicalHeight-iHeight)/2;
// Move the window into the correct position
MoveWindow(m_pApp->GetHwnd(),iXPos, iYPos,
                                   iNewWidth, iNewHeight, true);
//...function continues with DirectX operations
```

After assigning the values of the parameters to the class attributes, you determine values for iNewWidth and iNewHeight. You perform this work so that you can properly size the window as it appears on your screen. To properly size the window, you adjust your parameter values slightly so that the client area of the window (the area inside the border) is the size you designate with the parameter values.

To size the client area, you first use the Win32 GetClientRect() function to manage the dimensions of the window you intend to create. To work with the dimensions, you declare a RECT struct (rc), which stores the coordinates of the upper left and lower right of your window. When you use this approach to obtain the position of size of the window, Windows obtains dimensions for your window based on the size of the client area, not the size of the window.

Having the client area dimensions, you can then subtract iActualWidth from iWidth and iActualHeight from iHeight to get the adjusted size of the window as it is displayed on the screen. Given these dimensions, you can position the window in the center of the screen. To accomplish this, you first call the Win32 GetSystemMetrics() function with two defined values (SM_CXSCREEN and SM_CYSCREEN). The two defined values request that the system return the x and y dimensions of the screen. Again, you obtain these figures adjusted for resolution.

To position your application window in the center of the screen, you use a standard procedure. Your objective is to find the center of the screen and then subtract from this position half the width of the window to obtain the x coordinate value for the upper left corner. You then subtract half the height of the window to discover the y coordinate value for the upper left corner. You assign the resulting values to iXPos and iYPos.

Having established the coordinates of the upper left corner, you can then call the MoveWindow() function to position the window. The first parameter of this function is a handle to the window (HWND) you want to position. The second and third parameters set the upper left corner (iXPos, iYPos). The third and fourth parameters set the lower right corner using the adjusted values you obtained for the window height and width (iNewWidth, iNewHeight). The final parameter tells the function to repaint the window.

DirectX Object Creation

The first of the DirectX statements in the CGraphics::SetGFXMode() function involves using a powerful function called Direct3DCreate9() to create the interface object. The function returns a pointer to an IDirect3D9 object, m_pD3D.

```
// Create the Direct3D9 interface
m_pD3D = Direct3DCreate9(D3D_SDK_VERSION);
```

Keep in mind at this stage of the game that the pointer provides a place to store device and display parameters. More work remains to be done. Also, note that a standard defined value, D3D_SDK_VERSION, appears as the parameter of Direct3DCreate9(). This value can be described as a system value that conveniently identifies the current version of DirectX you are working with.

Presentation Parameters

By far the most complex struct involved in initializing the DirectX device is of the type D3DPRESENT_PARAMETERS. The CGraphics:SetGFXMode() function also takes on this task. The name of the instance of the struct, as noted previously, is m_d3dpp. Notice that the first action performed using the instance involves employing the Win32 ZeroMemory() function to clear the m_d3pp instance. The sizeof() function ascertains the size of the struct in bytes, and the ZeroMemory() function clears this number of bytes in the memory area for the struct. Here's the code from CGraphics:SetGFXMode():

```
// Set up presentation parameters up
    ZeroMemory(&m_d3dpp,sizeof(D3DPRESENT_PARAMETERS));
    // Use page flipping, windowed mode, and 1 backbuffer
    m_d3dpp.SwapEffect = D3DSWAPEFFECT_FLIP;
    m_d3dpp.Windowed = true;
    m_d3dpp.BackBufferCount = 1;
    // Get the current display mode from the desktop
    D3DDISPLAYMODE dmMode;
    m_pD3D->GetAdapterDisplayMode(D3DADAPTER_DEFAULT,&dmMode);
```

```
m_d3dpp.BackBufferFormat = dmMode.Format;
m_d3dpp.BackBufferWidth = m_iWidth;
m_d3dpp.BackBufferHeight = m_iHeight;
m_d3dpp.PresentationInterval = D3DPRESENT_INTERVAL_IMMEDIATE;
// Enable auto depth stencil, and set some
//other common values
m_d3dpp.EnableAutoDepthStencil = true;
m_d3dpp.AutoDepthStencilFormat = D3DFMT_D16;
m_d3dpp.hDeviceWindow = 0;
m_d3dpp.FullScreen_RefreshRateInHz = 0;
m_d3dpp.Flags = 0;
```

Following this clearing of the memory, the SetGFXMode() function proceeds to set the values of the elements of the struct. The following list names and describes the elements of the D3DPRESENT_PARAMETERS struct:

- **SwapEffect color.** The swap effect defines how your device will process data as it is moved from buffer to display. The defined value is D3DSWAPEFFECT_FLIP, which establishes that the back buffer is "flipped" to the buffer as soon as it is filled.

- **Windowed.** You can set this to true if you use a windowed application.

- **BackBufferFormat.** The back buffer format requires a little work to establish. Notice that first it is necessary to set up the display mode. The display mode is a struct of the type D3DDISPLAYMODE that defines the width, height, refresh rate, and the format used for surfaces. The instance of this struct is called dmMode, and as you can see, a call to the basic DirectX object (m_pD3D) using GetAdapateDisplayMode() provides information that is passed to a reference to the D3DDISPLAYMODE instance. The call to GetAdapterDisplayMode() employs a defined parameter for the display adapter, D3DADAPTER_DEFAULT. Then the format element of the D3DDISPLAYMODE instance is used to set the D3DPRESENT_PARAMETERS bBackBufferFormat element.

- **BackBufferWidth.** This is the size of the area that must be refreshed and corresponds to the size of the client area.

- **BackBufferHeight.** As with BackBufferWidth, this is the size of the area that must be refreshed and corresponds to the size of the client area.

- **PresentationInterval.** This value sets the maximum swap rate. The flag value assigned, D3DPRESENT_INTERVAL_IMMEDIATE, is one of several values that might be used. Generally, this establishes that a screen refresh operation accommodates a windowed application.

- **EnableAutoDepthStencil.** When you set this to true, DirectX takes care of setting up the depth-stencil for you. The stencil value controls the depth of the z buffer that is displayed.

- **AutoDepthStencilFormat.** The D3DFMT_D16 flag sets the default stencil depth to 16 bits.

- **hDeviceWindow.** This parameter sets the location and size of the back buffer on screen. By default, for windowed applications, it is set to the default target window.

- **FullScreen_RefreshRateInHz.** This parameter sets how fast the display adapter refreshes the screen. Since the application uses a window, the refresh rate is set to zero.

- **Flags.** Flags refer to the D3DPRESENTFLAG data type. Flags can be used to achieve a number of specific ends relating to swapping and buffers. Here, no such specific adjustments are needed, so the parameter is set to zero.

Device Capabilities and the Device

After you have set up the D3DPRESENT_PARAMETERS struct, you can then move on to set up the device capabilities. Again, the SetGFXMode() function performs this work. The work involves the use of the IDirect3D9 object (m_pD3D) and a call to the GetDeviceCaps() function. Here's the code:

```
// Get device caps
m_pD3D->GetDeviceCaps(D3DADAPTER_DEFAULT,
          D3DDEVTYPE_HAL, &m_d3dCaps);
```

The GetDeviceCaps()function populates the capabilities struct (D3DCAPS9 m_d3dCaps) using values you supply to it. The first parameter is of the UINT type and identifies the display adapter you want to use. Since you are likely to be using a single display, set this parameter to the default using a defined value (D3DADAPTER_DEFAULT). The second parameter sets the device type you want to use. To show that you prefer to use a hardware device, you set the DeviceType parameter to D3DDEVTYPE_HAL. For the last parameter, you use a pointer to the capabilities struct (m_d3dCaps).

As for the actual creation of the device, notice that the FAILED() macro surrounds the function that creates the device. The function that creates the interface is IDirect3D9::CreateDevice(). Example 4.1 shows you the code:

Example 4.1 (Listing04_01/CGraphics.cpp)

The SetGFXMode() function sets up the device, sets parameters, and assigns capabilities.

```
    // Create the actual Direct3D 9 device
    // Try creating a software device
        if(FAILED(m_pD3D->CreateDevice(D3DADAPTER_DEFAULT,
            D3DDEVTYPE_HAL, (HWND)m_pApp->GetHwnd(),
            D3DCREATE_SOFTWARE_VERTEXPROCESSING, &m_d3dpp,
            &m_pDevice)))
        {
```

```
                        SAFERELEASE(m_pD3D);
                        MessageBox(NULL, "Failed to create Direct3D Device, \
                                    make sure you have DirectX9 installed!",
                                    "Error!", MB_OK);
                        return false;
            }
    // Reset the device
    Reset();
    // Success
    return(true);
```

Here is the prototype Microsoft provides of the `CreateDevice()` function:

```
HRESULT CreateDevice(
    UINT Adapter,
    D3DDEVTYPE DeviceType,
    HWND hFocusWindow,
    DWORD BehaviorFlags,
    D3DPRESENT_PARAMETERS *pPresentationParameters,
    IDirect3DDevice9 **ppReturnedDeviceInterface
);
```

The following list summarizes the parameters of `CreateDevice()`:

- **Adapter.** This is set with `D3DADAPTER_DEFAULT`, which is the basic primary display adapter.

- **DeviceType.** As mentioned previously, `D3DDEVTYPE` indicates the desired device type.

- **hFocusWindow.** Here the `GetHwnd()` function from `CApplication` serves to return a handle to the application window. The return value is cast to ensure its validity.

- **Behavior Flags.** The value assigned here is `D3DCREATE_SOFTWARE_VERTEXPROCESSING`, which establishes that the device will perform software vertex processing. As Example 4.1 shows, two possible routes of device creation can be anticipated. The difference between the two approaches involves how you want to proceed with index processing. One approach is to refer some of the work to the hardware (`D3DCREATE_MIXED_VERTEXPROCESSING`) directly, while the other restricts index procession to software (`D3DCREATE_SOFTWARE_VERTEXPROCESSING`).

- **Presentation parameters.** This is a reference to the `D3DPRESENT_PARAMETERS` structure defined previously.

- **ppReturnedDeviceInterface.** The final parameter is a reference to the `IDirect3DDevice9` interface. The function sets the values that apply to the interface you are creating.

As you can see in the code sample given for the `CreateDevice()` function (Example 4.1), the final action performed in the `SetGFXMode()` consists of a call to the `Reset()` function. The `Reset()` function calls to the `IDirect3DDevice9::Reset()` function, which wipes memory surfaces and in other ways destroys any resources associated with the device.

As mentioned previously, the `SAFERELEASE()` macro calls the appropriate `Release()` function to decrement the reference count for the COM object you are using. This macro is defined in the utils.h file:

```
#define SAFERELEASE(x) if(x){x->Release();x = NULL;}
```

The x argument for the `SAFERELEASE()` macro is a pointer. If the `Release()` function does its work properly, it returns a "safe" value.

The `SAFERELEASE()` macro allows you to release both the `IDirect3DDevice9` and the `IDirect3D9` objects. Release in this context often applies to COM objects. A COM object cannot be destroyed directly, as you do when you destroy one of your class objects in C++. Instead, reference counts identify COM objects, and when you create or destroy COM objects, you increment or decrement a counter that applies to the object. The `Release()` function takes care of the incrementing and decrementing procedures. When you pass a `IDirect3DDevice9` and/or `IDirect3D9` to the macro, the appropriate `Release()` function is called.

Standard Operations

DirectX provides a set of operations that support the standard features of programs that control devices and what you see on the monitor. The features fall under the heading of *presentation*, which is what happens as items move from back to front buffers and are displayed. Most of the presentation functions are members of the `IDirect3DDevice9` interface. (See Table 4.1.) The `CGraphics` class encapsulates these operations:

- `CGraphics::BeginScene()`. This function encapsulates `IDirect3DDevice9::BeginScene()`. `IDirect3DDevice9::BeginScene()` tells Direct3D that you are about to begin rendering. This function confirms that surfaces exist for you to render to, and it sets a flag that notifies DirectX that a rendering operation is in progress.

- `CGraphics::EndScene()`. This encapsulates `IDirect3DDevice9::EndScene()` and `IDirect3DDevice9::Present()`. The `IDirect3DDevice9::EndScene()` function cleans up a scene. Among other things, it flushes data you have cached, and it verifies the validity of the surface to which you intend to render. It also works with the rendering flag, for it sets it so that it notifies `DirectX` that the rendering work is over. The `IDirect3DDevice9::Present()` function delivers from the back buffer for rendering.

- **CGraphics::Clear()**. This encapsulates `IDirect3DDevice9::Clear()`, which clears surfaces. It offers you a number of parameters to tune its activities. Among these is a parameter that allows you to adjust how you want to deal with the depth and stencil buffers.

- **CGraphics::Reset()**. This encapsulates `IDirect3DDevice9::Reset()`, which regulates what is known as the "swap chain." The swap chain refers to a chain of back buffers that can be brought forward sequentially and swapped with the front buffer.

- **CGraphics::Release()**. This function falls into the encapsulation category, but its route is not as direct as those mentioned previously. If you glance at the Utils.h file, you can find a `SAFERELEASE` macro.

GUI Events and Controls

If you access the AppFramework.sln file for Listing04_02 and compile the code, you see a window in which a button appears in the lower right of the client area. (See Figure 4.5.) After you have viewed the window, click the Exit App button. The window closes. The more general name for features like the Exit App button is *control*. To make it possible to create controls and program them so that they trigger actions, you augment the framework with code that processes GUI functionality. To help with this work, Microsoft has developed the DirectX Sample Framework.

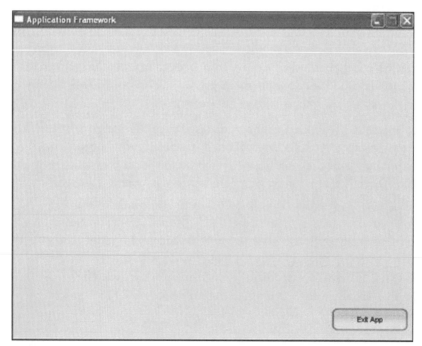

Figure 4.5 The code in Listing04_02 uses controls and GUI events.

DirectX Utility Files

To implement the DirectX features that support GUI controls and events, the best approach is to obtain the DirectX Sample Framework from Microsoft and make use of its features (http://msdn.microsoft.com/library). Figure 4.6 illustrates the files you obtain with the Sample Framework, which are all placed in the DXUtil directory. To view the specific files the project uses, open the Solution Explorer.

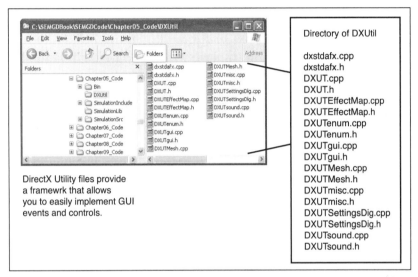

Figure 4.6 DirectX files are in the DXUtil directory.

This chapter makes use of relatively few features of the Microsoft framework, but it is best to include the whole set of framework files, for the files require relatively little disk space, and the dependencies that exist among them make including them all as a set the best policy.

n o t e

If you want to explore the DXUtil classes on your own, access the MSDN library at http://msdn.microsoft.com/library. Having accessed the MSDN library, search using the expression "sample framework" in the search field. You then see topic paragraphs for "Sample Framework Overview (DirectX 9.0 C++)" and "The Sample Framework (DirectX 9.0 C++)". Read the documentation associated with either of these topics to begin your exploration of the DirectX framework.

Based on the summary list Microsoft furnishes, the DirectX framework provides the following application support:

- Simplification of programming to create windows and devices.
- Graphical user interface controls.
- Support for event programming, including keyboard and mouse events.
- Help with windowed and full-screen modes of display.
- Help with the hardware abstraction layer (HAL).

Augmenting Messaging

Augmenting the framework so that it accommodates GUI events and controls requires that you implement new functionality to process events. This work you accomplish, to start with, in Main.cpp. The function you implement enhances the messaging processing capabilities of the program so that GUI events you generate using DirectX utility controls can be processed separately from windows events. The approach used to achieve this goal involves the addition of the following bit of code to the Main.cpp (See the Main.cpp file in Listing04_02):

```
void CALLBACK OnGUIEvent(UINT nEvent,
                         int nControlID,
                         CDXUTControl *pControl)
{
    if(g_pApp)
        g_pApp->OnGUIEvent(nEvent, nControlID, pControl);
}
```

The OnGUIEvent() function is a CALLBACK routine, like the WindowProc() function, and its purpose is to pass events to the CApplication class for processing. On the other hand, you see that inside the braces of the callback function, you see a call to the CApplication::OnGUIEvent() function. This second call allows you to process messages that your DirectX GUI controls generate. The parameters of the event include a UINT (integer) for the message, an integer that identifies the control, and a pointer to the control itself. This function is a part of the basic windows messaging circuit, so it is continuously in operation.

GUI Setup and Declaration

To see how the messaging process works, take a look at the code in CApplication.h of Listing04_02. At the top of the file, you can see the prototype of the Windows CALLBACK OnGUIEvent() function. Including the prototype in this file makes it easier to locate it. As for how application events relating to your DirectX controls are processed, examine the code a few lines later, in the CApplication class declaration:

```
// The dialog used for all our controls
CDXUTDialog m_GUI;
```

The CDXUTDialog data type originates with the classes included in the DirectX framework files. This data type allows you to create instances of the controls the DirectX framework offers. To set up the controls, a few lines later, in the functions section, notice that the class includes a GUI control initializer followed by the declaration of a handler for GUI controls:

```
//   Initialize the GUI for the application
    virtual void InitGUI();
// Processes a DirectX GUI event
    virtual void OnGUIEvent(UINT nEvent, int nControlID,
                              CDXUTControl *pControl);
```

The CApplication::ONGUIEvent function provides the functionality that allows you to process DirectX GUI events. The other function, InitGUI(), initializes the processes and components that comprise your DirectX GUI. Both of these operations receive further discussion in the next section.

Application Message Processing

In the CApplication.cpp file, you enable event processing for GUI controls. To accomplish this, you add a few lines to the CApplication::ProcessMessage() function. Here's the code:

```
// Pass the message on to the GUI first of all
if(m_GUI.MsgProc(hWnd, msg, wParam, lParam))
    return;
```

If the selection line detects a DirectX message, the CDXUTDialog::MSGProc() function processes the event (m_GUI is a CDXUTDialog object) and the ProcessMessage() function returns. Otherwise, the selection statement registers false and the rest of the code in ProcessMessage() is processed.

To see how your application receives messages, locate the CApplication::OnGUIEvent() function in the CApplication.cpp file. Here's the code:

```
void CApplication::OnGUIEvent(UINT nEvent, int nControlID,
                              CDXUTControl *pControl)
{
    if(nControlID == 0)
    {
        SetRunning(false);
    }}
```

For now, CApplication::OnGUIEvent() processes only one message. In time, it will process other events. The message you see processed is from the Exit App button. The control identification number for this message (nControlID) is zero (0). This identification might identify any control. Currently, however, the number identifies the button you saw when you compiled and ran the application. When the selection statement detects this control identifier, it sends a message of false to SetRunning(), which terminates the application.

Initializing Processes and Components

You cannot send messages unless you have something with which to send them. For this reason, you must initialize processes and components. To see how your program initializes processes and components, find the implementation of InitGUI() in CApplication.cpp. The code is as follows:

```
void CApplication::InitGUI()
{
    // Initialize dialogs
    m_GUI.SetCallback( ::OnGUIEvent );
    m_GUI.AddButton( 0, L"Exit App", m_iWidth-130,
    m_iHeight-50, 125, 40 );
}
```

The first line in the function calls to CDXUTDialog::SetCallback() and identifies the OnGUIEvent() function defined in global scope as the callback (or message processing) function. (Double colons [::] indicate global scope.) Next, the InitGUI() function calls CDXUTDialog::AddButton() to add a button. The first parameter is the button's ID, which is set to zero. The second parameter sets the button's text. The third and fourth parameters allow you establish the x and y client area coordinates that position the button (this is the upper right corner of the button). The last two parameters allow you to set the size.

note

To see the parameter information for the button, right-click on AddButton and select Parameter Info. If you want to test the parameters of the CDXUTDialog::AddButton() function, change the InitGUI() to appear as follows:

```
m_GUI.AddButton( 10, L"First Exit App", m_iWidth-130,
m_iHeight-100, 125, 40 );
m_GUI.AddButton( 0, L"Exit App", m_iWidth-130,
m_iHeight-50, 125, 40 );
```

Note that you have changed the First button's ID to 10. After you compile your application, the First button invokes no action in the CApplication::OnGUIEvent() function because no selection statement processes a message for the event. To change this situation, alter the code in the CApplication::OnGUIEvent() function so it appears as follows:

```
if(nControlID == 0){
    SetRunning(false);
}
if(nControlID == 10){
    //SetRunning(false);
}
```

Timing Issues

Events occur in time. Time is relative to the frequency of processing you set up in your application. To set up a frequency, you generally determine an interval between a start time and an end time. The frequency is the time between the two times. To see how time frequency can be generated, look at the CApplication::MessageLoop() function (see CApplication.cpp for Listing04_02). Here's the code:

```
float fTargetFPS = 30.0;
float fSecondsPerFrame = 1.0f/fTargetFPS;
DWORD dwLastFrame = GetTickCount();
//lines deleted...enter the loop
// Calculate the time since the last frame
DWORD dwCurrentTime = GetTickCount();
// Calculate the time difference and the time scale
DWORD dwTimeDiff = dwCurrentTime - dwLastFrame;
m_fTimeElapsed = (float)(dwCurrentTime - dwLastFrame)/1000.0f;
float fTimeScale = m_fTimeElapsed/fSecondsPerFrame;
dwLastFrame = dwCurrentTime;
```

The Windows `GetTickCount()` function acquires the speed of the computer. The first two lines of the excerpt code create a float value representing one-thirtieth of a second. To calculate the frames per second, you divide the elapsed time by the amount of time each frame has taken. You then set the time you started with to the time that has elapsed.

Rendering

After you have set up a frequency at which you can call on your application to make changes in its appearance, you can then use a set of functions to render these changes. You call the `UpdateScene()` function, and in succession, the `BeginScene()`, `Render()`, and `EndScene()` functions. Here is the code from `CApplication::MessageLoop()`:

```
// Update the logic and render the scene
UpdateScene(fTimeScale);
// Render the scene
m_pGraphics->BeginScene();
Render();
m_pGraphics->EndScene();
// Yield some time to Windows to keep it happy
Sleep(10);
```

The `UpdateScene()` function ultimately works as a controller of the rate at which you see things change in your graphical rendering. It works separately from the messaging cycle of the window, so you can slow things down or speed them up as you please. For the other functions, see the summary provided under the heading "Standard Operations" earlier in this chapter.

Beyond what occurs in the `MessageLoop()` function, notice that in the implementation of `CApplication::Render()` the following line is added:

```
m_GUI.OnRender(GetTimeElapsed());
```

`CDXUTDialog::OnRender()` calls `CApplication::GetTimeElapsed()`, which you can find implemented at the last of CApplication.cpp:

```
float CApplication::GetTimeElapsed()
{
    return m_fTimeElapsed;
}
```

The `OnRender()` function serves to govern the rate at which the application renders its graphical objects to the monitor. (Note that `m_fTimeElapsed` is an attribute of `CApplication` declared in CApplication.h.)

Creating a Console

Access the folder for Listing04_03 and compile the code. The code in Listing04_03 provides you with a basic console, which you see in the window shown in Figure 4.7. The rounded gray rectangle at the bottom of the window provides a work area that is distinct from the client area. This work area features a number of DirectX controls that resemble those common to most Windows applications. Among these are a text box, a list box, check boxes, radio buttons, and drop-down boxes.

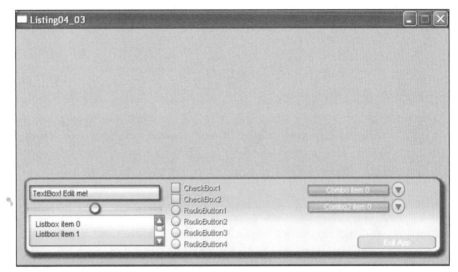

Figure 4.7 The code in Ch4_03 creates DirectX components that support the framework console.

Declarations for CApplication

The panel shown in Figure 4.7 is a CSprite object, and the declaration of CSprite occasions the addition of two new files to the project. These files consist of CSprite.h and CSprite.cpp. Subsequent sections of this chapter examine these files in detail, but for now it is helpful to inspect the attributes and function declarations in CApplication.h that relate to the additional capabilities. Example 4.2 shows selected lines from CApplication.h.

Example 4.2 (Chapter04/Listing04_03/CApplication.cpp)

A CSprite object and attributes for dimensions set up the console.

```
class CSprite *m_sprConsole;
// Position/Size of the console
int m_iConsoleX;
```

```
int m_iConsoleY;
int m_iConsoleWidth;
int m_iConsoleHeight;
//lines left out...
virtual void PreInitialize();
virtual void Cleanup();
virtual void ProcessMessage((/* deleted */);
virtual void MessageLoop();
virtual void UpdateScene(float fTimeScale);
virtual void Render();
virtual void InitGUI();
virtual void Initialize();
virtual void OnGUIEvent(/* deleted */);
virtual void DrawConsole();
```

As the lines in Example 4.2 show, the CSprite object is declared as a pointer. The CSprite object furnishes a way to display a DirectX entity that you define using a variety of attributes. Four integer attributes (m_iConsoleX, and so on) provide you with a way to control the size of the CSprite object.

With the exception of PreInitialize() and DrawConsole(), the functions you see consist of the set discussed previously. PreInitialize() provides a context in which resources such as textures and meshes, which require extensive loading time, can be processed. In this section, no such resources are used, so nothing beyond declaring PreInitialize() occurs. DrawConsole() provides a context in which you can draw the console. Other functions, such as InitGUI(), MessageLoop(), and Cleanup(), receive new code. Of these functions, InitGUI() receives the most attention, but the code added to it consists largely of predictable statements that create instances of the DirectX controls you see in the console panel. These changes receive attention in the next few sections.

Definitions for CApplication

As discussed previously, the updates to the functions in CApplication require only minor labors. For example, notice in CApplication.cpp that Initialize() becomes the setting in which two things occur. First, the C++ operator new allows you to create an instance of the CSprite class, which is assigned to the attribute m_sprConsole. Second, the CSprite object calls the Load()function to load the "bitmap" for the console. In this instance, the bitmap is not really a bitmap (a *.bmp file) but rather a *.png file, which provides an effective graphics format for use with DirectX because it incorporates an efficient compression algorithm. Here's the code for Initialize() from CApplication.cpp:

```
void CApplication::Initialize()
{
    m_sprConsole = new CSprite();
    m_sprConsole->Load(L"Console.png");
}
```

In addition to actions involving the construction of the console, you see also, in Cleanup(), that the program deletes objects. In this instance, the program puts to work the SAFEDELETE macro defined in Utils.h. The deletions involve the instances of CGraphics and CSprite created during the execution of the program. Here's the code:

```
void CApplication::Cleanup()
{
    SAFEDELETE(m_pGraphics);
    SAFEDELETE(m_sprConsole);
}
```

In the definition of DrawConsole() in CApplication.cpp, notice that the main work the function performs involves calling CSprite::Draw(). The specifics of this function receive attention in the next section. Notice for now that the parameters of the function account for the four coordinate attributes declared previously. Likewise, the CGraphics object, m_GUI, calls OnRender(), which in turn calls GetTimeElapsed() to control the speed of rendering. In the same context, notice that the Render() function, which receives definition immediately following DrawConsole(), calls the CGraphics::Clear() function to wipe the monitor to prepare it for the drawing of the console, which is accomplished with a call to DrawConsole(). Here's the code for these two function definitions:

```
void CApplication::DrawConsole()
{
    m_sprConsole->Draw(m_iConsoleX, m_iConsoleY,
                        m_iConsoleWidth, m_iConsoleHeight);
    m_GUI.OnRender(GetTimeElapsed());
}

void CApplication::Render()
{
    m_pGraphics->Clear(D3DCOLOR_XRGB(200,200,200));
    DrawConsole();
}
```

One other minor piece of work takes place in the MessageLoop() function. Notice at the top of the function that the call to Initialize() performs the groundwork needed to allow you to add graphical features to your application after you have initialized the message loop. The following excerpt shows the change:

```
void CApplication::MessageLoop()
{
    // lines deleted . . .
    // Start out running
    SetRunning(true);
    // lines deleted . . . now add additional graphical features
    Initialize();
            //lines deleted. . .
}
```

Initializing GUI Features

Before tackling the specifics of the main player in Listing04_03 (the CSprite class), some attention needs to go to the updates of the InitGUI() function. You saw in a previous section that you can employ this function to create instances of controls and assign integers to them that you then use later, in the OnGUIEvent() function, to process messages. Another activity of the InitGUI() is to position and size the console.

In the implementation of InitGUI() in CApplication.cpp, concern with the console becomes an immediate priority, for you need to assign values to several class attributes. Some of the assigned values result from simple calculations. The calculations allow you to position the console within the client area and to establish the size of the console.

With respect to initializing controls, much of this territory has been covered in the discussion of Listing04_02. It won't hurt to restate, however, that the parameters of the controls almost always involve assigning an integer to the message, setting a string for the value to be displayed, and then setting the size of the control. In some instances, these operations vary somewhat, and such variations can be discussed as they occur.

Here is an example of the code from InitGUI() showing values being assigned to class attributes so that the console (and other items) can be positioned and the instantiation of a few of the DirectX controls that appear in the console:

```
void CApplication::InitGUI()
{
    // Set up defaults for console size/position
    m_iConsoleWidth = m_iWidth;
    m_iConsoleHeight = 128;
    m_iConsoleX = 6;
    m_iConsoleY = m_iHeight - m_iConsoleHeight;

    int y=m_iConsoleY;

//code left out . . .Initialize controls
```

```
    m_GUI.AddButton(0, L"Exit App", m_iWidth-140,
                        m_iHeight-42, 125, 22 );
    m_GUI.AddEditBox(1, L"TextBox! Edit me!",
                        m_iConsoleX+10,y+=10,200,30,false,NULL);
    m_GUI.AddSlider(2,m_iConsoleX+10,y+=22,200,32,0,100,50,false,NULL);
//code left out. . .
}
```

Creating Sprites

Now it's time to proceed to the most significant feature of Listing04_03. As usual, it is best to begin with a discussion of the attributes. Notice in CSprite.h that a couple of DirectX features come into play:

```
//lines left out . . .
    static ID3DXSprite *m_pSprite;
    static int m_iReferenceCount;
    IDirect3DTexture9 *m_pTexture;
    int m_iWidth;
    int m_iHeight;
    RECT m_rcSource;
    D3DXIMAGE_INFO m_infImage;
```

Technically, a sprite is a 2D object, and as you can see from the declaration of m_pSprite, the framework being developed here uses the DirectX ID3DXSprite object to implement what will serve largely as a 2D object. Provision for the sprite's content comes with the use of the IDirect3DTexture9, which is the data type of m_pTexture. An object of the IDirect3DTexture9 type defines a texture. The functions associated with this data type help you load the texture data from its source file. In addition, notice that the declaration of CSprite includes a static integer identifier, m_iReferenceCount, which allows you to track the number of references to sprites you have created. A final attribute in this set is the D3DXIMAGE_INFO struct, which DirectX provides for obtaining and manipulating values relating to textures and images.

Regarding the behavior of the CSprite, as you can see a little further along in CSprite.h, a small set of member functions covers the bases:

```
    CSprite();
    ~CSprite();
    bool Load(wstring strFile);
    void Draw(int x, int y);
    void Draw(int x, int y, int w,int h);
    int GetWidth();
    int GetHeight();
```

The constructor for CSprite requires no arguments, but it still performs quite a bit of hidden work (as becomes evident in the discussion of its implementation later on). The visible work of using the CSprite class arrives with the use of the Load() and Draw() functions. Draw() provides two overloaded versions. One version allows you to accept the default size of a sprite when you render it. The other version allows you to scale the sprite dynamically to create a variety of effects.

As a final point, apart from the specific features of the CSprite class declaration, notice at the top of CSprite.h the #include directives for the two DirectX header files:

```
#include <d3d9.h>
#include <d3dx9.h>
```

These two header files provide links to a variety of DirectX services. You can find these files in the Include directory of DirectX. The d3d9.h header file contains #include directives to the core DirectX header files. The d3dx9.h header files contain type definitions and define statements for most of the items you use commonly, such as device interfaces, textures, and vertex buffers.

Implementing CSprite

If you examine CSprite.cpp, you'll see that at the top of the file the program assigns NULL to a static instance of CSprite (m_pSprite) and a zero to the reference counter, m_iReferenceCount. Here's the code:

```
ID3DXSprite *CSprite::m_pSprite = NULL;
int CSprite::m_iReferenceCount = 0;
```

The approach used in this application for displaying sprites involves creating instances of sprites as needed and tracking these instances using a reference counter. To accomplish this task, you employ both the ID3DXSprite identifier and the integer to track the number of CSprite references. These are declared as static.

CSprite Construction

The constructor of CSprite has a somewhat hidden agenda. The hidden agenda involves setting up the interface for the sprite using information derived from the global pointer to CApplication declared at the top of CApplication.h (g_App). The global pointer provides information relative to both Win32 and DirectX parameters. Notice the work of the cascaded function calls in CSprite::CSprite():

```
//cascading function calls. . .
D3DXCreateSprite(g_pApp->GetGraphics()->GetDevice(),&m_pSprite);
m_iReferenceCount = 0;
```

In the D3DXCreateSprite() function call, CApplication::GetGraphics() returns a reference to the CGraphics object, and the CGraphics::GetDevice() function returns a reference to the IDirect3DDevice9 object currently instantiated. The device values can then be used to set up the ID3DXSprite interface (m_pSprite). If this is the first instance of a CSprite object, the reference is set to zero.

The only constructor activities that follow setting up the device values of the CSprite object involve incrementing the reference count and setting the m_Texture attribute to NULL.

```
m_iReferenceCount++;
m_pTexture = NULL;
```

The constructor increments the reference count only when the selection statement [if (!m_Sprite)] indicates that the interface already exists.

CSprite Loading

The CSprite::Load() function shown in CSprite.cpp uses the D3DXCreateTextureFromFileEx() function, which is about as complex as you would expect it to be as a one-stop solution for loading a 3D sprite. So that you can view the context the Load() function provides, here is the call to D3DXCreateTextureFromFileEx() with most of the parameters left out:

```
bool CSprite::Load(wstring strFile)
{
    // lines left out . . .
    SAFEDELETE(m_pTexture);
     if(FAILED(D3DXCreateTextureFromFileEx(
        g_pApp->GetGraphics()->GetDevice(),
        //code left out …
        &m_infImage,
            NULL,
            &m_pTexture)))
    {
        return(false);
    }
    m_iWidth = m_infImage.Width;
    m_iHeight = m_infImage.Height;
    SetRect(&m_rcSource, 0, 0, m_iWidth, m_iHeight);
    return(true);
}
```

As for the parameters of the D3DXCreateTextureFromFileEx(), here is the prototype Microsoft provides:

```
HRESULT WINAPI
D3DXCreateTextureFromFileEx(
                            LPDIRECT3DDEVICE9 pDevice,
                            LPCTSTR pSrcFile,
                            UINT Width,
                            UINT Height,
                            UINT MipLevels,
                            DWORD Usage,
                            D3DFORMAT Format,
                            D3DPOOL Pool,
                            DWORD Filter,
                            DWORD MipFilter,
                            D3DCOLOR ColorKey,
                            D3DXIMAGE_INFO *pSrcInfo,
                            PALETTEENTRY *pPalette,
                            LPDIRECT3DTEXTURE9 *ppTexture
);
```

Table 4.2 provides a summary of the `D3DXCreateTextureFromFileEx()` parameters.

Following the population of the parameters for the `D3DXCreateTextureFromFileEx()` function, the `Load()` function proceeds to set the class attributes for the sprite's width and height. Using these values, the final lines of the `Load()` function establish the position of the rectangle that contains the sprite. To set the position, you use the Win32 `SetRect()` function (which winuser.h provides).

CSprite Drawing

Overloaded versions of the `Draw()` function of `CSprite` enable you to manipulate sprites in two ways, using either default or scaled values for its size. With the exception of the differing parameter lists and the addition of the statement that controls the scaling, both functions are the same.

From an analysis of the three-parameter version, how the two-parameter version works becomes evident. Here's the code for the three-parameter version of `CSprite::Draw()` as presented in CSprite.cpp:

Table 4.2 D3DXCreateTextureFromFileEx() Parameters

Parameter	Discussion
pDevice	The technique for obtaining the device values by calling cascading functions was presented previously under the heading "Sprite Construction." The pDevice is a LPDIRECT3DDEVICE9 object.
pSrcFile	The strFile parameter, of the type wstring (which is ultimately a LPCTSTR) provides the name of the source file for the sprite. Note that SAFEDELETE macro in CSpirte::Load() checks for the existence of the file.
Width	The type is UINT, and it designates the width in pixels. Note in CSpirte::Load() that the value is set to zero. When you set this value to zero, DirectX determines dimensions for itself by deriving values from the file and rounding them in a safe way.
Height	The type is UINT, and it designates the height in pixels. As with Width, note that this value is set to zero. As before, DirectX determines dimensions for itself by deriving values from the file and rounding them in a safe way.
MipLevels	This is an integer value (UINT) and sets the *mipmap* sampling level for your image. You can view the increments of resolution you select for the image—although the concept is more complex. If you set the value to D3DX_DEFAULT, DirectX sets up what it considers a consistent chain or series of resolutions for you.
Usage	This is a DWORD value, and you can use it to indicate that the surface is to be used as a render target. In the Load() functions, things are simplified by not setting a target surface.
Format	This parameter is of the typeD3DFORMAT and designates the requested pixel format for the texture. This defined value you see used in Load(), D3DFMT_A8R8G8B8, sets up a back buffer format.
Pool	This parameter is of the type D3DPOOL and designates the memory class into which the texture should be placed. In the Load() function, the D3DPOOL_MANAGED value establishes that DirectX will automatically copy resources to device-accessible memory.
Filter	This parameter is of the type DWORD and regulates how DirectX filters the image. If you specify D3DX_DEFAULT the result is the same as using the or'd expression: D3DX_FILTER_TRIANGLE | D3DX_FILTER_DITHER
MipFilter	This parameter is of the type DWORD. The value D3DX_DEFAULT is the equivalent of D3DX_FILTER_BOX. The general result is that DirectX computes the filter from the source image by using a 2_2(_2) pixel box.
ColorKey	This parameter is of the type D3DCOLOR. As you can see in the Load() function definition, the D3DCOLOR_XRGB() macro, with values of 255,0,255, sets this parameter.
pSrcInfo	This parameter is a pointer reference of the type D3DXIMAGE_INFO. The value used in Load() is a reference to the D3DXIMAGE_INFO attribute declared for CSprite (m_infImage).
pPalette	This parameter is a reference of the type PALETTEENTRY, which sets up a 256-color palette for color substitutions. The value for Load() is NULL, so no palette is used.
ppTexture	This parameter is a pointer reference of the type LPDIRECT3DTEXTURE9. The value used in Load() is m_pTexture.

```
void CSprite::Draw(int x, int y, int w, int h)
{
    float sx = (float)(w)/(float)(m_iWidth);
    float sy = (float)(h)/(float)(m_iHeight);
    D3DXMATRIX matScale;
    D3DXMatrixScaling(&matScale,sx,sy,1.0);
    m_pSprite->SetTransform(&matScale);
    D3DXVECTOR3 vecPos((FLOAT)x,(FLOAT)y,0);
    m_pSprite->Begin(D3DXSPRITE_ALPHABLEND);
    m_pSprite->Draw(m_pTexture,
                    &m_rcSource,
                    NULL,
                    &vecPos,
                    D3DCOLOR_XRGB(255,255,255));
    m_pSprite->End();
}
```

The first two lines of CSprite::Draw() establish the values that scale the sprite. Following the calculation of these values, the function declares a D3DXMATRIX struct (matScale). Following the declaration of the D3DXMATRIX struct, the D3DXMatrixScaling() function is called. This function builds a matrix that scales along the x axis, the y axis, and the z axis. The final parameter, which designates the z axis, is set to a "normal" value of 1.0. Setting the z axis to normal accommodates 2D sprites. The D3DXMatrixScaling() function uses the calculated scaling values to set up the matrix for transformation. The ID3DXSprite::SetTransform() function uses a reference to the D3DXMATRIX object (matScale) to set the transform, which scales, rotates, or transforms the sprite.   ♦

To use the parameters passed to CSprite::Draw(), a D3DXVECTOR3 struct comes into play following the SetTransform() function. The vector casts the x and y parameter values as floats and sets the z value to 0. The final three lines of CSprite::Draw() use the ID3DXSprite functions Begin(), Draw(), and End(). (Discussion of the function appears in Table 4.1.) The only notes that might be added concern a few of the parameters. Consider, for example, that you can set the alpha blending state using D3DXSPRITE_ALPHABLEND. In the call to ID3DXSprite::Draw(), the RECT struct (m_rcSource), in conjunction with the D3DXVECTOR3 object creates a context in which the sprite can be drawn.

Gearing Up for Action

Open Listing04_04 and compile the code. You see the window shown in Figure 4.8. The great difference between this and previous versions of the application the framework allows us to develop becomes evident when you look at the graphical images of the hammer and the many text indicators that show the values stored in or generated by the DirectX controls in the panel.

Figure 4.8 The code in Listing04_04 makes use of the `CSprite` control capabilities.

To arrive at a sense of how triggered events change the application, click the controls for Hammer1.png and watch the image of the hammer change. Likewise, click other controls, type a line in the TextBox! Edit me! field, and play with the slider.

Data and Constants

To provide for the different types of messages you see conveyed in the window Figure 4.8 illustrates, it is necessary to feed some data to the application. To accomplish this, the means available for now consist of a few values confined to the `CApplication` class. Attributes that accommodate these values are as follows (see CApplication.h):

```
int m_iSlider;
wstring m_strText;
wstring m_strListBox;
bool m_flgCheck1;/*lines deleted. . .*/
bool m_flgRadio1;/*lines deleted. . .*/
wstring m_strCombo1;/*lines deleted. . .*/
class CSprite *m_sprPicture1;/*lines deleted. . .*/
```

To make use of these values, you declare a number of static constants at the top of CApplication.cpp. These static constants identify controls and messages to be uniquely processed as the controls issue them. Here's a sampling:

```
static const int IDC_SLIDER = 0;
static const int IDC_TEXTBOX = 1;
static const int IDC_CHECKBOX1 = 2;/*lines deleted. . .*/
static const int IDC_BUTTON = 4;
static const int IDC_LISTBOX = 5;
static const int IDC_RADIO1 = 6;/*lines deleted. . .*/
static const int IDC_COMBOBOX1 = 10;/*lines deleted. . .*/
static const int IDC_STATIC = 12;/*lines deleted. . .*/
static const int EVENT_INITIALIZE = 1234;
```

The prefix IDC designates that the identifier stands for a control. Notice, also, that you use the EVENT_INITIALIZE constant to set an initial value for data rather than to identify a control. Use of this value becomes evident in the discussion of the selection statements in the OnGUIEvent() function.

InitGUI Updates

Given the data and constants mentioned previously, you can augment the controls instantiated in CApplication::InitGUI() so that they can process data and issue unique messages. Previous sections cover the specifics of how this happens, but to review, consider a few of the changed control statements in CApplication.cpp:

```
// Checkboxes
    y = m_iConsoleY;
    m_GUI.AddCheckBox(IDC_CHECKBOX1,
                      L"CheckBox1", m_iConsoleX + 220, y += 10, 100, 16);
    m_GUI.AddCheckBox(IDC_CHECKBOX2,
                      L"CheckBox2", m_iConsoleX + 220, y += 16, 100, 16);
    // Radio buttons
    m_GUI.AddRadioButton(IDC_RADIO1, 0,
                      L"RadioButton1", m_iConsoleX + 220,y += 16, 100, 16);
    m_GUI.AddRadioButton(IDC_RADIO2, 0,
                      L"RadioButton2", m_iConsoleX + 220, y += 16, 100, 16);
```

Notice that for each of the controls, one of the static constants declared earlier serves as a unique identifier. Mnemonic identifiers for the controls replace integer values. In this way, you can reduce the task of identifying the controls to a lookup system. This eliminates the irregular dependency on hard-coded integer values that results when you do not declare static constants in a convenient and visible place in the program.

OnGUIEvent Updates

Processing events for the controls becomes fairly straightforward when you use mnemonics to identify control messages. Consider a few lines of `CApplication::OnGUIEvent()`:

```
void CApplication::OnGUIEvent(UINT nEvent,
                              int nControlID,
                              CDXUTControl *pControl)
{
/*lines deleted. . .*/
else if(nControlID == IDC_TEXTBOX)
    {
        // Update the textbox variable
        CDXUTEditBox *pEditBox = (CDXUTEditBox *)pControl;
        WCHAR wszText[50];
        pEditBox->GetTextCopy(wszText,50);
        m_strText = wszText;
    }
    else if(nControlID == IDC_CHECKBOX1)
    {
        // Set the check box
        CDXUTCheckBox *pCheckBox = (CDXUTCheckBox *)pControl;
        m_flgCheck1 = pCheckBox->GetChecked();
    }
 /*lines deleted. . .*/
}
```

As you can see, in each of the selection statements, `CApplication::OnGUIEvent()` receives the `nControlID` value and uses it to determine which control's message should be processed. Next, for each control, the pointer to the `pControl` value allows you to access actions specific to each type of control. To make this happen, you cast the `pControl` value using a pointer for the type of control you want to access and then assign the result to a local instance of the control. For example, for an edit box, you use the following statement:

```
CDXUTEditBox *pEditBox = (CDXUTEditBox *)pControl;
```

Adding Open Dynamics Engine

Open the project for Listing04_05 and compile the code; the application you see does not differ from the one you created with Listing04_04 (see Figure 4.8). At this point, Listing04_05 allows you to glimpse only the basics of how to incorporate the Open Dynamics Engine (ODE) into your project. Toward this end, consider the `#include` statement in CApplication.h:

```
#include <ode/ode.h>
```

The directory for the ODE contains relatively few files compared to the numbers you encounter in the DirectX directories, but the usefulness of the ODE files remains considerable. Figure 4.9 illustrates the ODE directory and the files Listing04_05 accesses with the #include statement.

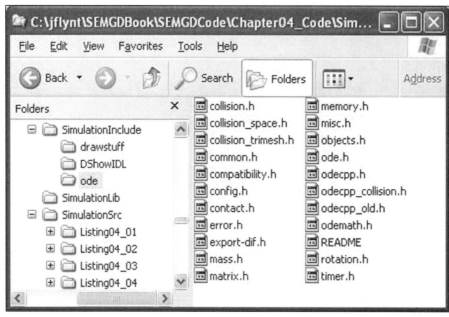

Figure 4.9 The ODE provides a rich set of capabilities in relatively few files.

Obtaining ODE

To obtain the files you see in the ODE directory shown in Figure 4.9, go to http://ode.org and follow the instructions provided. (For the projects included in this book, the ODE is included. For your own projects, you'll want to work from the website and download the most recent version of ODE.)

While the ODE code carries primary importance, you should also access the body of documentation that tells you how to use the ODE. Make sure that you download this along with the code. The best documentation is Russell Smith's *User's Guide.* Smith develops the ODE as an open-source product. You can download the *User's Guide* as a *.pdf file for convenient access. Here are strengths of the ODE that you can learn from the documentation:

- Simulates *articulated* rigid body structures. Another way of putting this is to say that the ODE allows you to work with rigid bodies of different shapes collected together as a single object.

- Suitable for interactive or real-time simulation. In other words, if you are working with moving objects and a changing environment, then the engine will be able to provide services so that you do not perceive irritating delays.

- Provides a highly stable integrator. This is basically a way to prevent errors in collision calculations from replicating to the point that you lose the ability to control objects.

- Provides *hard* contacts. This makes it so that when collisions are detected, the detection algorithm preserves the geometric integrity of the colliding objects.

- Furnishes a system for built-in collision detection for several types of entities. Among the entities for which the ODE has been developed are the following: sphere, box, capped cylinder, plane, ray, and triangular mesh.

Identifiers and Initializing the ODE

Among the few changes to the framework that Listing04_05 provides are those that commence the declaration of CApplication (in CApplication.h):

```
dWorldID m_dWorld;
dSpaceID m_dSpace;
```

Here you see two data types derived from the ODE. One is dWorldID. The other is DSpaceID. Later chapters review these and other ODE terms in greater detail, but for now, consult Table 4.3 to gain a sense of what these data types represent.

Table 4.3 A Few ODE Data Types

Data Type	Discussion
dWorld	This refers to a *dynamics* world. Such a world is a container for rigid bodies and joints. Objects in one world cannot interact with those in other worlds. A good reason underlies such insularity: You can simulate systems that operate at different rates.
dSpace	This is a *collision* space. The ODE accommodates several types of collision space. You can differentiate kinds of collision space using structures that geoms use and algorithms that perform collision culling.
dBody	This refers to *rigid body*. Such bodies can be connected to each other with joints. Likewise, each body can be viewed as containing an x-y-z coordinate frame that moves and rotates with the body.
dGeom	This refers to *geometry* (for collision). A *geom* might be viewed as the capacity of an object to detect collisions. Different objects can be furnished with different geoms, but any one geom can collide with any other geom.
dJoint	This refers to a *joint*. A joint might be said to resemble a regular old door hinge or a ball and socket joint in a robot set. It serves to connect two objects in a flexible way. A joint group is a special container that holds joints in a world.

Creating World and Space

For now, creating world and space for the application involves adding a line to the constructor for CApplication. The line calls CApplication::InitODE() (see CApplication.cpp):

```
CApplication::CApplication(const wstring &strName,
                           HINSTANCE hInstance,
                           int iWidth, int iHeight)
{
    /* . . . */
    InitODE();
}
```

As for the CApplication::InitODE() function, the main work of creating the function involves making calls to the constructors of the dWorld and dSpace objects:

```
void CApplication::InitODE()
{
    // Initialize ODE
    m_dWorld = dWorldCreate();
    m_dSpace = dHashSpaceCreate(NULL);
}
```

As you have read before, ODE will be discussed in greater detail to illustrate the specific uses of its functions. For now, however, the application contains ODE world and space objects and is for all practical purposes ready to begin collision detection.

The ODE allows you to track and calculate the movements and collisions of the objects you create with DirectX. DirectX provides you with the ability to control movements or to physically bring about the rendering of objects. The ODE allows you to impose mathematical order on the items you create, so that you can use them to create convincing simulations.

Reorganizing and Optimizing

Access Listing04_06 and open the project. Inspect the classes. You see a new, derived class, CMyApplication. This class allows you to have a more flexible framework for developing applications. Using this class, you shift the functionality formerly contained in CApplication to a specialized application class, CMyApplication. The shift makes it easier for you to create new instances of applications that address specific simulation objectives. Figure 4.10 illustrates the position of the new class in the project window.

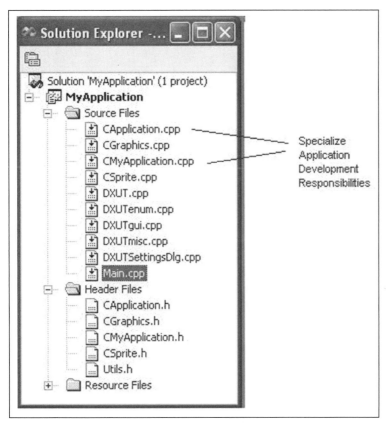

Figure 4.10 Specialization simplifies development activities.

CMyApplication Declaration

As you can see from the declaration of CMyApplication, everything the class contains derives from CApplication. For this reason, you need to learn little that is new about how to use CMyApplication. Example 4.3 shows you the declaration of the class. Notice that it publicly *inherits* the attributes and functions of CApplication.

Example 4.3 (Listing04_06/CMyApplication.h)

CMyApplication encapsulates the specific activities involved in implementing the controls and events of an application.

```
#include "CApplication.h"

// This is our custom application class, we override some of the key functions
// but we get to keep most of the functionality of the base application which
// makes things a lot simpler
```

```cpp
class CMyApplication : public CApplication
{
private:

    // These are constants for our GUI objects
    static const int IDC_SLIDER = 0;
    static const int IDC_TEXTBOX = 1;
    /*. . . Same as before. Lines deleted . . .*/
    static const int IDC_COMBOBOX1 = 10;
    static const int IDC_COMBOBOX2 = 11;
    static const int IDC_STATIC = 12;
    // The number of pictures we can load from our combobox
    static const int NUM_PICTURES = 5;
    // Define some data that can be modified by the application's GUI
    int m_iSlider;
    wstring m_strText;
    wstring m_strListBox;
    /*. . . Same as before. Lines deleted . . .*/
    bool m_flgRadio4;
    wstring m_strCombo1;
    wstring m_strCombo2;
    class CSprite *m_sprPicture1;
    class CSprite *m_sprPicture2;
public:
    // Initialize the application
    void Initialize();
    // Clean up the app
    void Cleanup();
    // Initialize our GUI
    void InitGUI();
    // Render the scene
    void Render();
    // Update the scene
    void UpdateScene(float fTimeScale);
    // This is our custom GUI event handler
    void OnGUIEvent(UINT nEvent,
                int nControlID, class CDXUTControl *pControl);
};
```

You have already received exposure to the attributes and member functions CMyApplication displays because you have studied the implementation of CApplication. All that changes is that you move the attributes that declare DirectX GUI controls from CApplication to CMyApplication. Further, you *override* the functions that allow you to implement the controls and their associated events. In addition, as you can see in Example 4.3, CMyApplication reduces the complexity of rendering graphical events because it allows you to override the Initialize(), Render(), and Cleanup() functions.

Generally speaking, despite the power it provides you as a developer, the CMyApplication class requires no explication beyond what already has been provided for the CApplication class. However, it is important to realize that CMyApplication provides a *patterned* approach to development. In other words, using the model it provides, you can proceed to develop your own class. To do so, you can use CMyApplication.h and CMyApplication.ccp as models. You create a class that you name as you please, declare identifiers for GUI controls and messages you want to process, and then implement the functions you see named in CMyApplication.h to process these messages. Likewise, you create the sprites you want to create and render them as you want them rendered. The pattern allows you to do all of this with relative ease.

Conclusion

In this chapter, the work has centered on implementation of DirectX features. Your work in this respect begins with the use of the IDirect3D9 and IDirect3DDevice9 interfaces. The IDirect3DDevice9 interface provides a large number of functions you use repeatedly as you develop an application for simulation. By encapsulating these functions in the interface of a class you create for yourself, CGraphics, you make it easier to put the power of DirectX to work for you.

The four main players in your startup activities with DirectX are the IDirect3D9 COM object, the IDirect3DDevice9 interfaces, and a couple of structs. The D3DPRESENT_PARAMETERS struct allows you to set device parameters. The D3DCAPS9 struct enables you to set device capabilities. To make use of these structs, you use the Direct3DCreate9() and IDirect3D9::CreateDevice() functions. These you encapsulate in the SetGFXMode() function of CGraphics.

After setting up a device and creating a class to process graphics using DirectX, you then proceeded to incorporate classes from the DirectX GUI utilities framework. This framework allows you to implement DirectX controls, such as buttons, text fields, and combo boxes. To instantiate controls, you make use of the InitGUI() function of CApplication, which allows you to make calls to the constructors of the DirectX controls. To process events from these controls, you set up selection statements in the OnGUIEvent() function of CApplication. Using unique identifiers for the messages and the controls, you are able to identify and process events for any control in your application.

To provide your application with 2D image processing capabilities, you add a `CSprite` class to the framework. `CSprite` makes use of the `ID3DSprite` class to create sprites. `ID3DSprite` uses the `D3DXCreateSprite()` function to tie the sprite to the device and application instances. Likewise, it uses the `D3DXCreateTextureFromFileEx()` to load the sprite file. Other functions, such as `ID3DXSprite::Begin()`, `ID3DXSprite::Draw()`, and `ID3DXSprite::End()`, when encapsulated by the `CSprite::Draw()` function, make it possible to readily introduce sprites to your application.

A few final touches involve anticipating future development efforts. First, you add connectivity to the Open Dynamics Engine. Then you create a derived class, `CMyApplication`, which serves as a pattern for development using the simulation framework. The `CMyApplication` class encapsulates the message and control identifiers you use in your application, and it overrides the six functions central to setting up graphics and message processing capabilities in your application.

Here are a few books that provide more information on the topics touched on in this chapter:

John P. Flynt, with Omar Salem, *Software Engineering for Game Developers* (Boston, Massachusetts: Thomson, 2004).

Wendy Jones, *Beginning DirectX9* (Boston, Massachusetts: Thomson, 2004).

Charles Petzold, *Programming Windows, Fifth Edition* (Richmond, Washington: Microsoft Press, 1999).

Richard J. Simon, *Microsoft Windows 200 API SuperBible.* (Indianapolis, Indiana: Macmillan, 2000).

Peter Walsh, *The Zen of Direct3D Game Programming* (Roseville, California: Prima Publishing, 2001).

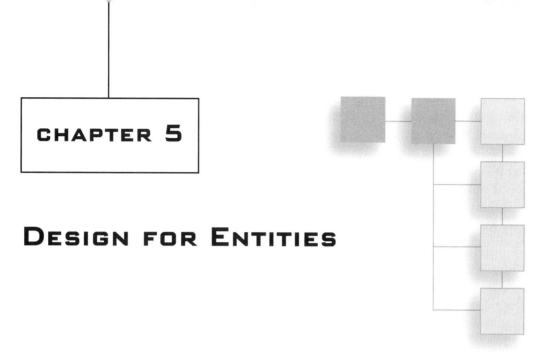

CHAPTER 5

DESIGN FOR ENTITIES

In this chapter, you add elements to the framework you developed in Chapters 3 and 4 so that you can work with entities. To start out, you'll explore some concepts that provide you with an essential foundation for designing and developing entities. You'll then turn to a discussion of how to use C++ and DirectX to create a basic entity. In this case, the entity is named Tiny and originates with some sample programs that Microsoft provides. To implement the code that allows you to see Tiny, you'll fold in a class that you can find in the source demonstration code Microsoft furnishes for developers who want to learn how to use DirectX. Here are a few of the topics the chapter covers:

- Identifying the primary properties of an entity
- Working with the design of an entity
- Understanding vertices, matrixes, and meshes
- Understanding light
- Understanding skeletons, bones, and skinned meshes
- Adding different types of animation
- Using the demonstration program

Basics of Entities

In Chapters 3 and 4, you saw how several components of a simulation framework might be implemented. This chapter continues that discussion, but along a more concerted line. In this chapter, the goal becomes one of finding approaches to creating entities. An *entity* can be described as anything that possesses distinction in a *world*. An *event* brings together an entity and a world and allows the entity to behave relative to the potentials the world creates.

So far, however, the framework has yet to provide you with the ability to create worlds. That remains for the next chapter. For now, the focus is on entities in isolation. Even in isolation, however, entities are characterized by interactions. Three such interactions are how an entity responds to commands you issue it, how an entity manifests behaviors (which are basically collections of events), and how such factors as lighting change the mood or appearance of an entity. If you can isolate an entity from its world by applying simple events to it, you'll have an easier time discerning the general potentials simulation and event modeling offer. You are then in a better position to consider the contexts of behavior a given world might offer.

Ultimately, the way you create an entity involves using a *mesh*. A mesh is a container that you create using vertices and groups of vertices. To this basic container you add such qualities as color characteristics and textures. The result is a dynamic creation that provides immense potentials for simulation activities.

Although the meshes this chapter presents represent human beings, it is important to keep in mind that anything can be viewed as an entity. When the discussion centers on an entity that resembles a human being, the intent is largely one of introducing something that is fairly challenging and that at the same time furnishes a set of characteristics that might be applied to a wide variety of animated and other entities.

Characteristics of Entities

Entities have characteristics. On an abstract level, meshes are humans, animals, inanimate objects, theoretical constructs, illustrations, graphs, charts, maps, and so on. When you work as a programmer to develop an entity, you undertake any number of actions to enhance the verisimilitude of the entity by enriching its characteristics. Several approaches to enhancing characteristics lie open to you. For example, if you work with game design, you can create rich narratives that guide the creation of the personality of the entity and the world the entity dwells in. If you work at implementing the features a graphics engine provides to create realistic simulations or imaginary universes, your job is to make use of the engine in the most refined way. If your work entails developing an engine, then your tasks are more fundamental, involving discovering effects worth pursing and creating and applying the math that creates such effects.

Ultimately with models such as those that have become familiar from such games as *Gran Turismo 4*, *Half-Life 2*, *Halo 2*, and *Metal Gear Solid: Snake Eater*, you face a situation in which expensive corporate efforts diminish to insignificance anything you can hope to achieve independently. Still, using basic tools such as DirectX and the framework developed in this chapter, you can gain a solid sense of the tasks and obstacles professional developers of games face as they create the simulations included in the games they work on. The principles of entity design ultimately combine intensive, close examination of intricately detailed scenarios with the technologies at hand for implementing simulations. In *Halo 2*, for example, when you see soldiers buzzing around a wrecked city fighting aliens, the machines, weapons, and creatures you encounter result from straightforward design techniques applied with rigor and consistency using a highly refined set of technical tools.

Designing an Entity

You can view an entity as an "actor" in a simulated or game world. Whether an entity is an inanimate object (for example, a model of a spaceship, an airplane, or an automobile) or an animate object (for example, a model of a human being, an elephant, or a centipede), the entity possesses interest for the person who interacts with it. The interest the entity possesses varies according to how you shaped it. You shape it so that its characteristics present an array of absorbing ways the person who interacts with it can, among other things, manipulate it, watch it grow, or establish circumstances that present problems for it. The interest such interactions generates depends on design.

Design issues can take you in any number of directions. Often, entities provide a medium through which the players of a game project themselves into the world the game presents. The same applies to simulations. Consider for example what you might do if you were asked to design a language training program that features an avatar that enters a barroom and interacts with a number of characters in the barroom in ways that challenge the player of the game to develop language skills.

If you consider some of the discussion in Chapter 3, you might immediately decide that the first thing you must accomplish as a simulation developer involves establishing an event model that incorporates a variety of devices and constraints that draw the player of the game into different language-learning scenarios. Consider the following:

- A pool table offers a way the player can call shots and interact with other pool players.
- The character can approach, converse, and sit with a prospective date at a table near the back of the bar.
- A shady character might be seated at a table in the back of the room. This sinister figure might create a situation in which your character encounters harsh language and yet must respond in a conciliatory (or at least reserved) way.
- A man seated at the bar likes to talk garrulously about sports with anyone who sits near. Disengaging from him is like pulling your hand from a bucket of honey.
- An inebriated writer seated in a booth drinks beer and whiskey and wants to talk about how he recently lost his job or could not find a buyer for a film script.
- The bartender, who can talk about many things, waits to serve the avatar upon demand and replies obsequiously to anything said, regardless of how inane.

You might employ use cases to explore fully the potentials for interaction and language use that your event model supports. As the potentials for interaction become more and more refined, the language your character uses might be reduced to highly concentrated but carefully filtered dialogues that offer a variety of thematic pathways. Likewise, as the player vicariously participates in these dialogues, the potentials for acquisition of new vocabulary items or syntax patterns might vary and increase according to the problems or challenges you offer in the context of play.

If you consider the types of interactions the language-acquisition scenario introduces, you might find that designing an entity's characteristics takes you in a few general directions. Consider the following:

- **Personal qualities.** The entity possesses abilities or qualities that allow it to interact with its world. The abilities and qualities can range from such things as physical prowess (leaping a given distance or being schooled in the martial arts), possessing background knowledge, or understanding a given vocabulary.

- **Complexity.** Complex simulations constrain characters in simple and complex ways. A very simple setting, such as what might arise when a character faces the problem of opening a door, might become intricately detailed. On the other hand, even if the world your character encounters contains a vast array of scenes and targets, it might remain that your character interacts with its world in a reductive way, such as by shooting a gun. In such a setting, interactions supported by complex coding efforts might involve such direct activity as navigating a terrain, finding a target, and destroying the target. In contrast, consider a situation in which the character explores a terrain, spends a great deal of time and effort identifying a problem, and solves the problem through extensive interaction. One such scenario might arise if you modeled a character as a physician. The character finds a prone man, asks questions, and offers a diagnosis.

- **Occasions.** The world offers a set of occasions for interaction, but then such occasions have significance only to the extent that the character can *engage* them. Even in a shooter scenario, if the character cannot aim a weapon and shoot, no interaction with targets occurs. The world the entity dwells in determines the occasions of interaction, but at the same time, the character passes through the world without interactions if you do not create ways characters actively engage their world. This is the basis of event analysis. Even the most simple of events can require extensive efforts of analysis.

- **Constraints.** The entity responds in specific ways to the interactions. Entities can resist blows, become dizzy, gain strengths, and generally learn in any way you program them to learn. Each of these behavioral patterns represents the implementation of a specific set of constraints. Initially, your work with constraints might be a bit one-sided. In other words, your efforts might be confined to just getting an avatar to walk back and forth or in a circle. In time, however, through the use of AI, physics, and collision detection, you can increase the complexity of the constraints with which you define interactions to an astonishing extent. In many respects, you can trace the history of games as revealing, along with increasing powers of graphical rendering, a corresponding increase in the complexity of the constraints applied to entities.

Figure 5.1 depicts the dynamics that characterize qualities, occasions, and constraints of entities in a simulation:

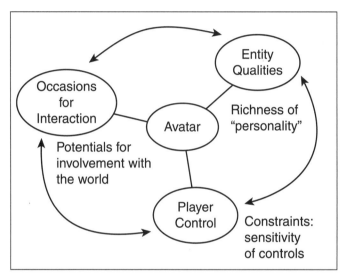

Figure 5.1 Constraints determine the richness of interactions.

Ends and Means

You can view an entity as an item that is an end in itself or as an item that is a means to an end. If you view an entity as a means to an end, you use the entity to achieve an effect that lies beyond the specific definition of the entity itself. For instance, suppose you want to create a game in which you show spectacular panoramas that bring to the player an increasing awareness of the flora and fauna of the Amazonian rain forest. The means to this end might be an entity you represent as a scientist, a simulated expert who examines and names flowers, insects, and other inhabitants of the forest. The knowledge the experiences introduce constitutes the primary objective of interaction. On the other hand, role-playing games (RPGs) provide scenarios in which the player becomes the avatar, so that the strengths and standing of the avatar merge with the psyche (or persona) of the player. In such worlds, the identity that the experience of playing the game creates becomes the primary end of the play.

Analysis of an Entity

You are likely to find an entity interesting when you find the behavior associated with the entity interesting. Such behavior is, among other things, involved, challenging, rewarding, and consistent. At the same time, you are unlikely to be conscious that an entity possesses interest for you unless the interactions the entity provides you with sustains the *experience of discovery*. Discovery consists of two phases. During the first phase, you become aware of a limitation. The awareness of *limitation* brings you a desire to escape or transcend the limitation. This leads to the second phase, which involves a search for information or experience that *increases your awareness* and removes the sense of limitation.

To create occasions of discovery, you first look at the constraints that apply to the entity you are dealing with. You ask yourself how the entity you are dealing with learns. Consider, for example, how an entity you set up as a news reporter might encounter a common urban edifice, such as a bridge.

The reporter passes over a given bridge inside your simulated world. How can you provide a learning experience, a challenge, or a sense of limitation to a character as cynical as a reporter? One of the simplest scenarios might involve creating a situation in which the bridge suddenly no longer furnishes a "normal" experience (that of driving or walking over a river or chasm). If the bridge collapses, for example, it creates a challenge. Suddenly, the thought of the bridge and the fact of its absence create a sense of limitation. To use a term from the writings of Sigmund Freud, it introduces the uncanny. The uncanny in this instance is something familiar to the point of being boring that suddenly creates, when taken away, a sense of emptiness (or limitation) that demands that you do something to compensate for it. To this sense of limitation you can add all sorts of complexities. Consider these:

- Protestors block the bridge when they stage a protest. To pass over the bridge, you must pass through a crowd whose members address you in specific ways and, perhaps, demand given types of politically charged responses.
- A gang war takes place on the bridge. Rival gangs battle it out, and to pass over the bridge, you have to dodge this way and that or join ranks with a group you can assist to become the victors in the war.
- As you approach the bridge, you see that a woman is giving birth to a child. You help with this activity, perhaps only on the periphery, but in the process gain new experience with life.
- As you attempt to pass over the bridge, you find that members of a local historical society have gathered on the bridge, legally closing down traffic for a few hours as its speakers relate historical details about the bridge. If you stop and listen, you learn about history.

Behavior Corresponds to Potentials

How you equip an entity to be receptive to a given type of behavior determines the potential it possesses for interest. Characters in a game might be equipped with qualities that remain concealed until they reach certain points of development. On the other hand, a character possesses enormous capacities for interaction right from the start, but until you arrive at a specific setting in the world the character inhabits, the capacities the character displays might seem superfluous. Further, when the tension that characterizes a sense of limitation provides you with an opportunity for discovery, you must take time to shape the interaction so that the growth in awareness or experience that the inter-action fosters naturally manifests potentials. All such progressions of activity constitute *behavior*. Behavior is basically a set of actions defined by a central theme.

Continuities of action embody *potentials*. You might view a potential as a kind of behav-ior that a character might or might not engage in, depending on whether the player discovers and learns how to guide the character through the behavior. Once again, constraints play a leading role in such scenarios. A character that cannot show grief, anger, or amusement cannot grow in these ways. A character that cannot show or exer-cise mathematical or scientific knowledge cannot make use of such knowledge. In each instance, constraints characterize interactions, and interactions characterize behaviors. Behavior, in turn, has significance according to how it enables you to become aware of new dimensions of experience—to learn.

Behaviors and Animations

Later on in this chapter, you'll have a chance to work with an entity so that you associate it with a set of behaviors. At first, you associate an entity with different behaviors using separate *animations*. Ultimately, an animation consists of a sequence of activities that unfold programmatically. For example, you see an entity taking a given stance, as though assuming a fighting position. This behavior might consist of one quick move. However, you can create complex behaviors by combining simple moves. The most ready example of this involves walking. As your simulations increase in complexity, your interactions with your entities come to involve more and more combinations and refinements of a large number of simple moves. Figure 5.2 shows that simple entity behaviors can be com-bined to create complex, or composite, behaviors. Ultimately, this is the basis of complex event development in a simulation.

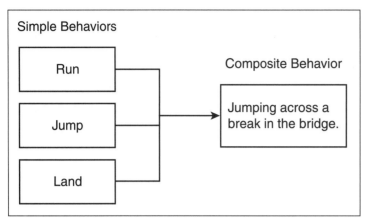

Figure 5.2 Simple events combine to form complex events.

Use Case Design Strategies

To design an entity so that it embodies complex behaviors, you can apply use cases. As you might recall from Chapter 2, software engineers frequently employ use cases to facilitate their efforts as they design software systems. Use cases prove appropriate for entity design efforts because they afford you a way to analyze complex behaviors so that you can identify simpler behaviors. When you find ways to increase the number of simple behaviors that combine to form a composite behavior, you increase the richness of the potentials for interaction your entity possesses. As Figure 5.3 illustrates, as you increase the number of simple behaviors you combine to create composite behaviors, you also multiply the instances in which you can vary a given scenario and introduce occasions for interaction. As the occasions of interaction increase, so does the potential for challenge and learning.

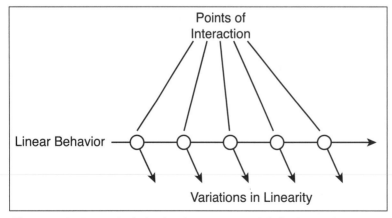

Figure 5.3 Composite behaviors increase potentials for interaction.

Getting to the core of an interactive scenario begins with assessing the scenario so that you discover a rich variety of ways that you can view the scenario as a collection of basic actions. You can view each action as an event, as a moment in which your entity changes in one way or another. Usually, you might find that you tend to view all behavior in a given situation as a natural set of occurrences, but consider how limiting this might be. For example, reflect on what happens in the language game when the character enters the bar. Figure 5.4 provides a use case (created using SmartDraw) in which you can see how a brief analysis of the character's overall behavior of moving through the bar can engender many simpler behaviors that offer occasions for interaction. If you apply use case analysis to identify the simpler behaviors, you can find even richer contexts of interaction.

Use Case Name: (UC 3) Character moves through bar

Requirement(s) Explored: NA

Player (Actor) Context: Create an occasion for talk

Precondition(s): (UC 2) Objective of learning about the lay of the city is established, together with knowledge of the patrons.

Trigger(s): Eye contact, gestures, anything that indicates a possible contact.

Main Course of Action: Character walks slowly and silently toward the back of the bar.
Character eyes the bartender.
Character eyes the pool players.
Character eyes the sports fan at the bar.
Character eyes the prospective date.
Character turns.
Character stops.
Character speaks greeting.
Character shakes hands.
Character orders drink for self.
Character orders drink for other.

Alternate Course(s) of Action:

Exceptional Course(s) of Action:

Figure 5.4 Uses cases allow you to explore the richness of composite behaviors.

Controlling Entities

After you analyze the behavior of your entity to discover ways in which you can increase the opportunities for interaction your entity offers and the qualities you must instill in your entity to make such interactions possible, your activity returns to the assessment of constraints. As was pointed out previously, controls constitute a form of constraint—as do the behaviors themselves. A control provides a means of interaction.

Generally, you apply a control to regulate a specific event, as when you press an arrow key to command a character to walk in a given direction. With complex entities, your controls often apply to segments of activity known as animations. An animation event, for example, consists of walking, jumping, stooping, reaching, turning, or any number of continuous but incremental behaviors.

To press a key and see an action result constitutes the most basic type of control sequence. As Chapter 2 discussed, such feedback loops form primary features of any event model. Consider, however, a few variations on rudimentary stimulus-response scenarios:

- The entity is in continuous motion and possesses its own impetus, so when you provide input, what you see you cannot necessarily interpret as a simple response to a command. For instance, to make a character turn, you must perform four or five separate actions, not just one.

- What happens depends not on your immediate control of the entity but on the forces or opportunities you introduce to the entity. Consider, for example, what might happen if you were to be in charge, not of the entity, but of a light that guides an entity as it walks. As you light candles or illuminate passages, your mesh moves accordingly. However, you do not control the entity directly.

- Only after you create the capacity to respond can the entity respond to your commands. For example, in some games you must teach your character to drive a car, fly a plane, or in some other way acquire the ability to perform a given type of activity. You anticipate far in advance the type of interactions you wish so see.

- An entity can move toward a determinate end, so that your assertion of controls becomes one of trying to divert or hinder the actions of the mesh. Such interaction amounts to a type of reverse behavior. You resist the set pattern.

In each of the instances the list presents, just as you can view behaviors as simple and composite, so you can view controls as simple and complex. It remains important to view all such interactions—visible behavior or control—as but different manifestations of the constraints you apply to your event model and the entities encompassed by it.

Creating Entity Graphics

Putting entities into simulations begins with the creation of graphical assets. The artistic and graphical design assets that you see in professionally developed games involve fairly significant team efforts and large budgets. If you work on your own resources, you are likely to have to settle for humbler items. However, regardless of how humble, if you employ such applications as Photoshop, MilkShape, Maya, and 3D Max in conjunction with DirectX, you are in essence working on a platform that equals that of professional studios. Tenacity and refinement determine the quality of the end product.

Most of the entities shown in this book have been created using such applications as Photoshop and Maya. To aid you in your own endeavors, here is a short list of information about these tools:

- **MilkShape.** You can download and use this application for free. If you want to use it extensively, a minimum investment might be necessary. The Internet site for downloading is http://www.swissquake.ch/chumbalum-soft/index.html.

- **Maya.** You can download a trial version of this application, but you are not allowed to create entities that you can use directly in your games or simulations until you purchase the application. The Internet site for information and demonstrations is www.alias.com/mayaple.

- **3DS Max.** You can download and begin using this application on a demonstration basis, which means that you are not able to implement fully the meshes you create until you purchase the product. The Internet site for obtaining a trial version is http://www4.discreet.com/3dsmax.

- **Photoshop.** Adobe, the maker of Photoshop, affords several ways you can explore Photoshop on a trial basis. As with the other commercial products, however, don't expect to be able to go very far until you purchase a fully functional product. The site for a trial download is http://www.adobe.com/products/photoshop/main.html.

In addition to strengths and weaknesses of different applications, keep in mind that different file formats exist for each of the applications. Even after you have created a mesh using MilkShape, Maya, or 3D Max, you cannot directly drop the result into an application created using DirectX. You must first convert the mesh to the Microsoft *.x file format. As of this writing, no easy way exists to accomplish this unless you are willing to invest in a commercial product. The free software Microsoft provides tends to be difficult to use and a bit defective. As an example of a commercial product for converting from Maya and 3DS Max formats to the *.x format for DirectX, consider Okino Computer Graphics at http://www.okino.com/default.htm.

Creating Entities Using DirectX

The framework you develop in this chapter allows you to manipulate entities using DirectX. To develop an entity, you implement a class that loads the resources necessary to create the entity. You also implement a class that allows you to apply controls and behaviors to the entity. As mentioned previously, you can also associate entities with sounds, voices, intelligence, and learning capabilities. For now, the main task must be that of working with DirectX to implement and control a complex type of mesh known as a skinned mesh. Such a mesh allows you to simulate such activities as walking and running. From this beginning, it becomes possible to expand the behavior of the mesh in any number of directions.

MSDN and the DirectX SDK

This and other chapters in this book extensively use the examples and discussions that Microsoft provides on its developer's resource site, which is called the Microsoft Developer's Network (MSDN). MSDN provides every imaginable resource you might require as you work with C++ and DirectX to develop simulations and games.

In this chapter, much of the discussion centers on the creation of functionality that supports skinned meshes. To find Microsoft documentation and sample code that relate to the discussion, you can follow two approaches:

- You can access the DirectX SDK help utility and then search for "skinned mesh." (A panel in Chapter 3 provides you with information on how to conduct such a search.)
- You can access the Microsoft MSDN on the web (http://www.msdn.microsoft.com/). When you access the site, you'll find that your browser displays a search panel, which Figure 5.5 illustrates.

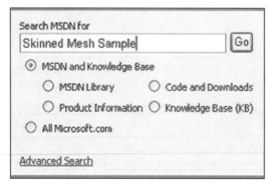

Figure 5.5 Use the MSDN search panel.

continued

The search expression you see in Figure 5.5 prompts the MSDN site to display the link you see in the upper left of Figure 5.6. If you were to access this link, you could click it to find the reference that appears in the lower right of Figure 5.6. Note that the information Microsoft provides refers you to documentation and code samples in the DirectX SDK.

Skinned Mesh Sample (DirectX 9.0 C++ Archive)
The Skinned Mesh sample shows how to load and render a skinned mesh.
http://msdn.microsoft.com/archive/en-us/directx9_
c/directx/graphics/programmingguide/TutorialsAndSamplesAndToolsAndTips/
Samples/skinnedmesh.asp

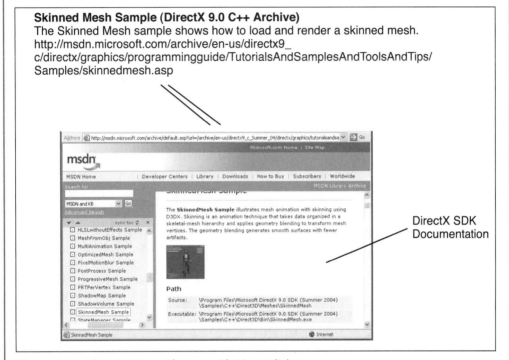

DirectX SDK
Documentation

Figure 5.6   The MSDN provides you with DirectX links.

Entities and Meshes

The starting point for an entity is a mesh. More specifically, for the uses you make of meshes in simulation, the starting point is a collection of meshes that work together to create an animation. Such a collection is known as a skinned mesh. Review Table 5.1 for a brief discussion of some of the concepts associated with meshes and DirectX.

Table 5.1 From Point to Skinned Mesh

Concept	Discussion
Vertex	A vertex in a 3D world consists of a set of three coordinates (x, y, z) that define a point and the color of the point.
Polygon	A set of three vertices is enough to create the most elementary shape—a triangle. A triangle can also be called a polygon. All of the more complex 3D shapes, whatever they may be, consist of triangles.
Face	If you create a 3D cube, the cube consists of six faces. Each face comprises a surface that represents a single side of the cube, and each face also consists of two polygons.
Vertex buffer	A vertex buffer points to an array of vertices. To create a vertex buffer, then, you first create an array of vertices. Then you assign the address of the array to a pointer. This creates a buffer.
Index buffer	An index buffer reduces the amount of memory you use as you manipulate vertex buffers. The best way to picture this is to view an index buffer as consisting of a set of numbers that uniquely identify the vertexes in a vertex buffer. You access the index rather than the vertex.
Matrix	A matrix is a multidimensional array of vertices. A matrix holds the values that describe the vertices with which you define a mesh.
Identity matrix	An identity matrix holds values for an object (whatever it may be) that allow the object to be positioned at the origin of the world it inhabits and to assume its original size (if it has been scaled).
Flexible Vertex Format (FVF)	The FVF is an object Microsoft provides to manipulate the information in a vertex buffer. For example, you might not want color information about a vertex. The FVF allows you to control color.
Reciprocal of Homogenous (RHW)	This term designates that the coordinates are already presented as screen coordinates.
Texture	A texture is a bitmap (or other form of image) that is "wrapped around" a mesh to give its faces some type of appearance.
Skinned mesh	A skinned mesh can be viewed as a collection of meshes that make it possible to create a complex animation. A collection of meshes that work together to create a single animation is sometimes called a *hierarchy*. Developers call what ties the meshes together a *skeleton*. The skeleton consists of *bones*. Generally, animating the skinned mesh involves, first, animating the skeleton. As each bone of the skeleton moves, the meshes associated with it are repositioned to accord with the movement of the bones.

Transformations and Space

Entities move around in the virtual world of your monitor because the meshes that you use to create and manipulate them are put through fairly involved manipulations that involve vector and matrix math. DirectX encapsulates the mathematical activities, but it remains important for you to acquire a clear view of the types of transformations you achieve through processes such as matrix multiplication and vector normalization.

When you make an entity so that it can move around in the virtual world of the monitor, your activity falls under the heading of *coordinate transformation*. The order in which you transform coordinates during the rendering process is controlled by the geometry *pipeline*. Transformation deals with making it possible for an object you have created to be rendered in the space of your game. The pipeline regulates the order of operations you perform as you effect transformations. In addition to transformation and pipeline operations, you should also give some consideration to the different spaces that characterize the entity in itself (local space), the virtual space of the monitor (global or world space), and the space that characterizes your view of the entity (camera space). Table 5.2 provides discussion of these three types of space.

Table 5.2 Space and Transforming Coordinates

Concept	Discussion
Model space	When you create a model using tools like MilkShape, Maya, or 3D Max, you usually center the model on its origin. In other words, the x, y, and z coordinates intersect at the center of the model. The space of the model unfolds relative to this scheme of things. Developers sometime refer to model space as local space. Given that at any moment many objects can populate your world, you can say that many model spaces can exist at any given moment in your world space.
World space	The space of your world has its origin at the center of the surface to which you render your models. Only one world space exists (generally speaking). The local spaces of the models that occupy the space are translated into world space.
Camera space	You can also have space that is relative to a viewer or camera. Such a space allows you to see some things becoming larger as you approach them while other things become smaller as you move away from them. A view port is relative to how you position your camera—what you can and cannot see. Likewise, a *projection plane* is relative to what you can see as you look through a camera.

Lighting for Entities

You can use DirectX to give lighting to both entities and the worlds that contain them. Lighting enormously impacts the appearance of entities, for it contributes to mood transformation, physical verisimilitude (whether it looks real), and dramatic highlighting (how light and other effects guide the viewer's attention). Table 5.3 provides discussion of some of the terms useful in understanding lighting effects. Under the discussion of CMesh, you can see how to implement some of these effects using DirectX. For now, it is enough to review the terms so that you are familiar with them when they come into play as the code is implemented.

Table 5.3 Lighting Sources

Concept	Discussion
Ambient lights	You can view ambient lighting as a type of general, non-directional lighting. It has no source, and it casts no shadows. Since it has no source, you do not need to designate its source. You basically just turn it on. You can change its color, however.
Directional lights	You can view directional light as light that comes from a given direction but travels in waves that are parallel to each other. You might picture light from the sun, for example, which originates so far away that its rays seem to strike the earth in straight lines, without any fanning effect. A directional light can have a source (to the left or right, for example, of the viewing area), and it can have color.
Point lights	If you picture a candle placed in the middle of a gymnasium and picture yourself walking the perimeter of the gymnasium and viewing the candle from different vantage points, you can get an idea of what point light involves. A bare light bulb in a room is a point light, also. A point light emits light in all directions, so it is directionless. However, it does have a position, and you can give it color.
Spotlights	A spotlight is a light that is enclosed on its back and sides and projects in one direction. As it projects, however it creates a cone. The light of a flashlight is an example of a spotlight (a later chapter features a flashlight-spotlight, in fact).

The Behaviors of Light

When you consider the four light sources that Table 5.3 names, it is helpful to consider the *behavior* of light as it relates to how you see what is illuminated. For example, the brightness of light diminishes with distance. When an entity casts a shadow, the position of the shadow indicates the position of the source of the light that creates the shadow. All such effects reveal the behaviors of light, and DirectX provides a number of functions that help you implement such behaviors. The basic behaviors DirectX helps you with are as follows:

- **Position.** Point and spotlights have positions. In other words, you can identify via coordinates where they originate.

- **Direction.** Spotlights and directional lights have direction. You might not be able to know their precise source, but an object placed in the paths of such light can cast a shadow.

- **Range.** You can change a point light or a spotlight so that its intensity diminishes with the illusion of distance.
- **Attenuation.** Light changes in intensity as you move farther from its source.
- **Theta, Phi.** These terms refer only to spotlights. Theta measures a spotlight's inner circle of light. Phi measures a spotlight's outer circle of light.
- **Falloff.** This term also refers only to spotlights. Falloff measures how much the intensity of the light decreases from the inner to the outer circles that define the cone.

Target Characteristics—Materials

Light strikes objects, and the objects the light strikes absorb or reflect the light that strikes them. The property that describes how an object reflects or absorbs light is called the object's *material characteristics*. Developers usually truncate this expression to *materials*. To understand materials, consider both what you see and what you understand as you see. In other words, say that you see something that appears to you to be metallic. Why do you think it appears to be metallic? Well, your answer might be that you see that it is shiny and silvery. This is a result of the entity's material characteristics. Material falls into four categories:

- **Diffuse.** This is the color of the light the object gives off. Diffusiveness, then, relates to the color and intensity of the light the object reflects.
- **Ambient.** Ambient light is the color of the light as you see it reflected. An object might be of a given color, but when it reflects light, you might notice that the color of the reflected light differs from the color of the object.
- **Specular.** Entities seldom appear simply flat and consistently of the same color. Rather, when you look at an object, you see highlights. For example, consider what you see when you look at the metal on a steel cylinder. It appears to be lighter in color (more silvery) at the point at which light strikes it most directly and darker (less silvery) in the shadowed areas that are not directly in the path of the light.
- **Emissive.** When you make an object look as though it is glowing with heat, you are dealing with emissive light. Emissive light is light that an object gives off.

The Geometry Pipeline

As mentioned previously, an important part of the process of rendering entities to the screen involves applying different mathematical processes to the entities. While DirectX hides the mathematical complexity of rendering processes by encapsulating these activities in a tidy set of functions you apply to the meshes you use to create your entities, it remains important to be aware of the general nature of what happens. Here is a summary of the basic operations:

- *Transformation (or setting the transformation)* occurs when you alter the values of the matrix that defines your mesh so that your mesh assumes a different position.

- *Translation* occurs when you move a mesh along one or another axis of a coordinate system.

- *Rotating* occurs when you turn a mesh around one of the axes that applies to it.

- *Scaling* occurs when you multiply the values in a matrix that define a mesh by the values stored in another matrix. The result is that the size of your mesh changes.

Orders of Operation

In addition to being aware of the functions DirectX provides to allow you to mathematically manipulate entities, you must also be aware of the *order* in which you apply the functions. Here is a summary of the functions and their order.

- **Rotate.** You always rotate first. When you rotate an entity, you apply mathematics to rotate it around the x, y, or z axis.

- **Scale.** After you rotate, you scale. When you scale an entity, you increase or decrease the size of the entity relative to its "normal" size. Generally, you can accomplish this by multiplying the values in the matrix that define the object by values in another matrix that represent the scaling factor.

- **Translate.** This involves moving the object along the x, y, or z axis. This can become fairly involved because you are moving an entity that is defined in a local coordinate space to a space that is defined by a world coordinate space.

The CMesh Class

To get down to making something happen with an entity, a somewhat traditional route for would-be Microsoft DirectX developers is to take a stroll with an entity named Tiny. Tiny is an entity Microsoft provides, and you can find her in the DirectX tutorials that you install with the DirectX SDK. See Figure 5.7 for a view of Tiny.

To give Tiny a place in the framework you create in this book, the first and largest addition to the framework you make consists of a class called CMesh, which provides the functionality you need to render an animated mesh. A complex animated mesh in this case is a skinned mesh. To control the mesh, CMesh makes use of a number of DirectX *helper*—or *utility*—functions.

Open Chapter05/Listing05_01 and compile the project. Figure 5.7 shows you the result. You see Tiny walking forward, into the camera. The console at the bottom has no purpose ⸍his point, but later features are added to it.

Figure 5.7 Tiny provides an example of an entity that you create using a skinned mesh.

To understand how you can put Tiny in your application, take a look at `CMyApplication`, in CMyApplication.h. Notice that a new attribute appears in the class:

```
// The test mesh
class CMesh *m_pMesh;
```

The attribute is of the type `CMesh`, which encapsulates all the functionality you require to load, render, and destroy a mesh object. The `CMesh` class is fairly complex, much more complex than the `CSprite` class shown in Chapter 4. To understand the complexity, turn to CMesh.h, where the `CMesh` class is declared. Here's the start of the code:

```
// enum for various possible skinning modes
enum SKINMETHOD
{
    D3DNONINDEXED = 0,
    D3DINDEXED = 1,
    NONE= 2
};
```

The first thing you see, just prior to the CMesh class declaration, is an enumeration (enum) called SKINMETHOD, which sets up some values that allow you to select the method you want DirectX to use for skinning a mesh. Skinning occurs when you use the bones of the mesh to update the vertices of the mesh to accord with its animation. You apply the values the enumeration provides as you render the mesh. In this instance, you use D3DNONINDEXED, which provides a way to make the code compatible with most video cards.

CMesh Attributes

Continuing on with the discussion of the code in CMesh.h, the next item to consider is the declaration of the CMesh class itself. Notice first that the class establishes a number of attributes. Here are the attributes and brief descriptions of each:

- LPD3DXFRAME m_pFrameRoot. This is a structure that provides the root frame for the *.X file. The root frame is the root of the entire hierarchy of the mesh. Another term for this is "parent node." Everything in the mesh ultimately refers to this frame. This frame has children and siblings. Another way of looking at it is to say that it is a tree that has branches and twigs.

- ID3DXAnimationController *m_pAnimController. This is a DirectX class that you instantiate when you create your mesh. It is the animation controller. It provides you with the capability to enumerate all your animations and set which animation you want to use. It offers a number of functions, such as AdvanceTime(), which allows you to move the animation forward.

- D3DXVECTOR3 m_vecObjectCenter. This is an object that DirectX provides for you. It stores the position of the center of your mesh in object space. The values you populate it with depend on how you want to create the mesh.

- float m_fObjectRadius. This value allows you to set the radius of a bounding sphere that appears around an object and contains it.

- D3DXMATRIXA16* m_pBoneMatrices. This is a pointer to an array of matrices for each bone. When you have a skeleton, you have to keep track of the transform for each bone. A transform can be any combination of translation, rotation, and scaling.

- UINT m_iNumBoneMatricesMax. This is a long integer that stores the number of bone matrices. It is provided here as a convenience measure and is not immediately used.

- IDirect3DVertexShader9* m_pIndexedVertexShader[4]. This is a set of pointers to the vertex shaders. A vertex shader is an object that transforms vertices. These are not used in the current application.

- D3DXMATRIXA16 m_matWorld. This is the world matrix. This matrix contains a transform ¨¨r the entire mesh, not just a particular bone. This is where you start rendering the ɔject; all other transformations are combined with this.

- DWORD m_dwBehaviorFlags. This is a 32-bit flag value that allows you to check 3D device compatibility. You might use it to force hardware rendering, for example. Here it is not put to any immediate use because software rendering is used.
- static bool SoftwareVP. You can find this value lower down in the file containing the class declaration. This value allows you to determine whether to revert to the software mode. It is a Boolean value that allows you to set the software vertex processing mode for maximum compatibility.
- static SKINMETHOD SkinningMethod. This is a declaration of the enumerated type you saw previously, which enables you to communicate with your video card.

CMesh Functions

The CMesh class provides a basic set of functions that allow you to perform the rendering activity associated with skinned meshes. For starters, consider the DrawMeshContainer() function. You call this function from DrawFrame(), which is explained momentarily. The DrawMeshContainer() function goes through all the vertices of your mesh, transforms them according to the values the bones provide, and renders them to the screen. Here's the code:

```
// Utility functions for setting up bones, etc
    void DrawMeshContainer( IDirect3DDevice9 *pd3dDevice,
                  LPD3DXMESHCONTAINER pMeshContainerBase,
                  LPD3DXFRAME pFrameBase );
```

DrawMeshContainer() has the distinction of actually drawing polygons to the screen. To accomplish this work, it has a fairly impressive set of parameters. The first, of the type IDirect3DDevice9, is your DirectX device, which was discussed in Chapter 3. As you recall, the device is your interface to the Direct3D object. Next, the parameter of the type LPD3DXMESHCONTAINER offers a massive struct that contains a mesh and the information about it. This container is a pointer (LP). As a pointer, it augments performance. In this instance, this struct is likely to contain a single part of the mesh hierarchy. For example, picture an arm moving in two segments, lower arm and upper arm. The final parameter type, LPD3DXFRAME, designates an object that points to the frame that contains the bones associated with the mesh transformation.

Following DrawMeshContainer(), you see the SetupBoneMatrixPointersOnMesh() function. A matrix pointer is a pointer that points to a transformation matrix. The pointer is "on" the mesh because it sets up an array for each mesh container that relates each bone to its transformation matrix. Doing things this way means that you do not have to search for the bone as you render. The SetupBoneMatrixPointersOnMesh() has only one parameter, of the type LPD3DXMESHCONTAINER, which is a pointer to the struct that contains information about parts of your mesh. Again, a "part of a mesh" is a piece of the hierarchy within the skinned mesh (Tiny) you see walking around the screen. Here is the code:

```
HRESULT SetupBoneMatrixPointersOnMesh(
                    LPD3DXMESHCONTAINER pMeshContainerBase );
```

The next function you see, `SetupBoneMatrixPointers()` has one purpose, which is to call `SetupBoneMatrixPointersOnMesh()` on every mesh container. The purpose, then, is to iterate through every piece of the hierarchy. Here's the signature line:

```
HRESULT SetupBoneMatrixPointers( LPD3DXFRAME pFrame );
```

After `SetupBoneMatrixPointers()`, you see the `DrawFrame()` function. This function renders a frame and then recursively calls itself on the frame's children and siblings. This effectively renders the entire hierarchy when you call it on the root frame. (You can see it used in the `Render()` function of `CMesh`.) As for the parameters of `DrawFrame()`, the first is an `IDirect3DDevice9` object. The second, is an `LPD3DXFRAME` object. These are the same parameters you saw at work in `DrawMeshContainer()`.

```
void DrawFrame(IDirect3DDevice9 *pd3dDevice, LPD3DXFRAME pFrame);
```

After presenting `DrawFrame()`, `CMesh` provides you with the `GenerateSkinnedFrame()` function. Here's the code:

```
HRESULT GenerateSkinnedFrame( IDirect3DDevice9 *pd3dDevice,
                    LPD3DXFRAME pFrame );
```

You use the `GenerateSkinnedFrame()` function to traverse the entire mesh hierarchy. To traverse the hierarchy, `GenerateSkinnedFrame()` calls `GenerateSkinnedMesh()` on each part of the hierarchy. You don't see `GenerateSkinnedMesh()` in the declaration of `CMesh` because it is both declared and defined in CMesh.cpp. It is a global function, but it is associated with a local scope. Hidden as it may be for now, however, `GenerateSkinnedMesh()` remains important because it converts the mesh to a skinned mesh before you apply animation functions to it. As a final observation, `GenerateSkinnedMesh()` calls the Direct3D function `ConvertToBlendedMesh()`. The code is complex, but in essence, it prepares a mesh for animation.

The next function you see in CMesh.h after `GenerateSkinnedFrame()` is `UpdateFrameMatrices()`. This function traverses the entire hierarchy and transforms the bone matrices in it. As a result of this function's work, you see the mesh move. For review, note that the type of the matrix passed in (`LPD3DXMATRIX`) designates the parent matrix. All of the children matrices automatically inherit the parent's transformations. Here's the function:

```
void UpdateFrameMatrices(LPD3DXFRAME pFrameBase,
                    LPD3DXMATRIX pParentMatrix );
```

As for the constructor of CMesh, notice that it is very simple. You call it in CMyApplication::Initialize(), and most of its preliminaries are taken care of with the Load() function.

```
// Constructor for the mesh class
    CMesh();
```

Accompanying the constructor, you find the class destructor, which is called in CMyApplication::Cleanup(). The destructor attends to freeing all of the memory associated with the mesh.

```
// Destructor for the mesh class
    ~CMesh();
```

Loading

An especially important function in the CMesh class is the Load() function. It has two parameters. The first parameter is a string designating the name of the *.x mesh file that you want to load. The second is the IDirect3DDevice9 device interface. The declaration in CMesh.h is as follows:

```
// Load a mesh from a .X file
    bool Load(wstring strFile, IDirect3DDevice9 *pd3dDevice);
```

You call the Load() function from CMyApplication::Initialize(). You can see this in CMyApplication.cpp. Here's the code for the call to Load():

```
void CMyApplication::Initialize()
{
    // Load our mesh
    m_pMesh = new CMesh();
    m_pMesh->Load(L"Meshes\\Tiny.x", m_pGraphics->GetDevice());
     //lines left out. . .
}
```

The Load() function uses a Microsoft *.x file stored in the Mesh directory. In this case, the mesh function's name is "Tiny."

In addition to the Load() function, the CMesh class also features the Update() function. The application calls the Update() function once per frame. To use the function, you pass in the amount of time elapsed from the last frame (fTimeElapsed), and Update() updates accordingly. You pass in the time so that you can set the same animation speed on every machine. Here's what the signature line for Update() (in CMesh.h) looks like:

```
// Update the animation
 void Update(float fTimeElapsed, IDirect3DDevice9 *pd3dDevice);
```

A final function in CMesh is Draw(). If you examine CMyApplication.cpp, you can see that CMyApplication::Render() calls this function. Draw() renders the mesh to the screen. Here's what the signature line for Draw() (in CMesh.h) looks like:

```
// Draw the mesh
 void Draw(IDirect3DDevice9 *pd3dDevice);
```

Reset Activities

Another important player involved in rendering your mesh is the CGraphics::Reset() function. You can find this function in CGraphics.cpp:

```
void CGraphics::Reset()
{
    m_pDevice->Reset(&m_d3dpp); // call to IDirect3DDevice9:: Reset()
    // Set up the default projection matrix
    D3DXMATRIX matProj;
    float fAspect = (float)m_iWidth / (float)m_iHeight;
    D3DXMatrixPerspectiveFovLH( &matProj, D3DX_PI/4,
                                fAspect, 1.0f, 1000.0f );
    m_pDevice->SetTransform( D3DTS_PROJECTION, &matProj );
    // Set up some default render states
    m_pDevice->SetRenderState(D3DRS_LIGHTING,TRUE);
    m_pDevice->SetRenderState(D3DRS_DITHERENABLE,TRUE);
    m_pDevice->SetRenderState(D3DRS_ZENABLE,TRUE);
    m_pDevice->SetRenderState(D3DRS_CULLMODE,D3DCULL_CCW);
    m_pDevice->SetRenderState(D3DRS_AMBIENT,D3DCOLOR_XRGB(64,64,64));
    m_pDevice->SetRenderState(D3DRS_NORMALIZENORMALS, TRUE);
    m_pDevice->SetSamplerState(0, D3DSAMP_MAGFILTER, D3DTEXF_LINEAR);
    m_pDevice->SetSamplerState(0, D3DSAMP_MINFILTER, D3DTEXF_LINEAR);
    // Initialize the dialog resource manager with our D3D device
    DXUTGetGlobalDialogResourceManager()->OnResetDevice();
}
```

CGraphics::Reset() sets up the render states to enable lighting, z-buffering, and texture filtering. As a reminder, z-buffering is a technique to track the depth of objects in a scene. Texture filtering allows your textures to look smooth as you enlarge them and move them around. CGraphics::SetGFXMode() calls CGraphics::Reset() on its final line.

To understand how CGraphics::Reset() works, first notice that you call the IDirect3DDevice9:: Reset() function (m_pDevice->Reset()), which resets the state of the Direct3D device. The parameter (m_d3dpp) is a reference to the D3DPRESENT_PARAMETERS object declared in the CGraphics.h file. Next, you see that a D3DXMATRIX object is set up to transform 3D vertices to 2D screen space. To accomplish this, you create a value for fAspect, which allows you to set the aspect ratio of the screen. (The aspect ratio is the ratio of the width to the height of the screen.)

The D3DXMatrixPerspectiveFovLH() function is a Direct3D function that generates a perspective matrix. "FOV" refers to "field of view," and "LH" refers to "left-handed coordinate system." As you might recall from the previous discussions, the left-handed coordinate system provides a z value that increases with depth. The FOV is the angle at which you can see objects. D3DX_PI/4 sets the field of view, and this value is fairly standard for games. Humans, however, actually have a much wider field of view.

After the call to D3DXMatrixPerspectiveFovLH(), the Render() function calls the SetTransform() function. This function instructs DirectX to use the matProj object as the projection matrix. Next, in the series of calls to SetRenderState() that follows the call to the SetTransform() function, you see the primary values set for lighting and texturing. The last call in the Reset() function resets the dialog manager, which controls the graphical user interface.

Initializing Lighting

The work of the CGraphics::Reset() function possesses great importance, but another function—located in the CMyApplication class—possesses equal importance. This is the Initialize() function. Here is the code:

```
void CMyApplication::Initialize()
{
    // Load our mesh
    m_pMesh = new CMesh();
    m_pMesh->Load(L"Meshes\\Tiny.x", m_pGraphics->GetDevice());
    // Set up the light - white diffuse
    D3DLIGHT9 light;
    D3DXVECTOR3 vecLightDirUnnormalized(0.0f, -1.0f, 1.0f);
    ZeroMemory( &light, sizeof(D3DLIGHT9) );
    light.Type       = D3DLIGHT_DIRECTIONAL;
    light.Diffuse.r  = 1.0f;
    light.Diffuse.g  = 1.0f;
    light.Diffuse.b  = 1.0f;
    D3DXVec3Normalize( (D3DXVECTOR3*)&light.Direction,
                       &vecLightDirUnnormalized );
    m_pGraphics->GetDevice()->SetLight(0, &light);
    m_pGraphics->GetDevice()->LightEnable(0, TRUE);
    // Initialize the application using the parent call
    CApplication::Initialize();
}
```

Working from the top of the Reset() function, after you use the Load() function to load the mesh you are going to use, the most important task is initialization. For now, this involves lighting. For this reason, after the Load() function call, the first thing you see is the declaration of a D3DLIGHT9 object. This is your light. You need to massage the light a little, so next you see the declaration of a D3DXVECTOR3 object (vecLightDirUnnormalized), which allows you to set the direction of the light. (The source of the light in this case is above and to the left.)

Given these two objects, you can then set the Type attribute of the D3DLIGHT9 object —in this case you request directional light (D3DLIGHT_DIRECTIONAL). Then you use elements of the Diffuse attribute to set the color of the light. The values you see applied to the light.Diffuse elements (r, g, and b) are between zero and 1.0. When you assign 1.0 to the three Diffuse elements, you create white lighting.

The call to D3DXVec3Normalize() normalizes the vecLightDirUnnormalized vector and stores the result in the direction element of the D3DLIGHT9 struct. The SetLight() function designates the light you have created as light 0. (Direct3D supports up to eight lights in a scene, and the numbering begins with 0.) Following designation of the light number, LightEnable() turns the light on. Finally, CApplication::Initialize() calls the Initialize() function of the parent class (CApplication) to handle any default initialization.

Adding a Camera

Open Chapter05/Listing05_02 and compile the project. If you position the cursor in the window and press the right mouse button, you'll notice that you can rotate Tiny around the x, y, or z axes. See Figure 5.8. You can use the right mouse button in this way because the application now possesses a camera. The camera has its own "space," as was discussed previously, so what you are doing as you work with the mouse amounts to changing your view of the mesh rather than the actual mesh itself.

CApplication Changes for the Camera

To make it so that the application has a camera, you implement an instance of CModelViewerCamera from the Direct3D utility library (dxutmisc.h). The CModelViewerCamera object provides an interface for viewing and rotating around a single mesh. (Tiny counts as a single mesh.) Here's the code that declares the CModelViewerCamera object in CApplication.h:

```
// Our D3D camera
CModelViewerCamera m_Camera;
```

Figure 5.8 Changing the camera changes the view of Tiny.

To see how you can accommodate the new CModelViewerCamera object, you need to turn to CApplication.ccp and take a look at the definitions of the InitWindow(), UpdateScene(), and ProcessMessage() functions. For starters, consider InitWindow().

Here's the code:

```
// Set up the camera. The LEFT button rotates the model.
   The mouse wheel zooms in and out.
   The RIGHT button rotates the camera.
    float fAspect = (float)m_iWidth / m_iHeight;
    m_Camera.SetProjParams(D3DX_PI/4, fAspect, 1.0f, 5000.0f);
    m_Camera.SetWindow(m_iWidth, m_iHeight);
    m_Camera.SetButtonMasks(MOUSE_LEFT_BUTTON,
                            MOUSE_WHEEL, MOUSE_RIGHT_BUTTON);
  // Set up the initial projection matrix.
    m_pGraphics->GetDevice()->SetTransform(D3DTS_PROJECTION,
                                    m_Camera.GetProjMatrix());
```

On the first line after the comments, notice that you create the value for the *aspect ratio* (fAspect). The value consists of the width divided by the height of the screen. You then set up the projection matrix for the camera using SetProjParams(). The *projection matrix* translates points from 3D world space to 2D screen space. The first parameter of SetProjParams() sets the field of view (D3DX_PI/4), which is the *viewing angle* of the camera. Imagine looking through the small end of a funnel to get a notion of what the viewing angle regulates. (When you look through the funnel, your view is restricted by the conic dimensions of the funnel.) You then set the aspect ratio (fAspect). After you set the aspect ratio, you set the third and fourth parameters to establish the near and far *clipping plane*. The clipping plane consists of a space that starts one unit away (1.0f) and runs to a distance 5000 (5000.0f) units away.

Now, after you set the projection parameters, you move on to use SetWindow() to set the *size* of the window. Setting the size of the window involves supplying parameters for width and height. Having set the size of the window, you use SetButtonMask() to set the *button masks*. A button mask allows you choose which buttons control different aspects of the camera movement. When you change the view of Tiny, you use the right button to control the camera. To set the button mask for this button, you assign MOUSE_LEFT_BUTTON to the first parameter of SetButtonMasks(). This is a defined value you obtain from DirectX.

The second parameter of SetButtonMasks() controls the *zoom*. Zoom pertains to how you move the camera toward and away from the entity. When you zoom the camera, you might notice that the entity (Tiny) increases or decreases in size depending on whether you are moving away or approaching it. You set this parameter as MOUSE_WHEEL because— well—this is a natural, convenient way to move in and out of a scene.

The third parameter of SetButtonMasks() controls how you rotate the camera around the entity. When you rotate the camera, imagine that you are sitting on a merry-go-round and watching the stationary center of the merry-go-round. The center (the entity) is actually not moving. You are moving. Picture yourself moving around the perimeter of the merry-go-round and in the process seeing the center from different angles.

The final call in InitWindow()—SetTransform()—sets the projection transform, which means that at this point all the parameters are established, and DirectX just needs to apply them.

Updating a Scene

The next great adventure in the CApplication class after working with the camera involves changing UpdateScene() so that Tiny can move in a smooth, consistent way. UpdateScene() is a fairly straightforward function. Your application calls it once per frame to update all the objects in a scene. Here is the code for CApplication::UpdateScene() in CApplication.cpp:

```
void CApplication::UpdateScene(float fTimeScale)
{
    // Call quick step for the ODE world
    if(m_fTimeElapsed>0)
        dWorldQuickStep (m_dWorld, m_fTimeElapsed);
    // Set up the view matrix using the camera
    m_Camera.FrameMove(m_fTimeElapsed);
    // Set up the view matrix from the camera
    m_pGraphics->GetDevice()->SetTransform(D3DTS_WORLD,
                                   m_Camera.GetWorldMatrix());
    m_pGraphics->GetDevice()->SetTransform(D3DTS_VIEW,
                                   m_Camera.GetViewMatrix());
}
```

The use of the Open Dynamics Engine (ODE) dWorldQuickStep() function has already received some discussion, but it does not hurt to repeat that you use the function to regulate the physics engine. (The physics engine receives extensive discussion in Chapter 7.) The selection statement regulating the call to dWorldQuickStep() uses m_fTimeElapsed. The m_fTimeElapsed attribute stores the time that elapses between the rendering of frames. You do not want to invoke the function if no time has elapsed. You calculate m_fTimeElapsed continuously to ensure that the motion you see occurs smoothly. FrameMove(), which you call right after dWorldQuickStep(), also makes use of m_fTimeElapsed.

Next, you use a couple of calls to SetTransform() to set the *world transform*, which keeps track of the world matrix. The left mouse button controls transforming of this type. Notice that you use the D3DTS_WORLD to set the world matrix. You use the D3DTS_VIEW to set the view matrix. The right mouse button controls the view matrix. Upon the completion of UpdateScene(), your application has set up the matrices that make possible the movement of the camera. No movement, however, has yet occurred.

Processing the Message

The final changes you make to CApplication() allow you to set up message processing activity for the camera. At the center of this activity is the ProcessMessage() function. The ProcessMessage() function takes care of raw Windows messages. You make one change to accommodate the camera. Here's the code added to ProcessMessage():

```
    // Handle camera messages
    m_Camera.HandleMessages(hWnd, msg, wParam, lParam);
```

The parameters for the HandleMessages() function received attention in Chapter 3. These messages are general Windows messages, but they supplement the work of the camera because they process all the incoming Windows messages. Among these are the messages you create when you use the keyboard and the mouse. This, then, is where you click the right mouse and move the camera so that your view of Tiny changes.

Attaching the Camera to the Model

One significant change remains if you are to control your camera's actions, and that is to attach the camera to the entity. This action takes place in the CMyApplication::Initialize() function. Here are the lines that have been added:

```
// Setup the camera's view parameters
float fRadius = m_pMesh->GetRadius();
  D3DXVECTOR3 vecEye(0.0f, 0.0f, -fRadius * 2);
  D3DXVECTOR3 vecAt (0.0f, 0.0f, -0.0f);
  m_Camera.SetViewParams( &vecEye, &vecAt );
m_Camera.SetRadius( fRadius * 2.0f, fRadius* 0.5f, fRadius * 10.0f );
```

Notice first that you set up the radius to enclose the entity using a call to CMesh::GetRadius(). This function returns the radius of the bounding sphere of the mesh. The bounding sphere is the 3D area that contains the mesh.

Next, you set vecEye using the fRadius value. The *eye vector* (vecEye) is the position of the camera. The three parameters of vecEye are the x, y, and z positions of the camera, respectively.

The next value, the *at vector* (vecAt), is the point at which the camera is looking. In this case, this is the origin of the world space (the place where the x, y, and z axes intersect). Again, the three parameters of vecAt are the x, y, and z positions of the camera, respectively.

After you populate the vecEye and vecAt vectors, you feed references to these vectors to SetViewParams(). This sets up the position and orientation of the camera (the view matrix).

SetRadius() finishes things off by setting up, as its first parameter, the distance the camera starts from the object. The second and third parameters of SetRadius() establish the minimum and maximum distances allowed for the camera. The minimum distance is the closest point relative to the entity to which you can use the mouse wheel to move the camera. The maximum distance is an arbitrary distance beyond which you cannot move the camera. You do not necessarily see the entity disappear at this distance, but you cannot move beyond it. Imagine a dog on a leash, and you probably have the essence of the matter.

Adding Lights

Open Chapter05/Listing05_03 and compile the project. Notice that different colored lights now come to bear on Tiny. The lights in Figure 5.9 are only in shades of gray, but if you look at the compiled version, you can see that Tiny's face is now green. In the previous version (see Figure 5.8), she lacked such coloration. Depending on how you move her using the mouse, you can see stronger and weaker tints of green and blue. All of these changes involve lighting.

Figure 5.9   Tiny gets some lights.

A few changes make possible the lighting changes that you can see. Your first stop in this regard is the CGraphics class. There, you add a function called SetDirectionalLight(). In addition, you make a few changes to the CMyApplication::Initialize() function. Subsequent sections discuss these changes.

Setting the Direction of the Light

If you open the CGraphics.h file and take a look at the class declaration for CGraphics, you'll notice the addition of a prototype:

```
// Sets up a basic directional light
void SetDirectionalLight(int iNum, DWORD dwColor, D3DXVECTOR3 dir);
```

This function sets up a light that has color and direction. The function also enables the light. If you go to the CGraphics.cpp file, you can see the definition of the function. Here's the code:

```
void CGraphics::SetDirectionalLight(int iNum, DWORD dwColor,
                                                D3DXVECTOR3 dir)
{
    // Set up the light
      D3DLIGHT9 light;
      ZeroMemory(&light, sizeof(D3DLIGHT9));
      light.Type = D3DLIGHT_DIRECTIONAL;
      // Set the diffuse color
    light.Diffuse = D3DXCOLOR(dwColor);
    // Set the position and range
      D3DXVec3Normalize((D3DXVECTOR3*)&light.Direction, &dir);
      light.Range = 1000.0f;
    // Set up the light on the device
      m_pDevice->SetLight(iNum, &light);
      m_pDevice->LightEnable(iNum, TRUE);
}
```

On the first line of CGraphics::SetDirectionalLight() after the opening brace, notice that you declare a D3DLIGHT9 object (light). This is a struct that contains information about lighting. Next, the Win32 ZeroMemory() function clears the reference to the light object and then employs the sizeof() function to appropriate the right amount of memory for it.

After setting up safe memory values for the D3DLIGHT9 object, you then set the Type element of the struct. The value you assign to this is D3DLIGHT_DIRECTIONAL, which is one of several defined values DirectX provides to set lighting types. (Others set such light types as point and spotlight.) Following the setting of the type, the function proceeds to set the Diffuse element of the struct. You use the D3DXCOLOR class to accomplish this. This class converts between all different types of color formats. In this case, the DWORD dwColor parameter might be almost any color format.

Next, you store the result of a casting procedure into the light direction. Here's the line:

```
D3DXVec3Normalize((D3DXVECTOR3*)&light.Direction, &dir);
```

Note that you use a reference to the direction vector of the D3DLIGHT9 object and cast it as a pointer to a D3DXVECTOR3 object. This then enables the D3DXVec3Normalize() function to store the result of the normalization in the D3DLIGHT9 light element.

In the last two lines of the function, you use SetLight() to assign a number (iNum) to your light. Beginning with 0, you can have up to eight lights. After you have numbered your light, you can turn it on. LightEnable() turns the light on.

Initializing the Light

To see how to initialize the lighting, turn to CMyApplication.cpp and look at a few lines in the Initialize() function. Here's a selection of the code:

```
void CMyApplication::Initialize()
{
  //lines left out . . .
  // Set up the lights
  m_pGraphics->SetDirectionalLight(0, D3DCOLOR_XRGB(255,255,255),
                  D3DXVECTOR3(0,-1, 1.0f));
m_pGraphics->SetDirectionalLight(1, D3DCOLOR_XRGB(0,255,0),
                    D3DXVECTOR3(0, 1 , 0));
m_pGraphics->SetDirectionalLight(2, D3DCOLOR_XRGB(255,0,0),
                    D3DXVECTOR3(0, 0, -1));
m_pGraphics->SetDirectionalLight(3, D3DCOLOR_XRGB(0,0,255),
                  D3DXVECTOR3(1, 0, 0));
  //lines let out . . .
  }
```

These lines use the SetDirectionalLight() function to set up lights in a scene. All of the calls to SetDirectionalLight() work the same, but each describes a slightly different light. Consider, for example, the first call to SetDirectionalLight(). The first parameter you see used in this call (2) designates the number of the light (this remains the same as before; you can have up to 8, and the values start at 0). Then you set the color of the light using the D3DCOLOR_XRGB() macro. The X in the macro name means that the macro does not have an alpha component. The values are, respectively, red, green, and blue values, and using 255 for all of them results in white light.

After setting the color, you then set the direction of the light using a D3DXVECTOR3 object. The parameters you use in the D3DXVECTOR3 determine the direction the light points in 3D space. For example, the first light (0, -1, 1.0f) points down on the y axis and into the screen on the z axis. You always see this as long as you are not looking up from the bottom of the object. The second light (0, 1, 0), in contrast, points up on the y axis. You see this unless you are looking at the top of the object. The third light (0, 0, -1) points out on the z axis, so to see it, you must move the camera around the back of the model. The final light (1, 0, 0) points down the x axis, and to see it, you look down the x axis from the left side of the model.

Conclusion

Working out the basic concepts of what you can do to make entities interesting and then using use cases and other tools to explore scenarios in which to place entities provides you with ways to create interesting simulations. A simulation becomes interesting when it induces you to perceive opportunities for learning. Learning can take place whenever your interaction with an entity allows you to perceive instances of limitation. If a simulated activity induces you to explore options to compensate for the absence of something you think should be evident in the world with which you are interacting, then you automatically find yourself motivated to remain involved with the application and to explore it. At the heart of this simple scenario lies the characteristics you provide to entities to make them interesting.

In this chapter, you have covered how you design an entity and the basic coding activities involved in bringing one to life. In the process, as a first step in bringing Tiny to life, you implemented a camera that allows you to see Tiny in different ways. The camera allows you to create the appearance of movement without actually moving an entity. Instead of moving the entity, you move a camera around in the space the world furnishes to you. Even this basic change offers a way to enhance the characteristics of an entity.

In addition to creating a camera, you set up lighting. Although the lighting at this point does not do much, it is still the case that you have a foundation that you can use to give your entity different moods or to impose different themes on it. Like the camera, the lighting allows you to change the appearance of the entity in simple ways to make it more interesting for someone who is interacting with it.

In this chapter, you also had the chance to continue exploring the use of controls. The controls remained simple. You programmed the framework so that it would process mouse messages to control the camera and lighting. As you further develop the framework in subsequent chapters, the work you have done here goes in many directions.

For further reading, consider the following sources:

André LaMothe. *Tricks of the Windows Game Programming Gurus, Second Edition* (Indianapolis, Indiana: Sams Publishing, 2002).

Mason McCuskey. *Special Effects Game Programming with Direct X* (Indianapolis, Indiana: Premier Press, 2002).

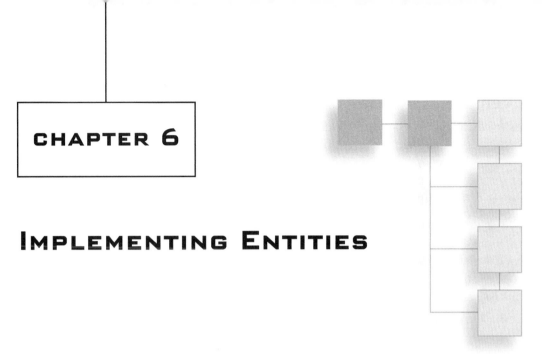

CHAPTER 6

IMPLEMENTING ENTITIES

In this chapter, you continue the work you started in Chapter 5. Your work centers on extending the basic properties of entities so that you can accommodate complex behaviors. To accommodate such behaviors, your first task is to add the ability to accommodate animations. Animations allow you to provide a single entity with different forms of behavior. For example, if you have a set of animations, you can turn an entity into a warrior who lunges, kicks, and strikes, among other things. While you continue to see one entity, you see the behavior of the entity extended in many interesting ways. In addition to extending the behavior of the entity, you also extend the interactive options of the person who interacts with the mesh. To accomplish this, you implement more sophisticated controls and process more involved messages.

Here are a few of the topics the chapter covers:

- Creating classes for clocks and events
- Adding a custom-build mesh to the framework
- Creating a class to embody the qualities of an entity
- Extending the capacity to control an entity
- Setting up sequences of events
- Working with skeletons, bones, and skinned meshes
- Automating mesh behavior
- Using the demonstration program

Events and Entities

As the discussion in Chapter 5, "Design for Entities," revealed, you can make entities more interesting if you give them a variety of characteristics that allow you to interact with them in different ways so that a multitude of possible behaviors result. To create different avenues of interaction, you must have a way that you can associate a given entity with different events, controls, and visible appearances.

You enhance the interest of an entity if you vary the way an entity responds to the controls you apply to it. For example, as you saw in the lighting examples in Chapter 5, you used the left and right mouse keys to directly induce a change in the entity. In addition to connecting an entity directly with a control and then having the control immediately invoke a change in the entity, you can provide the entity with its own agenda of possible responses to controls, so that even though you might use a given control in the same way on your entity, the entity's responses will differ from moment to moment.

Figure 6.1 illustrates some of the scenarios that might characterize entity control and response interactions.

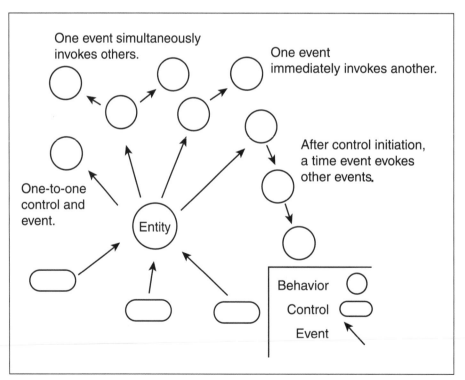

Figure 6.1 Control and interaction scenarios can vary according to the complexity of your entity.

In the sections that follow, you explore a number of techniques you can use to develop control and response characteristics for your entities. Chief among these is the capacity of the entity to respond in different ways to a given control stimulus. To make such responses patterns, you can use vectors to store information that the entity can divulge when it receives stimulus. While one type of information might allow the entity to trigger the actions of other entities, another type of information might lead the entity to change its own behavior. The possibilities extend in a multitude of directions.

To give entities the appearance of change, you can add a set animation to the store of characteristics that define a given entity. An animation is a unified set of behaviors, such as a running or walking motion. When you associate animations with a given entity, the entity can respond in complex ways to different types of stimulus. For now, things remain simple. You learn to control your entity to make it walk back and forth or in a circle. You can also speed up or slow down its walk. The behavior depends on how you combine events and controls.

Enumerating Animations

Open Chapter06/Listing06_01 and compile the project. Figure 6.2 shows you what you get after you click the left mouse button and pull the mesh around so that the profile and the lighting change. Try this as a preliminary exercise. In addition to positioning the mesh, click such options as "Dead," "Spear," and "Hurt" in the combo box you see in the panel.

To implement this functionality, it is necessary for you to be able to load different animations into your application. An animation differs from a lone mesh because it consists of what amounts to a set of instructions that cause the entity to move in different ways. To create such an animation, you use an application like Maya. In addition to seeing isolated behaviors, you also change behaviors (Dead to Spear, for example). Each time you see the behavior of the entity change, you are looking at a different animation. This approach to combining actions—if you remember the discussion from the start of the chapter—forms the starting point of creating complex entity behaviors.

Adding to CMesh

To make it possible for an entity to engage in different behaviors, it is necessary to load different animations of the same mesh (or entity). To accomplish this, you add a few new functions to CMesh. The new functions are GetAnimationName(), GetNumAnimations(), and SetAnimation(). All of these functions allow you to manipulate sets of animations. Here's the code in CMesh.h that shows the declarations of these functions:

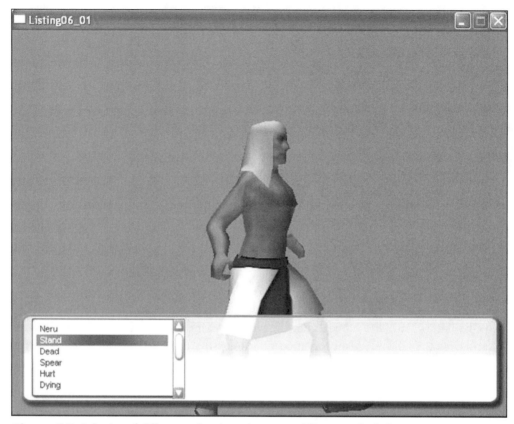

Figure 6.2 Selection of different animations shows you different entity behaviors.

```
// Gets the name for the requested animation num
wstring GetAnimationName(int iNum);
// Returns the number of animations for this mesh
int GetNumAnimations();
// Sets the animation to the specified name
void SetAnimation(wstring strName);
```

Setting the Animation

Setting the animation involves creating an animation controller. You initiate this activity by declaring an LPD3DXANIMATIONSET object. To see where you declare the object, go to CMesh.h and glance at the attribute list. Notice the following addition:

```
// The animation controller. Only on is needed.
ID3DXAnimationController *m_pAnimController;
```

To use the controller, you create an animation set object. In the CMesh.cpp file, you can see how this happens if you go to the SetAnimation() function. Here is the code for SetAnimation() in CMesh.cpp that shows this activity:

```
void CMesh::SetAnimation(wstring strName)
{
    LPD3DXANIMATIONSET pAnimSet = NULL;
    //Prepare to convert the name to ASCII
    char buf[255];
    ZeroMemory(buf, 255);
    WideCharToMultiByte(CP_ACP, 0, strName.c_str(),
                        (int)strName.length(), buf, 255, " ", false);
      m_pAnimController->GetAnimationSetByName(buf, &pAnimSet);
    // lines left out . . .
    // Set it on the current track
    m_pAnimController->SetTrackAnimationSet(0, pAnimSet);
    SAFERELEASE(pAnimSet);
}
```

An LPD3DXANIMATIONSET object represents a single animation. The object's name is pAnimSet. Eventually, you want to associate this object with the controller, but first you need to deal with issues that concern how to name your animations. The animation controller supports only ASCII names, and all of the strings in this application so far are Unicode. For this reason, you must use an ASCII array to name the animation.

After you have used the WideCharToMultiByte() to set up the appropriate character format for the name of your mesh, you use the animation controller object (m_pAnimController) to call to the GetAnimationSetByName() function, which uses the ASCII array you just created (buf) and a reference to the animation set (pAnimSet) to create a container for the data you have requested for the animation.

Note

One hazard you face when you create the buffer (buf) is that your path designation is now limited to 255 characters. As an alternative approach, you could use a wide character string to create a character buffer. The syntax for this takes the following form:

```
char* buf = new char[stringName.length) * 2]
```

Having used the new operator to create a pointer, you must remember to delete it.

You then make a call to SetTrackAnimationSet(), which sets the current animation to the one you have just requested (pAnimSet). The final action is to use the SAFERELEASE() macro on the animation set object.

Getting the Number of Animations

Your next duty after setting up the animation controller is to establish the number of animations you want to use. To accomplish this you call the CMesh::GetNumAnimations() function. Here's the code from CMesh.cpp:

```
int CMesh::GetNumAnimations()
{
    // Handle case of NULL animation controller
    if(!m_pAnimController)
        return 0;

    // Otherwise return the number of animations
    return m_pAnimController->GetNumAnimationSets();
}
```

Notice that the function centers on a single call to ID3DXAnimationController::Get-NumAnimationSets(), which obtains the number of animations from the animation controller. The function returns the number of animations, which is then used to populate the list box you create using the DirectX utility controls. If you view the code in CMyApplication::InitGUI() in the CMyApplication.cpp file, you can see the following bit of code that shows how you actually use the returned data:

```
// Add a list box with the animation names
m_GUI.AddListBox(IDC_ANIMLIST,25,m_iConsoleY+8,200,100);
for(int i=0;i<m_pMesh->GetNumAnimations(); i++)
{
    m_GUI.GetListBox(IDC_ANIMLIST)->AddItem(
                    m_pMesh->GetAnimationName(i).c_str(),NULL);
}
```

The GetNumAnimations() function returns the total number of animations, and this is used to control the for loop. Then, inside the for loop, you see a call to the GetAnimationName() function, which returns a string naming each of the animations you want to use.

Getting Animation Names

With respect to the GetAnimationName() function, you can see how it is laid out if you turn to CGrapics.cpp. Here is the code:

```
wstring CMesh::GetAnimationName(int iNum)
{
    // lines left out . . .
    //Get the animation set
    LPD3DXANIMATIONSET pAnimSet = NULL;
```

```
    m_pAnimController->GetAnimationSet(iNum, &pAnimSet);
    // lines left out . . .
    //Get the ASCII buffer
    LPCSTR szName = pAnimSet->GetName();
    // Convert to unicode
    WCHAR wszName[255];  //Again you create a path length limit
    MultiByteToWideChar( CP_ACP, 0, szName, -1, wszName, 255 );
    wszName[254] = L'\0';
    SAFERELEASE(pAnimSet);
    return(wszName);
}
```

As you can see from selected lines of GetAnimationName(), the code first sets up the LPD3DXAN-IMATIONSET object (pAnimSet) and then proceeds to use this object to obtain the name of the animation. It then converts the name to a string type that the DirectX GUI control can use.

Playing with Time

The importance of being able to time events cannot be underestimated. When you create complex forms of behavior for your entities, the behavior unfolds as a set of events you schedule in some type of succession. For example, if you want an entity to first assume a stance, then jump, then land, you must precisely schedule the firing of these events if you want to make the action look consistent. To make such consistency possible, you need a precise timer.

Open Chapter06/Listing06_02 and compile the project. Figure 6.3 shows you the result. The information that the window displays in the upper left corner tracks time values relative to the operation of your application. The values you see track the total time the application has been running, the time of the last frame, and the framerate. Although you have seen values for timing in previous versions of the framework, what you see now provides you with a higher precision timer and a cleaner interface for obtaining information about the time and scheduling events for your entities. To make the changes necessary to create this new functionality, you add a class called CClock. You then modify the CApplication class to use the functionality CClock provides.

If you examine the code used to declare CClock in CClock.h, you can see that the class provides a private constructor, which prevents you from directly invoking the constructor. When you want to use a CClock object, you use the GetClock() function, which returns a pointer to a CClock object. Such procedures characterize a Singleton class, which is a class designed to allow its users to create only one instance of it. Here is the code that declares CClock:

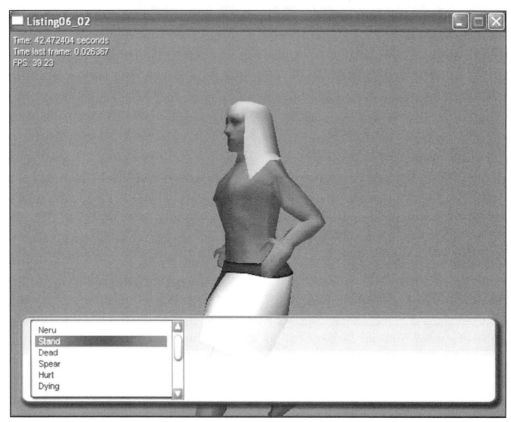

Figure 6.3 CClock and precise time measurements allow you to control events precisely.

```
class CClock
{
private:
    LARGE_INTEGER m_lFrequency;        // Frequency of the clock
      __int64 m_lStartTime;              // Time the system started up
    bool m_bHighFrequencySupport;      // Support high frequency?
    CClock();                          // Instantiate the clock object

public:
    // This is a singleton object, so the constructor is hidden.
      // Reference to the clock using the GetClock function
    friend CClock *GetClock();
    // Destroys the clock object
    ~CClock();
```

```
    // Returns the amount of time on the clock in seconds since
    // the clock has been started
    double GetTime();
};
```

The attributes of the CClock class deal largely with the large numbers you must have available to you when you work with extremely precise time values. For the most part, such values are 64-bit integers. The Microsoft compiler provides you with two data types you can use in this respect. The first type you see is a C union, which is basically a special type of struct that allows you to access the integer as two DWORD values or one LONGLONG (__int64). The __int64 data type is an integer capable of storing what amounts to a very large number (2^{63}). Given this large number, you can then track the time of your simulation to the level of picoseconds (or smaller).

As for the functions, notice only that the GetTime() function provides you with the number of seconds that have transpired since the opening of the application. You can use this function for a number of purposes, as already mentioned.

Clock Construction

Construction of a Singleton object requires that you use what is known as a friend function. A friend function is a function that has access to all the public, private, and protected members of a class. A friend class similarly has access to all members, regardless of the access level of the class declaring it a friend. Normally, the access point for a singleton is with a static function, which is a member function that can be called without an instance of the class (without the use of the this pointer). So the friend keyword in this case is usually replaced with static. The definition of the function is:

```
    CClock* CClock::GetClock()
```

You can then call this function as follows:

```
    CClock* clock = CClock::GetClock();
```

Note

When a function returns a pointer, it can be an invitation to disaster if someone else uses the function to return a pointer and then calls delete on the returned pointer. A safer implementation requires calling new in the creating function, making the destructor private, and creating a friend class that you can use to destroy the object. This is an example of the Destroyer pattern.

—Courtesy of John Hollis

In CClock.cpp, you can see that the GetClock() function serves as a surrogate for a direct call to the constructor. Here's the code:

```
CClock *GetClock()
{
    static CClock theClock;
    return(&theClock);
}
```

Notice that the GetClock() function creates a static instance of the CClock class and then returns a reference to this class instance. The static instance of the CClock class ensures that you can create only one instance of the clock during the life of your application.

To cover the preconditions of GetClock, you create a constructor in the private scope of the CClock class. Here's the constructor code from CClock.cpp:

```
CClock::CClock()
{
    // Get the frequency/check if high-frequency is supported
    QueryPerformanceFrequency(&m_lFrequency);
    m_bHighFrequencySupport = (m_lFrequency.QuadPart > 0);
    // Get the system start time using one of two methods
    if(m_bHighFrequencySupport)
    {
        LARGE_INTEGER lTime;
        QueryPerformanceCounter(&lTime);
        m_lStartTime = lTime.QuadPart;
    }
    else
    {
        m_lStartTime = timeGetTime();
    }
}
```

The first call in the constructor is to QueryPerformanceFrequency(), a Win32 API function. This function sets the value of a reference to the LARGE_INTEGER attribute of CClock (m_lFrequency). The next line checks the m_lFrequency.QuadPart element to ensure that you possess high frequency support. Given the truth of this condition, you use the QueryPerformanceCounter() function to obtain the start time of the application. You then access the lTime.QuadPart element and assign this to the class attribute m_lStartTime, which makes the start time available for determining, among other things, how long the application has been running. If it so happens that your machine cannot support the m_bHighFrequencySupport performance range, then the alternative selection option is to use a less precise timer (timeGetTime()) to set the start time (m_lStartTime).

Creating GetTime()

After you create the CClock() constructor and the GetClock() function, you create the
GetTime() function to provide the time since the start of your application. Here's the code
from CClock.cpp:

```
double CClock::GetTime()
{
    // Get the current time, and subtract the start time
    if(m_bHighFrequencySupport)
    {
        LARGE_INTEGER lTime;
        QueryPerformanceCounter(&lTime);
        __int64 lCurrentTime = lTime.QuadPart;
        // Subtract the system start time
        lCurrentTime -= m_lStartTime;
        // Now convert to seconds and return
        return((double)lCurrentTime/(double)m_lFrequency.QuadPart);
    }
    else
    {
        // Get the current time and convert to seconds, then return
        __int64 lCurrentTime = timeGetTime() - m_lStartTime;
        return(lCurrentTime/1000.0);
    }
}
```

The first call CClock::GetTime() is to QueryPerformanceTimer(), which as was mentioned
previously, is a Win32 API function. This function allows you to obtain the number of
clock ticks that have occurred since the start of the system.

The next significant event in CClock::GetTime() occurs when you subtract the start time of
the application (m_lStartTime) from the time at which you decide to take a reading
(lCurrentTime). The difference between the two times establishes the time the application
has been running. You then divide the time the application has been running by the
frequency (m_lFrequency.QuadPart) to obtain the time in seconds. The function returns this
value. The low frequency time (this is the second option on the selection statement) works
the same way, except that you use the timeGetTime() function along with a
frequency of a thousand ticks per second to generate the return value.

Creating Events

As was emphasized in the opening sections of this chapter, events define the behavior of entities, and the more complex the behaviors you create, the more interesting your entities become. For this reason, you require functionality in your simulation software that allows you to easily construct, combine, and control events so that you can form them into complex behaviors. The CEvent class addresses this need.

Open Chapter06/Listing06_03 and compile the project. When you compile the project, the first thing you'll notice is that a message box pops up (see Figure 6.4). The message box demonstrates an immediate event that the CEvent class creates for you and then triggers. Click on the OK button in the message box. After a short time, another message box appears. You can click the OK button on this box and close it. Finally, 20 seconds from the time you start the application, a message box that allows you to close the application appears. In each instance, you are seeing the CEvent class at work. The event you see relates to the controllers you apply to your entities. Later, the connection between the controllers and the entities receives extended discussion. For now, to understand how to implement the CEvent class, turn to the CEvent.h file.

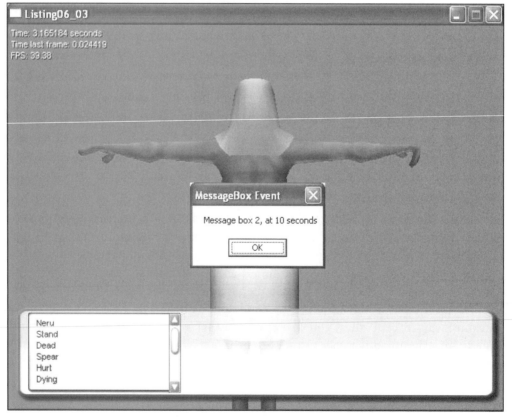

Figure 6.4 Events provide entities with behaviors.

Adding Events

In the CEvent.h file, you can see the declaration of the CEvent class. This is a class that is new to the framework. This class allows you to schedule custom events using the clock. To schedule an event, you create a local CEvent object in the Initialize() function of CMyApplication. It is possible, of course, to create CEvent objects in any number of places, such as in the code that responds to input from the keyboard or mouse in the ProcessMessage() function. Here, however, the events appear in the Initialize() function as a matter of convenience. Here is the code that appears in the Initialize() function in CMyApplication.cpp:

```
// Create an event to show a message box immediately,
  // and another one in 10 seconds
// then create an event to terminate the application in 20 seconds
CEvent *pMessageBox1 = new CEvent(L"MESSAGEBOX");
pMessageBox1->AddStringParam(L"Message box 1, immediate");
CEvent *pMessageBox2 = new CEvent(L"MESSAGEBOX",TIME_ABSOLUTE,10);
pMessageBox2->AddStringParam(L"Message box 2, at 10 seconds");
CEvent *pTerminate = new CEvent(L"TERMINATE",TIME_ABSOLUTE,20);
// Add the events to the queue
AddEvent(pMessageBox1);
AddEvent(pMessageBox2);
AddEvent(pTerminate);
```

As you can see from the first line after the opening braces and the comments, creating an event involves creating an instance of CEvent and assigning it to a CEvent pointer. The constructor uses the parameter MESSAGEBOX to create a pointer that is assigned to pMessageBox1. The parameter value you feed to the CEvent can vary, depending on the type of events you want to create. In this case, the event you want to create is a message box. Notice that in the subsequent calls to the constructor you use an overloaded version of the constructor that allows you to add to the basic message type designation information that refines your control of the execution of the event. (The use of these arguments is discussed at greater length a little later on.)

As you can see in the last three lines of code shown for the CApplication::Initialize() function, for each instance of CEvent, you use the CApplication::AddEvent() function. The sole parameter for this function is a pointer to a CEvent object, and the result of the function's call is to schedule the event in the life of your application.

Processing Events

The CMyApplication::OnEvent() function processes the events you set up in the CApplication::Initialize() function. Here is the code for CMyApplication::OnEvent(), which you can find in CMyApplication.cpp:

```
void CMyApplication::OnEvent(CEvent *pEvent)
{
    // Process message box event
    if(pEvent->GetName() == L"MESSAGEBOX")
    {
        // The first parameter sets the name of the message box
        wstring strText = pEvent->GetStringParams()[0];
        MessageBox(NULL, strText.c_str(),L"MessageBox Event", MB_OK);
    }
    else if(pEvent->GetName() == L"TERMINATE")
    {
        MessageBox(NULL,L"TERMINATE event fired (20 seconds),
            exiting", L"Exiting!",MB_OK);
        SetRunning(false);
    }
}
```

Scheduling Events

If you access the CEvent.h file in your project folder for Listing06_03, you can see, first, that just prior to the declaration of the class an enumeration appears. Here's the code:

```
enum TIMEMODE
{
    TIME_IMMEDIATE,
    TIME_RELATIVE,
    TIME_ABSOLUTE
};
```

The purpose of the TIMEMODE enumeration is to allow you to describe when events fire. You can do this in three basic ways. The first is immediately (TIME_IMMEDIATE), which means that if you employ this value, any event you set using it occurs as soon as possible. Next, if you want to specify that an event is to fire at a specific time from when you create the object for the event object, you can use TIME_RELATIVE. This time mode is "relative" to the time you create the event object. (You want, for example, a phantom to appear when your hero opens a door, but three seconds later, you want the phantom to vanish.) Finally, if you want to have an event fire at a specific time from the start of the application, then you can use the TIME_ABSOLUTE value. If you recall what the final message box did when you executed the application, for instance, you saw that the message box closed the application 20 seconds after the application started. This was an absolute period of time.

Event Construction

If you examine the CEvent class in CEvent.h, you can see that the first bit of activity involves creating the constructors. Here is the code.

```
// Initialize the event, including the time at which it should occur
CEvent(wstring strName, TIMEMODE TimeMode = TIME_IMMEDIATE,
                               double iProcessTime = 0);
// Destroy the event
~CEvent();
```

Notice that the CEvent constructor takes three arguments. The first argument is the name of the event. Any name you use for this parameter becomes a name you can later retrieve to associate actions with this event. Next, you see the use of the TIMEMODE data type, which you know from the previous discussion allows you to control how an event fires. By default, this parameter is set with the TIME_IMMEDIATE value. The last parameter of the constructor allows you to set the time the event fires. How the time value you provide the constructor affects the event depends on the TIMEMODE value you supply. For example, consider the use of the constructor in the Initialize() function:

```
pMessageBox2->AddStringParam(L"Message box 2, at 10 seconds");
    CEvent *pTerminate = new CEvent(L"TERMINATE",TIME_ABSOLUTE,20);
```

The integer value 10 follows the TIME_ABSOLUTE value. In this instance, the event occurs 10 seconds after the (absolute) start of the application. Were you to supply TIME_RELATIVE instead of TIME_ABSOLUTE, the events visible manifestation would follow the creation of the event by 10 seconds (rather than the creation of the application).

Event Controls

Returning to the CEvent class declaration as shown in CEvent.h, you see a fairly extensive set of functions that allow you, ultimately, to exert quite a bit of control over your events. Here's the code:

```
    void AddStringParam(wstring strParam);
    void AddIntegerParam(int iParam);
    void AddFloatParam(double dParam);
    void AddPointerParam(void *pParam);
    const vector<wstring> &GetStringParams();
    const vector<int> &GetIntegerParams();
    const vector<double> &GetFloatParams();
    const vector<void *> &GetPointerParams();
```

The `AddStringParam()` and its associated functions provide you with the ability to add information to the events that you can retrieve when the application fires the events. What does such information allow you to control? Suppose that you want to have one event trigger another with a given type of information. To do this, you have the event store the information you want it to communicate to other events.

Adding information to events involves pushing information into the vector attributes that accompany each `CEvent` class object. The parameters of the overloaded versions of the `AddIntegerParam()` feed information to the vectors. If you look at the last few lines of the `CEvent` class declaration, you can see the vector attributes that support this capability. Here are the lines:

```
// A vector of string parameters
vector<wstring> m_vecStringParams;
// A vector of integer parameters
vector<int> m_vecIntegerParams;
// A Vector of floating point parameters
vector<double> m_vecFloatParams;
// A vector of pointer parameters
vector<void *> m_vecPointerParams;
```

Given the use of the STL vector template for each of the data types, your ability to store information for an object is for all practical purposes unlimited. You could push a large set of dialog items into the `wstring` vector, for example, and pop these in succession according to the mapping of your event.

In addition to functions that store and retrieve information associated with events, you can also call a function that tells your application that an event should fire. This is the `ShouldProcess()` function. You use this function in the `CApplication::ProcessEvents()` function. Here's the code:

```
bool ShouldProcess();
```

The final function, `GetName()` returns a constant reference to `wstring`, which allows you to obtain the name of the event with which you are dealing:

```
const wstring &GetName();
```

As for the remainder of the `CEvent` class declaration, you find a group of refining attributes. Here they are

```
// The unique identifier for the next event
static unsigned long ID;
// The unique ID for this particular event
unsigned long m_iUniqueID;
// Time the event was created
double m_dCreationTime;
// Time the event should be processed
double m_dProcessTime;
// Which time mode are we using
TIMEMODE m_TimeMode;
// Name of the event
wstring m_strName;
```

The attributes serve the functions discussed previously. The attribute of the TIMEMODE type stores values related to absolute and relative times. The m_dCreationTime and m_dProcessTime attributes allow you to track when you create events and how long you want to take to process them. You can also see that the m_iUniqueID attribute allows the constructor to assign a unique long integer identifier to each event. The ID attribute allows your application to track the number of events it has created.

Processing Events

To view how the application processes events, take a look a the CApplication::Process-Events() functions in CApplication.cpp. Here's the code:

```
void CApplication::ProcessEvents()
{
    // Go through all events
    vector<CEvent *>::iterator i;  //vector CEvent declaration
    for(i = _vecEvents.begin();i != m_vecEvents.end();i++)
    {
        CEvent *pEvent = (CEvent *)(*i);  //retrieve events
        // If the event is ready to process, process it,
            // and then remove it from the list
        if(pEvent->ShouldProcess())
        {
            OnEvent(pEvent);
            // Erase the event
            SAFEDELETE(pEvent);
```

```
            //Remove from the vector and move the iterator back one
            m_vecEvents.erase(i);
            i--;
        }
    }
}
```

The MessageLoop() function of CApplication calls the ProcessEvents() function as every frame is processed. The call occurs inside the while loop after the loop while condition checks to see if the application should continue running. Part of running involves processing events. Here are a few lines from the MessageLoop() function:

```
while (IsRunning())
    {
        if(PeekMessage(&msg, 0, 0, 0, PM_REMOVE))
        {
// Lines left out . . .
        // Process all events
        ProcessEvents();

//lines left out . . .
}
```

Generally how quickly your application processes events depends on the framerate of your application, but a general ballpark figure is between 10 and 60 times a second. This gives you what might be viewed as an "event frequency" for accomplishing whatever it is that you want to accomplish using your application.

To see how the ProcessEvents() function works, look again at the code in ProcessEvents() and consider how the function uses the STL vector. The first line of ProcessEvents() declares an iterator for a vector:

```
vector<CEvent *>::iterator i;
```

Given the declaration of the iterator, the function can then proceed to use a for loop in conjunction with the begin() and end() functions of the vector class to iterate through all the events you have stored in your event vector. As each event emerges from the vector, you then cast it as a CEvent:

```
CEvent *pEvent = (CEvent *)(*i);
```

You then check to see whether the event should be processed, and if this is so, you then invoke CEvent::ShouldProcess() to trigger the event:

```
if(pEvent->ShouldProcess())
        {
            OnEvent(pEvent);
        //.. . lines left out
        }
```

The `CApplication::OnEvent()` function executes the event.

An Entity Class

One of the most important factors contributing to the success of simulation and event modeling involves being able to enrich the qualities of the entities you create. While it is important to represent entities using meshes, control entity actions using extremely precise time values, and set up events so that they can trigger each other, putting everything together for a simulation requires an encompassing entity class. To reach this goal, it becomes necessary to enhance the `CEntity` class.

Open Chapter06/Listing06_04 and compile the project. Figure 6.5 shows you the result. Use the mouse to move the entity around a little and then sit back and watch it rotate. What you are observing here is a new level of entity behavior. You are going beyond simply executing and animation. Now you are creating a behavior. `CEntity` provides you with the controls you need to achieve this end. Among the 3D operations that facilitate such behaviors are rotation, scaling, and translation.

To discover where the work of controlling an entity begins, take a look at the declaration of `CMyApplication` in CMyApplication.h. There you see the following lines:

```
// Our test entity
class CEntity *m_pEntity;
```

The declaration of the pointer `m_pEntity` allows you to create an instance of a `CEntity` in the `Initialize()` function of `CMyApplication`. Here's the code as shown in CApplication.cpp:

```
void CMyApplication::Initialize()
{
    // Load our mesh
    m_pEntity = new CEntity(L"Test Entity");
    m_pEntity->LoadMesh(L"Meshes\\multi_anim.x", m_pGraphics->GetDevice());
//lines left out. . .
```

Notice that the constructor of `CEntity` allows you to provide the entity with a name. Next, you use the `LoadMesh()` function of `CEntity` to load the animation for the mesh. You can create as many entities as you want in this manner. After you create them, you are in a position to associate controls and events with them as needed.

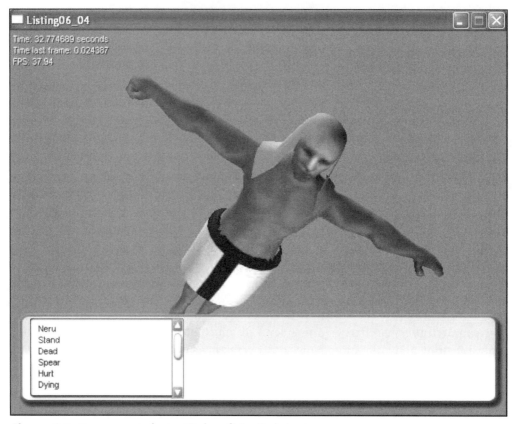

Figure 6.5 You can control an entity by refining its behavior.

Assigning Attributes to Entities

If you turn to CEntity.h in Listing06_04, you can see that the first thing that happens involves declaring the class attributes for CEntity. Here are the declarations:

```
// The name of the entity
wstring m_strName;
// The mesh which represents the entity
class CMesh *m_pMesh;
// A static ID # so the application can assign
  //each entity a unique ID
static unsigned int ID;
// The unique ID for this specific entity
int m_iUniqueID;
// Our message queue
vector<class CEvent *> m_lstEvents;
```

As you can see, the first attribute is a wstring that allows you to assign a name to your entity. Following the attribute that holds the entity name, you see a CMesh attribute—which might be said to give your entity a body. The work of the CMesh class has been covered in detail previously, but here it might be noted that the entity you see at this point, unlike the examples shown previously, can process events and is for this reason much more extensible. This is explained in detail as we go.

Next, the ID attribute is incremented each time you add an entity so that your application can track the number of entities it has created. Further, for each entity, you can assign a unique identification using the m_iUniqueID attribute.

Following the creation of identifiers for the entities, the class provides you with three attributes of the type D3DXVECTOR3. The first D3DXVECTOR3 attribute allows you to set and control the position of the entity. The second allows you to control the scaling of the entity. The final allows you to translate the entity in whatever manner you see fit. Here are the lines that declare the D3DXVECTOR3 attributes:

```
// Position, scale, rotation vectors for the entity
D3DXVECTOR3 m_vecPos;
D3DXVECTOR3 m_vecScale;
D3DXVECTOR3 m_vecRotAngles;
```

Controlling Entities

Following the declaration of attributes pertaining to the entities, the CEntity class provides you with a number of functions that allow you to create and control entities. The lines read as follows:

```
// Entity constructor
    CEntity(wstring strName);
        //lines left out . . .
    // Loads a mesh for the entity
    virtual bool LoadMesh(wstring strFile, IDirect3DDevice9 *pDevice);
    // Processes a CEvent
    virtual void OnEvent(class CEvent *pEvent);
    // Render the entity
    void Render(IDirect3DDevice9 *pDevice);
    // Update the entity
    void Update(float fTimeElapsed,IDirect3DDevice9 *pDevice);
    // Processes the events for the entity
    void ProcessEvents();
    // Add an event to the event list for this entity
    void AddEvent(class CEvent *pEvent);
```

The constructor for CEntity requires only that you assign a name to the entity. You can use the name to refer to the entity as you use it throughout your program. Next, you see the LoadMesh() function. For the first parameter, this function requires you to name the source file for the entity mesh. For the second parameter, it asks you to provide the pointer to the IDirect3DDevice9 object you declared in CGraphics::SetGFXMode(). You saw previously in CMyApplication::Initialize() the use of the CEntity constructor and the LoadMesh() function.

Following the LoadMesh() function, you see the OnEvent() function. The work of OnEvent() does not differ from what you saw with the CApplication::OnEvent() function discussed previously. The ProcessEvents() function has been added to CEntity so that entities can process their own events. This makes it possible for you to associate specific events with each entity. Here is the code:

```
void CEntity::ProcessEvents()
{
//lines left ...
        // Process the event
          if(pEvent->ShouldProcess())
            {
                OnEvent(pEvent);
                // Remove the event from the list if it's time to terminate
                if(pEvent->ShouldTerminate())
                {
                    SAFEDELETE(pEvent);
                    m_lstEvents.erase(i);
                    i--;
                }
                else
                {
                    // Otherwise update the time on
                            the event so it can be fired again
                    pEvent->UpdateTime();
                }
```

Notice that the if…else selection allows for a new type of event that automatically repeats itself over a given period, so you can, for example, create an event that repeats itself. The erase() function deletes the event after it is no longer active. The UpdateTime() function determines if period events are again scheduled to fire.

Updating

CEntity::Update() takes care of drawing and updating your transformations. Here are the first few lines of the Update() function, which you can find in CEntity.cpp:

```
void CEntity::Update(float fTimeElapsed, IDirect3DDevice9 *pDevice)
{
    // First of all, process all the events
    ProcessEvents();
    // Construct the matrices for our transformation
    D3DXMATRIX matWorld, matTrans, matScale,
                matRot, matRotX, matRotY, matRotZ;
    D3DXMatrixTranslation(&matTrans, m_vecPos.x, m_vecPos.y, m_vecPos.z);
    D3DXMatrixScaling(&matScale, m_vecScale.x, m_vecScale.y, m_vecScale.z);
```

The call to ProcessEvents() handles all the pending events for the entity. After ProcessEvents() finishes its work, you use the D3DXMatrixTranslation() and D3DXMatrixScaling() functions to construct the matrices that are to be used to translate and scale the entity. This activity is based on the vectors that you see declared as class attributes.

Next, you move on to use D3DXMatrixRotationX() and its associate functions to construct a matrix that describes the rotation "about" each axis:

```
    // Build the rotation matrices
    D3DXMatrixRotationX(&matRotX, m_vecRotAngles.x);
    D3DXMatrixRotationY(&matRotY, m_vecRotAngles.y);
    D3DXMatrixRotationZ(&matRotZ, m_vecRotAngles.z);
```

Then you move on to combine the three matrices you have set up into a single rotation matrix. You use two calls to D3DXMatrixMultiply() to accomplish this because you can only multiply two matrices at once. First you take care of the x and y axes. Then you multiply that result by the matrix associated with the z axis. This effect achieves the matrix multiplication X·Y·Z:

```
    D3DXMatrixMultiply(&matRot, &matRotX, &matRotY);
    D3DXMatrixMultiply(&matRot, &matRot, &matRotZ);
```

If you recall the order of operations discussed previously, you can see that the next set of operations is slated to involve scaling, translation, and rotation. Notice that although you see rotate last, it is still the case that you scale and translate after you rotate. The order appears to be backward. The reason for this is that the second argument to D3DXMatrixMultiply() is applied first:

```
// Multiply the matrices together to combine them
//scale and then translate
D3DXMatrixMultiply(&matWorld, &matTrans, &matScale);
//rotate
D3DXMatrixMultiply(&matWorld, &matWorld, &matRot);
```

The final lines of CEntity::Update() take care of getting a copy of the current world matrix generated by the camera and combining this matrix with the one used for the entity:

```
// Now get a copy of the original world matrix
 // so it can be combined with the new one. This
// is the matrix that transforms the model via
 // the mouse (from the camera class)
D3DXMATRIX matOrigWorld;
pDevice->GetTransform(D3DTS_WORLD,&matOrigWorld);
D3DXMatrixMultiply(&matWorld, &matWorld, &matOrigWorld);
// Now set the world matrix
pDevice->SetTransform(D3DTS_WORLD,&matWorld);
```

Creating Entity Events

Open Chapter06/Listing06_05 and compile the project. Figure 6.6 shows you the executable. You now see five buttons on the panel, along side the animation combo box. Also, to the right, you see a Clear events and an Exit app button. Try experimenting with the buttons to see what happens. Here is a short summary of the events the buttons initiate:

■ **Rotate X—10 seconds.** This rotates the entity around the x axis for ten seconds. The rotation you see involves changing the D3DXMatrixRotationX() values you saw at work in the previous section.

■ **Rotate Y—10 seconds.** This rotates the entity around the y axis for ten seconds. The rotation you see involves changing the D3DXMatrixRotationY() values you saw at work in the previous section.

■ **Rotate Z—10 seconds.** This rotates the entity around the z axis for ten seconds. The rotation you see involves changing the D3DXMatrixRotationZ() values you saw at work in the previous section.

■ **Scale up—5 seconds.** This causes the entity to increase in size for a period of five seconds. Watch out! If you click multiple times, the clicks are queued up and will continue to grow in size until you see the inside of the mesh. To adjust things, you can also use the mouse wheel. To accomplish this, you use the D3DXMatrixScaling() function you saw at work in the previous section.

- **Scale down—5 seconds.** This causes the entity to decrease in size for a period of five seconds. As before, if you click multiple times, the entity continues to shrink in accord with your commands, so it completely vanishes and then returns to a visible size upside down. This occurs because you have diminished the values in the matrices that define the entity so far that the values become negative. With the negative values, the application visually distorts (inverts) the entity. This effect is left here to illustrate what happens. When you create applications for general release, you can prevent such distortions if you limit the scaling to positive values only. This scaling, like the previous one, involves using the D3DXMatrixScaling() function you saw at work in the previous section.

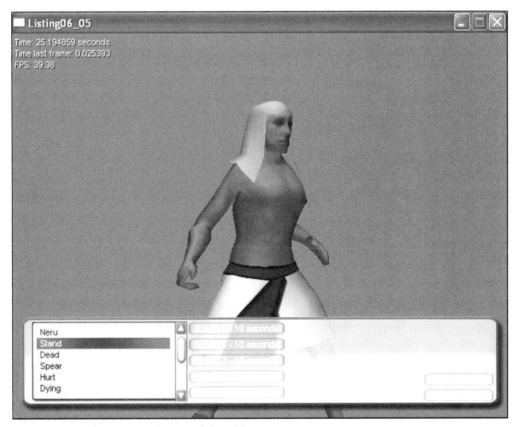

Figure 6.6 Behaviors now become fully evident.

Selecting Events

To create the effects you see in Listing06_05, go to CMyApplication.cpp and take a look at the OnGUIEvent() function. Here's the code:

```
void CMyApplication::OnGUIEvent(UINT nEvent, int nControlID,
                                              CDXUTControl *pControl)
{
    // Make sure our entity exists
    if(!m_pEntity)
        return;

    // Animation changed
    if(nControlID == IDC_ANIMLIST)
    {
        CDXUTListBox *pListBox = (CDXUTListBox *)pControl;
        m_pEntity->GetMesh()->SetAnimation(pListBox->
                                GetSelectedItem()->strText);
    }
    else if(nControlID == IDC_EXIT)
    {
        SetRunning(false);
    }
    else if(nControlID == IDC_CLEARALL)
    {
        m_pEntity->ClearEvents();
    }
    else if(nControlID == IDC_ROTATEX)
    {
        // Create a rotation event for the entity
        CEvent *pEvent = new
            CEvent(L"ROTATERELATIVE",TIME_PERIOD,.01,TIME_RELATIVE,10);
        pEvent->AddFloatParam(.01);
        pEvent->AddFloatParam(0);
        pEvent->AddFloatParam(0);
        m_pEntity->AddEvent(pEvent);
    }
    else if(nControlID == IDC_ROTATEY)
    {
        // Create a rotation event for the entity
        CEvent *pEvent = new  CEvent(L"ROTATERELATIVE", TIME_PERIOD,
                                .01, TIME_RELATIVE,10);
        pEvent->AddFloatParam(0);
```

```
        pEvent->AddFloatParam(.01);
        pEvent->AddFloatParam(0);
        m_pEntity->AddEvent(pEvent);
    }
    else if(nControlID == IDC_ROTATEZ)
    {
    //lines left out . . .
    }
    else if(nControlID == IDC_SCALEUP)
    {
        // Scales the entity
        CEvent *pEvent = new CEvent(L"SCALERELATIVE",
                            TIME_PERIOD, .05, TIME_RELATIVE,5);
        pEvent->AddFloatParam(.01);
        pEvent->AddFloatParam(.01);
        pEvent->AddFloatParam(.01);
        m_pEntity->AddEvent(pEvent);
    }
    else if(nControlID == IDC_SCALEDOWN)
    {
        //Scales the entity
        CEvent *pEvent = new CEvent(L"SCALERELATIVE",
                            TIME_PERIOD,.05, TIME_RELATIVE, 5);
        pEvent->AddFloatParam(-.01);
        pEvent->AddFloatParam(-.01);
        pEvent->AddFloatParam(-.01);
        m_pEntity->AddEvent(pEvent);
    }
}
```

Note

For programmers with a background in C++, note that a switch structure could be used in place of the series of if…else selection statements. To make your code more elegant, substitute switch statements where possible.

As you can see, the OnGUIEvent() function consists mostly of an extended group of selection statements. Depending on the value that proves true for the selection statement, the line after the first statement can assign a pointer to the CDXUTListBox object. Following this, the selection structure then continues to process messages relating to the buttons. The first one, for example, tests for IDC_EXIT. Subsequent tests deal with all of the other buttons you see in Figure 6.6.

Generally, the selection processes work in two ways. You see that one set of lines deals with rotation while the others deal with scaling. Here's the code that affects the rotation for the x axis:

```
else if(nControlID == IDC_ROTATEY)
{
    // Create a rotation event for the entity
      CEvent *pEvent = new CEvent(L"ROTATERELATIVE",
                        TIME_PERIOD, .01, TIME_RELATIVE, 10);
    pEvent->AddFloatParam(.01);
    pEvent->AddFloatParam(0);
    pEvent->AddFloatParam(0);
    m_pEntity->AddEvent(pEvent);
```

The selection statement checks for the truth of the IDC_ROTATEY event. After that, the first line creates a CEvent object. Then the following lines call the AddFloatParam() function to set the rotation. The three function calls work in a specific order. The first call applies to the x axis, and the last two apply to the y and x axes, respectively. The final call, to AddEvent(), stores the event in the vector you saw in the previous section (m_lstEvents), so the entity can process the event according to the parameters you apply to it.

The other set of lines applies to scaling. Here is the code:

```
else if(nControlID == IDC_SCALEUP)
{
    // Create a rotation event for the entity
    CEvent *pEvent = new CEvent(L"SCALERELATIVE",
                        TIME_PERIOD, .05, TIME_RELATIVE,5);
    pEvent->AddFloatParam(.01);
    pEvent->AddFloatParam(.01);
    pEvent->AddFloatParam(.01);
    m_pEntity->AddEvent(pEvent);
```

As with the previous set of lines, the statement tests for the truth of the message. In this case, the message consists of IDC_SCALEUP. If this proves true, then the first line assigns an object to a CEvent pointer. Following the assignment of the pointer, calls to the AddFloatParam() function set values for the scaling along the x , y , and z axes, respectively. Finally, the AddEvent() function adds the event to the vector, as you saw before.

You might also notice that one of the selections calls CEntity::ClearEvents(). This function flushes the event vector of all its pending events. You cannot process the events you clear from the vector because the function cancels them out.

Setting Up the GUI

To send messages to the application for selection, you create the buttons and other GUI objects to initiate events. You create the buttons in the CMyApplication class. To see how this is so, take a look at CMyAapplication::InitGUI() in CMyApplication.cpp. Here's the code:

```
// Add the rotation buttons
int y = m_iConsoleY+8;
m_GUI.AddButton(IDC_ROTATEX, L"Rotate X - 10 seconds",225,
                                        y,130,18);
m_GUI.AddButton(IDC_ROTATEY, L"Rotate Y - 10 seconds",225,
                                        y += 20, 130, 18);
m_GUI.AddButton(IDC_ROTATEZ, L"Rotate Z - 10 seconds", 225,
                                        y+=20, 130, 18);


// Add the scaling buttons
m_GUI.AddButton(IDC_SCALEUP, L"Scale up - 5 seconds",
                                    225,y+=20,130,18);
m_GUI.AddButton(IDC_SCALEDOWN, L"Scale down - 5 seconds",
                                    225,y+=20,130,18);


m_GUI.AddButton(IDC_CLEARALL, L"Clear events",
                        m_iWidth - 110,m_iHeight - 56,96,18);
m_GUI.AddButton(IDC_EXIT, L"Exit app",
                        m_iWidth - 110, m_iHeight - 36, 96, 18);
```

You create all of the buttons in the same way. In each case, you use the CDXUTDialogManager object (in this case, m_GUI) to call to the AddButton() function. The parameters of the AddButton() function begin with the message with which the button is associated (IDC_ROTATEX, for example). Next, you see the text on the button (for example, L"Scale down—5 seconds"). The third and fourth parameters set the x and y location of the upper left corner of the button on the screen. Finally, the last two parameters set width and height in pixels.

Setting Up Entity Behavior

At this point, it becomes possible to implement fully an application that allows you to interact with entities in a variety of ways. The controls you use for interaction include the mouse and such GUI controls as sliders and combo boxes.

Open Chapter06/Listing06_06 and compile the project. Notice that a number of new features now appear in the console. See Figure 6.7. You see two sliders and a drop-down list displaying the option "Stand still." For starters, move the sliders. The top slider provides more light to the entity. The bottom slider increases the speed of the animation.

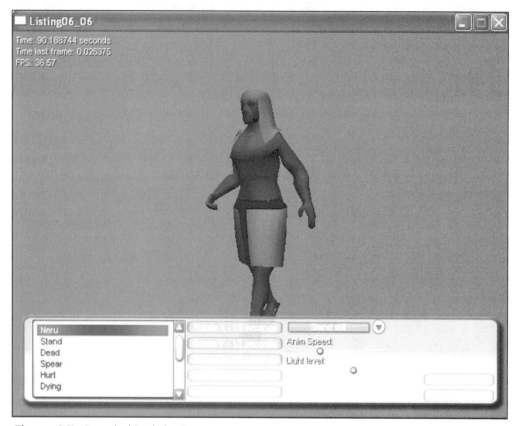

Figure 6.7 Controls drive behaviors.

Click on the icon to the right of the "Stand still" list item. Figure 6.8 shows you the options that you can then see. Select different options to see the behavior of the entity change.

Figure 6.8 Interaction allows you to select behaviors.

Setting Up Entity Behavior Using Sliders

In CMyApplication::OnGUIEvent in CMyApplication.cpp, look first at the code for the two sliders. One set of code controls speed, the other lighting. Here's the code you use to change the lighting:

```
else if(nControlID == IDC_LIGHTING)
    {
        // Set up the light
        CDXUTSlider *pSlider = (CDXUTSlider *)pControl;
                        m_pGraphics->SetDirectionalLight(0,
                            D3DCOLOR_XRGB(pSlider->GetValue(),
                                            pSlider->GetValue(),
                                            pSlider->GetValue()),
                            D3DXVECTOR3(0,-1,1.0f));
    }
```

After the selection statement checks for the IDC_LIGHTING value, the first line of the selected code assigns a pointer the CDXUTSlider object, which controls the lighting values at work on your entity. Then you make a call to the SetDirectionalLight() function of the CGraphics class. Recall that the first parameter, 0, designates the light number. Next, the D3DCOLOR_XRGB macro constructs a color with RGB values equal to the values you retrieve from the slider using the GetValue() function. Since the three calls to GetValue() return the same value, you always see a light that is a shade of gray. The final argument uses the values of a D3DVECTOR3 to designate the direction the light points.

The next section of the selection code tests for messages issued by the slider that controls the animation speed. Here's the code:

```
else if(nControlID == IDC_ANIMSPEED)
    {
        // Set up the animation speed
        CDXUTSlider *pSlider = (CDXUTSlider *)pControl;
        float fSpeed = (float)pSlider->GetValue()/100.0f;
        m_pEntity->GetMesh()->SetAnimSpeed(fSpeed);
    }
```

After the selection tests for the IDC_ANIMSPEED message, the code assigns a pointer to a CDXUTSlider object. It then creates a float value that ranges from 0 to 1 depending on the value you set using the slider. The statement divides the value of the slider by 100 to generate the final value for the speed (fSpeed). Finally, the CEntity::GetMesh() function calls to the CMesh::SetAnimSpeed() function, which employs the value stored in fSpeed to control the speed at which the animation occurs.

Using a Combo Box to Control Behavior

To control the different types of movements you see the entity perform, you use a combo box. The combo box, as you saw previously, allows you to select such behaviors as circular and back-and-forth walking. Each of these behaviors represents a type of animation that a message issued from the combo box invokes. To see how this happens, once again turn to a section of code from the `CMyApplication::OnGUIEvent()` function in CMyApplication.cpp:

```
else if(nControlID == IDC_MOVEMENT)
{
CDXUTComboBox *pCombo = (CDXUTComboBox *)pControl;
int iAction = *(int *)pCombo->GetSelectedItem()->pData;

// Set the movement mode
m_iMoveMode = iAction;

// Figure out something to do based on move type
if(iAction == MOVE_NONE)
{
    m_pEntity->SetPos(D3DXVECTOR3(0,
        m_pEntity->GetMesh()->GetRadius()/4,0));
    m_pEntity->GetMesh()->SetAnimation(L"Walk");
}
else if(iAction == MOVE_LEFTRIGHT)
{
    // Handle moving left to right
    m_pEntity->SetPos(D3DXVECTOR3(0,
        m_pEntity->GetMesh()->GetRadius()/4,0));
    m_pEntity->GetMesh()->SetAnimation(L"Walk");
    m_pEntity->SetRotAngles(D3DXVECTOR3(0,-D3DX_PI/2.0f,0));
    m_vecMoveDir = D3DXVECTOR3(-.03,0,0);
}
else if(iAction == MOVE_BACKFORTH)
{
    // Handle moving back and forth
    m_pEntity->SetPos(D3DXVECTOR3(0,
        m_pEntity->GetMesh()->GetRadius()/4,0));
    m_pEntity->GetMesh()->SetAnimation(L"Walk");
    m_pEntity->SetRotAngles(D3DXVECTOR3(0,0,0));
    m_vecMoveDir = D3DXVECTOR3(0,0,.03);
}
else if(iAction == MOVE_CIRCLE)
```

```
        {
                // Handle moving in a circle
                m_pEntity->SetPos(D3DXVECTOR3(-1,
                        m_pEntity->GetMesh()->GetRadius()/4,0));
                m_pEntity->GetMesh()->SetAnimation(L"Walk");
                m_pEntity->SetRotAngles(D3DXVECTOR3(0,0,0));
        }
```

The first selection statement relating to the combo box items processes the IDC_MOVEMENT message. When you select an item from the combo box, the combo box issues this message. When the selection statement receives the IDC_MOVEMENT message, it processes the statement that assigns a point to the CDXUTComboBox object. After you have a pointer to a CDXUTComboBox object, you can then call a number of functions to retrieve the unique identifier for the item you have selected. Here is the code for the combo box:

```
int iAction = *(int *)pCombo->GetSelectedItem()->pData;
// Set the movement mode
m_iMoveMode = iAction;
```

In this instance, pData is a void pointer that stores the unique identifier. You then cast this to an integer pointer, which you can dereference to retrieve the value and store the resulting value in the CMyApplication attribute m_iMoveMove. This now enables you to know which item you have selected when you update the entity.

The remaining code you see in the CMyApplication::OnGUIEvent() allows you to process messages for the messages you issue from the combo box to invoke different event behaviors. Consider, for example, the message that controls the back-and-forth movement of the entity. Here's the code, which you can find toward the end of the OnGUIEvent() function:

```
        else if(iAction == MOVE_BACKFORTH)
        {
                // Handle moving back and forth
                m_pEntity->SetPos(
                        D3DXVECTOR3(0, m_pEntity->GetMesh()->GetRadius()/4,0));
                m_pEntity->GetMesh()->SetAnimation(L"Walk");
                m_pEntity->SetRotAngles(D3DXVECTOR3(0,0,0));
                m_vecMoveDir = D3DXVECTOR3(0, 0, .03);
        }
```

After testing for the MOVE_BACKFORTH message, the code then uses the CEntity::SetPos() to assign a position for the entity to start at. Next, you use the CEntity::GetMesh() function to call CMesh::SetAnimation(), which allows you to choose the animation the mesh is to display. Following this call to SetAnimation(), you then use the CEntity::SetRotAngles() function to reset the direction the entity faces. Then, you finish the thing off by defining a D3DXVECTOR3 object that contains the direction in which the entity walks.

Adding GUI Controls

To interact with the functionality you have implemented to control the behavior of your entity, you must create a number of interface controls. To see how to create the controls, go to the CMyApplication::InitGUI() function in the CMyApplication.cpp file. Here is a sampling of the code that creates the interface for the combo box:

```
m_GUI.AddComboBox(IDC_MOVEMENT,355, y, 130, 20);
m_GUI.GetComboBox(IDC_MOVEMENT)->AddItem(L"Stand still",
                                    (void *)&MOVE_NONE);
m_GUI.GetComboBox(IDC_MOVEMENT)->AddItem(L"Walk in circle",
                                    (void *)&MOVE_CIRCLE);
m_GUI.GetComboBox(IDC_MOVEMENT)->AddItem(L"Walk back/forth",
                                    (void *)&MOVE_BACKFORTH);
m_GUI.GetComboBox(IDC_MOVEMENT)->AddItem(L"Walk left/right",
                                    (void *)&MOVE_LEFTRIGHT);
m_GUI.GetComboBox(IDC_MOVEMENT)->SetDropHeight(64);
```

Notice that the first line uses the CDXUTDialogManager::AddComboBox() function to create the combo box. The parameters allow you to set the message type for the combo box (IDC_MOVEMENT), the position of the upper left corner (355, y), and the size of the combo box (130, 20).

The lines that follow all perform the same basic set of actions. First, you retrieve the combo box using the GetComboBox() function. This function identifies the combo box using the ID (IDC_MOVEMENT) you have associated with it. Next, the combo box object you have retrieved calls to the AddItem() function, which assigns a string that identifies a selection item in the combo box. You see, for example, that the first two statements assign "Stand still" and "Walk in circle" to the combo box. Finally, each of the AddItem() calls store the address of the unique identifier for a given movement type. For example, (void *)&MOVE_BACKFORTH identifies the back-and-forth movement type.

After the code for the combo box, you have only to create the control sliders. You create two sliders. Here is the code:

```
// Add the speed slider
m_GUI.AddStatic(IDC_ANIMLABEL, L"Anim Speed:", 355, y+=20,100,12);
m_GUI.GetStatic(IDC_ANIMLABEL)->
                GetElement(0)->dwTextFormat = DT_LEFT|DT_TOP;
```

```
m_GUI.AddSlider(IDC_ANIMSPEED, 355, y+=12, 130, 16, 0, 100,33);

// Add the light slider
m_GUI.AddStatic(IDC_LIGHTLABEL, L"Light level:",355,y+=12,100,12);
m_GUI.GetStatic(IDC_LIGHTLABEL)->
                 GetElement(0)->dwTextFormat = DT_LEFT|DT_TOP;
m_GUI.AddSlider(IDC_LIGHTING, 355, y+=12, 130, 16, 0, 255, 192);
```

Consider the slider for setting light values. Notice that you first use the
CDXUTDialogManager::AddSlider(). Next you use CDXUTDialogManager::GetStatic() to add the
slider. The parameters, as before, allow you to assign the message type and to position and
size the slider (355, y+=12, 130, 16). In addition to the values that allow you to set the size
and position, the last two values allow you to set the minimum, maximum, and default
values of the slider (0, 100, 33).

You call CDXUTDialogManager::GetStatic() to set the format of the text for the label above
the slider. The zero assigned to GetElement() designates that only one element exists for
this CDXUTDialogManager object.

Updating Scenes

One goal of having the entity walk around is to make certain the entity faces the right
direction as it walks. The UpdateScene() function proves instrumental in this respect. The
UpdateScene() function changes the position of the entity based on the movement mode
you select using the combo box. The first line gets the animation speed for the mesh so
that we can slow down the movement to accord with the animation speed. The code is as
follows:

```
// Move our entity around based on the movement mode
    float fAnimSpeed = m_pEntity->GetMesh()->GetAnimSpeed();
```

If the movement mode is MOVE_LEFTRIGHT, you first update the position of the mesh by
adding m_vecMoveDir * fAnimSpeed to its current position:

```
if(m_iMoveMode == MOVE_LEFTRIGHT)
    {
        m_pEntity->SetPos(m_pEntity->GetPos()
                           + m_vecMoveDir * fAnimSpeed);
```

Since the mesh moves left and right, you check to see if its position is less than negative 1
or greater than 1 on the x axis. If this is the case, you reverse the movement direction and
rotate the entity 180 degrees (D3DX_PI radians) about the y axis to turn the entity around.
Here's the code:

```
if(m_pEntity->GetPos().x <= -1 || m_pEntity->GetPos().x >= 1)
      {
      // Change the movement dir, and add an event
            to turn the mesh around
         m_vecMoveDir *= -1;
         m_pEntity->SetRotAngles(m_pEntity->GetRotAngles()
             + D3DXVECTOR3(0,D3DX_PI,0));
      }
   }
```

Since the mesh moves left and right, you check to see if its position is less than negative 1 or greater than 1 on the z axis. If this is the case, you reverse the movement direction and rotate the entity 180 degrees (D3DX_PI radians) about the y-axis to turn the entity around. Here's the code:

```
else if(m_iMoveMode == MOVE_BACKFORTH)
   {
      m_pEntity->SetPos(m_pEntity->GetPos()
                         + m_vecMoveDir * fAnimSpeed);
      if(m_pEntity->GetPos().z <= -1 || m_pEntity->GetPos().z >= 1)
      {
         // Change the movement dir, and
               add an event to turn the mesh around
         m_vecMoveDir*=-1;
         m_pEntity->SetRotAngles(m_pEntity->GetRotAngles()
                  + D3DXVECTOR3(0,D3DX_PI,0));
      }
   }
```

You set a static float to designate the position of the mesh on a circle on the x—z plane. This angle is incremented by fAnimSpeed over a constant every frame.

```
else if(m_iMoveMode == MOVE_CIRCLE)
   {
      // Figure out which angle (from the origin) our entity is at
      static float fAngle = -D3DX_PI/2;
      fAngle+=fAnimSpeed/30.0f;
```

Given a radius and an angle of rotation, you can then generate an x—z position to place the entity as it walks around the circle. You do this beginning with the starting position of the mesh (vecOrigPos). Note how the initial x (-1) value corresponds to the initial value of the static angle variable (-D3DX_PI/2).

```
// The starting position of the entity
D3DXVECTOR3 vecOrigPos(-1, m_pEntity->GetPos().y,0);
D3DXVECTOR4 vecNewPos;
```

Now you want to transform the original using a rotation matrix. You generate the rotation matrix about the y axis to get a point in the x—z plane using D3DXMatrixRotationY(). Then you transform the original position into vecNewPos using the D3DXVec3Transform() function. Here's the code:

```
// Build a rotation matrix with our angle,
      and use it to transform
// the original position vector into a new position
D3DXMATRIX matRot;
D3DXMatrixRotationY(&matRot, fAngle);
D3DXVec3Transform(&vecNewPos, &vecOrigPos, &matRot);
```

To set the new position, you calculate the position using D3DXVec3Transform(). In the last step you set the rotation of the entity about the y axis so that it is always facing the direction in which it is walking.

```
// Set the position and rotation vectors
m_pEntity->
        SetPos(D3DXVECTOR3(vecNewPos. x, vecNewPos.
                                        y, vecNewPos.z));
m_pEntity->SetRotAngles(D3DXVECTOR3(0,fAngle,0));
}
```

Figure 6.9 shows you how the entity turns to face the direction in which it walks as it navigates its way around a circle.

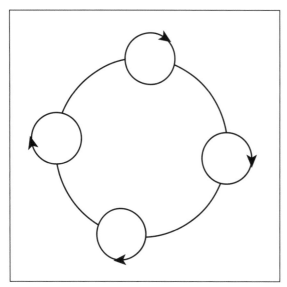

Figure 6.9 A mesh turns as it walks in a circle to face the direction it walks.

Conclusion

In this chapter, you started down a road that leads to many places. Working from concepts you first encountered in Chapter 5, you began developing an entity, not as a single mesh, but as a collection of animations that represented different behaviors of an entity. For this activity, you were able to explore an entity as a composite creature.

When an entity becomes a collection of animations you can set up to perform sequentially or in response to different controls, you introduce into your application the type of sophistication that characterizes games and advanced simulations. An entity suddenly becomes a creature capable of responding to stimulus in different ways.

To make it possible to increase the complexity of your entity, you continued the work begun in the last chapter with CMesh. In addition to the work on CMesh, you added CEvent and CClock, and CEntity. These classes provide you with the ability to load the mesh that becomes the visible manifestation of the entity you include in your application. The CEvent class allows you to associate events with entities by tying their actions to controls and automated routines. The CClock class allows you to obtain extremely accurate measurements of time so that you can both maintain a smooth refresh rate for your application and control the execution of events on a finely tuned basis.

The `CEntity` class provides you with a means of bringing all the functionality embodied in other classes into one primary container. This class allows you to store information that identifies an entity within the entity, so that as it encounters other entities or interacts with its world or those who use the application, it can, in effect, learn.

When you have brought into play the many features embodied in the `CMesh`, `CEvent` and `CClock`, and `CEntity` classes, you are in an excellent position to move a step farther, which takes you into an area of simulation development in which you begin to explore how entities relate to the world in which they dwell.

CHAPTER 7

CREATING A WORLD

In this chapter, you create a world that you populate with animated and static entities. From a programming perspective, creating a world involves minimal work. In essence, you create a container for your entities and an interface that allows you to put entities into and take entities from the container. Even with this fairly rudimentary programming activity, however, it remains that a world provides the functional area in which you begin to combine all the elements that make up an interesting, involved simulation, and for this reason, the creation of the software functionality that supports the world features marks a significant step toward creating comprehensive simulation programs. The path ahead requires the addition of many other features, among which are artificial intelligence and entity physics, but in this chapter a number of topics, in addition to the creation of a class that embodies your world, present themselves:

- The primary properties of a world
- How you programmatically interact with a world
- Considerations for enriching interactions
- Developing a world class
- Bounding spheres and the uses of meshes
- Creating hierarchies using child entities
- Laying out features of a world using hierarchies
- Enhancing control features

Basics of Creating a World

A world is simple to program but fairly complex to plan and use. It is analogous in many ways to a beautiful, difficult-to-reach valley located deep inside a lush island paradise. To get to it involves preparation for the journey and knowing how to navigate the path leading to the valley. When you arrive, everything seems simple. The valley lies open for you to explore. If you want to build a house in the valley, you can do so. Still, the fact that the valley is nested into such a beautiful, potential-laden place creates the problem of how to make the best use of the privilege that you have gained by reaching the valley.

Making the best use of a world involves charting the scope of the world and developing the functionality that supports the events, entities, and controls that occupy your world. When these items congregate in your world, the richness of the result depends on how you generate contexts that allow your user to sustain an involved set of interactions with your world.

As you saw in Chapter 2, "Specifying Events," and Chapter 3, "Designing an Application Framework," how you structure constraints determines to a great extent how much richness of effect you can hope to achieve as you translate an event model into the logic of a computer program. Carefully implemented constraints make transitions transparent, and when transitions are transparent, users become involved in a sustained experience. Consider the following list of concerns you face as you contemplate the factors involved in applying constraints:

- Entities emerge to visibility in a given order and within the scope of the world you present.
- The devices that characterize the interactions of the entities in your world provide a consistent experience for the user of your application.
- The potentials of each interaction remain approximate to or consistent with the potentials of other interactions.
- Events unfold according to a mapping that creates a convincing, logically and emotionally consistent experience for the user.
- Each entity possesses a distinct set of constraints. The user can move a character but not the building through which the character walks.
- All entities interact in some way, but the interactions differ. A character slams into a wall but converses with a compeer.

As you saw in previous chapters, creating entities that encapsulate events allows you to anticipate most of the interactions that unfold as you place entities together in a world. Figure 7.1 illustrates the properties you have worked with so far as you have created classes for controls, entities, and events. Generally, you associate events with entities. You allow automatic timer controls to govern the firing of events. You also equip entities with containers that can store information you can use to evaluate messages for processing. While you can view controls as manual devices that allow you to issue messages to entities, entities themselves can communicate with you and your application by issuing their own messages. Messages link controls, events, and entities.

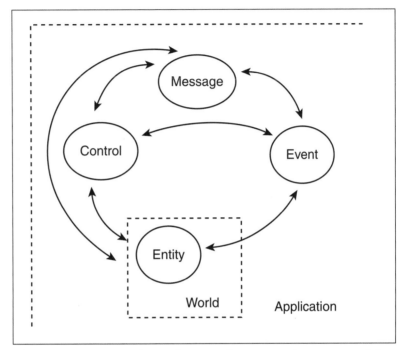

Figure 7.1 Messages tie together controls, events, and messages, and the world contains the entities.

World Elements

To implement a world, your main task reduces to creating a container that holds all the entities that appear in your world. The container allows you to access the interface you have designed to process the messages that relate to each entity. No great effort underlies this activity. You create a container of the entity type and assign entity pointers to it. You then iterate through the entity pointers and call to the operations the entity interface provides to process messages. As a result of the message processing, you initiate movements, load animations, or trigger events. Figure 7.2 illustrates the set of activities that processing events for entities within your world involves.

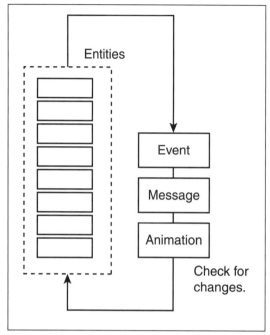

Figure 7.2 Entities contain most of the information, and the world associates them.

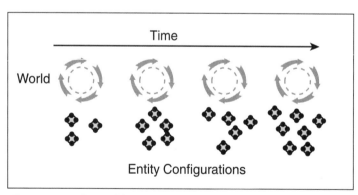

Figure 7.3 The world sustains entities and complexity over time.

You can use any number of approaches to controlling when and how entities enter your world. For example, you can schedule entities to appear in your world according to an agenda your event model provides. Picture, for example, a simulation that begins with a small number of entities. These entities bring with them a proportional number of possible interactions, events, and controls. The world that you see at first offers few entities and few interactions. As time goes on, however, the entities increase in number, and as the number of entities increases, there follows an accompanying increase in the richness and complexity of interactions the world sustains. See Figure 7.3.

The world you create sets a timeline of events that characterizes each entity's existence. To change the entities in your world, you use the interface your entity container provides. The interface allows you to create, manipulate, and destroy your entities. Here's a preliminary list of the operations that characterize the interface that a world container usually supports:

- Create the entity and add it to your world container.
- Load the meshes that you want to associate with the entity.
- Associate the entity with events.
- Load information that guides the behavior of the entity.
- Associate controls with the entity.

- Control the entity according to the mappings applied to it.
- Destroy the entity when its interactions conclude.

As you use the features of your entities, events, and controls, the world becomes a continuum of involved, dynamic changes. Figure 7.4 illustrates the primary actions that characterize this continuum.

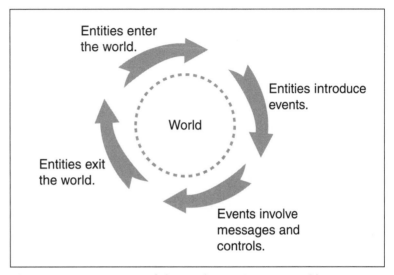

Figure 7.4 A continuum of change characterizes your world.

Your world and the program you create to sustain it foster a rich, complex set of interactions. Depending on the constraints you impose, you can load new entities into your world container or new events into your entities. You can change the information you supply to an entity so that its behavior changes. You can change the controls you associate with an entity. Contexts, event mappings, and event models guide what you do. Entities, events, messages, and controls come into and go out of scope, altering the terrain, the themes, and the overall description of the world.

The CWorld Class

To create a world, you create a container for the objects that you want to present in your world. To examine how you can accomplish this task, begin by opening Listing07_01 and compiling the project. Figure 7.5 provides a screenshot of the application you see. Use the mouse wheel to make the figures larger or smaller. Likewise, set the cursor on the figures and use the right or left mouse button to reposition them. They move together. As you move the figures, notice that the lighting changes.

Each of these figures is an entity you create using the CEntity class. To add these entities to your world, after you construct them, you insert pointers to them into a container you create in the CWorld class. When you want to control them, you then access the pointers to them and use these pointers to call CEntity functions to manipulate them.

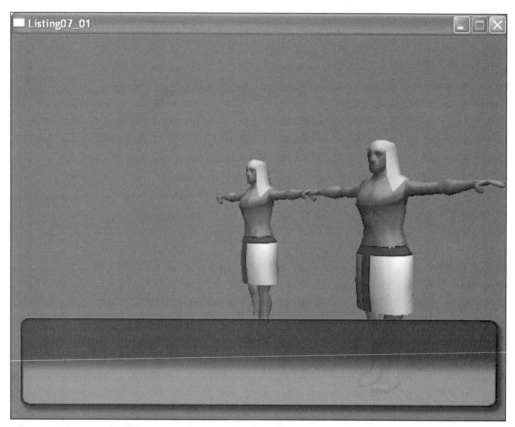

Figure 7.5 A world allows you to present multiple entities.

Defining the CWorld Class

A world in the simplest terms consists of a container of entities. The container you use in the CWorld class is an STL vector. Creating and then providing ways to operate on the container constitute the central responsibilities of a world class. To see how you begin to address these central responsibilities, take a look at the declaration of CWorld in CWorld.h:

```
class CWorld
{
public:
    // Destructor
    ~CWorld();
```

```
            // . . . a singleton object
        // provides a function to create objects rather
        //than an exposed constructor
        friend CWorld *GetWorld();
        // Load and create an entity
        void CreateEntity(wstring strName, wstring strMeshFile,
                                            IDirect3DDevice9 *pDevice);
        void AddEntity(class CEntity *pEntity);
        void RemoveEntity(class CEntity *pEntity);
        void Render(IDirect3DDevice9 *pDevice);
        void Update(float fTimeElapsed, IDirect3DDevice9 *pDevice);
        class CEntity *GetEntity(wstring strName);
private:
        // Constructor (private since this is a singleton)
        CWorld();
        // The container for the entities
        vector<class CEntity *> m_lstEntities;
};
```

The CWorld class is a *singleton* class. You can instantiate only one instance of it at a time. The world you create allows you to view all the activity in it as dramatically interlaced. The associations use controls, events, and messages to define a single, continuous series of actions. In practical terms, you restrict your application to one world at a time because this simplifies the processing of messages and events that take place during the life of your application. It is not necessary that you have only one world for the entire life of your application, of course, but for now, it is best to take this approach.

To create a CWorld object, you do not call the class constructor. Instead, you call a member function of CWorld, the GetWorld() function. This function is both static and a friend function. Since the function is static, you can call it without first creating an instance of CWorld. Since it is a friend function, you can use it as you please in other classes.

In addition to the GetWorld() function, the CWorld class provides you with the container in which you store the entities that populate your world. To find this container, examine the last few lines of the declaration of CWorld. The container attribute (m_lstEntities) is an STL vector. An entity comes into existence when you add it to this container. To interact with an entity, you iterate through this container, locate the pointer to the entity, and call one or another CEntity operation to change the entity. The sections that follow address these activities in detail.

Construction of a World Object

If you look at the code in the CWorld.cpp file, you can see that the constructor for the CWorld class consists of an empty set of braces:

```
CWorld::CWorld(){/*. . .*/}
```

In the declaration of CWorld, you declare the constructor for CWorld as private. Since it is private, you cannot use it directly to construct a CWorld object. Instead, you use a special function you create that takes care of construction activities for you. This type of construction activity characterizes singleton classes. A singleton class prevents you from constructing more than one instance of the class at a time. The function that takes care of construction is the GetWorld() function. As mentioned previously, since it is static and you declare it as a friend, you can call it without first having to declare a CWorld object. Here's the code for this function from CWorld.cpp:

```
CWorld *GetWorld()
{
    //create a static instance of the world
    static CWorld theWorld;
    return( &theWorld );
}
```

The first time you call the GetWorld() function, you create a static CWorld object. After that, a call to the function no longer creates a CWorld object but instead gives you access to the object already in existence. Here's a bit of code from the CMyApplication::Initialize() function in CMyApplication.cpp that shows you how you use the GetWorld() function. First, you create a world. Then you access the world so that you can add an entity to it:

```
//First call creates world and adds entity
GetWorld()->CreateEntity(L"Entity1",
                         L"Meshes\\multi_anim.x",
                         m_pGraphics->GetDevice());
//Second call accesses world and adds entity
GetWorld()->CreateEntity(L"Entity2",
                         L"Meshes\\multi_anim.x",
                         m_pGraphics->GetDevice());
```

How CreateEntity() works receives attention in the next section. For now, it is important only to see that GetWorld() both creates and retrieves the world object. The CreateEntity() function adds an entity to the world you have accessed through the GetWorld() function.

Adding Entities to Your Work

After you create a world, the first action you take toward it is to populate it with entities. You can add as many entities as you want. You add an entity as a part of the action of the CreateEntity() function. This function both creates a CEntity object and uses the AddEntity() function to add the object to the world container. Here is the code for CreateEntity() from CWorld.cpp:

```
void CWorld::CreateEntity(wstring strName, wstring strMeshFile,
                          IDirect3DDevice9 *pDevice)
{
    CEntity *pEntity = new CEntity( strName );
    pEntity->LoadMesh( strMeshFile, pDevice );
    AddEntity( pEntity );
    // Set managed to true so you delete the entity
    // when you destroy you world object
    pEntity->SetManaged( true );
    return(pEntity);
}
```

The CreateEntity() function calls the constructor for CEntity to create an entity. The first parameter (strName) of the CreateEntity() function allows you to assign a name to the entity, because you pass this parameter to the CEntity constructor. You pass the second and third parameters of CreateEntity() to the CEntity::LoadMesh() function. The strMeshFile parameter names the file that contains the mesh you want to use for your entity. The pointer to the IDirect3DDevice9 device allows you to access the device that you declare in the CGraphics.h file.

After loading the mesh, you use CWorld::AddEntity() to add the entity to your world container. AddEntity() inserts a pointer to an entity into your world container (m_lstEntities). Here's the code from CWorld.cpp that shows how this happens:

```
void CWorld::AddEntity(CEntity *pEntity)
{
    m_lstEntities.push_back(pEntity);
}
```

After you pass the CEntity pointer to the AddEntity() function, you insert it into m_lstEntities using the vector::push_back() function. This function pushes a pointer to the back (or end position) in the vector. The vector expands dynamically to accommodate the new pointer. After the entity pointer resides in the vector, you can access it to change the behavior of the entity it points to.

The CWorld::Create Entity() function performs one more task before reaching its closing brace. It calls the SetManaged() function. When you set SetManaged() to true for a given entity, you indicate that the destructor for CWorld is responsible for deleting the entity.

Removing Entities

You continuously usher characters (entities) into and out of existence. A typical scenario requiring creating and destroying characters might be the one you glimpsed in Chapter 5, "Design for Entities." Recall the main character moving through the barroom. As the main character progresses from the entrance toward the interior of the barroom, it encountered other characters, among which were a bartender, a garrulous patron who talked about sports, a pool player, a potential pick-up, and a seedy character who possibly posed dangers.

Each of these characters represents an entity, but all of them do not need to exist when your main character first enters the barroom. Instead, you can create them as your main character moves into the barroom. You might, for example, construct them only when they come into your main character's immediate view.

Figure 7.6 illustrates a possible mapping of events as the character walks toward the back of the barroom. Upon entering the barroom, the main character can see four other characters, but not until moving to the back of the barroom can the main character see those who sit at the rear tables. Such a mapping sets up a progression of events in which you might construct the characters at the back of the bar only after the main character has walked at least half the length of the barroom.

Along similar lines, if the main character moves to the back of the bar and takes up a conversation with the woman at the table, you might not want to keep other characters active in the scene. In fact, you might destroy all of the characters the main character is not communicating with directly. Entities can take up a great deal of memory and processing time, ultimately posing the risk of slowing the performance of your application.

To destroy entities, you use the CWorld::RemoveEntity() function. Here's the code for the RemoveEntity() function as shown in CWorld.cpp:

```
void CWorld::RemoveEntity(CEntity *pEntity)
{
    vector<CEntity *>::iterator itr;
    for(itr = m_lstEntities.begin(); itr != m_lstEntities.end(); itr++)
    {
        CEntity *pCurrent = (CEntity *)*itr;
        if(pCurrent == pEntity)
        {
            m_lstEntities.erase(itr);
            return;
        }
    }
}
```

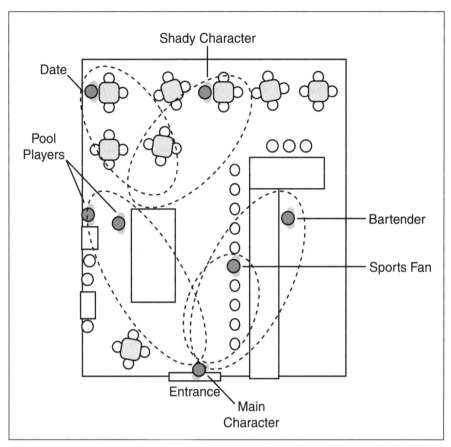

Figure 7.6 Create and destroy entities as you need them.

This function constitutes a first pass at what will become a familiar pattern. After the opening brace of RemoveEntity(), you declare an iterator for a vector using the template constructor with a pointer to CEntity as its argument. The iterator allows you to iterate through m_lstEntities, which is a vector that stores pointers to the world's entities. The begin() and end() functions in the for loop control statement are vector functions that identify the boundaries of the vector as you iterate through it. As you increment the iterator, you are able to examine each pointer in the vector.

```
CEntity *pCurrent = (CEntity *)*itr;
```

As you iterate through the vector, if the pointer you have passed to the RemoveEntity() function matches the pointer in the vector, then you remove the entity from the vector, destroying it as you do so with the vector::erase() function. Note that you have to cast the iterator as a CEntity pointer to be able to compare it to the RemoveEntity() parameter.

N o t e

In the C++ examples this book provides, the `std::vector<T>` class is used for almost all instances of collections. This is not always the best way to create a collection. The Standard Template Library provides a rich variety of collection classes. For example, if you use a collection you search often according to the order of the items in it, then you can use the STL set (`std::set<>`) class. This dramatically reduces search time. The scope of this book precludes coverage of STL collections. An excellent book on the STL is Nicolai M. Josuttis', The C++ *Standard Library: A Tutorial and Reference* (Biston: Addison-Wesley, 1999).

Accessing Entities

While accessing an entity always involves using a pointer, the procedure you employ for locating an entity might involve something other than simply comparing one pointer to another—which is what you saw in the discussion of the `RemoveEntity()` function. To use `GetEntity()`, you search for the entity you want to access, not with a pointer, but with a string that names the entity you are searching for. Here's the code for `GetEntity()` from CWorld.cpp:

```
CEntity *CWorld::GetEntity(wstring strName)
{
    for(int itr = 0; itr < m_lstEntities.size(); itr++)
    {
        if(m_lstEntities[itr ] &&
            m_lstEntities[itr]->GetName() == strName)
            return(m_lstEntities[itr]);
    }
    return(NULL);
}
```

To use the `GetEntity()` function, you provide the function with the name of the entity you want to access. This is a string (`strName`). The function passes the name to a selection statement that checks it against the name attribute of each `CEntity` object for which a pointer has been stored in the world container (`m_lstEntities`). The `GetName()` function retrieves the name. When the right name emerges, the function returns a pointer to the object that that name identifies. If no object emerges (for example, it has already been deleted or its name has been misspelled), the function returns `NULL`. To control the `for` loop that contains the selection statement, notice that you use the `vector::size()` function, which returns the number of items in the container.

Updating and Rendering

To make it possible for entities to change, you call the update functions associated with individual entities. If you were to update every entity arbitrarily, you would create quite a bit of work for yourself. To avoid having to perform this work, you can assume instead that every entity should be updated regularly and create functions that operate on the world level to apply changes to all of the entities in the world's scope.

The CWorld::Update() and CWorld::Render() functions allow you to automatically apply changes to all of the entities your world contains. When you update your entities, you change all of the events and behaviors associated with them. Here's the code for the Update() function in CWorld.cpp:

```
void CWorld::Update(float fTimeElapsed, IDirect3DDevice9 *pDevice)
{
    for(int itr =0; itr < m_lstEntities.size(); itr++)
    {
        if(m_lstEntities[itr])
            m_lstEntities[itr]->Update(fTimeElapsed, pDevice);
    }
}
```

The Update() function prepares the entity for rendering. The parameters you pass to the function are the time value you have created to control the pace of rendering (fTimeElapsed) and a pointer to the IDirect3DDevice9 device created in CGraphics.h (pDevice).

The for loop of the CWorld::Update() function goes through the world container (m_lstEntities) and calls CEntity::Update() for each entity in the container. The CEntity::Update() function processes events that apply to the entity and transforms the entity so that you can see changes in its behavior.

The CWorld::Update() function performs in tandem with the CWorld::Render() function. Once again, the function helps you avoid the work of having to arbitrarily address the actions of each entity in your simulation. The CWorld::Render() function draws the entities stored in the world entity container. To accomplish this task, it requires only one parameter value, a pointer to the IDirect3DDevice9 device you created in CGraphics.h. Here's the code for the Render() function in CWorld.cpp:

```
void CWorld::Render(IDirect3DDevice9 *pDevice)
{
    for(int itr = 0; itr <m_lstEntities.size(); itr++)
    {
        if(m_lstEntities[itr])
```

```
            m_lstEntities[itr]->Render(pDevice);
    }
}
```

As occurred in the Update() function, the for loop iterates through the entity pointers the world container holds. As it does so, calls to the CEntity::Render() function render every entity that populates your world. Generally, rendering involves first copying the entity to the back surface and then using CGraphics::EndScene() to flip it to the front or visible surface.

Destroying the World

Entities come into existence and after a time are destroyed. It also happens, however, that while you destroy entities, you can also destroy the worlds that contain entities. For example, you might decide that the complexity of the contexts of interaction illustrated in Figure 7.6 merits the creation of several worlds. You might create these worlds in succession, as the character moves into different contexts of interaction. Each time you create a new world, you destroy the old one. Figure 7.7 illustrates the situation.

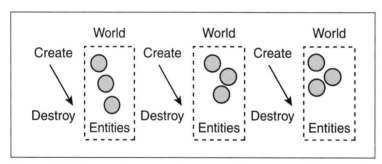

Figure 7.7 You can destroy and create worlds just as you destroy and create entities.

To remove a world from your application, you use the destructor for the CWorld class. Here's the code from CWorld.cpp for the CWorld destructor:

```
CWorld::~CWorld()
{
    // Delete all the entities in the container
    for(int itr = 0; itr < m_lstEntities.size(); itr++)
    {
        if(m_lstEntities[itr] && m_lstEntities[itr]->IsManaged())
            SAFEDELETE(m_lstEntities[itr]);
    }
    m_lstEntities.clear();
}
```

The CWorld destructor uses a for loop to iterate through the entity vector (m_lstEntities) to visit each entity the vector contains. As it moves through the vector, it applies two conditions to a selection statement. The first condition discovers whether the item resides in the vector. The second condition employs the CEntity::IsManaged() function, which determines whether the CWorld object is responsible for destroying the entity. If this is true, then the function calls the SAFEDELETE macro to remove the object. As a final measure, it calls the vector::clear() function to clean up the vector itself. This function reduces the memory allocated for the vector to a minimum.

Calling Entities in Your World

During a brief discussion earlier in this chapter (see "The CWorld Class"), you saw the declaration of the GetWorld() function. This function serves to create a static instance of the world object. When you create a static instance of an object, the object endures during the entire life of your application—unless you manually destroy it. In the application shown in this chapter, you create one world. To see where you create the world, take a look at CMyApplication.cpp, in the CMyApplication::Initialize() function:

```
void CMyApplication::Initialize()
{
    // Create the 2 entities.
    // The world manages the creation.
    GetWorld()->CreateEntity(L"Entity1",
                             L"Meshes\\multi_anim.x",
                             m_pGraphics->GetDevice());
    GetWorld()->CreateEntity(L"Entity2",
                             L"Meshes\\multi_anim.x",
                             m_pGraphics->GetDevice());
    // Transform the second entity
    GetWorld()->GetEntity(L"Entity2")->SetPos(D3DXVECTOR3(-1,0,0));
//lines left out. . .
}
```

The first lines of the Initialize() function create two entities using the CreateEntity() function. The calls to the CreateEntity() function each supply unique names to the entities they create. On the other hand, both calls use the same mesh file. The common mesh file poses no problem, however, for each entity retains a distinct copy of it. In addition to naming and assigning meshes to your entities, you register your entities with your IDirect3DDevice9 object. The CGraphics::GetDevice() function allows you to access the IDirect3DDevice9 object for this purpose.

The first call to GetWorld() creates a static instance of the CWorld class and then calls CreateEntity() to create the first entity. The second call to GetWorld() makes use of this instance of the CWorld class once again, for it calls CreateEntity() to create the second entity. Since the world already exists when you make the second call, you do not re-create it.

On the last line of CMyApplication::Initialize(), a cascading set of functions allows you to manually position the second of the entities you have created. You manually position the second entity because both entities, by default, appear in your world at the world's origin (0, 0, 0), so you must move one of them to be able to see them both. To accomplish this, after retrieving the CWorld object using GetWorld(), you make a call to the CWorld::GetEntity() function to retrieve a pointer to the second entity. Using the pointer to the second entity, you call the CEntity::SetPos() function to set the position of the entity. When you assign -1 to the x variable of the D3DXVECTOR3 array, you set the second entity to the left of the first entity as the application starts up.

Changes to the Application Classes

When you create classes that support animations, you develop interfaces that provide updating and rendering services. To characterize these two services, you can picture updating as having a slightly wider scope of operations than rendering. Updating might involve processing events other than those that change what you see on your monitor. Rendering, in contrast, almost always applies specifically to the graphical images you see.

The interfaces of the CApplication, CMyApplication, CEntity, and CWorld classes each offers rendering and updating services. Since CApplication is the parent class of CMyApplication, the services provided by CMyApplication represent a specialization of the services that CApplication provides. The interface that CWorld offers generalizes the updating and rendering of CEntity objects so that all of the entities in the world container are consistently processed. Figure 7.8 displays a UML diagram that represents how these classes relate to each other.

To ensure that your application consistently processes all of its updating and rendering tasks, you make calls from the CApplication and the CMyApplication class objects to the CWorld object. To see how this happens, it is necessary to examine the code in the UpdateScene() and Render() functions in CApplication.cpp and CMyApplication.cpp. The next few sections examine this code in detail.

Updating Your World

As you have seen in previous sections, the CWorld object contains all of the CEntity objects. To update the CEntity objects, you need to update the CWorld object on the broadest possible level. It ends up that the CApplication::UpdateScene() function provides you with this ability. Using calls to this function, you comprehensively address all of the entities in your application. Here's the code from CApplication.cpp for CApplication::UpdateScene():

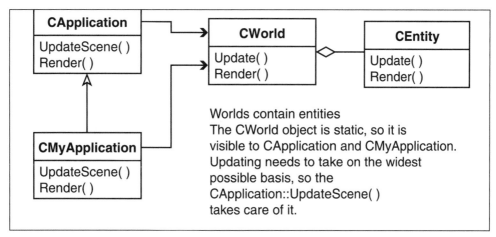

Figure 7.8 Updating through the parent class ensures consistency.

```
void CApplication::UpdateScene(float fTimeScale)
{
     GetWorld()->Update(fTimeScale, m_pGraphics->GetDevice());
}
```

The UpdateScene() function calls the CWorld::Update() function. You use the GetWorld() function to retrieve the static instance of the CWorld object. Then you apply the time and device values to the function to allow the update to take place.

Since the application you create is a CApplication object specialized as a CMyApplication object, when you update your application, you can do so using the CApplication::Update-Scene() function. If you have no need to overload the update operation, then you really have no need to put an UpdateScene() function in your CMyApplication class. Still, in CMyApplication.cpp, you see the following function, commented out:

```
//void CMyApplication::UpdateScene(float fTimeScale)
//{
//      // Call the parent update function,
//      CApplication::UpdateScene(fTimeScale);
//}
```

At this point, since you have no need to overload the function, you can comment it out. The code serves as a placeholder. Likewise, in CMyApplication.h, the declaration of the UpdateScene() function, for now, is also commented out.

Rendering Your World

As you saw in the discussions of CEntity and CWorld, updating encompasses a broader set of activities than rendering. This same generalization applies to updating and rendering at the application level. While you can wrap the update interface of the parent class (CApplication) in the update interface of the child class (CMyApplication), you must use restraint with rendering operations. To see how this works, consider the CMyApplication::Render() function. Here is the code from CMyApplication.cpp:

```
void CMyApplication::Render()
{
    // Clear the screen/ZBuffer
    m_pGraphics->Clear(D3DCOLOR_XRGB(96, 96, 96));
    // Draw the world
    GetWorld()->Render(m_pGraphics->GetDevice());
    // . . . lines left out
}
```

You perform rendering of your world in CMyApplication because you want to reduce rendering activity to as specific a context as possible. Since all of the actions that involve rendering employ a CApplication object, no need exists to render at the CApplication level.

Creating Bounding Spheres

Open Listing07_02 and compile the project. Figure 7.9 provides a screenshot of the resulting application. Use your mouse to manipulate the figure in the sphere. You can use the mouse wheel to enlarge the entity. As the entity increases or decreases in size, so does the sphere that surrounds it. The sphere that surrounds the entity is called a *bounding sphere*. When you create bounding spheres, you have an opportunity to investigate graphical primitives (which are meshes that you create programmatically, rather than with the use of data from files).

As you can see in Figure 7.9, the sphere identifies the entity's bounding sphere. The sphere consists of a mesh that surrounds the entity. When you create the sphere, you first place the entity in your world and then you create the sphere to surround it. The sphere always moves with the entity.

Game developers sometimes use bounding spheres to detect collisions because bounding spheres provide a convenient, relatively simple, and fairly accurate way to implement collision detection. Simple options for collision detection usually involve either a rectangle or a sphere. Rectangles are suitable for 2D applications, but when you move to 3D, you require something that more readily handles 3D collision detection, and this is where bounding spheres come into play.

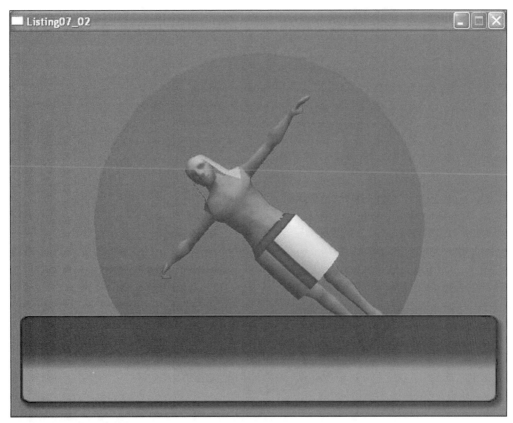

Figure 7.9 A bounding sphere surrounds your entity.

Note

In this text, instead of spheres, collision detection is accomplished using the collision detection interface of the Open Dynamics Engine (ODE). This topic is covered in Chapter 8, "AI and Physics for Simulation."

To color the sphere, you insert values to define the color properties of material you apply to your sphere. As is discussed further along in this chapter, you use a D3DXMESH object to define the properties of color. The next few sections discuss the bounding spheres in detail.

Changing CMesh

A bounding sphere is a *static mesh*. A static (or non-skinned) mesh differs from a skinned mesh because it is not animated, and it is simpler and easier to manipulate. A static mesh is also known as a *graphical primitive*. A graphical primitive is an object that you create using instructions in your program rather than information you take from a mesh file. The operations in CMesh provide the interface for working with static meshes. To begin a discussion of the interface for CMesh, consider the declaration of CMesh in CMesh.h:

```
class CMesh
{
protected:
    // The pointer to the mesh
    LPD3DXMESH m_pMesh;
    // The number of materials
    DWORD m_dwNumMaterials;
    // Pointer to an array of textures
    LPDIRECT3DTEXTURE9 *m_pTextures;
    // An array of materials for the mesh
    D3DMATERIAL9 *m_pMaterials;
    // The vector that points to the center of the mesh
    D3DXVECTOR3 m_vecObjectCenter;
    // The radius of the bounding sphere
    float m_fObjectRadius;
    // World matrix
    D3DXMATRIXA16 m_matWorld;
public:
    // Constructor for the mesh class
    CMesh();
    // Destructor for the mesh class
    ~CMesh();
    // Load a mesh from an .X file
    virtual bool Load(wstring strFile,
                      IDirect3DDevice9 *pd3dDevice);
    // Create a sphere object
    virtual void CreateSphere(float fRadius,
                      DWORD dwColor,
                      IDirect3DDevice9 *pd3dDevice);
    virtual void Update(float fTimeElapsed,
                      IDirect3DDevice9 *pd3dDevice);
    virtual void Draw(IDirect3DDevice9 *pd3dDevice);
    float GetRadius();
};
```

Moving down through the set of attributes visible in the declaration of the interface of CMesh, notice that while most of what you see remains the same as what you have seen in previous chapters, you do add a few attributes. Among these are a DWORD identifier that stores the number of materials you apply to the mesh you use for your entity, a LPDIRECT3DTEXTURE9 pointer to hold an array of textures, and a D3DMATERIAL9 pointer that allows you to create an array of materials.

In addition to providing a few new attributes that supplement your ability to process meshes, you also make changes to the class interface. One change visible to you in the declaration of the interface is the addition of the CreateSphere() function. Changes to the CMesh class not visible in the declaration of the interface involve the Load(), Update(), and Draw() functions. In addition to changes to these functions, you also make changes to the constructor and destructor of CMesh. The next few sections discuss these changes in detail.

Inheritance Issues

Before dealing specifically with the use of the CMesh class, it is important to note that a new class now does much of the work involved in creating animated entities. This is the CSkinnedMesh class, which appears for the first time in Listing07_02.

The code from the older version of CMesh now appears in CSkinnedMesh. CSkinnedMesh inherits the properties of CMesh. This is the same technique you saw applied when you created the CMyApplication class in Chapter 4, "Implementing the Framework." In the case of CSkinnedMesh, you can now deal at the specialized level with skinned meshes. You can use CMesh for primitives.

You might also notice that the code for CMesh and the CSkinnedMesh classes appears in the same files (CMesh.h and CMesh.cpp). This approach to setting up the code allows you to conveniently find in one place all of the code relating to mesh manipulations. Generally, however, be aware that this practice is not professionally sanctioned, for it tends to make declarations hard to find.

If you require a review of CMesh, you can turn to Chapter 5, which covers the functions CMesh provides. While these functions now appear in CSkinnedMesh, the names of the functions and their implementations remain the same.

From here on out, when you create a dynamic mesh (a skinned mesh) you call functions from CSkinnedMesh. A CSkinnedMesh object is still an object of the CMesh type, so the interface of CMesh is still at work in the background.

continued

Figure 7.10 uses a UML diagram to illustrate the relationship between CMesh and CSkinnedMesh. Notice that the interface of CSkinnedMesh has been specialized to accommodate the needs of skinned meshes and hierarchies. On the other hand, CMesh can also accommodate the needs of static meshes.

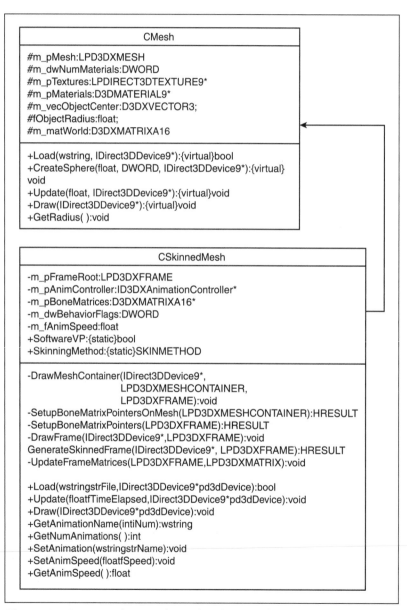

Figure 7.10 A UML diagram shows that the CMesh functions now reside in CSkinnedMesh.

Loading Meshes

As you know from previous discussions, the `CMesh::Load()` function serves as your primary vehicle for loading meshes. The revised `CMesh::Load()` function allows you to load meshes in a simpler way. Now, you no longer have to worry about animations and bones when you load your mesh. Here is the signature line of the `CMesh::Load()` function in CMesh.cpp:

```
bool CMesh::Load(wstring strFile, IDirect3DDevice9 *pDevice)
```

Following the opening brace, the function declares an `LPD3DXBUFFER` object, which stores information about the materials and textures associated with the mesh. Next, the function calls to the `D3DXLoadMeshFromX()` function, which makes use of the `Load()` function's `strFile` parameter and the pointer to the `IDirect3DDevice9` device to load a mesh from a Microsoft *.x file. This is a fairly complex function. Here is how it appears in CMesh.cpp as wrapped by the `CMesh::Load()` function:

```
if(FAILED(D3DXLoadMeshFromX(strFile.c_str(),
                            D3DXMESH_MANAGED,
                            pDevice,
                            NULL,
                            &pMaterials,
                            NULL,
                            &m_dwNumMaterials,
                            &m_pMesh)))
```

The parameters of the `D3DXLoadMeshFromX()` function are as follows:

- `LPCTSTR pFilename`. This is the name of the file that stores your mesh. The value you use is taken from `Load()` function `wstring` parameter. You use the `c_str()` function to convert the string to a constant.

- `DWORD Options`. This lets you specify options for your mesh, such as its location in memory. The value you see applied in the code is `D3DXMESH_MANAGED`.

- `LPDIRECT3DDEVICE9 pD3DDevice`. This is the device you declare in CGraphics.h. The value you see for this parameter is `pDevice`, which you obtain from the parameter list for the `Load()` function.

- `LPD3DXBUFFER *ppAdjacency`. If you use this parameter, the array your pointer designates is filled with information about those polygons in your mesh that share vertices. You use this information to optimize the performance of your mesh. Since this option is not used here, the value you see used for this parameter is `NULL`.

- `LPD3DXBUFFER *ppMaterials`. This is the buffer in which you store pointers to materials. The value you see applied to this parameter is `pMaterials`. This is the identifier `LPD3DXBUFFER` just declared within the scope of the `Load()` function.

- LPD3DXBUFFER *ppEffectInstances. If you are using effect files, this buffer is filled with information about them. An *effect* is usually a combination of vertex and pixel shaders. The value you see applied to this parameter is NULL since no effects are used.
- DWORD *pNumMaterials. This is the number of materials. You use the address of the class attribute m_dwNumMaterials to supply the value for this parameter.
- LPD3DXMESH *ppMesh. This is where you store the resulting mesh. The value you see applied to this parameter is m_pMesh.

Following the activity of loading the mesh, the Load() function creates arrays for materials and textures. The materials array is of the type D3DMATERIAL9. The texture array is of the type LPDIRECT3DTEXTURE9. Here's the code that creates these arrays:

```
// Create arrays for materials/textures
m_pMaterials = new D3DMATERIAL9[m_dwNumMaterials];
m_pTextures = new LPDIRECT3DTEXTURE9[m_dwNumMaterials];
```

Note that the m_dwNumMaterials value sets the size of the two arrays. Following the work of setting up the arrays, the Load() function obtains a D3DXMATERIAL buffer pointer using the GetBufferPointer() function. A buffer pointer is a pointer to the beginning of an array. The array stores the information about your materials and textures. Here's the code:

```
D3DXMATERIAL* d3dxMaterials =
            (D3DXMATERIAL*)pMaterials->GetBufferPointer();
```

Next, the Load() function employs a for loop to iterate through all of the materials in the D3DXMATERIAL array and copies the materials into the arrays you have created. You use the MatD3D element of the D3DXMATERIAL array to retrieve each material. You retrieve the value of the Diffuse (light) element and copy it into the materials Ambient element. You do this because *.x files do not store the ambient color. If you neglect to do this, your mesh will not appear as you expect it to. Here's the code for the first few lines of the for loop:

```
// Load the textures, set up the materials
for(int itr = 0; itr <m_dwNumMaterials; itr++)
{
      m_pMaterials[itr] = d3dxMaterials[itr].MatD3D;
      m_pMaterials[itr].Ambient = m_pMaterials[itr].Diffuse;
```

After the Load() function processes the materials, its moves on to set up the textures for the meshes. To accomplish this, it is necessary to first convert the texture filename from ASCII to Unicode using the MultiByteToWideChar() function. The primary parameter for this function is the pTextureFilename element of the D3DXMATERIAL array. Following this bit of work, it is necessary to strip the path. You strip the path because *.x files store an absolute path to a texture. You can use the absolute path only with great difficulty. To avoid difficulty, you use the PathStripPath() function to strip away the path. Since you store all of your textures in a directory called "Textures," you can remake the filename using a path to this directory. Here's the code:

```
WCHAR wszTextureFile[MAX_PATH];
  MultiByteToWideChar( CP_ACP, 0,
                          d3dxMaterials[itr].pTextureFilename,
                          -1, wszTextureFile, MAX_PATH );
    wszTextureFile[MAX_PATH - 1] = L'\0';
    // Strip the path off the buffer
    PathStripPath(wszTextureFile);
    // Now add the "Textures\" prefix to
    //the filename to make sure the
    // correct directory is being accessed
    wstring strTexturePath = wstring(L"Textures\\") +
                                wstring(wszTextureFile);
```

Having finished with the remake of the directory string, the Load() function calls the D3DXCreateTextureFromFile() function to load the texture. The parameters for the D3DXCreateTextureFromFile() function are those you already know. The first parameter is the IDirect3DDevice9 device passed in with the Load() function parameters. The second is the path you just re-created. The last parameter is the array of textures. When you are done with the D3DXCreateTextureFromFile() function, you set the current texture to NULL:

```
        if(FAILED( D3DXCreateTextureFromFile(
                pDevice,
                strTexturePath.c_str(),
                &m_pTextures[itr])))
                m_pTextures[itr] = NULL;
}//end of for loop
    // Release the material buffer
    SAFERELEASE(pMaterials);
```

Having set up the texture, you can use the SAFERELEASE macro to release the materials buffer. You do this so that you do not risk leaking memory. At this point, you have everything you need to render a mesh.

Calculating Bounding Sphere Radius

Within the CMesh::Load() function, you also perform the work needed to calculate the radius of the bounding sphere for your mesh. To accomplish this, you obtain a pointer to the vertices of the mesh and pass this pointer to a D3DX function that calculates the radius for you. To see how this happens, take a look at the concluding block of code in the Load() function in CMesh.cpp:

```
// Get the number of vertices
DWORD dwNumVerts = m_pMesh->GetNumVertices();
// Get the FVF format
DWORD dwFVF = D3DXGetFVFVertexSize(m_pMesh->GetFVF());
// Vertex pointer
VOID *pVertex = NULL;
// Lock the vertex buffer
if (FAILED(m_pMesh->LockVertexBuffer(0, &pVertex)))
    return(false);
// Compute the bounding sphere
```

First you use the `D3DXMESH::GetNumVertices()` function to obtain the total number of vertices in the mesh. You store the number of vertices in a `DWORD` identifier. You then obtain the format of the vertices in your mesh. To accomplish this, you use the `D3DXMESHL::GetFVF()` function. This function allows D3DX to step through each vertex in the array to calculate the radius of the bounding sphere. To obtain the size of each vertex (its number of bytes) you use the `D3DXGetFVFVertexSize()` function. The result is that you obtain the total byte size of the mesh.

Your next step is to lock the vertex buffer so that you can obtain a pointer to the starting point of the vertex buffer. Having obtained the starting point of the buffer, you can then use the `D3DXComputeBoundingSphere()` function to calculate the size of a sphere that can accommodate your mesh. Here's the code from the `Load()` function that performs this work:

```
if (FAILED(D3DXComputeBoundingSphere((D3DXVECTOR3 *)
                    pVertex,
                    dwNumVerts,
                    dwFVF,
                    &m_vecObjectCenter,
                    &m_fObjectRadius )))
        return(false);
    // unlock the vertex buffer
    if (FAILED(m_pMesh->UnlockVertexBuffer()))
        return(false);
    return(true);
}
```

Here are the parameters for the `D3DXComputeBoundingSphere()` function:

- `LPD3DXVECTOR3 pFirstPosition`. This is the pointer to the first vertex in your vertex buffer. The parameter value you see in the example is `pVertex`.

- DWORD NumVertice. This is the number of vertices in your buffer. The parameter value you see in the example is dwNumVerts.
- DWORD dwStride. This is the size of each vertex. The parameter value you see in the example is dwFVF.
- D3DXVECTOR3 *pCenter. This is a pointer that stores the set of coordinates the function determines to designate the center of the mesh. The parameter value you see in the example is m_vecObjectCenter.
- FLOAT *pRadius. This is the radius of the mesh. (In other words, it is the longest vector from the center of your mesh.) The value you see in the example is m_fObjectRadius.

After the call to the D3DXComputeBoundingSphere() function, the Load() function concludes its work by performing two simple actions. First, having locked the vertex buffer to perform calculations, it now unlocks it. When you unlock a vertex buffer, you let Direct3D know that you are done looking at the vertices so that it can then allow other processes to be applied to your mesh. The second action the Load() function performs involves reporting the success or failure of the unlock action. The Load() function returns a boolean value of true to indicate success. Here's the last of the code from the Load() function:

```
// unlock the vertex buffer
if (FAILED(m_pMesh->UnlockVertexBuffer()))
    return(false);
    return(true);
```

Creating a Bounding Sphere

The CreateSphere() function of CMesh allows you to create a mesh manually, as opposed to loading it from a file. It is sometimes more convenient to manually create an object rather than to use a mesh model for it. Usually, the objects you create in this way are graphical primitives, such as spheres, rectangles, and DirectX teapots. A bounding sphere is such an object.

To understand how the CreateSphere() function works, take a look at the CreateSphere() function in CMesh.cpp. Here's the signature line of the CreateSphere() function:

```
void CMesh::CreateSphere(float fRadius,
                         DWORD dwColor,
                         IDirect3DDevice9 *pDevice)
```

The parameters of CreateSphere() call for the radius of the sphere you want to create (fRadius), the color of the sphere (dwColor), and the IDirect3DDevice9 device (pDevice).

After the opening brace, the first lines of code in the CreateSphere() function call the DirectX D3DXCreateSphere() function to create a sphere primitive. Here is the code from CreateSphere() in CMesh.cpp:

```
// Create the sphere
D3DXCreateSphere(pDevice, fRadius,
                 25, 25,
                 &m_pMesh,
                 NULL);
```

The first two parameters of the D3DXCreateSphere() function call for the IDirect3DDevice9 device and the radius of the sphere. The third and fourth parameters allow you to set the resolution of the sphere (25, 25). The resolution of the sphere pertains to how many segments you want to create. The number of segments controls how many vertices represent the sphere. The greater the number of segments, the smoother the appearance of the sphere. The second to the last parameter supplies a reference to the sphere (m_pMesh) you are creating. The final parameter provides a reference to what is known as an *adjacency interface*. Such an interface is not used in this context, so a value of NULL is assigned to the parameter.

After creating the graphical primitive, the CreateSphere() function moves on to set the textures array to NULL. (This is necessary in this instance because this application does not support textures.) It then creates an array of the type D3DMATERIAL9 that can accommodate a pointer for one material. Finally, it sets the number of materials (dwNumMaterials) to 1 and immediately clears out the materials structure using the ZeroMemory() function. Here's the code:

```
m_pTextures = NULL;
m_pMaterials = new D3DMATERIAL9[1];
// Set the color
m_dwNumMaterials = 1;
ZeroMemory(&m_pMaterials[0], sizeof(D3DMATERIAL9));
```

The work in the CreateSphere() function continues, for now it uses the D3DXCOLOR object to convert the DWORD color parameter of the CreateSphere() function to a more understandable format. The more understandable format is a D3DCOLOR array called colMesh. Having completed this bit of work, it proceeds to copy the ARGB values from the color mesh into the properties of the Ambient element obtained when you use a D3DMATERIAL9 array. The first property (a) sets the alpha (opacity) value, and the following three parameters (r, g, b) set the color. Here's the code from the CreateSphere() function that performs this work:

```
D3DXCOLOR colMesh = D3DXCOLOR(dwColor);
m_pMaterials[0].Ambient.a = colMesh.a;
m_pMaterials[0].Ambient.r = colMesh.r;
m_pMaterials[0].Ambient.g = colMesh.g;
m_pMaterials[0].Ambient.b = colMesh.b;
m_pMaterials[0].Diffuse = m_pMaterials[0].Ambient;
m_fObjectRadius = fRadius;
m_vecObjectCenter = D3DXVECTOR3(0,0,0);
```

Having set the color of your mesh, the CreateSphere() function stores the radius of your mesh in the m_fObjectRadius member of the CMesh class for future reference. It also uses a D3DXVECTOR3 object to define the center of the mesh for the world space. To accomplish this, it creates a D3DXVECTOR3 object and assigns it values of 0, 0, 0. This set of values centers the mesh on its origin. The origin of the mesh is its center.

Drawing a Bounding Sphere

To make your bounding sphere visible, you must draw it. To accomplish this, you use the CMesh::Draw() function. This function works like the Render() function you have seen in previous sections. It places the mesh on the back buffer so that it shows up on the next flip of surfaces if you have defined its coordinates within the camera's viewport. The viewport, you recall, is the window of visibility that represents the final transformation of your 3D image into the world of the monitor.

If you look at the Draw() function in the CMesh.cpp file, you can see that the function requires only one parameter, a pointer to an IDirect3DDevice9 device. It requires the device because the device provides the interface that allows it to set the texture, material, and transform values of the meshes it draws. Here is the signature of the CMesh::Draw() function:

```
void CMesh::Draw(IDirect3DDevice9 *pd3dDevice)
```

Following the signature of the function, the Draw() function verifies the existence of the mesh by checking to see whether its identifier contains a NULL or zero value:

```
// Make sure the object exists
if(!m_pMesh)
    return;
```

After it establishes the existence of the mesh, the Draw() function proceeds to obtain the current world transform and store it in a D3DXMATRIXA16 struct called matWorld. To accomplish this, it calls the IDirect3DDevice9::GetTransform() function, which requires using the D3DTS_WORLD identifier as its first parameter and a reference to the resulting matrix as its second parameter. These two parameters indicate the transform the function is to retrieve. Here's the code for Draw() from CMesh.cpp:

```
// Set up world matrix, place the object in the
// center of the arc ball so it can be viewed
    D3DXMATRIXA16 matWorld, matCenter;
    pd3dDevice->GetTransform(D3DTS_WORLD, &matWorld);
```

Next, the Draw() function creates a matrix and translates the mesh based on the coordinates that designate the position of its center. To accomplish this, it calls the D3DXMatrixTranslation() function. The first parameter of this function is a D3DXMATRIXA16

reference to the matrix (matCenter) that stores the resulting matrix. The final three parameters represent the destination coordinates of the transformation. The destination
coordinates establish the local space position of the mesh that allows it to be translated to
world space. You establish the local space because when you create the mesh, the application with which you create the mesh (Maya or D3DMax, for example) aligns its coordinates
arbitrarily. When you translate the matrix, you supply negative values because you are
centering the mesh on the mesh's origin. Here's the code from the Draw() function:

```
// Translate and set the transform
D3DXMatrixTranslation(&matCenter, -m_vecObjectCenter.x,
                                  -m_vecObjectCenter.y,
                                  -m_vecObjectCenter.z);
```

After the Draw() function sets the local values, it multiplies the two matrices (&matCenter,
&matWorld) to combine them into the final world transform (&matWorld), which is represented by the first parameter passed to D3DMatrixMultiply(). Given this combination, Draw()
calls the SetTransform() function to inform Direct3D that this is the new world matrix.
Here, once again, you use D3DTS_WORLD to identify the transform you want to use:

```
D3DXMatrixMultiply(&matWorld, &matCenter, &matWorld);
pd3dDevice->SetTransform(D3DTS_WORLD, &matWorld);
```

At this point, the Draw() function has defined the world transform and is ready to draw
the mesh. To draw the mesh is no simple matter, however, for meshes can possess many
different components, each of which must be drawn separately. Each of these components
is called a *subset*. A subset is basically a group of vertices that shares the same material and
texture. To render each of these subsets separately, the Draw() function uses a for loop.
Here is the code from the Draw() function that shows the first part of the for loop:

```
// Draw the mesh, one material at a time
for(int itr = 0; itr < m_dwNumMaterials; itr++)
{
    // Set the texture
    if(m_pTextures)
        pd3dDevice->SetTexture(0, m_pTextures[itr]);
    else
        pd3dDevice->SetTexture(0, NULL);
```

As it renders the subsets with the for loop, the Draw() function controls the loop using the
number of materials (itr < m_dwNumMaterials). The number of materials, you recall, you
obtain using a call to D3DXLoadMeshFromX(). This function returns the number of subsets a
mesh contains.

Using the number of subsets as a control, the Draw() function then checks to see if the texture array exists (m_pTextures). If it exists, it calls the SetTexture() function to identify the texture that corresponds to the current subset. You set the first parameter of the SetTexture() function to 0 because you want to use only stage zero of the D3D rendering capability. (A stage is an aspect of multi-texturing.) As for the second parameter, to obtain the appropriate value, the Draw() function iterates through the m_pTextures array. When it does this, it accesses the texture of each subset so that it can place the appropriate texture on each subset of the mesh.

The second case (else) of the for loop in the Draw() function sets the texture to NULL in the event that the mesh has no textures. The SetTexture() function works the same as it did before, but this time the NULL value forces it to ignore the textures.

Following the selection statements and still within the braces of the for loop, the Draw() function proceeds to use the SetMaterial() function to access a materials element in the materials array (m_pMaterials) and apply it to the corresponding subset. Having now applied both the appropriate materials element and the appropriate texture, it then draws the current set of vertices using the

```
DrawSubset()
function:
        // Set the material
        if(m_pMaterials)
                pd3dDevice->SetMaterial(&m_pMaterials[itr]);
        // Draw the subset
        m_pMesh->DrawSubset(itr);
```

With this action, the Draw() function completes its work.

Adding Bounding Spheres

As was mentioned previously, you first create an entity and then add a bounding sphere to it. In this case, you add a bounding sphere to a dynamic entity. The dynamic entity is the figure in the sphere. The bounding sphere is a graphical primate. (Glance back at Figure 7.9 if you need a reminder.) To add a bounding sphere to your entity, you make a few changes to CMyApplication. These changes begin with a call to CWorld::CreateEntity() in the CMyApplication::Initialize() function. Here is the code from CMyApplication.cpp that shows the call:

```
CEntity *pEntity = GetWorld()->GetEntity(L"Entity1");
GetWorld()->CreateEntity(L"Sphere",
        pEntity->GetMesh()->GetRadius(),
        D3DCOLOR_ARGB(64,255,0,0),
        m_pGraphics->GetDevice());
```

The first thing you do in this bit of code involves using the GetWorld() and GetEntity() functions to obtain a pointer to an entity called "Entity1," which you assign to a CEntity pointer (pEntity).

Next, you use the GetWorld() and CreateEntity() functions to create a bounding sphere. The first parameter of CreateEntity() allows you to assign a unique name to the bounding sphere ("Sphere"). The second parameter allows you to set the radius of the bounding sphere. To set the radius, you use cascading calls to access the mesh that your bounding sphere contains (GetMesh()) and then to establish the radius of the mesh (GetRadius()).

The third parameter of CreateEntity() enables you to set the color of the bounding sphere, and you accomplish this using the D3DCOLOR_ARGB() macro. Notice that the "A" in the macro name indicates that you can use it to set the alpha component, which allows you to make the bounding sphere translucent. Since the alpha value (64) represents a value in the range of 0, for transparent, to 255, for opaque, the sphere will be more transparent than opaque.

To set the final parameter of CreateEntity(), call to the CGraphics::GetDevice() function to obtain a pointer to the IDirect3DDevice9 device you declared in CGraphics.h.

Scene Hierarchies

A scene hierarchy allows you to link entities together. You link entities together for a variety of reasons. One primary reason is that you want them to work as a single unit. For example, consider the problem of making an automobile model that allows you to simulate a door that opens and closes or tires that turn as the automobile moves. You can use a scene hierarchy to accomplish this task. Figure 7.11 illustrates a scene hierarchy that represents an automobile in this context.

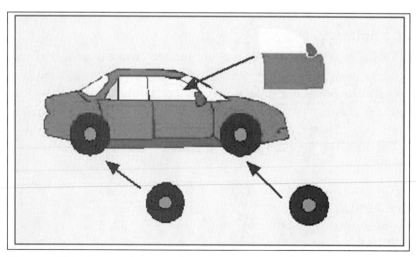

Figure 7.11 A scene hierarchy allows you to make entities work together as a single unit.

To create a scene hierarchy, you need to create children entities. A child entity is one that you can attach to a parent entity. A parent entity anchors other entities to its position so that all transformations performed on the child entity are combined with the transformations performed on the parent. For example, if you consider the hierarchy Figure 7.11 illustrates, if you rotate the parent entity (the car chassis), the child entities (the tires and the door) rotate also.

To begin investigating how to implement the code you require for creating scene hierarchies, open Listing07_03 and compile the program. Figure 7.12 shows you the result. Use the mouse wheel to enlarge the large figure. The large figure is the parent entity. The application features two child entities. The small figure is one of the child entities. The other is the bounding sphere that surrounds the small and large figures. The scene hierarchy, then, consists of one parent and two child entities.

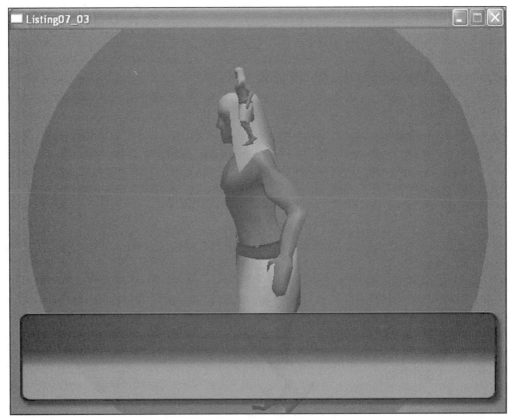

Figure 7.12 Scene hierarchies consist of parent and child entities.

Adding Children

To create a scene hierarchy, you first create a parent entity. Then you add children entities to the parent. To see how this happens, first take a look at the code in CEntity.h. Here is a sampling of the code you can find at the bottom of the class definition for CEntity in CEntity.h:

```
// List of children for this entity
vector<class CEntity *> m_lstChildren;
```

You set up a vector of the type CEntity that allows you to track child entities. Each CEntity object can be associated with one or more child entities. The child entities consist of CEntity objects of the same type as the parent. The only significant difference is that you designate one entity, the parent, as the root entity of the hierarchy. Like the parent entity of the hierarchy, the children entities can have their own children. Accessing the children of children involves using cascading function calls. This topic receives more attention further on.

Adding a Child Entity

To add a child entity to a parent entity, you create a function that allows you to automatically associate one entity with another. The name of the function is AddChild(). Here's the code that accomplishes this task in CEntity.cpp:

```
void CEntity::AddChild(CEntity *pChild)
{
    m_lstChildren.push_back(pChild);
    pChild->SetManaged(true);
}
```

The AddChild() function requires that you pass it one parameter value. The value consists of a pointer to the CEntity object you want to associate with the parent entity. The vector::push_back() function pushes the entity pointer to the back (or end) of the m_lstChildren vector, automatically resizing the vector as needed. Having included a pointer to the entity in the vector , you call the SetManaged() function to set the child's managed function to true so that when you want to destroy the parent, you can also destroy the children along with it.

To use this function, as you see a little later in this chapter, you make a call to it in CMyApplication::Initialize(), where after setting up the parent entity, you add child entities to the parent.

Updating and Rendering Child Entities

The functions you use to update and render child entities involve making a few modifications to the `CEntity::Update()` and `CEntity::Render()` functions to accommodate actions taken toward child entities. The situation is precisely the same you have seen before when dealing with meshes and skinned meshes. The next few sections discuss the specifics.

Updating Child Entities

As you saw in the discussions of meshes and skinned meshes, you usually update an entity's properties before you render the entity. The same applies to child entities. Here's the code from CEntity.cpp for the `CEntity::Update()` function:

```
// Update children
for(int itr=0; itr < m_lstChildren.size(); itr++)
{
    if(m_lstChildren[itr])
    {
        pDevice->SetTransform(D3DTS_WORLD, &m_matWorld);
        m_lstChildren[itr]->Update(fTimeElapsed, pDevice);
    }
}
```

To accommodate children, you add a `for` loop to the `CEntity::Update()` function. The `for` loop iterates through all the children you have added to the vector that holds pointers to the child entities. You control the vector using the `vector::size()` function. As the `for` loop progresses, an `if` selection statement checks to see whether any element in the `m_lstChildren` vector is `NULL`.

If the element in the vector is not `NULL`, then the next action involves calling the `SetTransform()` function to reset the world transform (`D3DTS_WORLD`) to the parent's world matrix. Setting the world transform involves resetting the world to a known state before the transformation occurs. You must reset the world matrix (or transform) to the parent's world matrix (`m_matWorld`). You must perform this operation every time the `for` loop iterates because each time it iterates it modifies the `D3DTS_WORLD` transform and sets it to an unknown state.

After you set the world transform, you call the child's `CEntity::Update()` function (`m_lstChildren[itr]->Update()`), which assigns to the child the same animation speed and devices parameters you assigned to the parent. You use the `fTimeElapsed` value to establish a constant animation speed. You pass the pointer to `IDirect3DDevice9` because without the device you cannot update the world transformations.

Rendering Child Entities

When you render child entities, you cause them to be displayed on the back buffer. You render child entities using the CEntity::Render() function. Here is the code for CEntity::Render() from CEntity.cpp:

```
void CEntity::Render(IDirect3DDevice9 *pDevice)
{
    // Restore transformation before each render, to
    // get back to a known state
    pDevice->SetTransform(D3DTS_WORLD, &m_matWorld);
    // Draw the mesh
    if(m_pMesh)
        m_pMesh->Draw(pDevice);
    // Render our children
    for(int itr=0; itr<m_lstChildren.size(); itr++)
    {
        if(m_lstChildren[itr])
        {
            m_lstChildren[itr]->Render(pDevice);
        }
    }
}
```

The sole parameter you pass to the Render() function is a pointer to the IDirect3DDevice9 device you declared in CGraphics.h. After the opening brace, your first action involves calling the SetTransform() function to set the transform (D3DTS_WORLD) to the matrix you generated in the Update() function (m_matWorld). Following this work, you then use an if selection statement to check for NULL values. (This is for safety measures. There should not be any such values.) If it is not NULL, you then call the Draw() function using your IDirect3DDevice9 device to draw the parent entity.

After you draw the parent entity, you draw the children of the parent entity. To accomplish this task, you use a for loop to iterate through the child entity pointers stored in the child entity vector (m_lstChildren). For each child entity pointer you find in the child entity vector, you call the CEntity::Render() function to draw the child entity to the back buffer.

Note

In this context, the CEntity::Render() function calls the CEntity::Render() function. This action does not constitute recursion (a function calling itself) in the usual sense of the term. Rather than the Render() function calling itself, it is the entities within the vector that call Render(), so the vector is in effect controlling how you call the function.

Changing the Application for Children

You add child entities to your application in the `CMyApplication::Initialize()` function. Generally, to add child entities, you create an entity that you want to use as the parent, you create child entities, and then you use the parent's `AddChild()` function to add the children.

If you look at the code in the `CMyApplication::Initialize()` function in CMyApplication.cpp, you'll see that the first thing you do involves retrieving `Entity1` from your world and assigning it to a local `CEntity` pointer, `pEntity`. This is your parent entity in the hierarchy you are going to create. Next, you call the `SetAnimation()` function to assign the "Walk" animation to this entity. Notice that to use `SetAnimation()`, you make use of the combination of `GetWorld()` and `GetEntity()` discussed previously. Notice that you must cast the mesh to a pointer to a `CSkinnedMesh` object to access the `SetAnimation()` function. Here's the code from the `CMyApplication::Initialize()` function:

```
// Get a pointer to the entity
CEntity *pEntity = GetWorld()->GetEntity(L"Entity1");
((CSkinnedMesh *)pEntity->GetMesh())->SetAnimation(L"Walk");
```

Having created the parent entity, you use a little magic to create an "incredible shrinking version" of the parent mesh to serve as the first of your child entities. (In Figure 7.10, the child entity stands on the shoulder of the parent entity.) To make this happen, you first create an instance of the "Small" entity. The parameter you assign, "Small", simply names the entity. After creating an instance of the entity, you then use the `LoadMesh()` function to associate a mesh file and a device with the entity. In this case, the mesh file you use is the same one you used for the parent entity. Here's the code from `CMyApplication::Initialize()` that performs this work:

```
//place a child to place on the shoulder of the parent
CEntity *pSmall = new CEntity(L"Small");
pSmall->LoadMesh(L"Meshes\\multi_anim.x", m_pGraphics->GetDevice());
```

After loading the entity, you then proceed to scale it using the `CEntity::SetScale()` function. This function sets up the size of the child entity. In this case, you use the value of 0.2 to scale the entity so that it is one-fifth the size of the original entity. You supply values to the `D3DXVECTOR3` struct to scale, respectively, the width, height, and depth (`x`, `y`, `z`) dimensions of the mesh. Here's the code:

```
        pSmall->SetScale(D3DXVECTOR3(0.2, 0.2, 0.2));
```

Having scaled the mesh, you can then position it. To position the mesh, you use the `SetPos()` function. You use a `D3DXVECTOR3` struct to set the values you use to position the mesh. The values you use, (`-0.10, 0.40, 0`), point, approximately, to a position in the parent's local space that designates a place roughly on the left shoulder. These values designate where the center of the child mesh is to be located. As a final touch, you set up the behavior of the entity using the SetAnimation() function. The procedure for this is the same as the procedure you used for the parent entity. Here's the code:

```
pSmall->SetPos(D3DXVECTOR3(-0.10, 0.40, 0));
((CSkinnedMesh *)pSmall->GetMesh())->SetAnimation(L"Walk");
```

Having stationed the child mesh on the shoulder of the parent mesh, your next bit of business is to create a bounding sphere. To create the bounding sphere, you call CEntity::CreateSphere(). This function creates a child entity of Entity1. As Figure 7.12 shows, both figures fit within the bounding sphere, but if the child entity were large enough, it would extend beyond the parent's bounding sphere. Here's the code from CMyApplication::Initialize() that sets up the bounding sphere:

```
// Create a sphere, and add it as a child to the main entity
CEntity *pSphere = new CEntity(L"Sphere");
pSphere->CreateSphere(pEntity->GetMesh()->GetRadius(),
                D3DCOLOR_ARGB(64,0,0,255),
                m_pGraphics->GetDevice());
```

Having done everything else, you are left to at last add the small entity and the bounding sphere to your hierarchy. To accomplish this, you use the AddChild() function to add the pointers that designate the two entities you have created. As the comments indicate, notice that the order in which you render entities determines whether they will be visible.

```
// Add the small entity first, and then the sphere.
//This is done because the sphere is translucent
// so it must be rendered last. If it is rendered first,
//it will write to the z buffer and the small
// entity will never be drawn since it fails the depth test.
pEntity->AddChild(pSmall);
pEntity->AddChild(pSphere);
```

Entities and World Events

A world takes on remarkable meaning when you are at last able to combine events, controls, and entities to implement complex scenarios. If you open Listing07_04 and compile the project, what happens when you implement a complex scenario becomes evident. Figure 7.13 shows you the results. If you click the button, you can see the ball move about in a random way. As the ball moves, the walking figure turns and begins moving toward it. When the walking figure reaches the ball, it stops walking and assumes a slightly stooped posture, as though reaching to pick it up. If you use the mouse wheel, you can change the location of the camera, so that the ball and the walking figure appear larger or smaller. Likewise, using the left mouse button, you can raise, lower, or pivot the camera with respect to the "stage." The stage is the grassy area on which the figure walks.

Figure 7.13 Combining events, entities, and controls creates interesting actions in your world.

Creating a Context of Events

To join a set of entities together into an interrelated system, you must combine them into a single context. A context is a system of some type in which entities respond to each other, to control messages, or to events that they trigger for themselves. If the activity that results manifests a given event model, you then have a context of events. In the `Initialize()` function of CMyApplication.cpp, you create a context of events by using three entities and a single, complex event to tie them together. Here's the code:

```
    // Create the stage entity
    GetWorld()->CreateEntity(L"Stage",
                             L"Meshes\\stage.x",
                             m_pGraphics->GetDevice());
```

```
// Create a green ball entity
CEntity *pBall =
            GetWorld()->CreateEntity(L"Ball",
                                      0.2,
                                      D3DCOLOR_XRGB(0, 255, 64),
                                      m_pGraphics->GetDevice());
//Move the green ball and change the default position.
pBall->SetPos(D3DXVECTOR3(-3,
                           pBall->GetMesh()->GetRadius(),
                           3));
// Create the walking entity. Leave the default position.
CEntity *pEntity =
            GetWorld()->CreateEntity(L"Entity1",
                                      L"Meshes\\multi_anim.x",
                                      m_pGraphics->GetDevice());
pEntity->SetAnimation(L"Walk");
```

This code sets up three entities. The first entity is a stage. The stage is the flat, square surface on which a walking entity and ball move. To create the stage, you use the static `GetWorld()` function to retrieve your world. You then use the `CreateEntity()` function to create the entity for the stage. The default values assigned to the entity position it in the center of your monitor.

After you create the state, you call an overloaded version of `CreateEntity()` to create a ball to place on the stage. Here is the signature for the overloaded version of `CreateEntity()` from CWorld.h:

```
// Create a sphere entity
class CEntity *CreateEntity(wstring strName,
                            float fRadius,
                            DWORD dwColor,
                            IDirect3DDevice9 *pDevice,
                            class CEntity *pParent = NULL);
```

Returning to the use of `CreateEntity()` in CMyApplication.h to create the second entity, the Ball, note that you do not assign an animation. You do not assign an animation because the overloaded function does not call for an animation. The ball is a static entity. The second parameter of the function sets the radius of the ball to 0.2. The parameter you see sets the device. The function declaration features another parameter, but in this case you do not see it assigned since it is not needed, and the so default value covers it (`class CEntity *pParent = NULL`).

Following the creation of the Ball entity, you then use the SetPos() function to designate the initial position of the entity. The first value you supply to the SetPos() function, -3, places the Ball at -3 on the x axis. You supply this value to move the ball away from the world origin. You do this to place the ball at a distance from the walking entity, which you create next.

You create the walker entity last. You do not need to set the position of this entity since by default it appears at the origin. To create the entity, you use a second overloaded version of the CWorld::CreateEntity() function. Here is the declaration of the overloaded CreateEntity() function from CWorld.h:

```
// Loads and creates an entity
    class CEntity *CreateEntity(wstring strName,
                               wstring strMeshFile,
                               IDirect3DDevice9 *pDevice,
                               class CEntity *pParent = NULL);
```

This second overloaded version allows you to supply a mesh (Meshes\\multi_anim.x) for your entity. You do so using the second parameter of the function (wstring strMeshFile). After you create the walking entity, you then assign a behavior to it. The behavior is in the form of an animated mesh. To set the animation, you call the SetAnimation() function to apply and apply the "Walk" animation to the entity.

Adding Events to the Context

After setting up the entities for your event context, you can then associate the entities with events. To accomplish this, things are made easy by the functions from the CEvent class. Here's the code from CMyApplication::Initialize() in CMyApplication.cpp that adds an event to your event context:

```
    // Create the "chase" event in the X/Z plane
    CEvent *pEvent = new CEvent(L"CHASE_XZ",
                               TIME_PERIOD, 0.01,
                               TIME_ABSOLUTE, CEvent::TIME_NEVER);
    pEvent->AddPointerParam(pBall);
    pEntity->AddEvent(pEvent);
```

With the first line, you create a pointer instance of CEvent called pEvent. With the first parameter of the constructor for CEvent, you name the event. With the second parameter, you assign the enumerated value TIME_PERIOD to designate the event should repeat indefinitely. The third parameter of the constructor, 0.01, designates that the event occurs one hundred times each second. The fourth parameter, TIME_ABSOLUTE, designates that the event begins with the instantiation of the event (rather than the start of the application). The constant value you retrieve from CEvent (CEvent::TIME_NEVER) designates that the event does not expire during the life of your application.

The CEvent::AddPointerParameter() function allows you to indicate that the pBall entity becomes the target of the action you want to initiate. For review, remember that the CEvent::AddPointerParameter() function consists of only one line of code. Here's the code:

```
void CEvent::AddPointerParam(void *pParam)
{
    m_vecPointerParams.push_back(pParam);
}
```

The function places a pointer to the Ball object in the vector you have created to hold pointer parameters for your event. You can pass in any number of objects, and then you can retrieve each of these objects when you want them to be associated with an event. In essence, then, as was illustrated in Chapter 4, an event involves associating entities in a way that allows you to create complex behaviors. In this case, the ball becomes the destination of the walker's path.

Following the call to CEvent::AddPointerParameter(), you then add the event to the walker's event list using a call to AddEvent(). From here on out, you call a CEntity() function to process events that relate to the walker.

Adding a Control

To interact with the context of events, you add controls. Controls allow you, the user, to have a role in the activity that unfolds in the context of events. You can create controls after you introduce entities and events into the context you are dealing with. You can then apply the controls to the entities and events. To accomplish this, you use the CMyApplication::InitGUI() and the CMyApplication::OnGUIEvent() functions.

The InitGUI() function, you recall, allows you to create any number of controls. In this case, the goal involves creating a single button that appears in the console area. You use the button to trigger an event that randomly places the ball in different locations on the stage. Here's the code in the InitGUI() function that creates the button:

```
void CMyApplication::InitGUI()
{
    // Call parent initialize
    CApplication::InitGUI();
    // Add the rotation buttons
    int y = m_iConsoleY + 8;
    m_GUI.AddButton(IDC_RANDOMBALL, L"Randomize Ball", 25, y, 130, 18);
}
```

After the opening braces, the CMyApplication::InitGUI() function calls CApplication::Init-GUI() to take care of the default initialization that occurs in the parent class. Next, you create a position (m_iConsoleY) for the upper left corner of the button you place in the console. When you call the `AddButton()` function, you use this value along with several others to name and position the button. The first parameter of the `AddButton()` function sets the message the button processes. The second parameter provides the text that appears on the button. The third and fourth parameters designate the upper left corner of the button. The final two parameters establish the dimensions of the button.

The creation of the control takes place in the `CApplication::Initialize()` function. This function calls the `CMyApplication::InitGUI()` function after it has created the console on which the button is to appear. The call to `InitGUI()` appears inconspicuous, but as you have seen in previous chapters, it can call a multitude of buttons and other controls into existence. Here's the code for the `Initialize()` function in CApplication.cpp:

```
void CApplication::Initialize()
{
    m_sprConsole = new CSprite();
    m_sprConsole->Load(L"Console.png");
    // Initialize the GUI
    InitGUI();
}
```

In addition to changes to the `Initialize()` function, adding a control also involves adding code that processes the message the control issues. In light of this, you make a few changes to the `OnGUIEvent()` function of `CMyApplication`. Here's the code:

```
void CMyApplication::OnGUIEvent(UINT nEvent,
                                 int nControlID, CDXUTControl *pControl)
{
    if(nControlID == IDC_RANDOMBALL)
    {
        // Get pointers to the ball and stage
        CEntity *pBall = GetWorld()->GetEntity(L"Ball");
        CEntity *pStage = GetWorld()->GetEntity(L"Stage");
        // Get the radius of the stage
        float fRadius = pStage->GetMesh()->GetRadius() * 0.6;
        float fRandX = ((float)rand()/RAND_MAX) * (fRadius*2) - fRadius;
        float fRandZ = ((float)rand()/RAND_MAX) * (fRadius*2) - fRadius;
        // Generate a random position
        pBall->SetPos(D3DXVECTOR3(fRandX , pBall->GetPos().y , fRandZ));
    }
}
```

As mentioned before, the `CMyApplication::OnGUIEvent()` function features three parameters. The first parameter supplies a unique event ID. The second parameter designates the number you assigned to identify the control. The final parameter provides a pointer to the actual control, which is of the `CDXUTControl` type.

The selection statement inside the CMyApplication::OnGUIEvent() function checks the control identifier you pass to the function against the constant value for the control you declare in the CMyApplication.h. Given that the selection statement selects this message, you then use the GetWorld() function in combination with the GetEntity() function to retrieve pointers to your entities by name (Ball and Stage). You assign the pointers you retrieve in this way to local pointer instances of CEntity.

After you have set up the local pointers to your entities, you can then proceed to ensure that the ball lies inside the stage. For this reason, the first thing you do is get the radius of the stage using the GetRadius() function. You multiply the value you retrieve by 0.6 to reduce it in size so that you can be sure that your entity will not walk over the edge of the stage.

Given these preliminaries, you can then calculate the x and y values that will repeatedly position the ball in different places on the stage. To set these values, you obtain a floating point value between 0 and 1 by dividing a randomly generated float value by a constant you obtain from the C library. You then multiply the values that result by the diameter of the foreshortened grass areas (fRadius*2). This gives you a value that lies between zero and the diameter of the foreshortened grass area. (You subtract the radius to move it into the range between -fRadius to fRadius, which is roughly the distance between the center and the edge of the foreshortened grass area.)

All of this comes together when you call the SetPos() function. The SetPos() function positions the ball according to the random x and z positions you have calculated. You leave the y position unchanged because you only want the walking figure to walk on the plane (defined by the x and z values), not above or below it (which is what happens when you change the y value).

Handling the New Event

To handle (or process) the events relating to the walker and the ball, you make changes to CEntity::OnEvent(). The code you require to process the event is somewhat involved, but in essence you determine the direction of the ball relative to the walker, turn in that direction, and then move the walker toward the ball. To locate the starting point for the processing of the chase event, locate the else if statement in CEntity::OnEvent() that tests for the "CHASE_XZ" value. Here's the first bit of code:

```
else if(strName == L"CHASE_XZ")
{
        // Get a pointer to the entity we are supposed to chase
        CEntity *pDest = (CEntity *)pEvent->GetPointerParams()[0];

        // Check for invalid arguments
        if(!pDest)
            return;
```

The first line returns the first element in the pointer parameter vector for the event you are processing (this is at index 0 of the vector). You assign the pointer to the element a pointer of the CEntity type. Next, you test the CEntity pointer to determine whether it is a NULL value. If it is NULL, you do nothing more.

If the pointer is valid, you can then proceed to determine the direction you need to move the walking entity. To accomplish this, you subtract the walking entity's position from the destination position (which is the position of the ball). To obtain these two positions, you use two calls to CEntity::GetPos(). The first is a call to the Ball entity. The second is to the walking entity. You use the C++ this keyword to access the walking entity. You then assign a 0 to the y element of the D3DXVECTOR3 vector. This prevents movement along the y axis. Here's the code:

```
// Get the direction we need to move in
D3DXVECTOR3 vecDir = pDest->GetPos() - this->GetPos();
vecDir.y = 0;
```

The next statement computes the length of the distance between the walker and the ball using the D3DXVec3Length() function, which takes a reference to your D3DXVECTOR3 vector (vecDir) as an argument. It returns the length of the vector—the distance to the ball. This you compare to the radius of the ball, which you retrieve using the GetRadius() function. Here's the code:

```
if(D3DXVec3Length(&vecDir) >= pDest->GetMesh()->GetRadius())
{
```

Given that condition returns true (the distance between the walker and the ball exceeds the ball's radius), you turn and move the walker toward the ball. The first step involves normalizing the direction vector so that its length equals 1. You do this so that the walker does not move faster as it proceeds away from the ball. (This would occur because as the walker moves away from the ball, the length of the vector that defines the direction to the ball becomes larger.) Here's the bit of code that accomplishes this:

```
// Normalize the direction vector
D3DXVec3Normalize(&vecDir, &vecDir);
```

After normalizing the vector, you make it so that the walker moves toward the ball at a constant rate of 0.01 units for each update. To accomplish this, you multiply the vector (vecDir) by 0.01 and then add the product to the current position of the walker:

```
m_vecPos += (vecDir * 0.01);
```

The next section of code determines the angle between the walker and the ball, so that you can rotate the walker appropriately (so it faces the ball). To rotate the walker, you first need to create a vector that represents the direction the walker faces in model space (vecFace(0, 0, 1)). Next you call the D3DXVec3Dot() function to calculate the dot product of the direction between the walker and the ball (vecDir) and the direction the walker faces in model space (vecFace). Here's the code:

```
// Now we need to calculate the angle we should be facing
// assuming all our models start out facing (0,0,1)
D3DXVECTOR3 vecFace(0, 0, 1), vecCross;
float fAngle = acos(D3DXVec3Dot(&vecDir, &vecFace));
```

Notice that you then use the C library acos() function to obtain the angle from the computed dot product. You assign this value to fAngle.

You then use the D3DXVec3Cross() function to obtain the cross product of the face and direction vectors. You store the result in the vector you have created for this purpose (vecCross).

```
D3DXVec3Cross(&vecCross, &vecDir, &vecFace);
```

The dot product gives you the angle between the two objects, but it does not give you the axis of rotation. To obtain the axis of rotation, you must calculate the cross product of the two vectors. In this instance, if the y element of the cross product is positive, you reverse the rotation around the y axis. Here's the code that accomplishes this feat:

```
// Switch the sign of the angle depending
    // on the values resulting
// from the cross product
if(vecCross.y > 0)
        fAngle *= -1;
```

Having calculated the angle the walker needs to be facing relative to its original direction, you then call the SetRotAngles() function to rotate the walker about the y-axis. The sole parameter of the SetRotAngles() is a D3DXVECTOR3 object, and to this parameter you assign the value for the angle (0, fAngle, 0). Given the completion of this work, you then assign the animation you want to use to show the walking behavior ("Walk"). Here is the code:

```
// Set the rotation angles, and the walk animation
        SetRotAngles(D3DXVECTOR3(0, fAngle, 0));
        SetAnimation(L"Walk");
    }
```

As a final bit of work in the CEntity::OnEvent() function, if the walker has reached its destination (it is within the radius of the ball), you set the animation back to standing. Here's the code:

```
        else
        {
                // We're done walking, just stand there
                SetAnimation(L"Stand");
        }
    }
```

Granted, the `OnEvent()` programming needed in the `OnEvent()` function to get the walking entity to walk on the stage in pursuit of the ball seems rather taxing for the limited activity you see. Still, the effort is justified, for after you establish the basic pattern of development required to create event contexts, you are on your way to almost any level of complexity you want to strive for. The key to success is to keep in mind that an event context emerges from the interaction of entities, events, and controls.

Conclusion

This chapter has taken you from the creation of a world to the implementation of a set functionality that allows you to combine entities, events, and controls to create a simple application that involves its user in an event context characterized by a pursuit scenario.

To reach this goal, you first saw how a world is fundamentally a container in which you store pointers to events. The `CWorld` class encapsulates a vector container in which you can store any number of entities you want to include in your world. To add an entity to your world, you programmed the `CreateEntity()` function, which ended up having two overloaded forms, one for entities that have animations associated with them, the other for entities that you create without animations.

You saw that when you create functions associated with a world, you tend to deal with all the entities in your world at once. To deal with all the entities at once, you make frequent use of `for` loops to iterate through the entities stored in the world container. After locating an entity, you then apply events, meshes, or controls to it.

To simplify the implementation of entities, you saw that it was possible to derive a class called `CSkinnedMesh` from the `CMesh` class—which you developed in a previous chapter. The `CSkinnedMesh` handles entities that use animated meshes. The `CMesh` class remains the primary class for processing simple entities. One such entity is the bounding sphere, which developers sometimes use for collision detection but in this chapter is shown only as a way of determining the size of the entities with which it is used.

A bounding sphere can be part of a scene hierarchy, which involves creating a parent entity and then associating other entities with the parent entity. The entities you associate with the parent mesh are called child entities. The actions of the children entities are always relative to those of the parent entity. Using a scene hierarchy, you can create complex sets of entities, such as those that might show an automobile with spinning tires and doors that open and close.

Given that you have the ability to add many entities to a world and to create hierarchies of entities, you can then proceed to associate entities and entity hierarchies with events and controls. In the event model applied to the entities in this chapter, the result is that you create an application in which a walking figure chases a ball. As an added feature, you created a stage on which the walking entity and the ball could move around.

After setting up the entities, you program the entities to process events and then interact with them according to a limited event model. The event model allows you to click a button that randomly repositions the ball. The event model allows the walking entity to interact with the ball because whenever it reaches the ball, it comes to a stop and stoops as though its about to pick up the ball.

To bring the event models to life, you apply events and controls to entities according to the contexts your event model generates for you. In this chapter, you ended up with a world that allows you to associate an entity with a ball. You move the ball around a stage and then have the entity pursue it. This marks a simple beginning but one that is well worth having in hand.

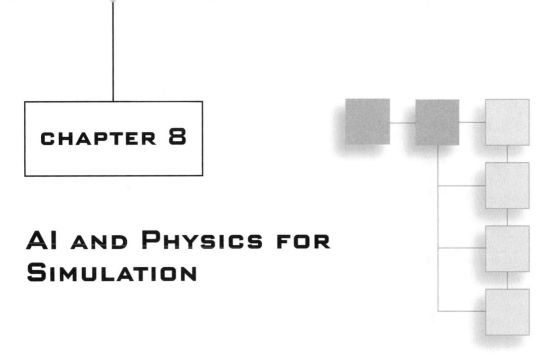

CHAPTER 8

AI AND PHYSICS FOR SIMULATION

I n this chapter, you add to the framework created in previous chapters in two significant ways. First, you make use of the functionality of the Open Dynamics Engine (ODE). You can acquire the ODE free of charge from its website and incorporate it into your project with a few simple `include` operations. All of this work has been done for you in this chapter, so you are ready to begin using it right off. The engine provides you with functions that allow you to simulate gravity and detect collisions between entities, among other things. After adding ODE functions, you add controls to your application so that you can interact with your entities in many ways. Given the inclusion of the ODE functions and controls, you enhance the capacity of your application to deliver simulation effects that mimic such physical properties as gravity and torque. In addition to the ODE and controls, you implement functionality that allows you to add intelligence to your application and, in the end, create a simple but absorbing game that might be described as a 3D version of *Pong*. Here are some of the core topics of this chapter:

- Understanding event models and artificial intelligence
- Adding physical properties to entities
- Setting up collision detection
- Creating complex interactions using events and controls
- Setting up a simple game scenario
- Refining the game scenario using complex event mapping

Thinking and Acting

So far, the book has built on the themes of events, entities, controls, and the world. Now it is time to go back and look at ways to make events more interesting. A way to make events more interesting is to add artificial intelligence (AI) to them. AI allows entities to process information and respond to events in complex ways. Among the ways that an entity can process information and respond to events are the following:

- An entity can receive information from other entities. The entity uses this information to make choices about how it interacts with other entities or how it responds to information you provide as the user of the application.

- Users can provide the entity with information. The user can provide information that allows the entity to select different AI elements that respond differently to different types of information.

- Entities can provide the users of an application with events that induce them to use controls in specific ways.

- Entities can behave differently in different event contexts. An event context emerges when a given set of entities interact, possibly prompted by a message that the application user issues.

When you develop an AI, you embed rules and information in the entities and events that characterize your event model. At the same time, you transfer the event model you have created for your application to the entities, events, and controls of your game.

Basics of AI

Defined in narrow terms, artificial intelligence is a set of rules. In broader terms, however, it is a context of behavior that a computer application can capture and sustain through a set of interactions. When you investigate the implications of artificial intelligence in broader terms, a number of implications arise:

- AI can be viewed as a property that makes events interesting.

- Intelligence can consist of a mapping of events you embed in an application and that the person who interacts with the application can discover.

- You can provide information that the AI uses.

- AI can allow an entity to extract information from other entities.

- When the event is triggered, the event can unfold according to intelligence embedded in the event.

- Intelligence works at different levels. Several triggers might apply to an event mapping. Not knowing which trigger is going to fire makes event contexts more interesting.

- Intelligence implies duration and consistency. Intelligence is not usually viewed as a property of random (chaotic) activity.
- Discovering purpose in what appears to be a random set of activities reveals intelligence.
- Mapping a single entity or a set of events in different ways reveals intelligence.

You might extend the list of such observations indefinitely, and one result might be that you would find that artificial intelligence can be understood in fairly flexible terms. Ultimately, intelligence might be viewed in relativistic terms. Intelligence emerges through interaction, and machines become intelligent when those who interact with them accept the interactions they foster as intelligent.

AI Interaction Networks

An interaction network in its barest manifestation consists of a system of events you associate with an entity. You feed information into the system and see how it proceeds from event to event until it reaches some type of destination or in some way brings closure to the interactions of the system. An interaction network provides a convenient way to visualize an event model.

Analysis of intelligence usually leads to the creation of an *interaction network*. In its elaborate form, such a network can be called a *neural network*. The expression interaction network designates a similar but conceptually simpler approach to analysis of event models. An interaction network consists of two primary elements:

- **Interaction points.** An interaction is a point in the network at which one of a set of results occurs depending on the information that you feed to the interaction. An interaction can also be viewed as an event.
- **Connectors.** A connector is a way to feed information to an interaction. A connector can be viewed causatively, in which case you can view an action as leading to a given consequence. Within the phenomenological framework set forward in Chapter 2, however, a connection establishes only an association between points of interaction. One event leads to another; it does not necessarily cause what comes next.

Figure 8.1 illustrates a generic interaction network. Any set of interactions that define a set of connectors can be viewed as a context of events (or event context). If you follow the pathway of connectors that link a set of interactions, you trace an event scenario.

Later in this chapter, this type of network provides a way to visualize the event model behind an elementary game that involves dropping a block onto a ground entity so that it rebounds and strikes a target entity. Interaction networks provide a way to show relationships between entities and to explore the event pathways that characterize different event mappings.

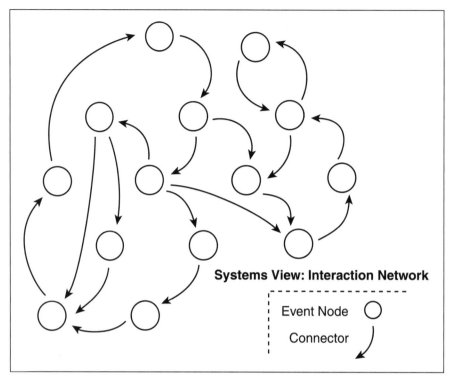

Figure 8.1 An interaction network allows you to establish associations between events.

Mapping Events Using AI

When you map events using AI, the complexity of what you accomplish depends on the events you seek to map. Mapping complex events requires complex intelligence. Here are a few items that increase the complexity of events:

- AI equips events so they have extended logics.
- Controls guide users to different applications of intelligence.
- Consoles offer users a way to input data.
- AI uses information to reach different event maps.
- AI allows you to understand an event model.
- Users can introduce intelligence through their interactions.
- Intelligence manifests itself in the interactions of entities.
- An interaction context can induce intelligence to emerge through different event mappings.

AI Event Contexts and Physics

It is important to keep in mind that events differ according to the objectives your event model establishes. Events can ostensibly map to the "realistic" physical properties of entities and how they behave within this relatively narrow definition of reality. However, while realistic physical events comprise an important, if not essential, aspect of the way entities interact, it remains that psychological and aesthetic extensions you add to realistic simulations of events can create experiences that participants in a simulation find much more valuable than those that strict realism fosters. In light of this observation, physics can become a means to an end.

Table 8.1 provides a short summary list of the some of the types of events that might accompany physical events to make them more interesting to those who interact with them.

This chapter focuses heavily on simulating a few realistic physical events. Physical events as applied here relate primarily to the physical properties explored in the study of classical physics, but it remains important to consider that artificial intelligence has to do with a large number of cognitive areas that do not easily reduce to such properties. Figure 8.2 illustrates how a simple collision can be extended to make its significance in experience emerge in a number of different ways. Some of the pathways of understanding that a person participating in an event might follow are named and described in Table 8.1.

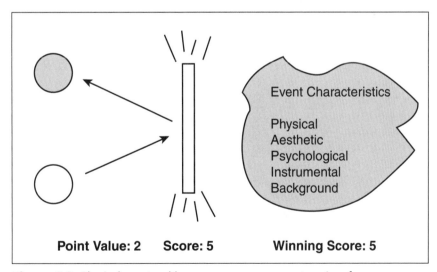

Figure 8.2 Physical events address one among many categories of understanding.

Table 8.1 Types of Events

Event Type	Description
Physical	Most physical events you represent in a simulation fall into the categories of physics that Isaac Newton set up. Such events deal with mass, force, and acceleration. You create such events by processing the information you feed to or extract from an entity's properties to make it move or interact with other entities according to the stipulations of Newton's law ($F = ma$).
Aesthetic	"Aesthetic" is an extremely broad term, but it suffices to cover the large set of visual, audio, and other qualities you can apply to an entity or group of entities to mark interactions. When you create a game that shows a ball colliding with a paddle, you can show the collision and apply the physical laws that govern the behavior of the ball and paddle after the collision. This provides an accurate but bland rendering of the physical event. On the other hand, you can also add sound and color effects to the physical event. You can hear a rapport from the collision, and you can see the ball paddle change color. This adds to the complexity and interest of the event.
Psychological	You might refer to this type of event as phenomenological, for it encompasses, generally, how viewers of an event understand an event. When you introduce psychological events, you provide the players of a game with information that allows them to interpret the event. When a ball strikes a paddle and rebounds, this is a physical event. If the ball changes colors, you have added an aesthetic dimension. If you add a score board to the interaction of the ball and paddle, you create a context in which the collision suddenly has psychological significance.
Instrumental	If you provide a way that the user can change the significance of a collision of the ball with the surface, you provide the user with a way to find the game more interesting. Interaction, as a general rule, enhances the interest of a simulated event. It changes the event from something characterized by observation to something characterized by *participation*.
Background	Event modeling allows you to create a background context for events. Background contexts almost always consist of a set of events that combine to create a synthetic effect. For example, if the ball and paddle change color, and the player can trigger a "shot" and set the significance of a "hit," then the background becomes a challenge accented by both rewards and wagers. If a "score" and a signal of "game over" appear to show the general context of the simulation, then the player finds a general and purposive context in which to pursue the activities the game offers. Likewise, visual images of a ball and paddle that change color as points accumulate add to the emotional intensity of the background.

Adding Physics

Access Listing08_01 and compile the project. Figure 8.3 illustrates the results. What you see is a collection of graphical primitives that the program generates above the world origin and that fall along the y axis at a rate determined by the force of gravity you apply to them. Initially, the force of gravity is roughly 9.8 units per second squared. You can control the gravity using the slider at the upper left of the console. As you move the slider to the right, the balls move faster because you increase the force of gravity you apply to them. Another way to say this is that you increase the acceleration of the objects.

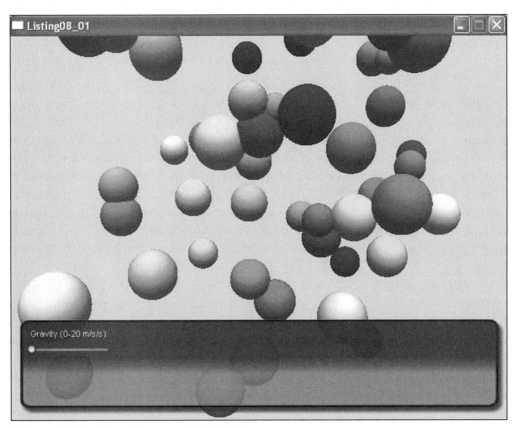

Figure 8.3 Apply gravity to graphical primitives.

To create the behavior of the balls you see in Figure 8.3, you use objects and functions from the Open Dynamic Engine (ODE) physics library. These objects and functions allow you to add simulated physical properties (*physics*) to the entities in your application's world. When you add physics to your application's world, properties you create in the world in which the entities exist begin to control the entities. After you have created these properties, you can then change the values you apply to them, and in this way, you can make your entities behave in a wide variety of ways.

To make it so that the ODE objects interact with the entities in your application, you add them to your entities and then use the interface they provide to pass information to them about your entities. The ODE objects then perform calculations using this information. The ODE objects perform calculations relative to the movement of your entities and at a rate that corresponds to the framerate you have set for your application. As the ODE objects perform these calculations, they pass the resulting information back to you, and you can put this to work in any number of ways to achieve different physical effects. The information most useful to you relates to the physical properties of *force, velocity, mass, acceleration, position,* and *rotation*. In the course of this chapter, each of these properties receives attention.

To implement the code for the ODE objects and functions that create the effects you see in Figure 8.1, you modify the code for the CEntity and CWorld classes. Changes to these two classes involve ODE world and space objects. You add ODE *world* and *space* objects to the CWorld class as class attributes. An ODE world object tracks the position and rotation properties of entities in your world. An ODE space object tracks collisions between entities. To track such collisions, ODE objects and functions use geometric information relating to the sizes, masses, and shapes of entities. Figure 8.4 shows you the general areas of responsibility of ODE world and space objects. The current section covers only the ODE world object. In the next section, you can find discussion of the ODE space object.

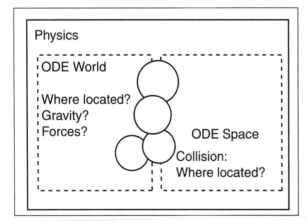

Figure 8.4 The ODE world and physics locate and control objects.

Adding ODE to the World

To add the ODE library to your application, first you add an include directive to the declaration of the CWorld class (in CWorld.h). Here is the include statement:

#include <ode/ode.h>

The path you see for the include statement directs you to the main directory for the ODE library. If you look at the directory for the ODE library, you see a large number of header files, but for most of the operations you perform using the library, you need to include only one, the ode.h file. The reason for this is that the ode.h file supplies include statements for all the other files in the ODE directory. Figure 8.5 provides a summary view of the ODE header files with the ode.h header file in bold.

After you have established contact with the ODE library using the *include* directive for the ode.h file, you can then declare two ODE objects that prove fundamental to all of the physics operations you perform using the ODE. These are the ODE world (dWorldID) and space (dSpaceID) objects. Here are the

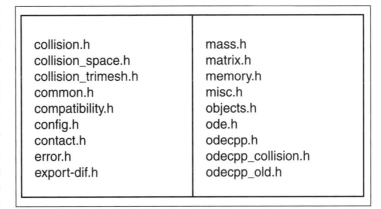

collision.h	mass.h
collision_space.h	matrix.h
collision_trimesh.h	memory.h
common.h	misc.h
compatibility.h	objects.h
config.h	ode.h
contact.h	odecpp.h
error.h	odecpp_collision.h
export-dif.h	odecpp_old.h

Figure 8.5 Include the ode.h header file to access the ODE library.

lines that declare the identifiers for these objects. You can find the lines in CWorld.h:

```
// Fundamental ODE objects
dWorldID m_dWorld;
dSpaceID m_dSpace;
```

As you can see in Figure 8.1, these two objects allow you to engage in two general types of activity. The dWorldID object allows you to obtain and regulate information about the properties of an entity that relate to such things as its mass and shape. The dSpaceID object allows you to obtain and regulate information about the location of your entity. In this section, the discussion concerns largely the use of the dWorldID interface, but in subsequent sections, the interface of the dSpaceID object comes extensively into play.

note

When you access the ODE library using the #include statement, all of the functions in the ODE library become available to you on a global basis. Because of this, you are free to call them at any point in your application code.

Given the declaration of dWorldID and dSpaceID identifiers, your next task is to access instances of these objects that you can use to reach the interfaces they provide. To accomplish this, you obtain pointers to the objects. To make obtaining pointers safe and convenient, you can add two accessor functions to CWorld, GetWorldID() and GetSpaceID(). Here's the code for the two functions as shown in CWorld.cpp:

```
dWorldID CWorld::GetWorldID()
{
    return m_dWorld;
}
dSpaceID CWorld::GetSpaceID()
{
    return m_dSpace;
}
```

Having declared identifiers for and created ways to access the dWorldID and dSpaceID objects, you are then ready to create instances of the objects. The ODE library provides you with constructor functions that allow you to achieve this objective. The CWorld constructor provides a convenient location in which to call these functions. Here are the lines from CWorld.cpp that show how you can call them:

```
CWorld::CWorld()
{
    // Initialize ODE
    m_dWorld = dWorldCreate();
    m_dSpace = dHashSpaceCreate(NULL);
    SetGravity(9.8);
}
```

You obtain access to the dWorldCreate() and dHashSpaceCreate() functions when you include ode.h. In both instances, the functions return pointers to the CWorld attributes for dWorldID and dSpaceID objects.

In addition to the two ODE constructor functions, the CWorld constructor calls SetGravity(). This function is a member of the CWorld class and, as the name implies, sets the force of gravity that applies to your world. In this instance, you see that it is set to 9.8, which simulates the gravity of Earth.

The SetGravity() function implemented in CWorld wraps a global function you obtain from the ODE library. The function you obtain from ODE is the dWorldSetGravity() function. Here is the code for the SetGravity() function from CWorld.h:

```
void CWorld::SetGravity(float fGravity)
{
    dWorldSetGravity(m_dWorld, 0, -fGravity, 0 );
}
```

The dWorldSetGravity() function requires four values. The first value is the ODE world object (m_dWorld). The second through the fourth parameters work together to represent a vector for the force of gravity. The second parameter represents the force of gravity in the x direction. The third parameter represents the force of gravity in the y direction. The fourth parameter represents the force of gravity in the z direction.

Along with adding the SetGravity() function, you make changes to the CWorld::Update() function to accommodate the use of an ODE object in your world. The change involves one line in the CWorld::Update() function. Here's the code from CWorld.cpp:

```
void CWorld::Update(float fTimeElapsed,IDirect3DDevice9 *pDevice)
{
    //Affiliated changes in the ODE and CWorld objects
    dWorldQuickStep(GetWorldID(), fTimeElapsed);
```

The ODE dWorldQuickStep() function goes through the ODE world and applies the physics of all the objects you have identified in it. To accomplish this feat, the dWorldQuickStep() function has two parameters. The first is a pointer to the ODE world, which you retrieve using the GetWorldID() function. The second is the amount of time that has elapsed since the last update (fTimeElapsed), which provides a convenient approach to updating entities independently of the framerate.

Adding ODE to the Entities

Just as you add ODE dSpaceID and dWorldID objects to your world to track the properties of your world, you add ODE dBodyID and dGeomID objects to individual entities to track their properties. The objects allow you to associate an ODE body and its accompanying geometry with each entity in your application. To accomplish this, you begin by adding two ODE attributes to CEntity. Here's the code from CEntity.h:

```
// The ID for the rigid body which represents
// this entity
dBodyID m_dBodyID;
// The geometry ID for this body
dGeomID m_dGeomID;
```

The m_dBodyID attribute allows you to represent a rigid body entity in your ODE world. For the purposes of this application, a rigid body entity is an object that is affected by the physics of the world (gravity). The m_dGeomID attribute allows you to describe the shape of the entities in your world. In both instances, you must set these values for each entity. You then use ODE functions to access the values of these attributes to retrieve position and rotation information about your entity.

After declaring dBodyID an dGeomID identifiers, you make a few changes to the constructor of the CEntity class to associate a world with your entity. Here are the changes to the CEntity constructor:

```
CEntity::CEntity(wstring strName)
{
    //lines left out . . .
    // Create an ODE body ID for this entity
    m_dBodyID = dBodyCreate(GetWorld()->GetWorldID());
```

The dBodyCreate() function is another global function you obtain from the ODE library. It associates the entity with the ODE world you have created. Given this association, the world knows the position and rotation of the entity.

Setting Up Geometry

After you have associated an entity with the ODE world, you then set up the geometry that describes the entity. To accomplish this, you make changes to the CEntity::CreateSphere() function. This function is a member of the CEntity class. The CreateSphere() function creates primitive graphical spheres such as those you see in Figure 8.2. The lines of the function that create spheres received attention in Chapter 7, "Creating a World," so the current discussion leaves these aside. Instead, the business of importance now concerns the ODE dCreateSphere() function. This function is a global function you obtain when you include ode.h. Its purpose, as the name implies, is to map the geometric properties of a sphere. Here is the call to the function as it appears in the CEntity::CreateSphere() function, which you can view in its entirety in CEntity.cpp:

```
void CEntity::CreateSphere(float fRadius, DWORD dwColor,
                           IDirect3DDevice9 *pDevice)
{
       //lines left out . . .
       // Create the information for ODE to use
       m_dGeomID = dCreateSphere(GetWorld()->GetSpaceID(), fRadius);
       dGeomSetBody(m_dGeomID, m_dBodyID);
}
```

The CreateSphere() function takes three parameters, as you might recall from previous discussions. The first is the radius of the sphere you want to create. The second is a value you use to determine the color of the sphere. The last is a pointer to the IDirect3DDevice9 device that you declare in CGraphics.h.

The ODE dCreateSphere() function takes two arguments. The first argument is a pointer of the dSpaceID type that you obtain when you declare the dSpaceID object in the CWorld class. The second parameter is taken from the parameter list of CreateSphere(). This is the radius of the sphere (fRadius).

The call to the dCreateSphere() function returns a dGeomID pointer, which you make use of on the next line when you call the dGeomSetBody() function. This function associates the geometry of the entity with the body (m_dBodyID) of the entity. Associating the geometry and the body is analogous to associating space and world: body takes care of the physical properties of the entity, while geometry takes care of its location.

Updating for Physics

To equip your entities to behave like physical objects, you make a few changes to the CEntity::Update() function. The changes allow you to retrieve information from the ODE engine that allows you to update the entity in accordance with the physical properties you assign to it. For example, the physics engine provides you with information about a given entity that takes into consideration such things as the mass and force you have applied to it. After the entity possesses a given mass, it accelerates according to the force that you apply to it.

Figure 8.6 provides a short review of the physics of this type of interaction. The same force acts on two balls in different ways because the balls possess different masses. Given the application of the same forces and the same amounts of friction, the ball with the greater mass (A) moves only a short distance, while the ball with less mass (B) moves farther.

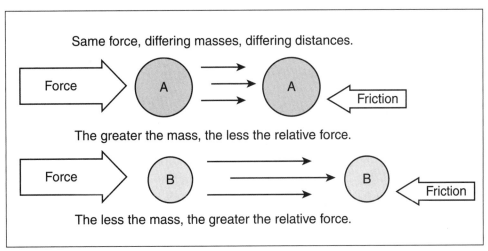

Figure 8.6 Isaac Newton established that force and mass are related to each other.

To set up the updating operations for the physics of an entity, you first obtain pointers to the position and rotation of the entity. You obtain this information from arrays that the ODE geometry object (dGeomID) provides. To access this information, you make calls to the ODE dGeomGetPosition() and dGeomGetRotation() functions:

```
void CEntity::Update(float fTimeElapsed, IDirect3DDevice9 *pDevice)
{
        //lines left out
        // Get the position and rotation from ODE
        const dReal *fPos = dGeomGetPosition(m_dGeomID);
        const dReal *fRot = dGeomGetRotation(m_dGeomID);
```

As the name implies, the dGeomGetPosition() function returns the position of the entity, which is in the form of an array containing the x, y, and z coordinates of the entity. The arrays are of the type dReal, which is a data type the ODE provides that designates floating point values. To make it possible for the function to return the position, you pass the function a pointer to the dGeomID object. To obtain the rotation of the entity, you use a call to the ODE dGeomGetRotation() function. As with the dGeomGetPosition() function, you supply the dGeomGetRotation() function with a pointer to the dGeomID object. In both cases, the functions return pointers to arrays (fPos, fRot).

The two arrays (fPos and fRot) allow you to create two matrices, for position and rotation. To use the values from the arrays to create Direct3D matrices, however, you must convert them to the Direct3D format. Here is the code from CEntity::Update() that attends to this chore:

```
// Matrices for transformation
D3DXMATRIX matWorld, matTrans, matRot
// Convert the rotation matrix from ODE format to DirectX format
D3DXMatrixIdentity(&matRot);
matRot._11 = fRot[0];
matRot._12 = fRot[4];
matRot._13 = fRot[8];
matRot._14 = 0;

matRot._21 = fRot[1];
matRot._22 = fRot[5];
matRot._23 = fRot[9];
matRot._24 = 0;

matRot._31 = fRot[2];
matRot._32 = fRot[6];
matRot._33 = fRot[10];
matRot._34 = 0;
```

Following the declaration of three local D3DXMATRIX matrices that you use to scale and transform the entity, the first function call is to the D3DXMatrixIdentity() function, which initializes the D3DXMATRIX matrix that tracks rotation. After you initialize the rotation matrix, you then make use of the values from the dReal matrix to populate it.

Populating the D3DXMATRIX matrix involves assigning the values for the fRot matrix to the matRot matrix. The indexes used by the D3DXMATRIX matrix allow you to access the rows and columns of the matrix with single elements. For example, _11 represents row 1 and column 1 (hence, 11). As for the zeros you assign to the fourth elements of each of the D3DXMATRIX matrices, you do this as a precautionary measure to eliminate bogus values.

After you populate the D3DXMATRIX matrix, you translate its values based on the x, y, and z positions of the entity stored in the fPos array. Here is the code for CEntity::Update() that takes care of this:

```
// Generate the translation and scaling matrices
   D3DXMatrixTranslation(&matTrans, fPos[0], fPos[1], fPos[2]);
   D3DXMatrixScaling(&matScale, m_vecScale.x,
                                m_vecScale.y,
                                m_vecScale.z);
```

Note that the first parameter of the D3DXMatrixTranslation() function uses a reference to the D3DXMATRIX matrix you declared locally, as does the D3DMatrixScaling() function. For its second, third, and fourth parameters, the D3DXMatrixTranslation() function uses values from the dReal matrix you created previously to set the position of the entity (fPos[0], fPos[1], fPos[2]). These values designate the origin of the entity. With the D3DMatrixScaling() function, the final three parameters represent the size of the entity after you transform it. To set the values for the scaling, you use the elements of the D3DXMATRIX you declared earlier.

Assigning Events to Entities

Before you can transform entities, you must attend to their creation, and after you have created entities, you must be able to destroy them. These are two events that characterize the life of every entity. On the other hand, to refer again to Figure 8.3, the entities you see are primitive—spheres that appear to fall across space. To make it possible for the spheres to behave this way, you associate them with a physical event that is characterized by the application of force. Another such event, dealt with later in this chapter, occurs when the spheres collide with each other. The laws of physics governing these events allow you to regulate the motion of entities through space and how they behave when they collide with each other. Other changes, such as those dealing with color and size, can be related to physical events to make them more interesting to observe as you interact with them.

Initialization of the Event

To create and destroy entities, you add code to the CMyApplication class. For the event cycle you see illustrated in Figure 8.3, the spheres come into existence at a point that is just above the origin of the world space. The spheres emerge to view at a constant rate and then "fall" in the direction that gravity exerts on them. You can change this direction by using the mouse button. Figure 8.7 illustrates the event sequence.

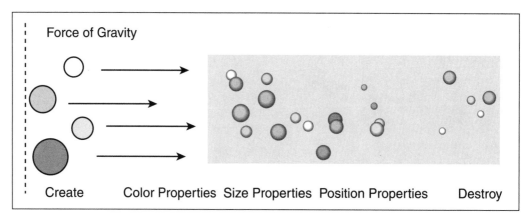

Figure 8.7 Spheres emerge and then fall with gravity.

To cause the spheres to appear to your view and then fall in the direction their gravity dictates, you set up a periodic event. The periodic event creates spheres at a constant rate. As the event creates the spheres, it assigns them gravity, color, position, and size. This activity has its beginning in the CMyApplication::Initialize() function, where you call the CEvent constructor. The name of the event is "CREATE". Here is the code from CMyApplication.cpp that shows the creation of the event:

```
void CMyApplication::Initialize()
{
//lines left out
    // Set up an event to create balls every .1 seconds
    CEvent *pCreateEvent = new CEvent(L"CREATE", TIME_PERIOD, 0.1,
                                TIME_RELATIVE, CEvent::TIME_NEVER);
    AddEvent(pCreateEvent);
```

The parameters you assign to the event constructor first name the event ("CREATE") and then designate an enumerated value (TIME_PERIOD) to specify that the event should be periodic. The third parameter (0.1) sets the event to occur every tenth of a second. The fourth parameter establishes the expiration schedule of the event, and in this case, you supply the enumerated value of TIME_RELATIVE. It remains, however, that since this event never expires, the expiration schedule receives no use. The value, then, appears only as a place holder. The final parameter value (CEvent::TIME_NEVER) specifies that the event repeats for the life of the application. The constructor returns a pointer to the CEvent object, which you assign to pCreateEvent. Following the call to the CEvent constructor, you call the AddEvent() function to add the newly created event to the event list of the application. The pointer the CEvent constructor returns serves as the sole parameter of the AddEvent() function.

Handling the Created Event

To handle the event you have created, you add code to the CMyApplication::OnEvent() function. Handling the event involves creating spheres with random colors, radii, and positions, as Figure 8.7 illustrates. Here is the code from the CMyApplication::OnEvent() function in CMyApplication.cpp that accomplishes this work:

```
void CMyApplication::OnEvent(CEvent *pEvent)
{
    wstring strName = pEvent->GetName();
    if(strName == L"CREATE")
    {
        // Create a new ball entity with random radius and position
        float fRadius = (((float)rand()/RAND_MAX) * 0.2) + 0.2;
        float fRandomX = ((float)rand()/RAND_MAX - 0.5) * 5;
        float fRandomY = ((float)rand()/RAND_MAX + 5);
        float fRandomZ = ((float)rand()/RAND_MAX - 0.5)*5;
        DWORD dwColor = D3DCOLOR_XRGB(rand()%255,
                                     rand()%255,
                                     rand()%255);
```

After the opening brace of the OnEvent() function, first you use the pointer you have passed to OnEvent() to call the CEvent::GetName() function, which retrieves the name of the event you want to process. This you store in the strName identifier. Next, given that the selection statement selects the CREATE event, you create values to use for the radius, position, and color values of the sphere.

To create the value to be used for the radius, you use the C library rand() function to generate a random number that you divide by the RAND_MAX constant (again from the C library). You then adjust the value by multiplying it by 0.2 to ensure that the size of the sphere is greater than or equal to 0.2. You use a similar approach to generate values to use for the x, y, and z variables that position the sphere.

Given that you have defined the values to be used for the radius and the position, you then create a value to be used to set the color of the sphere. To accomplish this, you use the C library rand() function along with the modulus operator to randomly generate three numbers between zero and 255 (representing red, green, and blue).

Having attended to the creation of values for the size and color of the sphere, you can then proceed to create the sphere itself and to position it in your world. To accomplish this, you add a few more lines to the CMyApplication::OnEvent() function in CMyApplication.cpp. The primary focus of this activity involves a call to the CWorld::CreateEntity() function, followed by a call to the SetPos() function. To illustrate this activity, here's another sampling of the code from the CMyApplication::OnEvent() function:

```
// Create the ball and set its position
CEntity *pBall = GetWorld()->CreateEntity(L"BALL",
                                    fRadius, dwColor,
                                    m_pGraphics->GetDevice());
pBall->SetPos(D3DXVECTOR3(fRandomX, fRandomY, fRandomZ));
```

To create the entity, you call to the CreateEntity() function, which returns a reference to a CEntity pointer identifier (*pBall). Following this call, you then use the SetPos() function to position the entity. The SetPos() function takes a single parameter, a D3DXVECTOR3 vector, which receives the three random values you created above.

Scheduling Events

Given that you have created the entity, you want to allow it to exist for only a given amount of time (in this case five seconds). To accomplish this, you create another event using a call to the CEvent constructor. In this case, as the first parameter of the constructor shows, a good name for the event is "DESTROY". The life of the event falls under the TIME_RELATIVE rubric, which means that the duration of the event's life is relative to its beginning. As the final parameter of the CEvent constructor shows, the event fires five seconds (5) after you create it. Here are the lines that accomplish this work in the Initialize() function:

```
    // Now create an event to destroy this ball in 5 seconds
    CEvent *pDestroy = new CEvent(L"DESTROY", TIME_RELATIVE, 5);
    pDestroy->AddPointerParam(pBall);
    AddEvent(pDestroy);
}//end of selection for CREATE
```

After the call to the CEvent constructor, you call the AddPointerParam() function to identify the entity that needs to be destroyed when the event fires. You then call AddEvent() to place the event in the application event list.

Handling the Destroy Event

After you create events, you must destroy them. To destroy events, you add a few lines of code to the CMyApplication::OnEvent() function. The lines of code you add implement a selection statement for the DESTROY event. Here is the code:

```
else if(strName == L"DESTROY")
{
    // Get a pointer to the entity to remove
    CEntity *pEntity = (CEntity *)pEvent->GetPointerParams()[0];
    GetWorld()->RemoveEntity(pEntity);
}//end of selection for DESTROY
```

After the opening brace of the selection statement, you use a pointer to the entity to call the GetPointerParams() function, which retrieves a vector that contains the entities in the entity's destroy entity list. In this case, the entity you seek falls in the 0 index position. You assign a reference to this entity to a CEntity pointer (*pEntity), which you cast first to restore its integrity. You then call the CWorld::RemoveEntity() function to remove the entity from the world.

Adding Intelligence and Gravity

Given that you have associated physical properties with entities and events, you can now proceed to create ways that you can interact with the entities to make them respond to messages that you send to them. One way to interact with entities involves creating a slider that allows you to change the rate at which the spheres you see in Figure 8.3 fall. You can make them fall faster or slower according to the value you set for the gravity that applies to them.

Using the slider, combined with the functions from the ODE, allows you to create a context in which a dynamic of interaction emerges, and you become conscious, in the process, that you are dealing with intelligence. The intelligence encompasses what you see, the laws that apply to what you see, and your use of the slider to regulate events. Figure 8.8 illustrates the dynamic at work.

Supplementing AI with Controls

Extending the dynamic of interaction that exists between the spheres, the gravity applied to them, and how you control the simulation involves creating a slider for the application panel. The slider enables you to vary the gravity of the world, which in turns affects the spheres as they fall. You also create a label to identify the slider. To create the label for the slider, you use the CDXUTDialog::AddStatic() function. To create the slider

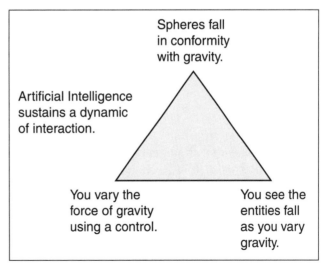

Figure 8.8 Artificial intelligence sustains a context of interaction.

itself, you use the CDXUTDialog::AddSlider() function. You accomplish this work in the InitGUI() function of CMyApplication. Here is the code for the function as it appears in CMyApplication.cpp:

```
void CMyApplication::InitGUI()
{

//lines left out
    // Create a gravity slider
    m_GUI.AddStatic(IDC_STATIC,
                        L"Gravity (0-20 m/s/s):",
                        25,m_iConsoleY+10,100,20);
    m_GUI.AddSlider(IDC_GRAVITY, 25,
                        m_iConsoleY + 30, 100, 20, 0, 200, 98);
}
```

Adding Control Event Handlers

Having created the label and the slider to guide your interactions with the spheres and the gravity applied to them, you create a handler for the message that the slider issues. To accomplish this, you make a few changes to the CMyApplication::OnGUIEvent() function. Here is the code:

```
void CMyApplication::OnGUIEvent(UINT nEvent,
                                int nControlID, CDXUTControl *pControl)
{
    // Allow the user to control the level of gravity
    if(nControlID == IDC_GRAVITY)
    {
        CDXUTSlider *pSlider = (CDXUTSlider *)pControl;
        float fGravity = (float)pSlider->GetValue()/10;
        GetWorld()->SetGravity(fGravity);
    }
}
```

In the first line after the opening brace of the condition, the if selection statement tests whether the nControlID value contains a value that equals the IDC_GRAVITY constant. If this is true, then you use the OnGUIEvent() pControl parameter to obtain a reference to the slider object. You assign this reference to a CDXUTSlider pointer identifier (pSlider). You then use the pSlider pointer to call the CDXUTSlider::GetValue() function, which returns the integer value for gravity that the slider issues as you adjust it. You cast this value to a float and divide by ten to translate the integer value to a floating decimal range that lies between 0 and 20. (The original range extends from 0 to 200.) You assign the resulting value to fGravity. Using the value stored in fGravity, you then set the CWorld gravity attribute using the CWorld::SetGravity() function. At this point, the gravity that governs the fall of the object accords with the value you have issued from the slider.

Adding Collision Detection

Probably one of the biggest events in game history falls under the heading of collision detection. The primary set of events characterizing collision detection involves setting an object into motion and placing another object in its path. If the first object strikes the second, a collision occurs. When the collision occurs, you detect it by discovering whether the space occupied by the first object encroaches on the space occupied by the second object. Figure 8.9 illustrates the elements at work in collision detection.

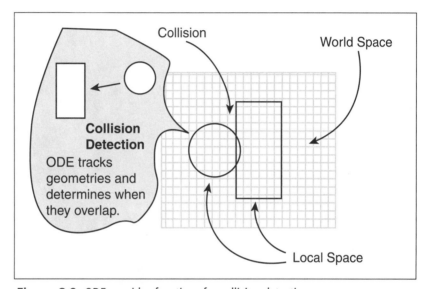

Figure 8.9   ODE provides functions for collision detection.

You can effectively implement collision detection for graphical primitives by using the functions the ODE provides. When ODE performs collision detection, it uses the space and world properties you have already introduced to your application. To set up the ODE functions for collision detection, you attend to four rudimentary chores:

1. Add a callback function to check for collision between two entities when their geometries overlap.

2. Register the callback function with ODE and allow it to process all collisions.

3. Update the positions of entities based on the collisions that occur.

4. Remove collisions after each iteration of the scene.

Given these preliminaries, if you open Listing08_02 and compile the solution file, Figure 8.10 shows you the result. If you press the left mouse button and pull the rectangular entity down a little, you can re-create the scene you see in Figure 8.10. You use the slider, as before, to set the gravity of the world in which the spheres exist. The spheres fall to the rectangular surface and strike other spheres. When struck, the target spheres roll away from the point of impact. The point of impact marks a point of collision. The ODE functions detect this collision.

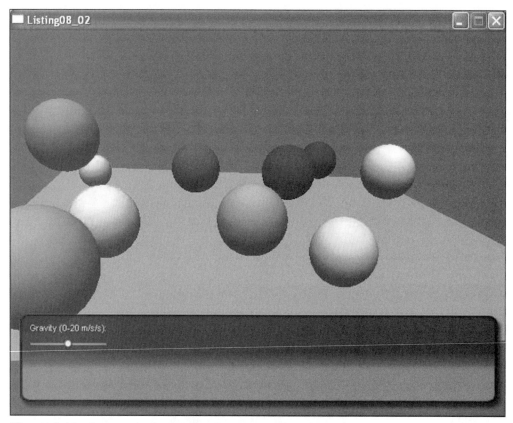

Figure 8.10 The ODE provides functions for collision detection.

NearCallback

As Figure 8.10 shows, when entities encroach on each other's space, a collision occurs. To detect collisions, you implement the NearCallback() function. The NearCallback() function is static and global, and you place its definition in CWorld.cpp. The NearCallback() function has two parameters. The first, a pointer to a void data type, can be used to pass in any type of data you might find useful as an extension of your collision detection activities. This parameter remains unused in this context. The second and third parameters represent the two objects between which you want to detect collision. These are dGeomID objects. As you recall, dGeomID is an ODE data type used to identify the geometry of an entity, and the geometry of an entity is essentially its shape. Here are the first few lines of NearCallback() as they appear in CWorld.cpp:

```
static void NearCallback (void *data, dGeomID o1, dGeomID o2)
{
    int itr;
    // exit without doing anything if the two
      //bodies are connected by a joint
    dBodyID b1 = dGeomGetBody(o1);
    dBodyID b2 = dGeomGetBody(o2);
      if (b1 && b2 && dAreConnectedExcluding(b1, b2, dJointTypeContact) )
          return;
```

After the opening brace of the NearCallback() function, you declare an integer identifier (itr) to use as an iterator. Following the declaration of the iterator, you use the dGeomID objects passed to NearCallback() to create two local dBodyID objects. The dGeomID objects represent shapes. The dBodyID objects represent other properties, such as velocity, torque, mass, and force.

Next, you attend to eliminating detection activity for unwanted joints. (A joint is basically any way that you join two objects.) To accomplish this, you create an if selection statement to determine whether common joints connect the objects you are dealing with. In the first part of the condition, you use the Boolean AND operator with b1 and b2 to check that both bodies exist. Then you use the ODE dAreConnectedExcluding() function to check if the two common joints connect the two bodies.

When you use the ODE dAreConnectedExcluding() function, you provide the two dBodyID objects for the first two parameters. (The order does not matter.) In the third parameter slot you insert an enumerated value you obtain from the ODE, dJointTypeContact. This value designates the type of joint you want to detect. In this case, you want to detect joints common to two bodies. You want to ignore all such joints. For example, if you have a table top, you want to ignore any common joints ("collisions") between the table top and the legs. The if statement checks for such joints and excludes them (using the return keyword action) from further processing.

Characterizing Collisions

To continue the discussion of NearCallback(), after you have eliminated common joints, you declare an array (contact) of the ODE dContact type to store information about collisions between objects. When you create the contact array, you set the size of the array using CWorld::MAX_CONTACTS. This establishes the maximum number of contacts you want to allow between two objects. The maximum depends on how much realism you want to strive for. An extremely high number would be 1000. In the current context, the demand is fairly minimal, so you set the maximum at 4. Here is the line that declares the contact array:

```
dContact contact[CWorld::MAX_CONTACTS];
```

After you set the maximum number of contacts, you then use a for loop to set up default properties for each of the collisions the array stores. The dContact data type provides several properties you use to characterize collisions. Here's the code for the for loop showing the properties:

```
for (itr=0; itr < CWorld::MAX_CONTACTS; itr++)
{
    contact[itr].surface.mode =
        dContactBounce | dContactSoftCFM;
    contact[itr].surface.bounce = 1.5;
    contact[itr].surface.bounce_vel = 1.6;
    contact[itr].surface.soft_cfm = 0.01;
}
```

The for loop allows you to iterate through all the collisions in the contact array and set their properties individually. One of the most important details to attend to involves defining the characteristics of the *surface*—how bouncy the collision is and how much energy is absorbed when two entities collide. You set this property using the surface.bounce element.

The ODE allows you to define surface characteristics extensively. To see the full list of the properties you can set, visit the ODE documentation site at http://ode.org/ode-latest-userguide.html. The following list provides details on the properties you see addressed by the code in NearCallback():

- **surface.mode**   If set, the bodies possess elastic qualities and so bounce off each other. You set this value using a flag, such as dContactBounce and dContactSoftCFM. The dContactBounce flag controls the amount of bounce. With the dContactSoftCFM flag, CFM refers to "constant force mixing," and the effect of the flag is to soften the surface.
- **surface.bounce**   This is a dReal type. Zero (0) means that the surface is not bouncy at all. If set to 1, then the surface bounciness is at its maximum.
- **surface.bounce_vel**   This is a dReal data type, and it designates the minimum incoming velocity necessary for bounce (in m/s). Incoming objects below this velocity effectively have a bounce parameter of 0, which means that they do not bounce. You use this value if the corresponding flag in the mode element is set to dContactBounce.
- **surface.soft**   If you have set the surface characteristics for bounciness, you can use the soft_cfm parameter to make the surface soft. This parameter controls the elasticity of the surface, so an object bouncing off it will bounce so that either more or less of its energy is absorbed.

Processing Collisions

After setting the parameters for the surfaces, your work in the NearCallback() function comes to an end with the actual detection of the collisions that apply to your objects. To reach this end, you first iterate through the contacts and identify the collisions that occur between them. To accomplish this, you set up a for loop that calls the ODE dCollide() function. Here is the code for the for loop:

```
if (int numc = dCollide(o1, o2, CWorld::MAX_CONTACTS,
                                &contact[0].geom,
                                sizeof(dContact)))
{
    for (itr=0; itr<numc; itr++)
    {
        dJointID jcon = dJointCreateContact(
                            GetWorld()->GetWorldID(),
                    GetWorld()->GetJointGroupID(),
                    &contact[itr]);
        dJointAttach(jcon, b1, b2);
    }
}
```

The dCollide() function requires a fairly extensive list of parameter settings. The first two consist of the two dGeomID objects between which you want to detect collisions. The third parameter sets the number of contacts you want to investigate (CWorld::MAX_CONTACTS). In the slot for the fourth parameter, you insert a reference to the contact array (contact[0]), with an index set to zero to indicate the first element. You call the geom element of the dContact data type. This element describes the substructures that come into play during collision detection. The final parameter is the size, in bytes, of each element in the contact array. You store the number of collisions in an integer identifier, numc. If numc is greater than zero, a collision has occurred.

The if selection statement contains a for loop. The for loop goes through each collision and creates a contact joint using the ODE dJointCreateContact() function. The parameters for this function are first, a pointer to your dWorldID object, and second, the dJointGroupID object that identifies the current set of joints. To obtain the set of joints, you call CWorld::GetJointGroupID(), an accessor function. The final parameter is a reference to the current contact in the contact array. The return type for this function is dJointID, which notifies you that a collision has been detected. After the call to dJointCreateContact(), your final step is to call the ODE dJointAttach() function to associate the newly created contact joint with the dBodyID objects.

Updating for Collisions

Changes to the CWorld::Update() function allow you to calculate collisions and then, having updated the positions of the objects using the collisions, clear the collisions out. This is accomplished with two calls. Here is the code from CWorld.cpp:

```
void CWorld::Update(float fTimeElapsed, IDirect3DDevice9 *pDevice)
{
    // Process collision detection
    dSpaceCollide(GetSpaceID(), NULL, &NearCallback);
      //lines left out . . .
      // Remove the contact joints
    dJointGroupEmpty(GetJointGroupID());
}
```

The call to the ODE dSpaceCollide() function involves three parameters. The first parameter is a dSpaceID object. The CWorld::GetSpaceID() function returns the dSpaceID object declared in CWorld.h. This object tracks the size and space of bodies in the application world. The second parameter can be used to pass arbitrary data to the NearCallback() function. It is not used in this context, so you see NULL inserted. The last parameter of the dSpaceCollide() function is the address of the NearCallback() function itself. You call it by reference.

When the Update() function calls the dSpaceCollide() function, the dSpaceCollide() function calls the NearCallback() function to detect collisions between all the objects in the scene. If a collision occurs, the ODE engine regulates the movements of the affected objects to accord with the appropriate laws. Since you do not want to apply collisions twice, you call the dJointGroupEmpty() function to remove the collisions from the joint group after you have processed them.

Initializing for Collisions

When objects you create fall through space, they strike the ground plane and bounce off. To ensure that the ground plane does not move when other objects strike it, you disable its gravity. The work of disabling the ground plane's gravity involves changes to the CMyApplication::Initialize() function. Specifically, you call the CEntity::SetEnabled() function to disable the effects of the physics engine on the ground plane. Here is the code in the CMyApplication::Initialize() function that performs this work:

```
void CMyApplication::Initialize()
{
     //lines left out...
    // Prevent the ground form falling
    pGround->SetEnabled(false);
```

Note

To make the ground fall when the first ball hits it, uncomment this bit of code in CMyApplication.cpp, in the `Initialize()` function.

```
// pGround->SetEnabled(true);
```

```
// pGround->SetGravity(false);
```

Applying Mass and Force

In this section, you apply mass, force, and torque to your objects. These properties of physics add behaviors to your entities that make them appear much more realistic and allow you to work with them to simulate activities that are involved and interesting. To see what results from the addition of mass, force, and torque to entities, compile Listing8_3. Figure 8.11 illustrates what you see.

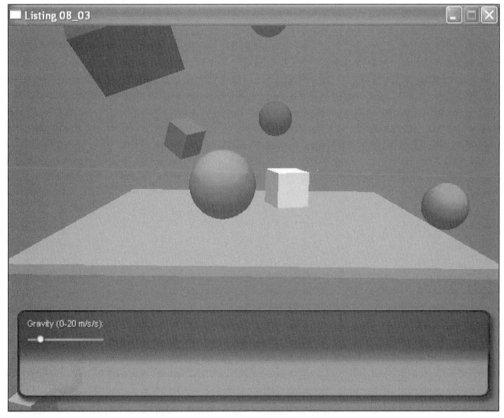

Figure 8.11 Force, mass, and torque vary the behavior of objects.

When you adjust the slider to the left, you decrease the force of gravity, so the shapes appear to strike the surface with less force and move slower as they rebound. Along the same lines, as the entities move toward and rebound from the surface, they rotate. The rotation manifests the *torque* applied to them. Torque is rotational force.

In each case—mass, force, and torque—you make use of the interface of the Open Dynamics Engine (ODE) to add physical properties to your objects. The functions the ODE interface provides regulate the motions of your entities so that they behave in accordance to the laws of physics. The difference between what you see in the real world and the world you create through simulation using the ODE rests on the values you supply to the interface. Using the ODE, for example, you can adjust the mass of any given object along an almost infinite range of values. You might set the gravity of objects to accord with the gravity of the moon. In this case, a block of fairly solid material might appear to have the consistency of Styrofoam.

Modifying CEntity

The first modification you make to implement torque involves the `CEntity` class. Your first task in this respect is to create an enumeration that identifies the shapes of entities. You use the shape of the entity to determine how to distribute its mass. When you distribute the entity's mass, you determine the characteristics of the entity in relation to how it responds to forces and collisions. For example, another entity might rebound from it in a sharp, brittle way. Or it might rebound in a bouncy way. How entities rebound from each other depends on how you distribute their masses.

To set up the entity type enumeration, you can create an enumerated data type, `ENTITY_TYPE`, and a few shape tokens. The code that accomplishes this appears in CEntity.h:

```
// Track different types of entity
enum ENTITY_TYPE{
     SPHERE,
     BOX,
     MESH
};
```

You might enumerate any number of shapes, but those common in the current application consist of a set of three:

- **SPHERE**   A sphere distributes the mass evenly from the center and toward the surface described by the radius of the sphere.
- **BOX**   A box distributes mass so that it is distributed evenly in a cube.
- **MESH**   A mesh designates an entity that has an irregular shape. The distribution of the mass for such an entity involves complex calculations. For now, a bounding sphere can be used to approximate the shape and mass of the mesh.

After enumerating the entity types, your next step is to create an object that can store mass properties. To accomplish this, you add an attribute to the CEntity class. Here are the lines in CEntity.cpp that declare the attribute:

```
// Store the mass of the body
dMass m_dMass;
```

The ODE dMass object (m_dMass) allows you to track the distribution of the mass of an entity. It also allows you to identify the center of mass of an entity and how much an entity weighs.

Following the declaration of the dMass object, you use the enumerated type, ENTITY_TYPE, to create an attribute to identify the shape of the entity (m_iType). The ENTITY_TYPE attribute allows you to conveniently identify the shape of the entity when you profile its mass. Here's the code:

```
// Type of this entity
ENTITY_TYPE m_iType;
```

As is shown in the next section, you set the values of the ENTITY_TYPE attribute with calls to the Create() and Load() functions of the CEntity class.

Following the declaration of the ENTITY_TYPE attribute, you create a D3DXVECTOR3 vector to store the values that you use to define the bounding spaces (spheres or boxes) of your entities. In this case, the space is a bounding box:

```
// Bounding box
D3DXVECTOR3 m_vecBoxSize;
```

The m_vecBoxSize vector stores the width, height, and depth of the entity's bounding space. You employ a bounding box in the same way that you use a bounding sphere. In other words, you can use it to detect collisions or to locate an entity relative to other entities in space.

Functions to Regulate Force, Torque, and Mass

Along with attributes for mass, shape, and bounding space, you add three function prototypes to the CEntity class. Here are the signature lines for the prototypes as shown in CEntity.cpp:

```
// Adds a relative force to the entity
void AddForce(D3DXVECTOR3 vecForce);
// Adds a relative torque to the entity
void AddTorque(D3DXVECTOR3 vecTorque);
// Set the mass of the entity
void SetMass(float fMass);
```

Each of these functions receives greater explanation in the sections that follow. For now, note that you use the `CEntity::AddForce()` function to apply a force to the entity. The force causes the entity to move. The more force, the higher the acceleration of the object. (Newton's equation that relates mass, force, and acceleration is $F=ma$).

The `CEntity::AddTorque()` function applies torque (rotation) about the given axis of the entity. When you apply torque, you cause an entity to spin. For instance, the cubes and spheres you see in the application (see Figure 8.11) rotate as they move. The rotation results from the way you apply torque to the body of the entity.

The `CEntity::SetMass()` function regulates the mass of the entity. Mass determines how force causes an entity to accelerate. For example, if two cubes collide, the cube with the greater mass rebounds from the collision more slowly than the cube with less mass. Acceleration indicates, generally, how much an entity resists changes in its state of motion.

Setting Mass and Type for Spheres

To change the `CEntity` class so that it can accommodate mass, force and shape type, you first focus on the `CEntity::CreateSphere()` and `CEntity::Load()` functions. A good place to begin is with the `CreateSphere()` function. Here is the code for the function from CEntity.cpp:

```
void CEntity::CreateSphere(float fRadius, DWORD dwColor,
                           IDirect3DDevice9 *pDevice)
{
    // Lines left out. . .
    m_iType = SPHERE;

    // Set a default mass of 1.0
    SetMass(1.0);
    dBodySetMass(m_dBodyID, &m_dMass);
}
```

The `CreateSphere()` function, as mentioned previously, takes three parameters. The first establishes the radius of the sphere you want to create. The second sets the color of the sphere. The last parameter identifies the `IDirect3DDevice9` device that you declare in CGraphics.h.

Following the opening brace of the `CreateSphere()` function, you set the `CEntity` attribute that identifies the entity type (`m_iType`) to `SPHERE`. You do this so that you can later retrieve the shape of the entity using the `CEntity` `ENTITY_TYPE` attribute. After setting the shape of the entity, you call `CEntity::SetMass()` with a default parameter value of `1.0` to set up the mass of the entity. Initially, all entities you see in the application have this same mass, but it is not necessary that the masses of the entities remain the same, for the mass range for entities stretches from zero to infinity, and you can change the mass you assign to entities to accord with your needs.

Having set the default mass for the entity you are to create, you call the ODE dBodySetMass() function to associate the mass with the body of the entity. The first parameter of this function is the dBodyID attribute (m_dBodyID) of CEntity. The second parameter is a reference to the dMass (m_dMass) attribute of CEntity. After you associate the mass of the entity with the dBodyID object, you then use ODE functions to calculate values you use to control the behavior of the entity.

Setting Mass and Type for Boxes

The entities you see in Figure 8.11 are spheres and cubes. You can also refer to the cubes as boxes. The CEntity::CreateBox() function produces the boxes. The procedure you use to produce the boxes resembles the one you saw at work in CEntity::CreateSphere(). Here is the code for CreateSphere() from CEntity.cpp:

```
void CEntity::CreateBox(float fWidth, float fHeight, float fDepth,
                   DWORD dwColor, IDirect3DDevice9 *pDevice)
{
     // Lines left out. . .
     // Set up the bounding box
     m_vecBoxSize = D3DXVECTOR3(fWidth, fHeight, fDepth);
     m_iType = BOX;
     // Set a default mass of 1.0
     SetMass(1.0);
     dBodySetMass(m_dBodyID, &m_dMass);
}
```

The difference between the CreateSphere() and CreateBox() functions begins with the parameter list. When you create a box, you require information for the height, width, and depth of the box (its *cubic* properties). The first three parameters supply these values. The fourth parameter provides the color of the box. The last parameter furnishes the IDirect3DDevice9 device you declared in CGraphics.h.

After the opening brace of the CreateBox() function, you use the constructor of the D3DXVECTOR3 object to create a vector to store the size of your entity. You assign this vector to a CEntity D3DXVECTOR3 class attribute, m_vecBoxSize. The three parameters of the D3DXVECTOR3 object account for the width, height, and depth of the box, and these you retrieve from the parameters of the CreateBox() function. You store this information at this point so that you can use it later in the SetMass() function to calculate how to evenly distribute the mass of the entity.

Since you are creating a box entity, you set m_iType to BOX. Having set its type, you then call SetMass() to assign the box a default mass of 1.0. As in CreateSphere(), you call dBodySetMass() to associate the dBodyID object with the newly defined dMass object. As before, this function associates the mass of the entity with its body.

A Closer View of Setting Mass

You employ the CEntity::SetMass() function to establish the properties of the mass of the entity. Here is the code for this function as it appears in CEntity.cpp:

```
void CEntity::SetMass(float fMass)
{
    // Make sure the mesh object is not NULL
    if(!m_pMesh)
        return;

    // If sphere or mesh, set the mass based on a spherical model
    if(m_iType == SPHERE || m_iType == MESH)
        dMassSetSphereTotal(&m_dMass, fMass, m_pMesh->GetRadius());
    // Otherwise use a box model
    else
        dMassSetBoxTotal(&m_dMass, fMass,
                                        m_vecBoxSize.x,
                                        m_vecBoxSize.y,
                                        m_vecBoxSize.z);
}
```

The single parameter of SetMass() is the float value that designates the entity's mass. After the opening brace, you test to discover whether the mass the m_pMesh attribute supposedly identifies is NULL. If it is NULL, then you exit the function with no further ado.

Following the check for NULL, an if…else selection statement verifies the type of the entity (m_iType) and sets its mass according to its type. If the type is SPHERE or MESH, you call the ODE dMassSetSphereTotal() function to evenly distribute the mass of the entity. The first parameter of this function is of a reference to a dMass structure (&m_dMass), which provides information about the mass of the body. The second parameter is the floating point value stored in fMass, which you retrieve from the float parameter of the SetMass() function. The final parameter is the radius of the sphere, which you obtain by calling CMesh::GetRadius().

If the type of the entity is anything other than SPHERE or MESH, then you call the dMassSetBoxTotal() function. This function employs a cubical model to distribute the mass of the entity. The first parameter of this function is a reference to a dMass object (m_dMass). The second parameter is the mass of the entity (fMass). The last three parameters are the width, height, and depth of the box, which you obtain from the CEntity D3DXVECTOR3 class attribute, m_vecBoxSize.

Adding Force

As mentioned in the discussion of the declaration of the CEntity class, to apply a force to an entity, you implement the AddForce() function. Here's the code for this function as presented in CEntity.cpp:

```
void CEntity::AddForce(D3DXVECTOR3 vecForce)
{
     dBodyAddRelForce(m_dBodyID, vecForce.x, vecForce.y, vecForce.z);
}
```

The single parameter for the AddForce() function is a D3DXVECTOR3 structure (vecForce) that provides the direction and magnitude of the force you wish to apply to the entity. Elements of the D3DXVECTOR3 structure provide information to the ODE dBodyAddRelForce() function. The first parameter of the dBodyAddRelForce() function is a pointer to the dBodyID object to which you are applying the force. The next three parameters supply the values that you derive from the D3DXVECTOR3 structure. These values define a directional vector for the force (vecForce.x, vecForce.y, vecForce.z). After you apply the direction of the force to the entity, the ODE automatically updates the position and velocity of the entity.

Adding Torque

The ODE also supports adding torque to entities. Adding torque to an entity causes the entity to spin around a given axis. In order to make it convenient to add torque to an entity, you create the CEntity::AddTorque() function. Here's the code for this function as it appears in CEntity.cpp:

```
void CEntity::AddTorque(D3DXVECTOR3 vecTorque)
{
     dBodyAddRelTorque(m_dBodyID, vecTorque.x,
                                  vecTorque.y,
                                  vecTorque.z);
}
```

The definition of the AddTorque() function stipulates the use of a single D3DXVECTOR3 vector parameter, which defines the torque you wish to apply to the entity. Using this vector, you set the *x*, *y*, and *z* force values that establish the direction of the torque. To set the torque, you pass these values to the ODE dBodyAddRelTorque() function. The first parameter of the dBodyAddRelTorque() function is the dBodyID attribute of the CEntity class. This attribute identifies the body to which you intend to apply the torque. The next three parameters establish the direction of the torque. To set these parameters, you retrieve the values stored in the D3DXVECTOR3 object passed to the AddTorque() function.

Modifying CMyApplication

To see the effects of the changes you have made to your entities, you make a few changes to the CMyApplication class. The first change involves the CMyApplication::OnEvent() function. Here is the code for the function as revealed in CEntity.cpp:

```
void CMyApplication::OnEvent(CEvent *pEvent)
{
        wstring strName = pEvent->GetName();
//Lines left out . . .
// Create a new ball or box entity with random radius and position
        else if(strName == L"CREATE")
        {
                float fRadius = (((float)rand()/RAND_MAX) * 0.2) + 0.2;
                float fRandomX = ((float)rand()/RAND_MAX - 0.5) * 5;
                float fRandomY = ((float)rand()/RAND_MAX + 5);
                float fRandomZ = ((float)rand()/RAND_MAX - 0.5) * 5;
                DWORD dwColor = D3DCOLOR_XRGB(rand()%255 ,
                                             rand()%255 ,
                                             rand()%255);
```

After the opening brace, you make a call to the CEntity::GetName() function to retrieve the name of the event and assign it to a wstring identifier (strName). A few lines later, the else if selection statement uses the strName identifier to determine whether the event passed to the OnEvent() function is a "CREATE" event. If the event is a "CREATE" event, then the first order of business involves generating a set of random values that can be used to define the radius, position, and color of the entity. The specific mechanics involved in generating these values involves the same operations discussed previously, under "Handling the Created Event."

Given the existence of the size, color, and position values, you then create a pointer to a CEntity object (pEntity) and set it to NULL. To determine whether the entity becomes a sphere or a box, you employ the rand() function from the C library to obtain a number between 0 and 99. If the number is less than or equal to 50, you create a sphere. If the number is greater than 50, then you create a box. Here are the lines from the CEntity::OnEvent function that accomplish this work:

```
                CEntity *pEntity = NULL;
                if(rand()%100 <= 50)
                {
                        pEntity = GetWorld()->CreateEntity(L"ENTITY",
                                                 fRadius, dwColor ,
```

```
                                    m_pGraphics->GetDevice());
    }
    else
    {
        pEntity = GetWorld()->CreateEntity(L"ENTITY",
                                    0.5, 0.5, 0.5,
                                    dwColor,
                                    m_pGraphics->GetDevice());
```

In either case, you assign the entity you create to the pEntity. Using pEntity, you then employ the random values you have created above (fRandomX, fRandomY, fRandomZ) to set up a D3DXVECTOR3 vector to represent the torque you want to apply to the entity. Having created the torque vector, you then call the AddTorque() function to apply the torque to the entity. Here is the code from the CMyApplication::OnEvent() function that accomplishes these tasks:

```
D3DXVECTOR3 vecRandomTorque(fRandomX, fRandomY, fRandomZ);
pEntity->AddTorque(vecRandomTorque);
```

Position, Mass, and Destruction

Having applied torque to your entity, your next few changes are to the final lines of the CMyApplication::OnEvent() function. Here you set the position and the mass of the entity. Then you destroy the entity. Here are the lines from the OnEvent() function in CMyApplication.cpp that show the changes:

```
// Set the random position
pEntity->SetPos(D3DXVECTOR3(fRandomX , fRandomY , fRandomZ));
// Create a random mass
float fRandomMass = (((float)rand()/RAND_MAX) * 2) + 1.0;
pEntity->SetMass(fRandomMass);
// Now create an event to destroy this ball in 15 seconds
CEvent *pDestroy = new CEvent(L"DESTROY", TIME_RELATIVE, 15);
pDestroy->AddPointerParam(pEntity);
AddEvent(pDestroy);
```

On the first line, you call the SetPos() function to designate the position of the entity using the random values created previously. You populate a D3DXVECTOR3 vector as the argument for the SetPos() function. After you designate the position of the entity, you then generate a random value using the C library rand() function in conjunction with the RAND_MAX constant. This value lies between 0 and 1, and you assign it to a float identifier, fRandomMass. You multiply the number by two and shift it by one to create a random mass between 1 and 3. You then provide this value to the CEntity::SetMass() function to assign a mass value to the entity.

Given that the entity has been created, positioned, and assigned a mass and had torque applied to it, you can then destroy the entity. To accomplish this task, you first create a reference to an event and assign the reference to a CEvent pointer identifier (pDestroy). When you create the reference, you set the parameters of the CEvent constructor so that the event is named "DESTROY", the time of execution for the event is relative to its creation, and the event executes 15 seconds after its creation. You then call the AddPointerParam() function and supply this event as its argument. This leaves you one last task, which is to call the AddEvent() function to queue up the event for execution. Upon execution, the entity is destroyed.

Building a Game Using Physics

Given the flexibility you now possess to simulate physical events, you can now begin to create a game that makes use of such events. To see how this works, access Listing08_04 and compile it. Use the mouse wheel and the left mouse button to position the ground entities so that they resemble those shown in Figure 8.12. The button control at the bottom of the panel causes a box to fall onto the ground plane. The sliders allow you to set the torque of the box. When a box falls onto the ground entity, it rebounds from it. If you adjust the sliders, you can eventually make it so that the box rebounds and strikes the target plane.

Setting Up a Game Scenario

Figure 8.13 illustrates an interaction network for the event model for a game that makes use of the physical properties the ODE offers. The event model requires that you designate the box as a block, the larger of the rectangular entities as a "ground," and the smaller of the rectangular entities as a "target." You then set about creating a game that allows the block to be dropped on the ground. When the block strikes the ground, you initiate an event that causes it to rebound. You regulate the behavior of the block after it rebounds using the ODE physics engine. When the block rebounds, for example, its path is determined by the torque you apply to it. If you generate the torque using random values, the block rebounds in a consistent but playful way. Given this situation, you can make it so that hitting the target becomes the object of a game. The player of the game adjusts the torque and gravity to make the block strike the target.

Listing08_04 possesses many of the features of the event model Figure 8.13 maps out. To implement the features of the event model, you create functions that detect when the block collides with the ground and target rectangles. You must also add controls to the application that enable you to control when the box comes into existence. The sections that follow discuss these activities. The discussion of Listing08_05, later in this chapter, shows you how to add a score board and a few other features to the application.

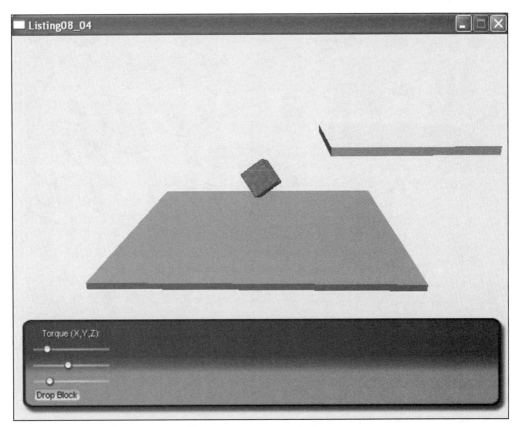

Figure 8.12 Combining events allows you create a preliminary event context.

Identifying Entities for Collision

The application Figure 8.13 illustrates incorporates three entities: a box entity and two ground entities. After you release the box from the top of the application's world space, it falls to the ground plane. When it strikes this plane, it rebounds. As the box rebounds, its path can carry it to three general destinations: It can repeatedly bounce around on the ground plane; it can bounce off the ground plane and into the infinite distance; or it can rebound from the ground plane and strike the target. Whatever the destination of the box, accounting for its behavior requires you to detect its collisions.

To detect collisions, you make several changes to the application. One way to start involves continuously searching the world for the entities it contains so that you can detect the collisions between them. To accomplish this, you add a function, GetEntity(), to the CWorld class. Here's the code for GetEntity() as presented in CWorld.cpp:

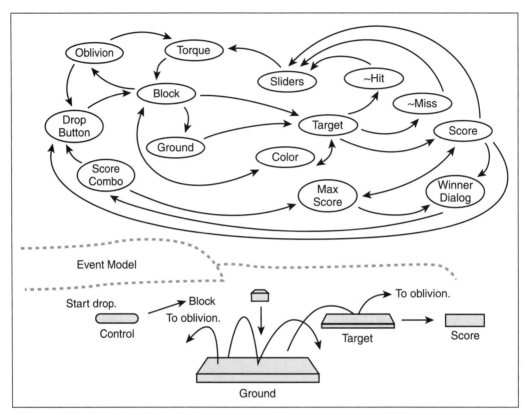

Figure 8.13 The event model calls for a block and targets.

```
CEntity *CWorld::GetEntity(dGeomID dGeometry)
{
    for(int itr=0; itr<m_lstEntities.size(); itr++)
    {
        if(m_lstEntities[itr] &&
            m_lstEntities[itr]->GetGeomID() == dGeometry)
            return(m_lstEntities[itr]);
    }
    return(NULL);
}
```

This function takes an ODE `dGeomID` object as its sole parameter. The `for` loop inside the function iterates through all of the entities contained in the world's entity list (`m_lstEntities`), and the `if` statement inside the `for` loop uses the `dGeomID` object to determine if the entity exists. To arrive at the determination, the `if` statement performs two operations. First, it establishes that the iterator (`itr`) does not designate a `NULL` value. Second, it verifies that the `dGeomID` value of the entity in the world entity list matches the dGeomID value (dGeometry) that you have fed to the GetEntity() function. To retrieve the dGeomID values of the entities from the world entity list, you make calls to the CEntity::GetGeomID() function. If the dGeomID value in the world entity list matches the dGeomID value you retrieve from the GetGeomID() parameter, you return the matching entity. If you do not find the dGeomID value, you return NULL.

Identifying Entities and Collisions

After you have a way to iterate through all the entities in your world, you can then begin to detect collisions between them. To accomplish this, you modify the global NearCallback() function in the CWorld.cpp file. Here's the signature and the first few lines of code for the function:

```
static void NearCallback (void *data, dGeomID o1, dGeomID o2)
{
    // Lines left out . . .
        // Get pointers to the entities
        CEntity *pEntity1 = GetWorld()->GetEntity(o1);
        CEntity *pEntity2 = GetWorld()->GetEntity(o2);
```

As has been mentioned previously, the NearCallback() function features three parameters. The first parameter is of a void type and allows you to pass any message you like to the function. For now, this parameter receives little use. The next two parameters present a different story, however, because they allow you to identify objects between which collisions might occur.

Following the opening brace of the function, you make calls to CWorld::GetEntity() to obtain pointers to the entities you want to compare. The calls to GetEntity() use the dGeomID objects (o1, o2) as their parameters and assign CEntity references to local pointer instances of CEntity (pEntity1 and pEntity2).

You can now determine whether the two entities collide with each other. An extensive selection statement attends to this task:

```
            // This represents a collision between the target and the block
            if(pEntity1 && pEntity2 &&
                ((pEntity1->GetName() == L"Target" &&
                  pEntity2->GetName() == L"Block") ||
                 (pEntity1->GetName() == L"Block" &&
                  pEntity2->GetName() == L"Target")))
```

The first part of this selection statement verifies that neither of the CEntity objects (pEntity1 and pEntity2) is NULL. Then the selection statement checks to see if the first entity is named "Target" and the second entity is named "Block". Since you don't know the order in which these objects are passed into this function, you cannot assume that pEntity1 is named "Block" and pEntity2 is named "Target". Having both orders ensures that you detect the possible combinations of block and target.

Enhancing Collisions

At this point in the NearCallback() function, if the selection statement establishes that a collision has occurred between the entities named "Block" and "Target", you can make the collision more interesting by adding some psychologically intensive qualities to it.

In addition to drawing the user into interacting with the application by clicking the button that causes the block to fall toward the ground entity, you can also provide the user with a reward for causing the collision. Toward this end, you make use of the CMesh::SetColor() function in the NearCallback() function to create color effects. Here are the lines you add to NearCallback() to accomplish this task:

```
if(...)
{
    // Set a random color for entity 1
    pEntity1->GetMesh()->SetColor(D3DCOLOR_XRGB(rand()%255,
                                               rand()%255,
                                               rand()%255));
    // Set a random color for entity 2
    pEntity2->GetMesh()->SetColor(D3DCOLOR_XRGB(rand()%255,
                                               rand()%255,
                                               rand()%255));
}
```

Employing pointers to the block and target entities, you make cascading calls to the GetMesh() and SetColor() functions. For each of the calls to the SetColor() function, you provide an instance of the D3DCOLOR_XRGB() macro. To address the parameters of the macro, you provide randomized values that you generate using the C library rand() function. The result is that when a collision occurs, the block and target objects change colors.

Creating a Ground Entity

Even though you have seen how you can detect a collision between two entities, it remains that you still need to create the entities. You need a block entity, a ground entity, and a target entity. Creating these entities begins with a few changes to the code in the CMyApplication::Initialize() function. Here are the lines you add for the target:

```
// Create the target entity
CEntity *pTarget =
        GetWorld()->CreateEntity(L"Target", 2, 0.1, 2,
                           D3DCOLOR_XRGB(0,255,128),
```

```
                              m_pGraphics->GetDevice());
   pTarget->SetPos(D3DXVECTOR3(2, 2,-2));
   pTarget->SetEnabled(false);
```

To create the target entity you call `CWorld::CreateEntity()`. The string you supply to the first parameter, `"Target"`, names the entity. This name matches the name you check for in the `NearCallback()` function. After naming the entity, you then set its size. The width of the entity you set at 2, the height at 0.1, and the depth at 2. You set the initial color of the entity using the `D3DCOLOR_XRGB()` macro, and the values you supply are 0, 233, and 128. The final parameter passed in to `CreateEntity()` is a pointer to the `IDirect3DDevice9` object declared in CGraphics.h.

After assigning a reference to the target entity to a pointer of the `CEntity` type (`pTarget`), you use this pointer to call the `CEntity::SetPos()` function, which establishes the initial position of the target entity. Because the initial position of the ground entity is at the world's origin (0,0,0), the call to the `SetPos()` function moves the target entity away from the ground entity 2 units in the x direction, 2 units in the y direction, and 2 units in the negative z direction.

To finish off your target-creation activities, you make a call to `CEntity::SetEnabled()` to disable the effects of physics on the target box. This is because you do not want the target to be affected by gravity or move around when the block strikes it.

Controls and the Block

The creation of the target marks an important step in finishing the implementation of the game, but quite a bit of work remains to be done. You have yet to create the block, for example, and work remains to be done on the ground entity. Before turning to those tasks, it is worthwhile to set up ways of controlling the block. The controls allow you to change the torque applied to the block and to initiate the dropping of the block.

Names, a Block, and Controls

To add the controls and the messages that apply to them, you must declare a few constant values. You declare these values as private attributes of the `CMyApplication` class. Here is the code for these attributes that you add to CMyApplication.h:

```
static const int IDC_DROP = 0;
static const int IDC_STATIC = 1;
static const int IDC_TORQUEX = 2;
static const int IDC_TORQUEY = 3;
static const int IDC_TORQUEZ = 4;
```

These constants identify the controls you use in the application. For example, the first identifier, IDC_DROP, names the "Drop Block" button. The next identifier, IDC_STATIC, names the label for the torque sliders. The last three identifiers name sliders you use to control the x, y, and z torque values.

To set up the block, you add yet another private attribute to the CMyApplication class. The identifier is for a pointer to a CEntity object. Here is the code from CMyApplication.h:

```
// The block
  class CEntity *m_pBlock;
```

The sliders you add to your application are CDXUTSlider objects, and to accommodate these objects you add three more private attributes to CMyApplication. These attributes are pointers to CDXUTSlider objects:

```
// Three sliders for torque (X,Y,Z)
CDXUTSlider *m_pTorqueX;
CDXUTSlider *m_pTorqueY;
CDXUTSlider *m_pTorqueZ;
```

Creating Controls

Given that you have added attributes to the CMyApplication class for the controls, you can begin taking care of the details of implementation. You implement a label, three sliders, and a button. The CMyApplication::InitGUI() function accomplishes this work:

```
void CMyApplication::InitGUI()
{
    // Call parent initialize
    CApplication::InitGUI();
    // Create a label for the sliders
    m_GUI.AddStatic(IDC_STATIC,        //ID
                    L"Torque (X, Y, Z):", //Label text
                    25, m_iConsoleY + 10,  //upper left coordinates
                    100, 20);              //width and height
    // Create the three sliders for torque (x, y, z)
    m_GUI.AddSlider(IDC_TORQUEX,           //ID
                    25, m_iConsoleY + 30, //upper left corner
                    100, 20,              //width and height
                    0, 100, 50,           //min, max, default
                    false,                //focus
                &m_pTorqueX);         //torque value
    m_GUI.AddSlider(IDC_TORQUEY, 25, m_iConsoleY + 50, 100, 20, 0,
                    100, 50, false, &m_pTorqueY);
    m_GUI.AddSlider(IDC_TORQUEZ, 25, m_iConsoleY + 70,100, 20, 0,
```

```
                              100, 50, false, &m_pTorqueZ);
       // Create the button for dropping the block
         m_GUI.AddButton(IDC_DROP, L"Drop Block",
                                25, m_iConsoleY + 90, 64, 18);
}
```

As the code comments indicate, the implementations in the `CMyApplication::InitGUI()` function fall into three categories. In the first category of control is the static label that identifies the torque slider. You create this label using the `CDXUTDialog::AddStatic()` function. The first parameter for this function is the ID of the label (`IDC_STATIC`). The second parameter is the text to be displayed (`"Torque (X, Y, Z)"`). The final four parameters position the upper left corner of the label and then set its width and height.

The second category of control in the `CMyApplication::InitGUI()` function consists of sliders. To create the sliders, you make three successive calls to the `CDXUTDialog::AddSlider()` function. In each instance, the first parameter of the `AddSlider()` function is the ID of the slider (for example, `IDC_TORQUEX`). The second and third parameters (`f25` and `m_iConsoleY + 30`) set the x and y coordinates for the upper left corner of the slider in the client area. The fourth and fifth coordinates set the width and height in pixels (100, 20).

After you set the values for the size and position the slider, you set the parameters of the `AddSlider()` function for the minimum, maximum, and default values of the slider (0, 100, and 50). The second to the last value enables you to indicate whether you want the slider to receive the window's focus by default. For the `IDC_TORQUEX` slider, this value is set to `false`. The last parameter is a reference to the `CDXUTSlider` object. The reference allows you to `assign` `m_pTorqueX`, `m_pTorqueY`, and `m_pTorqueZ` pointers to the slider.

The third category of control is a button. To create a button, you make a call to the `CDXUTDialog::AddButton()` function. The first parameter for this function is the ID of the button (`IDC_DROP`). The second parameter is the text the button displays ("Drop Block"). The final four parameters position the upper left corner of the button and then set its width and height.

Dropping the Block

Given that you have a button that can initiate a drop and sliders that you can use to set the torque that applies to the block as it collides with the ground entity, your next task is to implement the code that causes the block to drop. All of this work takes place in the `CMyApplication::OnGUIEvent()` function:

```
void CMyApplication::OnGUIEvent(UINT nEvent, int nControlID,
                              CDXUTControl *pControl)
{
    if(nControlID == IDC_DROP)
    {
```

```
            // Destroy the old block
            GetWorld()->RemoveEntity(m_pBlock);
            // Create the new block
            m_pBlock = GetWorld()->CreateEntity(L"Block", //name
                                0.5, 0.5, 0.5,              //size
                                D3DCOLOR_XRGB(255,0,0),     //color
                                m_pGraphics->GetDevice()); //device
            // Create a vector for the values obtained from torque sliders
            D3DXVECTOR3 vecTorque(
                                (float)m_pTorqueX->GetValue()/10.0f - 5.0f,
                        (float)m_pTorqueY->GetValue()/10.0f - 5.0f,
                        (float)m_pTorqueZ->GetValue()/10.0f - 5.0f);
            // Add torque to the block
                m_pBlock->AddTorque(vecTorque);
            // Set the block's initial position
            m_pBlock->SetPos(D3DXVECTOR3(0, 6, 0));
        }
    }
```

The OnGUIEvent() function takes three parameters. The first parameter furnishes the unique identifier of the event. The second parameter provides the identification of the control that applies to the GUI event. The last parameter is a pointer to the control itself.

After the opening brace, the function uses an if selection statement to determine the type of the event. In this case, the objective is to establish that the event has been triggered by the drop button, so the nControlID value needs to be IDC_DROP. If the nControlID type proves correct, then you call the CWorld::RemoveEntity() function to destroy any existing blocks. The value you supply this function is the CMyApplication attribute that stores a pointer to the block (m_pBlock). Your application supports only one block at a time, so before you click the button to create a new block, you must destroy the old one.

After destroying the old block, you call the CWorld::CreateEntity() function to create a new block. You are probably fairly familiar with the CreateEntity() function by this time, but it does not hurt to review the parameters. The first parameter names the entity ("Block"). The next three parameters set the height, width, and depth dimensions of the block (0.5, 0.5, 0.5). The second to the last parameter sets the color of the block. The final parameter is a pointer to the IDirect3DDevice9 object declared in CGraphics.h.

After you create the block entity, you create a D3DXVECTOR3 vector (vecTorque). The D3DXVECTOR3 object requires three values, and in each case, you obtain the values from the torque sliders. These values establish the torque to be applied to block. To obtain these values, you employ the name of the slider (m_pTorqueX, for example) to call the

`CDXUTDialog::GetValue()` function to obtain the integer value the slider provides. You then divide the integer value by 10 to get a floating point value between 0 and 10. (The range of values the sliders provide runs from 0 to 100.)

Having populated the `D3DXVECTOR3` vector using the values from the sliders, you apply the vector to the block (`m_pBlock`) using a call to the `CEntity::AddTorque()` function. When you apply the values in the torque vector to the block, you cause the block to spin in accordance with the value.

In the final line of code in the `OnGUIEvent()` function, you call the `CEntity::SetPos()` function. The argument you supply to the `SetPos()` function is a `D3DXVECTOR3` vector. The vector provides x, y, and z coordinate values. When you set the y value to 6, you position the block above the ground plane. Under the influence of gravity, the block then falls toward the ground entity. Having accumulated momentum, the block bounces. Depending on the torque you have applied to it, the block then rebounds and possibly strikes the target.

Final Touches

At this point, you can extend the work you have done on Listing08_04 and fully implement the game that Figure 8.13 maps out. As a refresher, Figure 8.14 provides an essential view of the event model for the game.

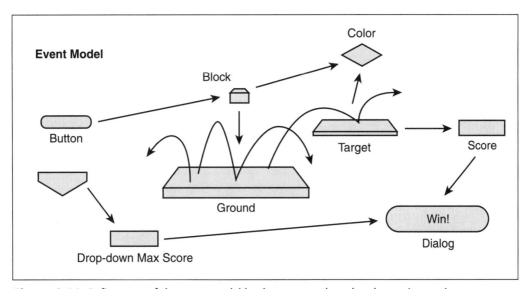

Figure 8.14 Refinement of the event model leads to a score board and more interaction.

To view the results you achieve by extending Listing08_04, access the project for Listing08_05 and compile it. Figure 8.15 illustrates the result. To play the game, first adjust the ground entity and the target entity so that they resemble what you see in Figure 8.15. Next, set the X, Y, and Z torque values using the sliders. Then select the level of score you want to try to obtain. (Your choices are 20, 50, and 100.) Having attended to preliminaries, click the Drop Block button.

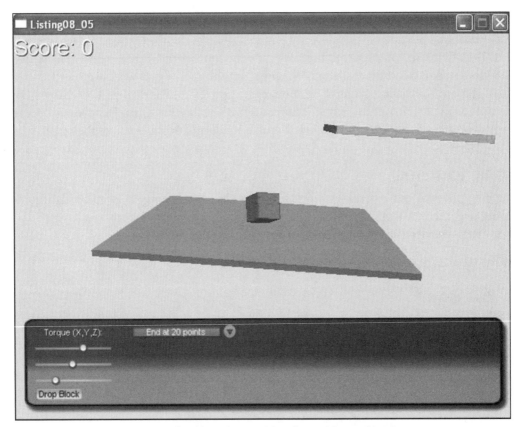

Figure 8.15 Set the torque, select the score, position the entities, and begin.

Figure 8.16 A dialog rewards your efforts.

If you succeed in adjusting the torque and positioning the ground and target entities correctly, you eventually win. When you win, a dialog box appears telling you of your victory. If you click the OK button of the dialog, you can begin another game. To close the game, you click the control on the application window. See Figure 8.16.

Emergent Intelligence

As the discussion in Chapter 2 emphasized, a system sustains a multitude of feedback loops. In terms of the event model that governs the interactions of the block game, the AI, console, and entity properties each involve some type of feedback loop. Each loop provides ways to enhance the potentials of the game. As a review, consider the following occasions (or nodes) of interaction:

- **Ground.** The player can use the mouse wheel and the left mouse button to position the ground entity in world space. Likewise, the AI governs the fall of the block, so that the block can strike and rebound from the ground entity in accordance with the forces of gravity and torque that have been applied to the block.

- **Target.** The player can use the mouse wheel and the left mouse key to position the target entity in world space. The AI governs the path of the bouncing block, so it can strike the target in a semi-random fashion. When the block strikes the target, the color of the target changes.

- **Button.** The player can click the drop button at will to trigger the fall of the block.

- **Block.** AI governs some of the physical properties of the block, so it behaves as though under the influence, for example, of gravity. The player's interactions with the game also govern the block. The player initiates the drop of the block. When the player successfully sets the torque of the block and the block bounces and strikes the target, then the block changes color.

- **Color.** Color and light both set the mood of the game and accentuate events of the game. When the block strikes the target, a change of color signals success.

- **Score.** The score provides the activity of the game with a purpose, a destination. The destination governs the player's interactions because, after the score becomes a factor in the play of the system, the play takes on characteristics of duration and intent.

- **Max Score.** When the player can assign different maximum scores, the game can be considered to have different levels of duration and difficulty.

- **Torque Sliders.** The player can introduce information into the AI of the game to vary the events that the physics of the game generate.

- **Dialog.** The dialog provides a way that a player can both see the results of a sequence of play and initiate another round of play.

All of these features combine to give shape to a complex of events. The complex of events forms a system, and when you participate in the system, you extend your experience as the event model the system creates allows you to extend your experience. When you explore the system through its interaction network, you eventually arrive at a sense that the system can have closure if you smooth out the pathways of events leading from the moment the player clicks on the button to drop the block to the moment the player realizes the significance of the overall context of play. An event that can bring things to closure in an elementary way is the assignment of a score to the proceedings. A score is a gauge of progress, a quantitative indicator of the cumulative value of the play the system fosters.

Creating a Scoreboard

To be able to track the play the game fosters in a quantitative fashion, you begin by adding attributes to the CMyApplication class:

```
static const int IDC_SCORE = 5;
static const int IDC_ENDSCORE = 6;
  // Track the score
int m_iScore;
// Set the score
int m_iEndScore;
```

The two static const int attributes allow you to identify the objects you add for the scoreboard and the controls that apply to it. The int attributes allow you to set and track the score of the game. In addition to tracking and setting the score, you require an attribute that allows you to continuously audit when a block occasions new game points. Each block you drop should allow you to augment the score only once. Here are the lines that add this Boolean attribute:

```
// Did the current block already score
bool m_bScored;
```

Showing the Score

To provide for the visual display of the score, you create a static GUI object to which you can assign text that bears the current score. To add this object, you make changes to the CMyApplication::InitGUI() function. Here are the lines from the InitGUI() function in CApplication.h that perform this work:

```
// Add the static label for the score
m_GUI.AddStatic(IDC_SCORE, L"Score: XX", 0, 0,200,200);
m_GUI.SetFont(1, L"Arial", 32,0);
m_GUI.GetStatic(IDC_SCORE)->GetElement(0)->SetFont(
                1, D3DCOLOR_XRGB(255,255,255), DT_LEFT);
```

You create the label for the score using the CDXUTDialog::AddStatic() function. The first parameter for this function is the ID of the label (IDC_SCORE). The second parameter is the text you want to initially display ("Score XX"). The final four parameters position the label in the upper left corner of the client area and its width and height at 200 each.

Following the creation of the score label, you then make a call, CDXUTDialog::SetFont(), to create a font face appropriate for the label. The arguments to the function are, first, the ID of the font you are setting. The second parameter supplies the name of the font ("Arial"). The third parameter sets the point size of the font. The final parameter designates the font weight (0 represents normal).

Given that you have set up the score label and the font you want to use to display the score, you can then call the CDXUTDialog::GetStatic() function to apply the font to the label. To accomplish this, you use a series of cascading calls.

Setting Maximum Scores

Another piece of work you perform in the CMyApplication::InitGUI() function involves creating a combo box that allows you to set the maximum score you want to allow for your game. Here are the lines in the CMyApplication::InitGUI() that perform this work:

```
// Create the combo box for the ending score
m_GUI.AddComboBox(IDC_ENDSCORE, 150, m_iConsoleY + 10, 140, 20);
m_GUI.GetComboBox(IDC_ENDSCORE)->AddItem(
                             L"End at 20 points",(void *)20);

m_GUI.GetComboBox(IDC_ENDSCORE)->AddItem(
                             L"End at 50 points",(void *)50);
m_GUI.GetComboBox(IDC_ENDSCORE)->AddItem(
                             L"End at 100 points",(void *)100);
m_GUI.GetComboBox(IDC_ENDSCORE)->SetDropHeight(70);
```

The call to CDXUTDialog::AddComboBox() creates the combo box. The first parameter associates the combo box with its ID (IDC_ENDSCORE). The next four parameters set the position and size of the combo box.

After creating the combo box, you then make three successive calls to the CDXUTDialog::AddItem() function to add the items you want to display as combo box options. In this case, you designate options for 20, 50, and 100 points. The AddItem() function takes two parameters. The first parameter provides the text the combo box displays for the item. The second is a pointer to data associated with the new item. You cast an integer value to a void pointer type so that the value can be retrieved later.

Having set the values for the combo box items, you call the CDXUTDialog::GetComboBox() function to retrieve a pointer to the combo box object and then use this, in turn, to call SetDropHeight(), which sets the height of the drop-down menu in pixels.

Updating

After setting up the static control that displays the score, you alter the CMyApplication::UpdateScene() function so that it updates the score. Also, you add a statement to check for the end-of-game condition. Here's the code:

```
void CMyApplication::UpdateScene(float fTimeScale)
{
    //Lines left out . . .
    // Update the text
    TCHAR wszBuf[80];
    wsprintf(wszBuf, L"Score: %d", m_iScore);
    m_GUI.GetStatic(IDC_SCORE)->SetText(wszBuf);
    // End the game
    if(m_iScore >= m_iEndScore)
    {
        MessageBox(NULL, L"Game over - you win!",
                        L"Game over!", MB_OK);
        //SetRunning(false);
        m_iScore = 0;
        wsprintf(wszBuf, L"Score: %d", m_iScore);
        m_GUI.GetStatic(IDC_SCORE)->SetText(wszBuf);
    }
}
```

After the opening brace, you create a wide-character buffer (wszBuf) to store the text for the score. You then call the wsprintf() function to place the score in the buffer. The resulting string consists of the word "Score:" followed by the value of the variable m_iScore. Having created the score string, you call the CDXUTStatic::SetText() function to feed the score text to the score label (IDC_SCORE). To retrieve the label, you call the CDXUTDialog::GetStatic() function.

Having set up the score display, you then use an if selection statement to determine whether the game has ended. If the current score exceeds the end-game score, you call the MessageBox() function to display a message box that notifies the player that the game is over. The message box pauses the game for a moment. If the player clicks the OK button in the message box, the next line resets the score to zero and displays it in the score label.

Note

The code for CApplication::SetRunning() is commented out. If you remove the comments, the Boolean value of false that you supply to SetRunning() terminates execution of the program.

The Score Event

To add a score event to the game, you make changes to the CMyApplication::OnEvent() function. These changes allow you to augment the score when the block collides with the target. Here is the code from the OnEvent() function in CMyApplication.cpp that accomplishes this work:

```
void CMyApplication::OnEvent(CEvent *pEvent)
{
    // Process the score event
    if(pEvent->GetName() == L"SCORE" && !m_bScored)
    {
        // Increase the score
        m_iScore+=10;
        m_bScored = true;

        // Randomize the mass of the block so the player
        // can not just use the same parameters over and over
        float fRandomMass = ((float)rand()/RAND_MAX) * 2-1;
        GetWorld()->GetEntity(L"Block")->SetMass(fRandomMass);
    }
}
```

The OnEvent() function takes one parameter, a pointer to a CEvent object. After the opening brace, you insert an if selection statement to determine if the event passed to the function is of the SCORE type. You also evaluate m_bScored to determine whether points scored by the current block have already been added to the score. If the condition of the if statement is true, you increment the score by 10 and set the m_bScored flag to true.

After setting the score, you then call the rand() function to generate a random value for the mass. This ensures that the block does not move in the same way every turn. To finish up, you assign the mass value to the block entity by calling the CEntity::SetMass() function.

Adding the Score Event

For the score event to occur, you must cause it to fire. To accomplish this, you modify the NearCallback() function in CWorld.cpp. Here is the code:

```
// Create an event to represent the collision
CEvent *pEvent = new CEvent(L"SCORE", TIME_IMMEDIATE, 0);
g_pApp->AddEvent(pEvent);
```

To create an event, you call the constructor for the CEvent class. The first parameter of the constructor allows you to name the event ("SCORE"). The second parameter of the constructor allows you to set the event to fire immediately (TIME_IMMEDIATE). Having created the event, you then call CApplication::AddEvent() to add the event to the application's event list.

Changing the End-Game Score

To make it so that you can set the maximum score for the game, you modify CMyApplication::OnGUIEvent() so that the combo box messages can be processed. Here's the code you add:

```
if(nControlID == IDC_DROP)
{
    // Lines left out. . .
}
else if(nControlID == IDC_ENDSCORE)
{
    // Get the new end-game score
    CDXUTComboBox *pCombo = (CDXUTComboBox *)pControl;
    m_iEndScore = (int)(pCombo->GetSelectedData());
}
```

To set up the handler for the combo message, you add a selection statement for IDC_ENDSCORE. When the OnGUIEvent() function receives a message for this event, it creates a pointer to a CDXUTComboBox object and then uses the pointer to call the CDXUTComboBox::GetSelectedData() function. This function retrieves the data associated with the item selected from the combo box. To use the data, you must cast it to an integer. As you might recall, the data type of the value retrieved from the combo box is void.

Conclusion

This chapter has covered topics that deal with creating events that possess realistic physical qualities, but it has also explored how other, complex qualities can supplement realism to give expression to varying event models. Artificial intelligence plays heavily into the objectives you might set for event modeling that incorporates realistic physical properties. Intelligence emerges from the interplay of events, and realism adds to the force with which this occurs.

The Open Dynamics Engine (ODE) proves a useful tool for implementing realistic physical effects. It provides a large set of functions that help you create behaviors that reflect such physical properties as mass, gravity, acceleration, and torque. To implement the functionality the ODE offers, you make use of dWorldID and dSpaceID objects. Using these objects to enhance CEntity and CEvent objects tremendously augment effects you can achieve as you engage in simulation programming.

When you create artificial intelligence, you can look at what you do in broad terms. Rather than applying rules to behavior or thought, artificial intelligence can be viewed as an activity that involves discovering occasions in which meaningful events converge to create rewarding experiences. Intelligence, then, becomes a quality of experiences that emerges from interaction, and creating simulation applications that foster interaction can be one way to explore the workings of artificial intelligence.

As the two iterations of the block game show, through successive experimental passes at developing the game's functionality you can gradually enhance the features of the game to include a variety of constraints that make the game more interesting to play. With the first pass, you were able to visualize the most fundamental ways in which simulation embodies a closed system of interaction. By adding a few simple constraints to the game during the second pass, such as rules that apply to scoring and a score board to display the results of play, you expanded the game until it became a fully implemented vehicle of interaction.

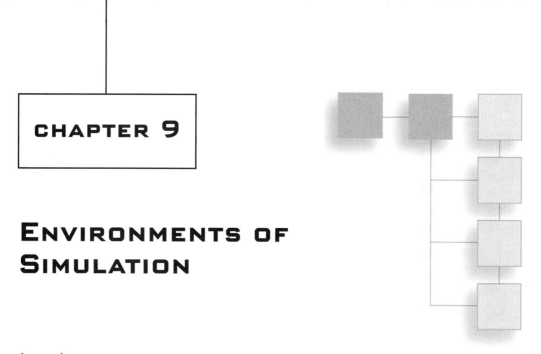

CHAPTER 9

ENVIRONMENTS OF SIMULATION

The information you encapsulate in a simulation is necessarily selective. Likewise, how you apply constraints determines how the user of your application can access the information you encapsulate in the application. The information you select for inclusion and how you allow the user to access this information together underlie the experience the user has with your application. Generally, when a game player or simulation participant receives enough information from a context of interaction to achieve what is known as cognitive saturation, the experience that results is accepted as convincing and realistic. This type of experience results from the application of iconic logic, which is logic that emerges from the interactive context that generates it.

Iconic logic allows you to apply constraints to a simulation in a way that effectively enhances the experience the simulation brings without becoming bogged down in troublesome struggles to discover when a scene is appropriately realistic or possesses enough detail. When you understand that the logic of a scene governs what counts as realism, you can refine your event model so that by implementing a few selected effects, such as those achieved through lighting, you can create a satisfying experience for the simulation participant. This chapter explores a number of topics related to exploring iconic logic and using lighting constraints:

- Different forms of reason
- Iconic logic as a model for modeling scenes
- Cognitive saturation
- Drawing upon light for constraints
- Setting up a scene and introducing play
- Making use of collisions and changes in constraints

Systems and Environments

An environment surrounds you. When people were searching for a term to use to describe the interrelatedness of all physical processes on Earth, they began to employ the term "environmental." When you think about things environmentally, you ultimately follow the path of ethical thought that the philosopher Kant mapped out, for he contended that to fully explore the significance of a given ethical concern, you should discuss it in its broadest possible context. Since science provides a universal way that people can discuss the issues they face, it provides an excellent medium for discussing ethical concerns. It is probably for this reason that many environmentalists tend to be scientists and many scientists tend to be environmentalists.

The centrality of mathematics to science contributes a major factor to the discussion of why the most universally acknowledged approach to settling the problems humanity faces tends to be scientific. Regardless of where you live, what your economic class, political, artistic, or religious affiliations might be, or what language or languages you might speak, you can measure the mass of a hydrogen atom using the same mathematical techniques and experimental tools that others have used and arrive at an answer that you can easily confirm or challenge using the findings others have provided.

The work of science, then, might not provide a final and irrefutable set of answers to the issues that human beings face, but it can at least provide a way that all human beings, given a little training in such subjects as math, physics, chemistry, and biology, can debate issues in a broad, encompassing context.

Relative Systems

Science might provide a broad, encompassing context in which to explore ethics, but it remains that superstition, prejudice, hatred, and ignorance still abound. A multitude of computer games use as their back stories the difficulties that arise from this situation. Gangsters, corrupt politicians, war lords, corporate fascists, and terrorists abound and lay the groundwork for struggles in which the goal is to survive and prevail.

When greed, lust, avarice, or insanity (among other things) become the prevailing "reason" in an imagined world, the play such a world fosters when it becomes a computer game tends sometimes to garner great stores of fans and generate large profits in sales. As contradictory as it might seem, then, not the continuity of science, math, and reason but systems belief and action based on relative standards ultimately make life interesting for many millions of people who enjoy health, security, and plenty due to the exertion of science, math, and reason.

In the world of film, rather than referring to relative systems of belief, filmmakers refer to "suspension" of belief. You accept for the duration of the film the premises the film lays down. You do this for the sake of entertainment. What you desire in return for your theater ticket is escape from reality. You allow the emotional context of the film to guide your understanding for the duration of the film.

During the middle decades of the twentieth century, the prevalence of the film industry led anthropologists, sociologists, and the academic critics involved in film, art (painting and sculpture), and literary studies (among others) to develop a vast body of writings relating to ways to interpret contexts of experience that do not require that all elements of experience be subordinated to a single, prevailing system of interpretation.

In light of these undertakings, a number of interesting, involved approaches to explaining how people experience art arose. One significant result is that a body of critical theory in art that relates to computer games is now emerging. A game, like a film, sculpture, painting, or novel, establishes its own context of understanding, its own "logic" of interpretation. A game, like any work of art, "deconstructs" what might be viewed as a generalized view of reality. At the same time, it constructs a specific logic that can be far more demanding and uncompromising than anything science or mathematics have to offer.

Logic

Logic is a way of thinking about things that allows you to understand that one thing results from another or that two things differ from each other or are the same. Logic is best viewed as a way to make experience consistent with itself. It requires that you put aside momentary inclinations to leap to given conclusions about experience on the basis of how things appear at first sight. Instead you reduce your assertions about experience to small units of information that you evaluate in the light of a single way of understanding.

It ends up that what happens in the context of a simulation, a film, or a game possesses logic but is also not the type of logic you encounter in science and math. The reason the logic you find at work in games, simulations, and film differs from the logic of science and math is that when you begin to participate in a work of art, you suspend beliefs that might lead you to instantly challenge everything you see and embrace, at least temporarily. The emotional and contextual forces that prevail in the work of art determine the logic.

The logic that prevails in a game, a simulation, or a film is *iconic*. An icon is an image that usually calls upon you to interpret the image in the light of a context of understanding you sustain as you behold the image. The meaning of the icon emerges from the feelings and thoughts that characterize your encounter with the icon. In the same way, the meaning of a work of art emerges from the interplay of feelings and thoughts that characterize your experience of the work of art.

Critical theorists who have written about iconic logic usually discuss it in terms of scenes in films. For example, consider an action film like *Alien Vs. Predator*. If you do not tacitly accept the validity of iconic logic, you might immediately begin asking an endless series of questions about given scenes. The more you apply reasoning drawn from science and mathematics to the events of the film, the more implausible and even ridiculous the given scenes can become.

Plausibility should not form a major factor in a serious science fiction or fantasy film. Energy beams can penetrate the atmosphere and punch kilometer-deep holes in the Antarctic ice without as much as forming a small puddle or a puff of steam, and an alien creature encased in thick sheets of a metal that clearly represents a mass greater than that of tons of lead can run across brittle snow and leave foot prints no deeper than those of a woman warrior whose weight is less than a hundred kilograms.

Two Forms of Logic

Two forms of reason prevail. Two approaches to reality prevail. The first approach to reality fosters the type of thinking that has characterized the history of science and the emergence of the modern world. The second approach to reality is much older (pre-Socratic) but at the same time has received through the film and game industries a new and powerful presence in the world. The first approach might be referred to as reflecting *inferential logic*. The second approach might be viewed as reflecting *iconic logic*. See Figure 9.1.

When inferential logic prevails, you evaluate your experiences in terms of a prevailing type of reason (one mode) that you apply to all experiences on a fairly equal basis. Inferential logic requires that you distance yourself from the events that you investigate. It requires that you first objectify the events you experience before you accept your interpretation of them as valid. The events you experience existentially generate a multiplicity of ways that a given situation might be logically investigated (multiple modes).

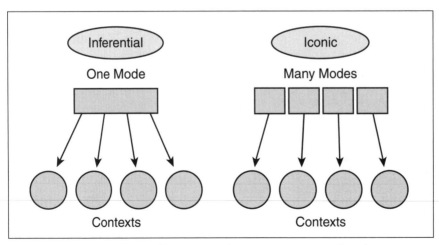

Figure 9.1 Different types of logic govern how experience is mediated.

When iconic logic prevails, you evaluate your experiences in terms of the effects on your thoughts and feelings during the moments of the experience. Iconic logic requires that you immerse yourself in the events that you investigate. The events might be said to have their own logic. You subject yourself to the events, and the logic follows. The events merge into a single, isolated (iconic) moment that you do not attempt to evaluate in the light of an objective standard of reason.

In language that was once popular, iconic logic might be viewed as another manifestation of the subordination of reason to romance. On the other hand, iconic logic involves much more than the subordination of reason to romance. Hollywood films and console games tend to involve technology that is so forceful in its psychological implications that traditional categories fall to the wayside.

Some critics refer to the result as "neurophysiological mainstreaming." Experience is injected with *Matrix*-like diabolism directly into your mind. Such pronouncements are in many ways exaggerated, but the point is still valid. As any number of film and game critics have said, film and game producers put extremely powerful mind-manipulation technologies into the entertainment productions that characterized the market today.

Note

Formal academic studies distinguish between inferential logic and multi-modal logic. The assertion that films and computer games represent a wholly original modern use of non-inferential forms of reasoning proves unfair. In fact, philosophers, logicians, and cognitive scientists over the past century or more have created a vast literature on multi-modal, diagrammatic, pre-Socratic, or iconic forms of logic. Chief among the figures in this respect is Charles Sanders Peirce (1833-1914), who is generally recognized as the founder of post-inferential logical studies. See Chapter 1, "What Is Simulation?" for a more involved discussion of iconic logic.

Cognitive Saturation

The logic of a film, simulation, or game does not need to be external to the logic of the context that sustains the logic. A film draws your attention into a context of events that allows you to be fully satisfied that everything is accounted for regardless of how much of what you witness might appear utterly illogical when evaluated according to the lessons you have learned from your studies of science, math, or other "rational" forms of knowledge. This is the nature of iconic logic. Iconic logic saturates your cognitive channels to the point that you do not or cannot distance yourself from the context of immediate experience. (See Figure 9.2.)

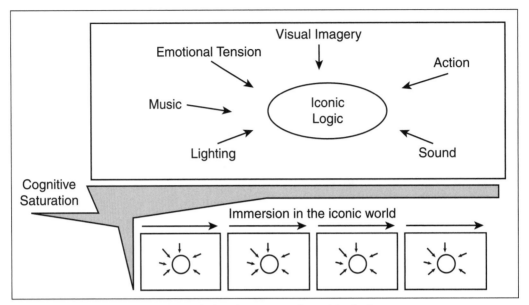

Figure 9.2 Cognitive immersion underlies the success of cognitive logic.

Systems and Interpretation

Implementing iconic logic brings with it a number of hazards. If you fail to saturate a given setting with the imagery and sound that induces the audience to fully relinquish its distance from the event, you can end up with something that appears ridiculous. In fact, such half-distancing is an extremely effective comedic device, and the technical term applied to such entertainment media is "spoof."

When you develop a simulation program, as Chapter 2, "Specifying Events," emphasizes, whether you are developing a serious simulation or a spoof, you develop an event model that determines the scope and depth of the details you include in the simulation. When you undertake the effort of gathering requirements, you quickly discover that achieving your end, regardless of its description, involves appropriately selecting events from a large potential store. Any simulation effort requires that you leave out some details while exaggerating or emphasizing others.

The details you decide to use, together with the constraints that you impose on the details, determine how the participant in a simulation can experience the simulation. A successful simulation—or game or film—is open to a variety of interpretations. Variety of interpretation depends on how the events that comprise the simulation can be logically connected. Iconic logic often proves the chief force at work in allowing the events to be connected.

Few people have either the cognitive speed or mathematical agility to reason through the physics at work when a huge space vehicle crashes into an asteroid. On the other hand, when you see enormous explosions and huge plumes of lava or steam, you get the message.

Selection of details allows interpretation to take place, and iconic logic, as much as classical logic, can create contexts in which almost any selective use of information can appear perfectly—well, reasonable. Consider a fairly dry, detailed set of systems interaction network diagrams that represent some type of economic or environmental system. In Figure 9.3, you see the events of a single system interpreted in two distinct ways. Interpretation 1 provides a close, detailed view of the interactions of the system. Interpretation 2 provides a refined view of the system, one that leaves out close detail.

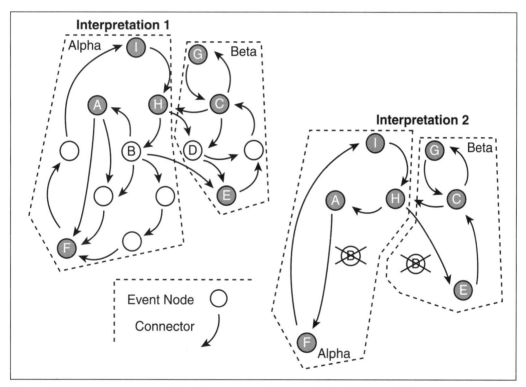

Figure 9.3 Interpretations provide different perspectives on the significance of different event contexts.

As Figure 9.3 shows, the two interpretations of the interaction network alter the roles different nodes play. In Interpretation 1, for example, an analyst might view the role of node A in subsystem Alpha as fairly insignificant. Node B appears to be responsible for creating the link between the two subsystems. In Interpretation 2, however, the diagram of system Alpha does not show node B at all, and so node A appears to be interpreted in an exaggerated way.

Along similar lines, consider node D in subsystem Beta. Interpretation 2 shows that node D has lost its significance, However, in Interpretation 1 node D interacts far more with other nodes than does node C. Again, the interpretation seems to present an exaggeration.

If a body of selected data were added to the representations of subsystems, you might be able to understand that the exaggerations are useful and reasonable. Consider, for example, constraints representing simple quantitative assessments. In Figure 9.4, the connector symbols appear darker and letters now identify them. The constraints represent quantitative values (not shown). Given this adjusted perspective, it now becomes possible to begin to find a logic for Interpretation 2.

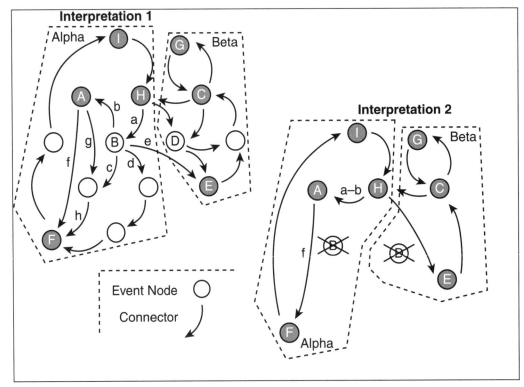

Figure 9.4 Recognizing that connectors bear significance as great as nodes increases the complexity of interpretation.

Consider what happens when constraints are imposed in the form of doubled connectors. As Figure 9.5 illustrates, the connectors *a*, *b*, and *f* in subsystem Alpha gain significance in Interpretation 1. You can impose any number of dramas that might make the systems more interesting to think about and allow you to more clearly rationalize the way Interpretation 2 refines the connectors. For example, suppose that the interaction network map shows accumulations of hazardous materials in a given ecological system. The doubled lines signify highly toxic flows of such materials. Subsystem Beta might then represent a reasonable and important streamlining of the activity shown in subsystem Alpha.

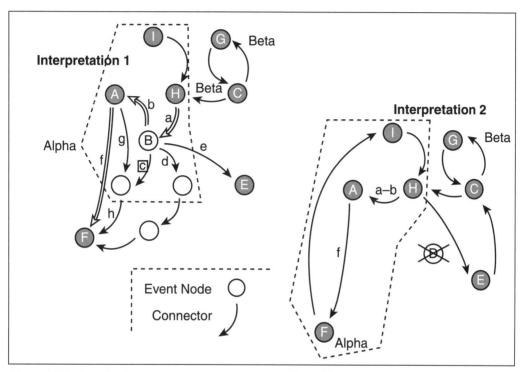

Figure 9.5 Quantitative assessment of connectors justifies refining the interpretation.

Figures 9.3 through 9.5 illustrate how you might apply different logics to any number of systems. If you view a system from an iconic perspective, then the constraints you apply to it must allow you to understand the system on its own terms. If you view a system from a more generalized system of logic, then your view of the system emerges objectively, through a process of reason that might not be at all apparent in the system. Either way, the constraints applied to events instill the events with significance.

Significance and Lighting

The application featured in this chapter provides a fairly simple interaction network that plays on the significance of different lighting effects. A figure walks around a graveyard. The background story might involve a fantasy setting in which a warrior searches through rows of tombstones for a single tombstone that possesses magical powers. Discovery of the magic tombstone might involve interpreting the meaning lighting effects impose on the scene. Consider the following lighting effects:

- **Brightness of ambient lighting.** If the warrior passes through the graveyard during the day, the tombstones might remain in the background. The warrior sees no significance in the tombstones beyond colliding with them when they lie in his path.

- **Source of directional lighting.** As the ambient light diminishes, it might be that a lantern or torch the warrior carries casts light on the tombstones and causes them to reflect light of varying intensities. Variation of intensity among groups of stones might serve as a guide to the warrior as he searches for the magic tombstone.

- **Source of effusive lighting.** A significant stone might glow. In other words, beyond reflecting light or being visible amid ambient light, it might be phosphorescent. As an object that glows on its own accord, it possesses significance over objects that do not.

- **Color of lighting.** Several tombstones might glow, but some might glow with colors of greater richness or appeal than others. If a tombstone appears only to glow with a haunting white presence, the meaning of the flow might be a background effect. But if the tombstone begins to glow with an urgent, sanguine hue, then the meaning might be of immediate and fatal significance.

- **Shadows.** When objects cast shadows, the significance of the shadows can go in many directions. When shadows darken a scene, hidden meanings begin to reside in it. Shadows can hide enemies or conceal allies.

- **Fog or visibility effects.** Fog serves, like shadows, to conceal meanings. Fog proves an effective way of reducing the horizon of events to the distance of a few steps without at the same time forcing a scene to be confined to a room, a hallway, or a natural setting with, for example, trees or vegetation that hide features more than a few steps away.

Graveyard Lighting

Lighting is but one of many possible ways you can make it possible for the events in a simulation to receive selective or filtered significance. With the addition of sound, you can extend the effects of lighting enormously. In addition to light and sound, you can also bring into play different character behaviors. Character behaviors interact with those of sound, lighting, and camera movement to create a realm of nearly endless interaction in which the player of a game or the user of a simulation application can thoroughly explore a context of events.

In this chapter, rather than dealing with economic or ecological systems, the event model encompasses restraints that apply to a simple scene from a game in which an entity proceeds through an eerie setting in search of a treasure. See Figure 9.6.

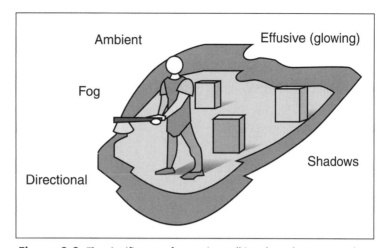

Figure 9.6 The significance of a warrior walking through a graveyard can be altered in a number of ways to accord with different event models.

Realism and Cognitive Saturation

Ultimately, you perceive as real what appears real, and when something appears real to you, it appears real because it draws your attention to it and becomes the central focus of your conscious activity. Psychologists and psychiatrists have noted for centuries that human beings tend to have one center or focus of consciousness. Consciousness is singular. At the same time, it is possible to conduct experiments in which two or more activities simultaneously demand your attention. When this happens, evolution seems to have put in place a mechanism that automatically filters out one event and allows you to dedicate your full attention to the other.

This generalization lies behind the performance of magic tricks. To perform a magic trick, you create a distraction that demands the observer's attention as you perform the trick. When you create a distraction, its demand on the observer's attention has a mesmerizing effect, drawing the observer into a narrowed frame of awareness. The observer concentrates on the distraction while you perform the trick, and when you finish, you appear to have performed magic.

If you think that you can simultaneously pay attention to two events, you can always consider the duck-rabbit illustration. This illustration became famous in the writings of the philosopher Ludwig Wittgenstein, when in his *Philosophical Investigations* he proposed that the duck-rabbit image revealed that language ultimately cannot be reduced to a system of meaning other than the system of meaning its speakers create as they speak. See Figure 9.7.

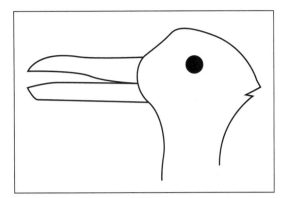

Figure 9.7 You can see one or the other, duck or rabbit, and *what* you see depends on *how* you see.

Experimenting with the duck-rabbit image in Figure 9.7 drives home the point that when something appears realistic, its realism is still relative to the attention of the observer. Attention, in turn, might be described as a *cognitive threshold* at which you receive enough information from a given experience that you consider what you see to be realistic or convincingly self-evident. No absolute standard exists for determining when something emerges to consciousness in this way. When do you see a rabbit? When do you see a duck?

In the context of a game or a simulation, this topic might be discussed in terms of the different constraints you bring into the event context you are working with. Consider, for example, how the few lines in Figure 9.7 create a simple game. You look at the lines one way, and you see a rabbit. You look at them in another, and you see a duck. The vacillation never ends, and the slight pause that marks the change from one way of seeing to the alternate way of seeing tends to induce a change of awareness.

A scene in a game does not differ. If you consider the cognitive saturation depicted in Figure 9.2, you see a different approach to the theme the duck-rabbit presents. A scene is a game that provides you with a number of activities that draw your attention. You might focus on using arrow keys to move a character around a graveyard in search of a grave containing gold, but if the lighting and shadows change as you go, you find that your attention leaps round, overwhelmed by the diversity of events you witness. The total involvement that the play induces leads to a sense of realism, a sense of being completely absorbed by the scene at hand.

Creating a Context of Reality

Access Listing09_01 and compile the project. When the application first starts, you see the character standing on a reddish ground area and facing away from the camera. See Figure 9.8.

Use the left mouse button and the mouse wheel to reposition the character to accord with what you see in Figure 9.9. To see the fog, first adjust the slider setting for the slider on the left so that it is positioned on the left of the slider track. Then go to the slider on the right and make the fog roll forward and back by moving the slider to the left and right. Finally,

Figure 9.8 The initial setting provides a contrast.

adjust the two sliders until they are in roughly the positions you see in Figure 9.9. When you make these changes, the result is a scene in which fog partially obscures the ground and the character, and the definitive boundaries of the scene disappear.

What effect do these changes have on you? Although responses differ, one thing you might note is that when you add fog and remove boundaries, you immediately contribute a set of constraints to the scene that heighten your expectations and draw you into the scene in ways that a clearly defined scene would not. Such changes form the beginning of a context in which an iconic logic begins to emerge. The character now exists in a world in which fog obscures horizons. The logic of the setting draws the character into the foreground and immediately imposes a mood of expectation. What lies hidden in the fog is an unknown, so the character now becomes an adventurer, someone who explores mysteries.

In this section, the goal is to create the basics of the effects you see in Figure 9.9. To accomplish this task, it is necessary to first make a few changes to the physics engine. Then you add entities to the scene to create the ground plane and the character. Following this, you

Figure 9.9 You can add fog and remove boundaries.

implement the fog and the controls for the fog. Given this starting point, you can then proceed to enhance the scene to add features that allow you, as subsequent sections show, to animate the mesh and add complexities to its world.

Disabling Physics

In this section, the goal is to use fog and lighting to set the mood of a scene. In later sections, you extend this activity to create shadows and other effects to enhance the mood. Such activities do not require the use of the physics engine, and for this reason, it is reasonable to turn off the physics engine. To do this, you add an attribute to the CWorld class. Here's the code from CWorld.h that adds the attribute:

```
// Enable physics?
bool m_bPhysics;
```

The m_bPhysics attribute is a Boolean, and it tracks whether or not physics should be processed. To set this attribute, you add a mutator function:

```
// Enable/Disable the physics engine
void SetPhysicsEnabled(bool bEnabled);
```

The SetPhysicsEnabled() function takes in a single Boolean argument that establishes whether the physics of the application should be processed. The function sets m_bPhysics equal to the argument bEnabled. Here is the code for the function in CWorld.cpp:

```
void CWorld::SetPhysicsEnabled(bool bEnabled)
{
        m_bPhysics = bEnabled;
}
```

After attending to the creation of an attribute to govern whether the physics engine is active, you set up a way you can check the flag before trying to perform physics operations. To accomplish this, you modify CWorld::Update(). Here's the code for this function:

```
void CWorld::Update(float fTimeElapsed, IDirect3DDevice9 *pDevice)
{
    if(m_bPhysics)
    {
        // Process collision detection
        dSpaceCollide(GetSpaceID(), 0, &NearCallback);
        dWorldQuickStep(GetWorldID(),fTimeElapsed);
    }
    D3DXMATRIX matOrigWorld;
    pDevice->GetTransform(D3DTS_WORLD, &matOrigWorld);
    for(int itr =0; itr < m_lstEntities.size(); itr++)
    {
        if(m_lstEntities[itr])
        {
            m_lstEntities[itr]->Update(fTimeElapsed, pDevice);
            pDevice->SetTransform(D3DTS_WORLD, &matOrigWorld);
        }
    }
    if(m_bPhysics)
    {
        // Remove the contact joints
        dJointGroupEmpty(GetJointGroupID());
    }
}
```

The changes to the function involve the addition of two if selection statements that check for the truth of m_bPhysics before calls to the ODE functions can be made. Since the three functions, dSpaceCollide(), dWorldQuickStep(), and dJointGroupEmpty(), account for all the calls your application makes to the physics engine, you need only these two selection statements to exclude all ODE activities.

Setting Up Lighting

After attending to the preliminaries of excluding operations performed by the physics engine, you set up the functions that provide the lighting for the scene. To make these changes, you alter a few lines of CMyApplication::Initialize(). Here's the code for this function:

```
void CMyApplication::Initialize()
{
    // Set up two lights
    m_pGraphics->SetDirectionalLight(0,
                D3DCOLOR_XRGB(220, 120, 255),
                D3DXVECTOR3(0, -1, 1.0f));
     m_pGraphics->SetDirectionalLight(1,
                D3DCOLOR_XRGB(128, 250, 128),
                D3DXVECTOR3(0, -1, 1.0f));
    // Lines left out. . .
}
```

These two calls to SetDirectionalLight() create two directional lights. The first argument for SetDirectionalLight() is the index of the light you want to set. The second argument is the color for the light. You use the D3DCOLOR_XRGB() macro to set the color. The final argument is a D3DXVECTOR3 vector that determines the direction the light points. The first of the color values creates a light that is blue. The second of the color values creates a light of less intensity. Both lights have the same origin.

Adding Fog

You create fog by selectively coloring pixels so they obscure the client area of your window. You can vary the density and color of the fog. As you might expect, the darker and more dense the fog, the less you see of the images the fog covers. To create fog, you treat the fog as though it were light and project it into the area you want it to affect.

Setting the Render State of Fog

To add fog to your application, you make changes to the CGraphics class. The function you add is called SetFog(). Here's the code as it appears in CGraphics.cpp:

```
void CGraphics::SetFog(DWORD dwColor, float fStart, float fEnd)
{
        // Enable fog
        m_pDevice->SetRenderState(D3DRS_FOGENABLE, true);
        // Enable ranged fog
        m_pDevice->SetRenderState(D3DRS_RANGEFOGENABLE, true);
        // Set the fog color
        m_pDevice->SetRenderState(D3DRS_FOGCOLOR, dwColor);
        // Set the mode to linear
        m_pDevice->SetRenderState(D3DRS_FOGVERTEXMODE, D3DFOG_LINEAR);
        // Set the start and end of the fog
        m_pDevice->SetRenderState(D3DRS_FOGSTART, *(DWORD*)(&fStart));
        m_pDevice->SetRenderState(D3DRS_FOGEND, *(DWORD*)(&fEnd));
}
```

This SetFog() function takes in three parameters. The first is the color of the fog. The second is a floating-point value that represents the distance from the camera at which the fog should start accumulating. The final argument is a floating-point value that sets the distance at which the fog should stop accumulating.

After the opening brace, the SetFog() function features six successive calls to the IDirect3DDevice9::SetRenderState() function. These calls all work in the same way. First, they use a token of the enumerated DirectX type D3DRENDERSTATETYPE. There are around one hundred different enumerated tokens of this type. Each token helps you in some way set an attribute that applies to the device render state. After you set the token for the render state type, the second parameter of the SetRenderState() function allows you to in some way tune the token. Table 9.1 provides a summary of the values you feed to the SetRenderState() function within the scope of the SetFog() function.

Initializing Fog

After you define the render state of the fog, you then create the attributes and functions needed to initialize the values that relate to the fog. Toward this end, you first declare the identifiers needed to set the start and end values of the fog. You declare these identifiers in the CMyApplication class. Here are the lines from CMyApplication.h that accomplish this work:

```
// Start and end values for the fog
float m_fFogStart;
float m_fFogEnd;
```

Table 9.1 Render State Function Values

Render State Value	Description
D3DRS_FOGENABLE	This token applies to the basic activity of setting up fog for your application. Fog consists of a blend of the colors that apply to the objects rendered in your application and the painted pixels of the fog. This token sets up the render state for fog blending. By default, when you use this token, it is set to false, so the second argument in SetRenderState() is true.
D3DRS_RANGEFOGENABLE	This token applies to fog that is vertex based. This type of fog is referred to as range-based fog. With this type token, the visual effect of the fog results from a calculation based on the distance of the object in the fog from the viewer. By default, when you use this token, it is set to false, so the second argument in SetRenderState() is true.
D3DRS_FOGCOLOR	This token sets the color of the fog. You use a color identifier of the type D3DCOLOR to assign a color to it. The D3DCOLOR is a typedef type derived from DWORD. When you set color for fog, the alpha value is left out. In the SetRenderState() function, the second value is the color you want to use, and in this case, the color is taken from the first parameter of SetFog() (dwColor).
D3DRS_FOGVERTEXMODE	This token identifies the way the fog is to be applied to vertices. The second value of the SetRenderState() provides a flag of the enumerated type D3DFOGMODE, which provides five different values you can apply to the vertex mode. In this instance, the linear mode is set using D3DFOG_LINEAR. When set to linear, the fog tends to intensify as you move from its start point to its end point.
D3DRS_FOGSTART	This token establishes the depth at which the effects of the fog begin. It applies to the linear mode of fog. The default value is 0.0f, and the values you use to set it are floating-point. However, since the SetRenderState() function accepts DWORD values, you must cast the variable that contains the value as a DWORD. For this reason, you see the cast as *(DWORD*) (&fStart). You obtain the float value (fStart) from the second SetFog() parameter.
D3DRS_FOGEND	This token establishes the depth at which the effects of the fog take full effect. It applies to the linear mode of fog. The default value is 1.0f. As with D3DRS_FOGSTART, since the SetRenderState() function accepts DWORD values, you must cast the variable that contains the value as a DWORD. For this reason, you see the case as *(DWORD*) (&fEnd). You obtain the float value (fStart) from the second SetFog() parameter.

Having set up the fog start and end attributes for the CMyApplication class, you then need to make some changes to the Initialize() function to determine how the values will be applied to the fog scene. In addition, you set up the ground plane and define the meshes that appear in the scene. Here is a selection of code from CMyApplication::Initialize():

```
void CMyApplication::Initialize()
{
     // Lines left out. . .
     // Create the ground plane
      CEntity *pGround = GetWorld()->CreateEntity(L"Ground",
                                             L"Meshes\\Stage.x",
                                             m_pGraphics->GetDevice());
     // Create the mesh for the character
      CEntity *pCharacter = GetWorld()->CreateEntity(L"Character",
                                             L"Meshes\\multi_anim.x",
                                             m_pGraphics->GetDevice());
     pCharacter->SetAnimation(L"Stand");
     // Set default fog start and end parameters
     m_fFogStart = 5;              //units from the camera
     m_fFogEnd = 8;                //units to saturation
     // Set up the fog
     m_pGraphics->SetFog(D3DCOLOR_XRGB(0,32,64),
                           m_fFogStart, m_fFogEnd);
     // Set a default camera position
     D3DXVECTOR3 vecEye(0, 1, -5);
     D3DXVECTOR3 vecLookAt(0, 0, 0);
     m_Camera.SetViewParams(&vecEye, &vecLookAt);
     // Lines left out. . .
}
```

The first two function calls of the Initialize() function are to the CWorld::CreateEntity() function. The first of the CreateEntity() function calls loads the mesh for the rectangular ground entity you see in Figure 9.8. The name of the entity is "Character", and the name of the mesh you use to create the entity is "Stage.x". The second call to the CreateEntity() function loads the mesh for the character you see in Figure 9.8. The name of the entity is "Stage", and the name of the mesh you use to create the entity is "multi_anim.x". For both calls, you use the CGraphics class attribute inherited from CApplication class to call the CGraphics::GetDevice() function, which returns a pointer to the IDirect3DDevice9 device your application uses.

Both calls to CreateEntity() originate with the CWorld object for your application. The static GetWorld() function retrieves a pointer to the CWorld object. Since CreateEntity() returns a CEntity reference, you declare two CEntity pointers to which to assign the references. For the stage entity, you assign the reference to pGround, and for the character entity, you assign the reference to pCharacter.

The two CEntity pointers differ slightly, because the character entity is animated, while the stage entity is stationary. To set the animation of the character entity, you call the CEntity::SetAnimation() function. The sole parameter for this function is a string value that provides the name of the animation. In this instance, the animation is called `Stand`. Before you finish this chapter, you will see two other animations in addition to this one. The `Stand` animation allows the character entity to assume a position that is typified by battle posturing.

After you take care of the two entities, you then assign values to the start and end values that define the dimensions of the fog. You set the `m_fFogStart` variable to 5 and the `m_fFogEnd` variable to 8. When you set the start position to 5, the result is that the fog begins to form 5 units away from the camera. When you set the end position to 8, the fog reaches its saturation point when it is 8 units away from the camera. You then call `CGraphics::SetFog()` to apply these parameters to the fog. You apply these parameters using the second and third parameters of `SetFog()`. For the first parameter, as was discussed previously, you provide a color definition. In this case, the definition is `D3DCOLOR_XRGB(0, 32, 64)`, which has a bluish theme.

As a final bit of work in the `Initialize()` function, you attend to the initial position of the camera. To accomplish this, you create two vectors and then pass them to the `CModelViewerCamera::SetViewParams()` function. The effect of this activity, first, is to make it so that the camera does not start out parallel to the ground plane. If this were to happen, the ground would be invisible upon startup. Of the two vectors you pass to the `SetViewParams()` function, the first (`vecEye`) represents the eye point of the camera. The second (`vecLookAt`) represents the point at which the camera is directed. You initialize the `vecEye` vector to (0, 1, -5), which places it slightly above the ground and 5 units out on the z axis. You initialize the `vecLookAt` vector at the origin of the world, so the camera looks directly at point (0, 0, 0).

Updating the GUI

At this point in the development of the application for Listing09_01, you have done what anyone would consider a good day's work. You have made is so that you can disable physics operations. You have set up the lighting for the scene. You have used six tokens to set the render state of the fog. You have added two entities, one for the stage and one for the character. And you have used the begin and end values for the fog to actually create the fog. This seems like it should be enough for one section, but still just a little bit of work remains to be done. The work is easy and rewarding, however, for it involves creating two labels and two sliders. The sliders control the front and back fringes of the fog. The labels tell you what the sliders are about. You can see these labels and sliders on the control panel in Figure 9.8.

Fog Labels and Sliders

To add these controls and the functionality associated with them, you work with the code in the `CMyApplication::InitGUI()` function. Here is a sampling of the code, which you can find in CMyApplication.cpp:

```
void CMyApplication::InitGUI()
{
    // Lines left out
    // Label and slider for begin
    m_GUI.AddStatic(IDC_STATIC_S, L"Fog Start(0-10):",
            25, m_iConsoleY + 10, 105, 18);
    m_GUI.AddSlider(IDC_START,
            25, m_iConsoleY + 30, 100, 20, 0, 100, 50);
    // Label and slider for end
    m_GUI.AddStatic(IDC_STATIC_E, L"Fog End (0-10):",
            275, m_iConsoleY + 10, 105, 18);
    m_GUI.AddSlider(IDC_END,
            275, m_iConsoleY + 30, 100, 20, 0, 100, 80);
}
```

You have seen the `AddSlider()` and `AddStatic()` functions before. The interface for the `CDXUTDialog` class furnishes these functions. The calls occur in two sets. Each set first creates a label and then a slider. The first set creates for the start slider, which sets the point at which the fog starts. The second set creates the end slider, which sets the intensity of the fog as it forms in relation to the starting point.

The `AddSlider()` and `AddStatic()` functions call for a name identifier as their first parameter. You declare the constant values that provide these identifiers in CMyApplication.h along with the other class attributes. Here are the lines that accomplish this work:

```
static const int IDC_START = 0;
static const int IDC_END = 1;
static const int IDC_STATIC_S = 2;
static const int IDC_STATIC_E = 3;
```

The second parameter of the `AddStatic()` function requires a string for the text the label displays. You see, then, "Fog Start" and "Fog End" as the text for the labels. Following the definition of the text for the labels, you see the two coordinates that establish the position of the upper left corner of the label. The first label, for example, is set `25` units from the left and `m_iConsoleY + 10` units from the top. The remaining two parameters of the `AddStatic()` function set the width and height of the label.

The parameters of the `AddSlider()` function resemble those of the `AddStatic()` function. After the name identifier, you see the two values that set the coordinates for the upper left corner and the values that set the height and width of the slider. The last three parameters of the `AddSlider()` function set, first, the starting value of the slider, then the end value of the slider, and finally the default setting of the slider. You might notice that the default values of the sliders are set at `50` and `80`. You have seen these values before, when you assigned them to `m_fFogStart` and `m_fFogEnd` in the `Initialize()` function.

Fog Control Messages

Having set up the controls that issue the messages, it is time to set up the functionality that processes the messages. To accomplish this, you visit the code in the CMyApplication::OnGUIEvent() function. You can find this function in CMyApplication.cpp:

```
void CMyApplication::OnGUIEvent(UINT nEvent, int nControlID,
                                 CDXUTControl *pControl)
{
      // Change starting fog value
      if(nControlID == IDC_START)
      {
            CDXUTSlider *pSlider = (CDXUTSlider *)pControl;
            m_fFogStart = (float)pSlider->GetValue()/10.0f;
      }
      // Change ending fog value
      else if(nControlID == IDC_END)
      {
            CDXUTSlider *pSlider = (CDXUTSlider *)pControl;
            m_fFogEnd = (float)pSlider->GetValue()/10.0f;
      }

      // Apply the settings
      m_pGraphics->SetFog(D3DCOLOR_XRGB(0, 32, 64),
                          m_fFogStart,
                          m_fFogEnd);
}
```

OnGUIEvent() function has three parameters. The first parameter designates the unique identifier of the event the function processes. The second parameter identifies the message associated with the event. The third parameter takes a pointer to the control that issues the message. After the OnGUIEvent() function receives a message, it identifies it and then performs the appropriate action in response to it.

In this case, the OnGUIEvent() function processes only two messages—those that the two sliders issue. As you can see from the selection statements, one message is from the start slider (identified with the IDC_START ID). The other message is from the end slider (identified with the IDC_END ID).

In both cases, to process messages, you first declare two local pointers to CDXUTSlider objects and assign the addresses of the fog sliders to them. You obtain the address using the CDXUTControl parameter (*pControl) of the OnGUIEvent() function. You have to cast the control addresses before assigning them to the pointers.

Using the `CDXUTSlider::GetValue()` function, you can obtain the value of the message the control issues. In this case, you obtain floating-point values between 0 and 10. You store these values in the appropriate class attributes you have declared to hold fog values (`m_fFogStart` and `m_fFogEnd`). These have been discussed previously.

Having obtained the slider values, you then call `CGraphics::SetFog()`. The first parameter of `SetFog()` is the color you want to assign to the fog. The second and third parameters are the start and end value for the fog.

At this point, you can execute the program and use the sliders to position the fog so that it rolls up over the character and, if you move the slider far enough, completely obscures it. Short of completely obscuring the character, you can create effects that bring added psychological dimensions to the scene, and these, as was mentioned at the beginning of the chapter, ultimately allow you to extensively shape the logic that defines the character's world.

Shadows

In the last section, you created fog and applied it to the character's world in a way that allowed you to introduce new and involved psychological dimensions into the scene. Fog is but one of many possible effects. Another set of effects involves shadows. Shadows have a variety of purposes. One is to add realism to scenes. Another is to further extend the psychological dimensions of the scenes you develop.

To get a sense of what shadows are about, access the code for Listing09_02 and compile the program. Figure 9.10 shows you the result. The sphere in the foreground casts what is known as a planar shadow. A planar shadow is one of the simplest types of shadows you can create. Such a shadow can be cast only on a predefined plane (thus the term *planar*). In this instance, the predefined plane is the surface of the ground, which remains stationary relative to the sphere. Although simple, planar shadows can provide your scenes with realism and tremendously enhance the visual appeal they have for their viewers.

The Shadow Function in Its Entirety

One of the longest functions described in this book results from the development of the code that supports shadows. This is the `DrawShadow()` function. To make it a little easier to understand the explanations that follow, Example 9.1 shows you the entirety of the `DrawShadow()` function. Take a minute to familiarize yourself with the code. In the sections that follow, the explanations break the function into pieces. If you become disoriented, refer back to Example 9.1.

As an aid to understanding, here is a summary of the headings for the next few sections and the discussion provided. Again, all of these headings sequentially dwell on different sections of the `DrawShadow()` function:

Figure 9.10 Shadows contribute to the mood of your world.

- **Validating meshes and enabling lights.** You check the validity of the mesh, and you enable lights.
- **Setting textures, z buffers, and materials.** You make it so you can transfer the lighting to the world matrix, and you set the materials for the objects in the scene.
- **Selecting and retrieving lights.** You set the properties for the lights that apply to the scene.
- **Setting normal and plane calculations and light types.** You designate the direction of the lights and determine the type of light you want to apply.
- **Selecting and Retrieving Lights.** You enable lights and associate them with the appropriate shadow vectors.
- **Transforming and drawing the shadow matrix.** You transfer the values you have created to the shadow matrix.
- **Rendering the state and enabling lights.** You draw the shadow and call the rendering function.

The reason that rendering shadows becomes complicated begins with the need to bring lights, the world, textures, materials, and the entities that cast the shadows all into harmony with each other. To complete the undertaking even for planar shadows, you have to be willing to take time to attend to the factors involved. To aid you with some of the terms that occur in the next few section, Figure 9.11 illustrates the work of directional lighting, the entity as a mesh, the planar surface (again, a mesh), and the shadow.

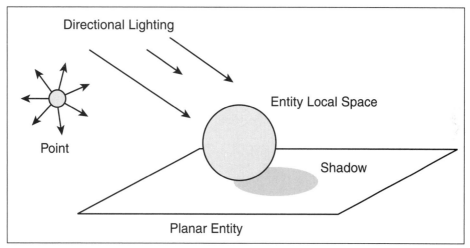

Figure 9.11 You need to apply material properties to the entity that casts the shadow and then translate the shadow to the planar surface.

Example 9.1 (Listing09_02/CMesh.cpp)

The DrawShadow() function performs the work of creating shadows.

```
void CMesh::DrawShadow(IDirect3DDevice9 *pd3dDevice)
{
    // Make sure the objects exist
    if(!m_pMesh)
        return;
    // An array to store the original "enabled" value of the lights
    BOOL bEnabled[8];
    for(int itr=0; itr<8; itr++)
    {
        // Store the value, and then turn off the light
        pd3dDevice->GetLightEnable(itr, &bEnabled[itr]);
        pd3dDevice->LightEnable(itr, false);
    }

    // Disable z-buffer checking
```

```
pd3dDevice->SetRenderState(D3DRS_ZENABLE, false);
// Shadows have no texture
pd3dDevice->SetTexture(0, NULL);
// Set up a material for the shadow (65% opacity, black color)
D3DMATERIAL9 materialShadow;
ZeroMemory(&materialShadow, sizeof(D3DMATERIAL9));
materialShadow.Diffuse.a = 0.35;
// Set the material
pd3dDevice->SetMaterial(&materialShadow);

// Loop through all the lights
for(int itr=0; itr < 8; itr++)
{
      // If it is not enabled, skip the rest
      if(!bEnabled[itr])
            continue;
      // Get the copy of the light
      D3DLIGHT9 Light;
      pd3dDevice->GetLight(itr, &Light);
      // Create the light vector
      D3DXVECTOR4 vecLight;
      D3DXPLANE Plane;
      //If this is a point light, set the w component to 1,
      //otherwise set it to zero, also
      //need to invert the plane depending on the light type
        if(Light.Type == D3DLIGHT_POINT)
        {
              Plane = D3DXPLANE(0, 1, 0, 0);  // w to 1
              vecLight = D3DXVECTOR4(Light.Position.x,
                                     Light.Position.y,
                                     Light.Position.z, 1);
        }
        else{
              Plane = D3DXPLANE(0,-1,0,0);
              vecLight = D3DXVECTOR4(Light.Direction.x,
                                     Light.Direction.y,
                                     Light.Direction.z, 0);
        }//end else

      // Create the shadow matrix
      D3DXMATRIX matShadow;
      D3DXMatrixShadow(&matShadow, &vecLight, &Plane);
```

```
        // Copy the original world matrix
        D3DXMATRIXA16 matOrigWorld, matWorld;
        pd3dDevice->GetTransform(D3DTS_WORLD, &matOrigWorld);
         // Apply the shadow matrix, set the transform
        D3DXMatrixMultiply(&matWorld, &matOrigWorld, &matShadow);
        pd3dDevice->SetTransform(D3DTS_WORLD, &matWorld);

        // Draw the mesh, one material at a time
        for(int iSubset=0; iSubset < m_dwNumMaterials; iSubset++)
        {
               // Draw the subset
               m_pMesh->DrawSubset(iSubset);
        }//end material for
     }//end light for

     // Re-enable the z-buffer
     pd3dDevice->SetRenderState(D3DRS_ZENABLE, true);
     // Turn the original lights back on
     for(int itr = 0; itr < 8; itr++)
      {
             pd3dDevice->LightEnable(itr, bEnabled[itr]);
      }
}//end DrawShadow()
```

Validating Meshes and Enabling Lights

To attend to creating shadows, you call the DrawShadow() function, which requires only one parameter, a pointer to a IDirect3DDevice9 device. This is the device you declare in the CGraphics.cpp. You can call the DrawShadow() function from a number of places (CEntity::Render(), CWorld::Render(), for example), but as a later section in this chapter shows, it is most convenient, for starters, to call it from CMesh::Draw().

The DrawShadow() function operates on the LPD3DXMESH attribute of the CMesh class (m_pMesh), so one of the first tasks you attend to involves checking the validity of the LPD3DXMESH attribute. The if selection statement determines that the value stored in m_pMesh is not NULL. If the value is NULL, then the statement forces the function to return. Here are the first few lines of DrawShadow() as they appear in CMesh.cpp:

```
void CMesh::DrawShadow(IDirect3DDevice9 *pd3dDevice)
{
     // Make sure the objects exists
     if(!m_pMesh)
            return;
```

After you have established the validity of the LPD3DXMESH attribute, you can then attend to the lighting of the scene. You first store the enabled status of the lights. Then you turn them off. As has been noted elsewhere, you can have up to eight lights in a scene. To check for enabled lights, you employ a for loop to iterate through the lights and discover if they are currently enabled. Here is the code that accomplishes this task:

```
// An array to store the status of the lights
BOOL bEnabled[8];
 //iterate to detect the status
for(int itr=0; itr < 8; itr++)
{
      // Store the value, and then turn off the light
      pd3dDevice->GetLightEnable(itr, &bEnabled[itr]);
      pd3dDevice->LightEnable(itr, false);
}
```

To store the information you retrieve about the status of the lights, you create a Boolean array (bEnabled[8]). To detect the value of the lights, you access the IDirect3DDevice9 device passed to DrawShadow() and call the IDirect3DDevice9::GetLightEnable() function. This function provides two parameters. The first is an index to the number of the light you want to check. The second is a reference to the Boolean array (&bEnabled) you have created to store the results of the check.

You then once again make use of the IDirect3DDevice9 device passed to DrawShadow(). This time, you call the IDirect3DDevice9::LightEnable() function. This function also offers two parameters. The first parameter identifies the number of the light you want to change. The second provides the Boolean value you want to apply to the light. A value of false turns the light off (disables it). You disable the lights so that they do not spoil the effects you achieve when you create shadows. Shadows should appear black.

Z Setting Textures, Z Buffers, and Materials

After turning the lights off, you next attend to setting up the appearance of the shadow. To accomplish this, you have three main tasks. The first is to turn off any lights that might distort the shadow. The second is to ensure that the shadow appears on top of whatever surface it strikes. The third is to provide the shadow with a velvety, raven material appearance. Here is the code that performs this work:

```
// Disable z-buffer checking
pd3dDevice->SetRenderState(D3DRS_ZENABLE, false);
// Shadows have no texture
pd3dDevice->SetTexture(0, NULL);
// Set up a material for the shadow (35% opacity)
D3DMATERIAL9 materialShadow;
```

```
ZeroMemory(&materialShadow, sizeof(D3DMATERIAL9));
materialShadow.Diffuse.a = 0.35;
// Set the material
pd3dDevice->SetMaterial(&materialShadow);
```

The first call to the SetRenderState() function disables the use of the z buffer. To accomplish this, you access the D3DRS_ZENABLE flag to set the first parameter of SetRenderState(). This flag tells SetRenderState() that you want to attend to the status of the z buffer. In this case, you want to disable the z buffer, and this you accomplish by setting the second parameter of SetRenderState() to false. The z buffer establishes the depth of the objects you want to render. You disable the z buffer because you want the shadow to draw over the ground plane. A shadow does not have the same depth value as the ground plane. When you disable the z buffer, you ensure that the shadows are always drawn over the ground plane.

Following your work with the z buffer, you call the IDirect3DDevice9::SetTexture() function. You call this function because you need to prevent the shadow object from being rendered with a texture. Shadows do not have textures. Instead, they have only colors that you assign to them. To eliminate the texture, you supply the SetTexture() function with values that cancel out the texture. The first value indicates the sampler number (or register) that a texture, if assigned, would occupy, and in this case the value you assign is 0. The second parameter designates a IDirect3DBaseTexture9 object (a texture). Since there is no texture to designate, you assign NULL for the second value.

A second chunk of work involved in setting up the shadow encompasses associating it with materials. Materials account for how objects reflect light, so when used with a shadow, materials help you give the shadow an inky ebon quality. To create the material you apply to the shadow, you first define a D3DMATERIAL9 structure (materialShadow). Having created the structure, you call the ZeroMemory() function to fill the structure with zeros. The two arguments for the ZeroMemory() function are the object you want to zero out (in this case the materials structure) and the size of the memory space the object requires (which you use the C library sizeof() function to obtain). Filling a structure with zeros is a precautionary measure programmers usually take when creating structures, but in this case, the zeros have a dual purpose. The color of the shadow is to be black, so to designate this color, you assign zeros to the elements of the materials structure. (The RGB values for black are 0, 0, 0.)

Having colored the material black, you again visit the D3DMATERIAL9 materialShadow structure to set its Diffuse element. The D3DMATERIAL9 material structure features four elements that store information about the four basic types of light. (See the sidebar, "The D3DLIGHT9 Structure.") Like other elements of the D3DMATERIAL9 structure, the Diffuse element defines a color, and the color type is D3DCOLORVALUE structure. Each D3DCOLORVALUE element itself contains four elements (r, g, b, and a), and the alpha component (a) takes a value between 0 and 1.0.

The alpha component determines the degree to which an object is transparent. If the value of the alpha component is 0, the object is completely opaque. For the current application, you set the transparency to 0.35, which makes the shadow 35% opaque (or 65% transparent). The value you assign to the alpha component depends on the effect you want to achieve. The higher the value, the more absorbing the shadow. You call the IDirect3DDevice9::SetMaterial() function to tell the device to apply the material transparency you have defined as it renders the shadow.

The D3DMATERIAL9 Structure

If you need a review of topics relating to light, see Chapter 5, "Design for Entities," and go to the heading titled "Target Characteristics—Materials." All of the elements of the D3DMATERIAL9 structure, save the last (Power) are of the D3DCOLORVALUE type. Here is the basic layout of the D3DMATERIAL9 material structure:

```
typedef struct _D3DMATERIAL9 {
        D3DCOLORVALUE Diffuse;    //all of these are color
        D3DCOLORVALUE Ambient;    //designations
        D3DCOLORVALUE Specular;
        D3DCOLORVALUE Emissive;
        float Power;              //this has a default value
} D3DMATERIAL9;
```

Selecting and Retrieving Lights

After setting up the materials for the shadow, your next major task is, first, to enable the appropriate lights and, second, to associate the shadow vector with the plane on which the shadow is to appear. A large for loop in the DrawShadow() function encloses the code that accomplishes this labor. Here is the first section of the code in the for loop:

```
for(int itr=0; itr < 8; itr++)
{
        // If it is not, continue
        if(!bEnabled[itr])
                continue;
        // Get the copy of the light
        D3DLIGHT9 Light;
        pd3dDevice->GetLight(itr, &Light);
        // Create the light vector and the plane struct
```

The for loop iterates through the lights of the scene. As was mentioned previously, DirectX supports up to eight lights. Within the for loop, the first action involves applying an if selection statement to verify that a light in the light array (bEnabled) has been enabled. You want no *disabled* lights to cast shadows, so the `if` statement asserts a nega-tion. If the negation proves true, revealing a disabled light, then the `continue` keyword forces the loop to the next iteration, and no further processing is performed on the light.

For *enabled* lights, life goes on, and the next step necessitates calling the `IDirect3DDevice9::GetLight()` function to retrieve the light from the DirectX device. Before you call the `GetLight()` function, you perform a preliminary task that consists of declaring a `D3DLIGHT9` structure that you name, appropriately, Light. You use the `D3DLIGHT9` structure (`Light`) to store the values you retrieve when you call the `IDirect3DDevice9::GetLight()` func-tion. This function requires that you provide it with two parameter values. The first is an integer that designates the light about which you want information. The second is a refer-ence (`&Light`) to the `D3DLIGHT9` structure, and the `GetLight()` function stores the information it retrieves in this reference.

The `D3DLIGHT9` Structure

The `D3DLIGHT9` structure consists of a vast assortment of light properties. For extended discussion of these properties, see Chapter 5. Here is the definition of the `D3DLIGHT9` structure with a few comments to briefly explain its features.

```
typedef struct _D3DLIGHT9 {
    D3DLIGHTTYPE Type;          //spot, point, directional
    D3DCOLORVALUE Diffuse;      //emitted color
    D3DCOLORVALUE Specular;     //emitted color
    D3DCOLORVALUE Ambient;      //emitted color
    D3DVECTOR Position;         //position in world space
    D3DVECTOR Direction;        //direction in world space
    float Range;     //distance light is effective
    float Falloff;    //difference between inner and outer cone intensity
    float Attenuation0;   //change of light over distance
    float Attenuation1;   //change of light over distance
    float Attenuation2;   //change of light over distance
    float Theta;          //spot light definition of inner cone
    float Phi;            //spot light definition of outer cone
} D3DLIGHT9;
```

Normal and Plane Calculations and Light Types

Having retrieved information on a light, you next set about assigning to it the direction you want it to point. Ultimately, the direction of the light determines the direction in which the shadow is cast. To attend to this chore, you involve yourself in a subtle set of calculations that allow you to determine the position of the light relative to the plane on which the shadow is cast. The calculations require that you declare a `D3DXVECTOR4` vector to identify the position of the light and a D3DXPLANE structure to set points on the plane that you measure relative to the points in the light vector. The sets of coordinates you use to identify points on the plane make use of what is known as a *homogenous point*, so coordinate sets on the plane possess x, y, z, and w values. The w value creates the homogenous point.

What happens next depends on the type of light you are dealing with. Generally, two types of light apply to the scene. One type is point light, which originates at a specific location and radiates out from it. The other type is directional, which means that rather than originating at a point and radiating outward, it somewhat resembles rain falling from a cloud and so has only direction. In either case, you have to designate the appropriate way to calculate the shadows for the light. To deal with the different types of light, you set up a selection statement. Here is the code:

```
// . . .  continuing the for loop . . .
D3DXVECTOR4 vecLight;
D3DXPLANE Plane;
 if(Light.Type == D3DLIGHT_POINT)
  {
        Plane = D3DXPLANE(0, 1, 0, 0);  // w to 1
        vecLight = D3DXVECTOR4( Light.Position.x,
                                Light.Position.y,
                                Light.Position.z,
                      1);

  }
  else{
        Plane = D3DXPLANE(0, -1, 0, 0);
        vecLight = D3DXVECTOR4(Light.Direction.x,
                               Light.Direction.y,
                               Light.Direction.z,
                               0);
  }//end else
```

If the light is of type D3DLIGHT_POINT (point light), the statement creates a D3DXPLANE structure. The arguments passed to the D3DXPLANE structure (0, 1, 0, 0) define the ground plane. (The equation the D3DXPLANE structure sets reads, $ax + by + cz + dw = 0$, so the y coordinate is the second argument.) The ground plane lies on the x-z axis and has a y value equal to zero. (See Figure 9.12.)

After establishing values for the ground plane, you create a vector to identify the light's position. To accomplish this, you make use of the D3DLIGHT9 Light structure you created prior to the loop, extracting values from its first three elements to populate a D3DXVECTOR4 object. For now, you assign 1 for the final value because, when you position the light, you also designate the light type, and this value serves to designate D3DLIGHT_POINT (point) lights.

That takes care of the first selection statement. There remains, however, the else clause. If the type of the light is directional (D3DLIGHT_DIRECTIONAL), you make the plane face the opposite direction (which is also called inverting it). To make the plane face the opposite direction, you assign a value of -1 to the y element of the D3DXPLANE structure. Following your work with the constructor, you then attend to the light's position. Since directional light has no fixed point of origin (as is the case with point light), you deal with position as a property that describes the direction in which the light moves. To accomplish this, you use the same means you employed with point light, a D3DXVECTOR4 structure. As you did before, when setting the point light, you use the D3DLIGHT9 Light structure to retrieve the light values, but in this case you set the fourth parameter of the constructor to zero instead of a one. This tells DirectX that the type of light this vector represents is directional.

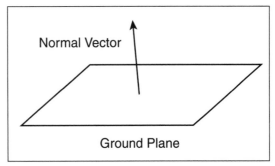

Figure 9.12 The normal vector is relative to the ground plane.

Transforming and Drawing the Shadow Matrix

In the previous work within the DrawShadow() function, you have established the materials properties of the shadow and set the light so that it can strike the plane in the right way. Now you must attend to transforming the shadow matrix, which is the set of coordinates that places the shadow on the plane, and then draw it on the plane. Here is the code that accomplishes these tasks:

```
// . . . continuing the for loop . . .
// Create the shadow matrix
D3DXMATRIX matShadow;
D3DXMatrixShadow(&matShadow, &vecLight, &Plane);

// Copy the original world matrix
 D3DXMATRIXA16 matOrigWorld, matWorld;
 pd3dDevice->GetTransform(D3DTS_WORLD, &matOrigWorld);
 // Apply the shadow matrix, set the transform
D3DXMatrixMultiply(&matWorld, &matOrigWorld, &matShadow);
pd3dDevice->SetTransform(D3DTS_WORLD, &matWorld);

// Draw the mesh, one material at a time
for(int iSubset = 0; iSubset < m_dwNumMaterials; iSubset++)
{
        // Draw the subset
```

```
                    m_pMesh->DrawSubset(iSubset);
            }//end material for
    }//end light for
```

To transform the shadow plane, you first declare an identifier of the D3DXMATRIX (matShadow). The matrix stores information that allows you to spread the shadow out on the plane. To populate the D3DXMATRIX, you call the D3DXMatrixShadow() function, which takes the values for the shadow and flattens them so they can appear on the plane. This function requires values for three parameters. The first is a reference to the resulting shadow matrix (&matShadow). The second is a reference to the D3DXVECTOR4 structure (&vecLight) you have set up to describe the light that casts the shadow. The final is a reference to the D3DXPLANE structure (&matShadow) that you have set up to describe the plane the shadow is cast on.

Having flattened out the shadow, you now copy your world matrix so that you can return to its original state after applying light. To accomplish this you first declare two D3DXMATRIX16 matrices for the worlds you are dealing with. You then call the GetTransform() function to retrieve the state of the device. Of the two parameters of this function, the type of the first is D3DTRANSFORMSTATETYPE, which tells how you want to transfer data to your device. In this case, you use the world matrix flag (D3DTS_WORLD). The next parameter is of the type D3DMATRIX, and for this parameter, you provide a reference to the world matrix you just declared (&matOrigWorld).

The last bit of work involves combining the shadow matrix with the world matrix. To accomplish this, you call the D3DXMatrixMultiply() function to multiply the world by the shadow matrix. This function takes three parameters. The parameters' values are references to the two worlds you are dealing with—the original and the transformed shadow matrix. The resulting matrix is stored in the first parameter (&matWorld). Having multiplied the two matrices, you then call the IDirect3DDevice9::SetTransform() function to set up the world transformation on the device. The final matrix is the second parameter (matWorld). The first parameter type is D3DTRANSFORMSTATETYPE, which tells how you want to transfer data to your device. As before, the flag is D3DTS_WORLD.

When you draw the shadow, you do so using a for loop that gives you access to the materials you want to apply to the shadow. The for loop iterates over all of the subsets of the mesh. A subset, you recall, refers to an area of a complex mesh that can be recognized as representing a distinct group of features (among which are materials). In most cases, you might find that you deal with only one subset; in this application, however, the mesh possesses more than one subset. To access the subsets, you call the D3DXMesh::DrawSubset() function. The single parameter this function uses takes an integer that designates the subset you want to access.

With this task completed, the main for loop of the DrawShadow() function is complete, but you still have just a little bit of work before you are done with the function itself. The work left to perform involves rendering the lights.

Rendering the State and Enabling Lights

Here is the code at the end of DrawShadow() that renders the lights:

```
// Re-enable the z-buffer
pd3dDevice->SetRenderState(D3DRS_ZENABLE, true);

// Turn the original lights back on
for(int itr=0; itr<8; itr++)
{
        pd3dDevice->LightEnable(itr, bEnabled[itr]);
}
```

To render the lights, you first reset the device for rendering. To accomplish this, you call the IDirect3DDevice9::SetRenderState() function. The first parameter of this function designates the render state (D3DRENDERSTATETYP), and in this case, the render state is D3DRS_ZENABLE, which allows you to place the shadow on a flat plane. The second parameter is a Boolean value, and this you set to true. After setting the render state, you then use a for loop to iterate through the lights of the scene and turn them back on.

To turn on the lights, you make a call to the IDirect3DDevice9::LightEnable() function. The two parameters of this function identify, first, the number of the light you want to enable and, second, the value that indicates whether the light is to be enabled. In this case, you retrieve the values you stored in bEnabled array. This array provides an "enable" flag for each of the lights you want to enable while leaving the others turned off.

Setting the Stage

Even after you create the DrawShadow() function to take care of details like applying materials to the shadow, transferring the shadow to the world, and turning lights on and off, you still need to create a way to call DrawShadow(). This work entails modifying the CMesh::Draw() function. The goal of the work is to have this function automatically render the shadow for the mesh. Here is the code for the Draw() function from CMesh.cpp:

```
void CMesh::Draw(IDirect3DDevice9 *pd3dDevice)
{
      // Lines left out. . .
      // Set up world matrix
       D3DXMATRIXA16 matWorld, matCenter;
       pd3dDevice->GetTransform(D3DTS_WORLD, &matWorld);
```

```
        // Draw the shadow
        DrawShadow(pd3dDevice);
        // Lines left out. . .
}
```

To set the stage for calling the DrawShadow() function, you first call the GetTransform() function. This function retrieves the state of the device. The type of the first parameter is D3DTRANSFORMSTATETYPE, which tells how you want to transfer data to your device. The flag you apply is D3DTS_WORLD, which designates the world matrix. The next parameter is of the type D3DMATRIX, and for this parameter, you provide a reference to the world matrix you declare locally (&matWorld). When you at last call the DrawShadow() function, shadows are created for all the simple meshes in your world.

Testing the Drawing of Shadows

To render the shadows, you create a sphere entity in the CMyApplication::Initialize() function. Here is the code from CMyApplication.cpp that creates the sphere:

```
        // Create a ball for testing shadows
        CEntity *pBall = GetWorld()->CreateEntity(L"Ball", 0.5,
                                    D3DCOLOR_XRGB(255, 255, 255),
                                    m_pGraphics->GetDevice());
        pBall->SetPos(D3DXVECTOR3(1, .5, 1));
```

You use the CWorld::CreateEntity() function to create an entity named "Ball". The first two parameters of the function set the radius to 0.5 and the color to white (255, 255, 255). The final parameter designates a pointer to the Direct3D device declared in CGraphics. The call to SetPos() moves the ball to a point away from the origin. When you set the sphere in this position, you ensure that it avoids collision with the character in the scene.

With the creation of the "Ball" entity, your work to set up the functionality that allows you to have shadows in your application is completed. You can now see the scene illustrated in Figure 9.8.

Creating a Graveyard Scene

Fog and shadows provide extremely effective ways to introduce constraints into the event models you implement as simulations. Fog, for example, constrains a scene so that its potentials for mystery become evident. Shadows accentuate entities so that they have a presence and resonance of meaning that they do not posses when they lack shadows. Realism enters into the scene, and what you see on your computer screen begins to reveal the full potentials of 3D graphics.

A further dimension awaits you when you begin extending the concept of point lights to those of equipping a character that you control with the power to light the objects that lie in his path. When you can accomplish this feat, your efforts become analogous to those of a cinematographer who can bring objects in a scene into the penumbra of light or focus in order to show you what a character might be seeing as he explores a specific setting. Controlling what emerges to visibility enables to constrain the psychological dimensions of your simulation in a number of fascinating, absorbing ways.

In this portion of the chapter, the project becomes one of equipping an animated character with the ability to cause objects around him to come into visibility through illumination. If you open Listing09_03 and compile the project, Figure 9.13 shows you the result. Ultimately, the programming involves assigning a point light to the character's position that changes as the character moves, illuminating objects that lie within a set perimeter of the character. In this section, you do not make it so that the character moves. That is a task left for the next section.

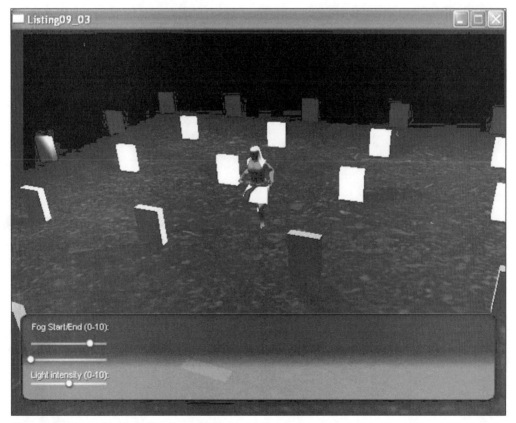

Figure 9.13 A character illuminates the surrounding area.

Modifying the World for Shadows

Before attending to assigning a point light to the character's potion, some preliminary work remains to be performed. Although you might not have noticed it after you executed the program for Listing09_02, when you positioned the character so that it stood in the path of the shadow, the shadow would overlie the character. See Figure 9.14. This is a feature that calls for correction.

Figure 9.14 The shadow encroaches on the character.

The improper appearance of the shadow results because the scene is not drawn in the correct order. When you rotate the camera, the features of the scene should appear so that the shadow covers the character only if the character is in the path of the shadow. To correct the situation, you must change the code so that the application draws objects in the correct order. The correct order calls for the ground plane to be drawn first. Following the ground plane, you then draw the shadows. After the shadows have been drawn, you can then draw other objects in the scene, among which is the character. To implement these changes, you change the code in the Render() function of the CWorld class. Here is the changed code from CWorld.cpp:

```
void CWorld::Render(IDirect3DDevice9 *pDevice)
{
        // Save the original camera transform.  The transformation matrix
        // is reset to this one after each object is drawn
```

```
D3DXMATRIX matCamera;
pDevice->GetTransform(D3DTS_WORLD, &matCamera);
int iStartEntity = 0;



// Render the ground plane, which must be the first object
if(m_lstEntities[0] && (m_lstEntities[0]->GetName() ==
    L"GROUND" || m_lstEntities[0]->GetName() == L"Ground"))
{
    m_lstEntities[0]->Render(pDevice);
    iStartEntity = 1;
}

// Next, render all shadows
for(int itr = iStartEntity; itr < m_lstEntities.size(); itr++)
{
    // Reset the transformation matrix
    pDevice->SetTransform(D3DTS_WORLD, &matCamera);
     if(m_lstEntities[itr])
        m_lstEntities[itr]->RenderShadows(pDevice);
}

// Now, render the rest of the entities
for(int itr = iStartEntity; itr < m_lstEntities.size(); itr++)
{
    // Reset the transformation matrix
    pDevice->SetTransform(D3DTS_WORLD, &matCamera);

    if(m_lstEntities[itr])
        m_lstEntities[itr]->Render(pDevice);
}
}
```

In the first few lines of the function following the opening brace, you declare a D3DXMATRIX structure to hold camera values. You then call the IDirect3DDevice9::GetTransform() to retrieve the current world transform. You obtain the transform information so that you can use it as needed in the operations that follow.

Following retrieval of the transform values for the camera, you write code that prevents the ground plane from being rendered more than once. To accomplish this, you first declare an integer identifier (iStartEntity) to track the indexes of entities stored in the entities vector (m_lstEntities). Having declared an entity counter, you then set up an if statement to determine if a non-NULL entity resides at element zero in the vector. The if statement also verifies whether this object equals "GROUND" or "Ground". If an entity does reside in the vector and does equate to either of the forms of "ground," then the code immediately renders it and sets iStartEntity to 1. This action prevents the ground plane from casting a shadow or being rendered in the loops that follow.

After you have taken care of the conditions involved in rendering the ground plan, you then create two for loops to render the shadows of entities other than the ground plane. To accomplish this, after passing over the ground plane, the first for loop iterates through the entities in the m_lstEntity vector and renders the shadows for each entity. To render the shadows, you first call the IDirect3DDevice9::SetTransform() function to set the transformation to the original camera matrix (matCamera). Following the setting of the transformation, you provide an if selection statement to determine whether the entity at the current index of the vector exists. If it exists, you call the CEntity::RenderShadows() function to render the shadow that corresponds to each entity.

The second for loop renders entities over the shadows that the first for loop has laid down. The operations within this loop work almost the same as those in the first for loop. The only difference is that you call the CEntity::Render() function instead of the CEntity::CRenderShadows() function. The CRender() function renders the entities so that they appear on top of the shadows. With this action, the problem Figure 9.14 illustrates disappears.

Adding Shadows to Entities

In the previous section, you might have noticed that you made calls to a function that you have not yet seen implemented. This is the CEntity::RenderShadows() function. Now is as good a time as any to remedy this situation. The purpose of the function is to allow the CEntity class to render its own shadows. Here is the code for the function from CEntity.cpp:

```
void CEntity::RenderShadows(IDirect3DDevice9 *pDevice)
{
    // Now set the world matrix
    pDevice->SetTransform(D3DTS_WORLD, &m_matWorld);

    // Draw the mesh
    if(m_pMesh)
        m_pMesh->DrawShadow(pDevice);

    // Lines left out. . .
}
```

The function's only parameter requires a pointer to a `IDirect3DDevice9` device. Following the open brace, you make use of the device to call the `IDirect3DDevice9::SetTransform()` function. This function sets the `D3DTS_WORLD` transformation so that it matches the matrix stored in `m_matWorld`. Matching matrices constitutes a safety precaution that ensures that you apply the correct world matrix prior to rendering. Unless you apply the correct world matrix, you get unexpected results.

You employ the `if` selection statement to determine whether the `m_pMesh` object exists. If the object exists, then you call the `CMesh::DrawShadow()` function to render the shadow associated with the object.

Adding the Tombstones

Now that you can properly place shadows beneath entities, you can proceed to add a variety of entities to the scene that can cast shadows. One scenario is grim but somewhat appropriate for fully revealing the potentials shadows hold for set designers. This involves placing the character among rows of tombstones. Here is the code from the `CMyApplication::Initialize()` function that you add to achieve this goal:

```
void CMyApplication::Initialize()
{
      // . . . Lines left out . . .
      // Create a 5 x 5 yard of tombstones
      for(int x = -5; x <=5; x += 2)
      {
            for(int z = -5; z <= 5; z += 2)
            {
                  CEntity *pStone = GetWorld()->CreateEntity(
                                    L"Tombstone", .35, .5, .10,
                                    D3DCOLOR_XRGB(64, 64, 64),
                        m_pGraphics->GetDevice());
                  pStone->SetPos(D3DXVECTOR3(x, 0.25, z));
            }
      }
      // . . . Lines left out . . .
}
```

The sole call to the `Initialize()` function occurs in the `CApplication::MessageLoop()` function, when you set up the assets for your application. Given this situation, it is appropriate that you should lay out both the ground plane, the character entity, and the tombstones.

To set up the tombstones, you create inner and outer `for` loops so that you can place the tombstones in a five-by-five array. One item you might notice involves the values of the `for` loop controls. For example, you set the initial value of the x control, in the outer loop, to -5. You set the control to -5 because it represents the x coordinate of the ground plane. The outer loop starts x at the value of -5 and increments it in jumps of two until its value is greater than 5, in this way setting up the x coordinate positions for the tombstones. The same operation characterizes the inner loop. The counter for this loop, z, starts at -5 and increments by jumps of two until its value is greater than 5. Again, this counter positions the stones on the z coordinate of the ground plane. To apply these values, as is discussed in greater detail momentarily, you call the CGraphics::SetPos() function.

To create the tombstones, you call the CWorld::CreateEntity() function. Each time you invoke the CreateEntity() function, you assign a pointer to a CEntity identifier (pStone). You then use the identifier to call CEntity::SetPos() to position the tombstones using the x and z values you have created with the for loops. The second parameter of the SetPos() function sets the y coordinate of the tombstone's position. You set the y coordinate to 0.25 so that the tombstone appears on top of the ground plane. The value of 0.25 is half of the height of the tombstone.

Setting and Enabling Lights

To add effects to the graveyard scene you began to construct in the last section, you can make it so that each tombstone's position relative to the character determines the amount of light it receives. Since a strong point light originates with the character, the sides of the tombstones facing the character can glow in a ghostly fashion while the other sides remain either dimly lit or dark. Along with these effects, the tombstones can cast shadows in line with the light they receive. To make these changes, add a point light to the scene. In order to create the point light, you add a function called SetPointLight() to Graphics. Here is the code from CGraphics.cpp for this function:

```
void CGraphics::SetPointLight(int iNum, DWORD dwColor,
                              float fRange, D3DXVECTOR3 pos)
{
        // Set up the light
          D3DLIGHT9 light;
          ZeroMemory(&light, sizeof(D3DLIGHT9));
        light.Type = D3DLIGHT_POINT;
    // Set the diffuse color
        light.Diffuse = D3DXCOLOR(dwColor);
    // Set the position and range
            light.Position = pos;
            light.Range = fRange;
    // Set up the light on the device
            m_pDevice->SetLight(iNum, &light);
            m_pDevice->LightEnable(iNum, TRUE);
}
```

The `CGraphics::SetPointLight()` function features four parameters. The first parameter is of the integer (int) type and sets the index of the light you want to set. The second parameter is of the DWORD type and indicates the color you want to apply to the light. The third parameter, of the float type, establishes how far you want the light to project into space (its range). The type of the final parameter is D3DXVECTOR3, and the values you provide with this vector allow you to position the light.

After the opening brace of the function, you declare a D3DLIGHT9 structure (light). This structure holds information about the light you are modifying. Having declared the light structure, you call ZeroMemory() to set the elements in the structure to zero so that you can safely use the structure. After setting its elements to zero, you then assign a D3DLIGHT_POINT flag to the Type element of the light structure. You perform this action to create a point light.

In the following lines, you set four more elements of the light structure. To set the Diffuse element, you use the dwColor from the SetPointLight() parameter list. To make use of this value, you employ the D3DXCOLOR() constructor to convert the values you receive from dwColor to those that the D3DLIGHT9 object uses. These values are of the D3DCOLORVALUE type.

Following the Diffuse element of the light structure, you set the Position element. As the name implies, this element sets the position of the light. To set the position, you use the D3DXVECTOR3 parameter (pos) from the SetPointLight() parameter list. Given that you have positioned the light, your only remaining task is to assign it a range. This you accomplish by assigning it the value of fRange, which you also obtain from the parameter list.

With the complete definition of the D3DLIGHT9 (light) structure comes the prerogatives to set and enable the light. To perform these tasks, you make two function calls. You first call the IDirect3DDevice9::SetLight() function to set the light at the appropriate index. Next, you call LightEnable() to instruct Direct3D to turn on the light.

Creating a Control

To fully appreciate the features you have implemented with the addition of the point light, you can add a control to regulate the intensity of the light. To achieve this goal, you begin by adding three attributes to the definition of CMyApplication. The attributes help you to identify the controls for and to process messages relating the intensity of the light. Here is the code from CMyApplication.h:

```
static const int IDC_INTENSITY = 3;
static const int IDC_STATIC2 = 4;
// Intensity of the light source (range)
float m_fIntensity;
```

The two `static const` attributes allow you to identify controls and process messages for the control you set for the light. The value you store in the `m_fIntesity` attribute pertains to the range of the light. To implement the control for the range, you amend a few lines of the `CMyApplication::InitGUI()` function:

```
void CMyApplication::InitGUI()
{
      // Lines left out. . .
      // Add the light control
      m_GUI.AddStatic(IDC_STATIC2, L"Light intensity (0-10):",
                         25, m_iConsoleY + 70, 105, 18);
      m_GUI.AddSlider(IDC_INTENSITY, 25,
                         m_iConsoleY + 80, 100, 20, 0, 100, 20);


}
```

The call to the `CDXUTDialog::AddStatic()` function creates the label for the control. The first parameter of `AddStatic()` makes use of the `IDC_STATIC2` class attribute to identify the label. The remaining parameters provide its text, its position, and its size. The call to `CDXUTDialog::AddSlider()` creates the slider control itself. This call uses the `IDC_INTENSITY` class attribute, which enables you to identify messages for the control when you process messages. In addition to setting the position and size of the slider, the remaining parameters set the range from 0 to 100 and the defaults to 20.

Processing Messages

To process the message the slider generates, you make a few changes to the `CMyApplication::OnGUIEvent()` function. Here is the code that shows the changes:

```
void CMyApplication::OnGUIEvent(UINT nEvent,
                                int nControlID,
                                CDXUTControl *pControl)
{

      // Lines left out. . .
      else if(nControlID == IDC_INTENSITY)
      {
            // Change intensity of the light source
            CDXUTSlider *pSlider = (CDXUTSlider *)pControl;
            m_fIntensity = (float)pSlider->GetValue()/10.0f;
      }
      // Lines left out. . .

}
```

Several portions of the selection structure (if…else if) are left out of the code sample for OnGUIEvent(), but it should still be clear that the selection statement determines whether the value from the value of nControlID matches the value of the IDC_INTENSITY control identifier. If the two values match, then you retrieve the reference in pControl and cast it as a pointer to a CDXUTSlider object, which you then assign to pSlider. You then use pSlider to call GetValue(), which retrieves the value of the intensity the slider provides. You divide this value by 10 so that you can obtain a floating-point value that lies in the range of 0 to 10. You then assign this value to m_fIntensity, the class attribute. When the value is stored in the class attribute, it is ready for use by the functions that update the light.

Updating the Scene for the Light

To make use of the value you store in m_fIntensity, you make a few changes to CMyApplication::UpdateScene() function. These changes allow you to retrieve the value stored in m_fIntensity to change the intensity of the light. Here is the code:

```
void CMyApplication::UpdateScene(float fTimeScale)
{
    // Set up the torch light (positioned above the character)
    m_pGraphics->SetPointLight(0, D3DCOLOR_XRGB(128, 128, 128),
                          m_fIntensity,
                               D3DXVECTOR3(0, 1.25, 0));
    // Lines left out. . .
}
```

To apply the intensity value, you call the CGraphics::SetPointLight() function. The third parameter of this function accepts the value you store in m_fIntensity. As for the other parameters, the first designates the point light index, and you set this to 0. Next, you set the color of the light using the D3DCOLOR_XRGB() macro. Following the application of the intensity value (the third parameter), the final parameter allows you to position the light. You position the light using values the D3DXVECTOR3 structure provides. In this case, you assign a value of 1.25 to the y coordinate, which elevates the light 1.25 units above the world origin. When you run the application, you can discern the position of the light by looking at the way the shadows trail away from the source of the light. To cap things off, use the slider that controls the intensity of the light to see how the shadows lengthen and diminish according to how you have adjusted the slider.

Searching for Gold

Every event model should strive to provide the user of an application with a scenario that possesses closure. Closure in this case involves allowing you to navigate the character around the graveyard until he makes contact with a gold tombstone. Figure 9.15 shows you the character walking through the graveyard searching for the gold. To work with the application, open Listing09_04 and compile it. Use the arrow keys to navigate the character. You can also click on the buttons to watch the character turn in different directions.

In this section you implement controls that allow the character to move. When the character moves, the light source moves along with him. As a result, you can watch the shadows move according to the location of the light. When he approaches a tombstone, he kneels to read the inscriptions. The tombstones also impede his progress. Although you have disabled the ODE physics model, you still have collision detection. The detection code uses bounding spheres.

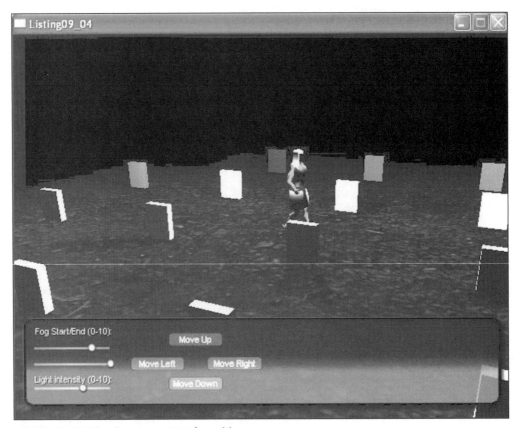

Figure 9.15 The character quests for gold.

Modifying the CWorld Class

Consistency in the character's behavior depends on whether he stops when he encounters tombstones and must walk around them as he makes his way to his goal (explained momentarily). Such behavior emerges only for collision detection, a form of intelligence you instill in the character. To create this intelligence, you make a few changes in the CWorld class. A significant change is the addition of the IsCollision() function, which serves as the primary vehicle for detecting collisions. Here is the code for the function from CWorld.cpp:

```
bool CWorld::IsCollision(wstring strName, D3DXVECTOR3 vecPos)
{
      // Examine each entity
      for(int itr = 0; itr < m_lstEntities.size(); itr++)
       {
            // Obtain a pointer to the entity
            CEntity *pEntity = m_lstEntities[itr];
            // Ensure names match
            if(pEntity && pEntity->GetName() == strName)
            {
                  // Ascertain the difference between
                  // the two objects
                  D3DXVECTOR3 vecDiff(vecPos - pEntity->GetPos());
                  float fDiff = D3DXVec3Length(&vecDiff);
                  // For an object within the bounding sphere,
                  // flag a collision
                  if(fDiff <= pEntity->GetMesh()->GetRadius())
                      return true;
            }
       }
      // When no collision occurs
      return false;
}
```

The CWorld::IsCollision() function has two parameters. The first parameter, of the wstring type, identifies the name of the object that you want to examine for a collision. After the name of the target object, the function provides a parameter that allows you to identify a point that might pass inside the target object. The type of this second parameter is D3DXVECTOR3, which accommodates the coordinates of the point.

Following the opening brace, you initiate a for loop that iterates through all the entities stored in the world entity vector (m_lstEntities). For each entity in the world entity vector, you return a pointer to the locally declared CEntity identifier (pEntity). After you retrieve the identity of the entity, you then employ an if selection statement to determine if the entity is non-NULL and to determine if its name equals the name stored in strName. If these conditions prove true, you construct a D3DXVECTOR3 object (vecDiff) to store the difference between the position of the entity and the position argument (vecPos). The sole argument for the D3DXVECTOR3 constructor is the difference you obtain by subtracting the vector position of the entity from the vector position of the point.

Given that you now have a D3DXVECTOR3 object that contains the difference (if any) between the two positions, you can call the D3DXVec3Length() function to determine the length (or magnitude) of the difference. This is the distance between the two objects (fDiff), and if this distance is less than or equal to the radius of the entity (which you obtain by calling the CMesh::GetRadius() function), then the function returns true, indicating that a collision has occurred. You can use the radius of the entity because each entity possesses a bounding sphere, and the distance from the center of the entity to the surface of the bounding sphere provides the radius that the GetRadius() function returns. After iterating through all of the objects the world vector contains, if you find that the centers of no two entities lie closer together than the distances their radii describe, then you can report no collision, so you return false.

Making Stones of Gold

Every event mapping can furnish the substance of a closed system. Economists sometimes contend that all systems involving human behavior achieve closure (purpose) over the notion that human activities possess the potential of generating wealth. In the case of the warrior in the graveyard, this notion remains valid, for the behavior involves a search for treasure. To make this search possible, you create a new function, CMyApplication::CreateStones(). Here's the code from CMyApplication.cpp:

```
void CMyApplication::CreateStones()
{
    // First remove the previous stones
    CEntity *pEntity;
    while(pEntity = GetWorld()->GetEntity(L"Tombstone"))
        GetWorld()->RemoveEntity(pEntity);

    // Remove the gold
    pEntity = GetWorld()->GetEntity(L"Gold");
    GetWorld()->RemoveEntity(pEntity);

    // Pick a random position for the gold tombstone
    int iGoldX = (rand()%2 - 1)*2 - 1;
    int iGoldZ = (rand()%2 - 1)*2 - 1;

    // Create some tombstones
    for(int x = -5; x <= 5; x += 2)
    {
        for(int z=-5; z<=5; z+=2)
        {
            CEntity *pStone;
```

```
            if(iGoldX == x && iGoldZ == z)
            {
                    pStone = GetWorld()->CreateEntity(L"Gold",
                                                      0.35, 0.5, 0.10,
                                        D3DCOLOR_XRGB(128, 128, 0),
                                        m_pGraphics->GetDevice());
            }
            else
            {
                    pStone = GetWorld()->CreateEntity(L"Tombstone",
                                                      0.35, 0.5, 0.10,
                                        D3DCOLOR_XRGB(64, 64, 64),
                                        m_pGraphics->GetDevice());
            }
            pStone->SetPos(D3DXVECTOR3(x, 0.25, z));
        }
    }
}
```

The CreateStones() function requires no parameters because it operates on class entities and its purpose is to deal solely with the stones that you have set up in the Initialize() function. The Initialize() function creates a graveyard full of regularly spaced tomb-stones, one of which is colored gold. To make it possible for the application to repeatedly change the position of the gold tombstone, you make the CreateStones() function.

To begin the activity of changing the position of the gold tombstone, you create a while repetition loop at the start of the function to iterate through all the entities in the world and identify any named Tombstone. When you find such an entity, you call the CWorld::RemoveEntity() function to remove it. Having removed all the regular Tombstone entities, you then call the GetEntity() and RemoveEntity() functions to eliminate the Gold tombstone entity. At this point, you have cleared the graveyard of tombstones and can replace them with a new configuration of tombstones.

To begin the activity of replacing the tombstones, you create random x and y coordinate positions (iGoldX and iGoldZ). You accomplish this task by calling the C library rand() function. The random values you create in this way lie in the range of -3 to 3. The numbers must be odd since you place the tombstones on a grid represented by odd numbers from -5 to 5.

To create the new set of tombstones, you implement two for loops, one inside the other. As you saw before with the Initialize() function, these loops iterate through the odd numbers between -5 and 5 on the xz plane. You declare a pointer to a CEntity object within the inner for loop to keep track of the tombstones as you create them.

Tracking tombstones in this context requires that if the current xz position of a tombstone equals the randomly generated position for the gold (iGoldX, iGoldZ), then you call CreateEntity() to generate a tombstone entity named "Gold". The tombstone is a yellowish or gold color (RGB 128,128,0), so it stands out from other tombstones in the scene. If the xz position does not match the randomly generated coordinates, then you call CreateEntity() to create a gray Tombstone entity.

When you have set up the tombstone, you call the CEntity::SetPosition() function to set its position correctly on the xz plane. As in the Initialize() function, the value of the y coordinate (0.25) elevates the tombstone above the surface of the plane.

Adding Buttons

Tombstones of gold are one thing, finding such things are another. For this reason, you need next to modify the CMyApplication class to add controls that allow you to move the character. To perform this bit of work, you change CMyApplication::InitGUI(). Here's the code from CApplication.cpp:

```
void CMyApplication::InitGUI()
{
    // Lines left out. . .

    // Create the four buttons for moving the entity
    m_GUI.AddButton(IDC_UP, L"Move Up", 200, m_iConsoleY + 20,
                                        75, 20, VK_UP);
    m_GUI.AddButton(IDC_LEFT, L"Move Left", 150, m_iConsoleY + 50,
                                        75, 20, VK_LEFT);
    m_GUI.AddButton(IDC_RIGHT, L"Move Right", 250, m_iConsoleY + 50,
                                        75, 20, VK_RIGHT);
    m_GUI.AddButton(IDC_DOWN, L"Move Down", 200, m_iConsoleY + 75,
                                        75, 20, VK_DOWN);
}
```

The code in the InitGUI() function creates four buttons. In each case, you create the button by calling CDXUTDialog::AddButton(). The first parameter of the AddButton() consists of a constant identifier that you declare in the header file of CMyApplication:

```
    // Four buttons for moving the mesh
    static const int IDC_UP = 5;
    static const int IDC_RIGHT = 6;
    static const int IDC_DOWN = 7;
    static const int IDC_LEFT = 8;
```

The second and third parameter values of the AddButton() function set the xy coordinates of the upper left corner of the button. The last three parameters establish the size of the button and the identifier for the button. The last argument designates a hotkey that allows you to associate the button with the keyboard. In this way, for example, when you press the up arrow key to the left of the number pad, your action is the same as if you clicked on the button.

Messages That Move

Having added buttons that can issue messages that cause the character to turn in different directions as he moves, you introduce a few changes to the CMyApplication::OnGUIEvent() function to process the messages the buttons issue. This function consists of two large sections. The first section processes the message to discover which way the character should turn. The second guides the character's actions in the event that a collision has occurred. Here's the code that accomplishes this work:

```
void CMyApplication::OnGUIEvent(UINT nEvent, int nControlID,
                                            CDXUTControl *pControl)
{
    // A vector containing the direction the character is moving, as
    // well as a pointer to the character
    D3DXVECTOR3 vecDelta(0,0,0);
    CEntity *pEntity = GetWorld()->GetEntity(L"Character");

    // Change starting fog value
    if(. . .)
    {
    //Lines left out . . .
     }
    else if(nControlID == IDC_UP)
    {
        // Vector moving in on the Z axis
        vecDelta = D3DXVECTOR3(0,0,.05);
        pEntity->SetRotAngles(D3DXVECTOR3(0,0,0));
    }
    else if(nControlID == IDC_DOWN)
    {
        // Vector moving out on the Z axis
        vecDelta = D3DXVECTOR3(0,0,-.05);
        pEntity->SetRotAngles(D3DXVECTOR3(0, D3DX_PI, 0));
    }
    else if(nControlID == IDC_LEFT)
    {
```

```
            // Vector going left on the x axis
            vecDelta = D3DXVECTOR3(-.05,0,0);
            pEntity->SetRotAngles(D3DXVECTOR3(0,-D3DX_PI/2,0));
      }
      else if(nControlID == IDC_RIGHT)
      {
            // Vector going right on the x axis
            vecDelta = D3DXVECTOR3(.05,0,0);
            pEntity->SetRotAngles(D3DXVECTOR3(0, D3DX_PI/2,0));
      }

      // See if movement should occur (vecDelta != 0)
      if(D3DXVec3Length(&vecDelta) != 0)
      {
            D3DXVECTOR3 vecNewPos = pEntity->GetPos() + vecDelta;

            // Check for a collision with the regular tombstones
            // as well as the gold
            if(GetWorld()->IsCollision(L"Tombstone", vecNewPos))
            {
                  pEntity->SetAnimation(L"Stand");
            }
            else if(GetWorld()->IsCollision(L"Gold", vecNewPos))
            {
                  MessageBox(NULL, L"You found the gold!",
                                       L"Winner!", MB_OK);
                  pEntity->SetPos(D3DXVECTOR3(0, 0, 0));
                  CreateStones();
            }
            else
            {
                  pEntity->SetPos(vecNewPos);
            }
      }//end if

      //Lines left out . . .
}
```

After the opening brace of the OnGUIEvent() function, you create a D3DXVECTOR3 structure (vecDelta) to store the values that indicate the direction the character moves. You initially set values of this structure to zero (0, 0, 0). These values change if you press one of the buttons.

Following the declaration of the D3DXVECTOR3 structure, you then call the CWorld::GetEntity() function to retrieve a pointer to the character that you can employ to alter the character's behavior using the directions the messages provide.

Accessing the directions the messages provide involves using a series of four if-else selection statements, each of which determines if the message identifier passed to the OnGUIEvent() nControlID parameter matches one of the constant message identifiers (IDC_UP, IDC_RIGHT, IDC_DOWN, IDC_LEFT). In each instance, the actions the selection statements introduce involve the same basic set of function calls. First, you use the D3DXVECTOR3 constructor to set the value of the direction vector (vecDelta) to correspond to the direction the button message designates. For example, the selection statement that processes the IDC_UP message creates a vector that moves the character in the positive z direction (0, 0, 0.5). The selection statement that processes the IDC_LEFT message creates a vector that moves in the negative x direction (-0.5, 0, 0).

After you have set the direction the character is to follow, you must also turn the character so that he faces the direction in which he walks. To reach this objective, you call the CEntity::SetRotAngles() function. Your task involves rotating the character around the y axis, so that as he turns, he more or less pivots on his heels. To make this possible, you make use of a 360-degree arc of rotation. When you want to turn the character in a given direction, then, you select a portion of this arc of rotation, which you define in 90-degree segments defined in pi values. To make the character face right (IDC_RIGHT), for example, you rotate him by D3DX_PI/2, or 90 degrees.

The if-else statements take care of turning and rotating the character, but you still have before you the labor of determining whether the character *should* walk, stop, or stoop. If the character encounters no tombstones, he walks. If he encounters the side of a tombstone, he stops. If he encounters the face of a tombstone, he stoops to read its inscriptions. How's that for intelligence!

But then you need to program these events into his intelligence, and to accomplish this, you require yet another if selection statement. This statement first calls the D3DXVec3Length() function to determine if the magnitude of the direction vector (vecDelta) is something other than zero. If the magnitude is zero, then you know that none of the buttons has been pressed.

Having checked for the magnitude of the direction vector, you create a new vector (vecNewPos) to store the position to which the character moves when you do press a button. To determine the values for vecNewPos, you add the values stored in vecDelta to the character's current position. To obtain the character's current position, you call the CEntity::GetPos() function.

Given that you have set the distance the character is to move, you can then determine whether the character's movement leads to a collision. To perform this labor, you call CWorld::IsCollision(). You check for two types of collision. The first type of collision is with a normal Tombstone entity. If you detect a collision will occur (IsCollision() returns true), then you call CEntity::SetAnimation() to replace the "Walk" animation with the "Stand" animation. The second type of collision marks the closure of the event mapping, for in this case, the character encounters the Gold tombstone. In this case, the IsCollision() function checks for an impending collision with the "Gold" tombstone. If this collision will occur, you call the Win32 MessageBox() function to inform the player that victory has been achieved.

As glorious as it might be to find the gold, it remains that every good game allows players the opportunity to repeat the experience the game fosters. Given this precept, following the display of the victory dialog, you reposition the character so that the quest can begin again. To reposition the character, you call the CEntity::SetPos(). The values you assign to this function are those with which you started, namely all zeros (such is the plight of even those who find the greatest wealth). In addition, to make the new game a challenge, you call the CreateStones() function to randomly place the stones again.

As an anti-climactic ending, you might wonder what you do if the character neither collides with a tombstone nor finds the gold. Well, this is easy enough. In this case, you update the position of the entity to the proposed position (vecNewPos). The character moves toward this position. You effect the move with a call to the CEntity::SetPos() function. And the quest goes on…

Using the Keyboard

As much as the world might seem to be complete with the processing of messages, it remains that you have just a pinch of work left to do to connect the keyboard to the message handler. This work involves adjusting the Windows event handler in the CMyApplication::ProcessMessage() function so that it detects messages the keys issue. The goal involves being able to hold down arrow keys to force the character to move. Here's the code:

```
void CMyApplication::ProcessMessage(HWND hWnd, unsigned int msg,
                                    WPARAM wParam, LPARAM lParam)
{
      // Map the arrow keys to the correct GUI event, so that you
      // can hold down a key to cause the character to move.
      if(msg == WM_KEYDOWN)
      {
            // If you press an arrow key, set the "walk" animation.
            if (wParam == VK_UP || wParam == VK_DOWN ||
```

```
            wParam == VK_LEFT || wParam == VK_RIGHT)
            GetWorld()->GetEntity(L"Character")
                                ->SetAnimation(L"Walk");
        if (wParam == VK_UP)
            OnGUIEvent(0, IDC_UP, NULL);
        else if(wParam == VK_RIGHT)
            OnGUIEvent(0, IDC_RIGHT, NULL);
        else if(wParam == VK_DOWN)
            OnGUIEvent(0, IDC_DOWN, NULL);
        else if(wParam == VK_LEFT)
            OnGUIEvent(0, IDC_LEFT, NULL);
    }
    // Call parent process
    CApplication::ProcessMessage(hWnd, msg, wParam, lParam);
}
```

After the opening brace, you check whether the msg parameter of ProcessMessage() conveys a WM_KEYDOWN message. This occurs whenever you press a key on the keyboard. What's more, the system issues the message as long as you continue to press the key. This is a fortunate situation for your character, because it means that as long as you want him to move in a given direction, you need only to hold down one of the arrow keys.

To make it so that the character can move, you access the message identifier stored in wParam to determine if a walk message has been issued and then set the animation for the character to "Walk". Following this action, you then again access the wParam value in one of four successive if selection statements to translate the key messages (prefixed with VK) to application messages (prefixed with IDC). You accomplish the translation by calling the OnGUIEvent() function. In each case, you use one of the message identifiers you declared in the header file for CMyApplication as an argument for a selection statement. The selection statement translates the key message (such as VK_UP) into a button message (such as IDC_UP). The result is that the button handler processes the message received from the key.

Updating the Light Source

Well… the story is almost over for this chapter, except that you still need to attend to ensuring that your character's actions take place within a context of events. The context of events emerges from the character's visual realm. As the character moves, he carries with him a power that illuminates tombstones—but only for a limited distance, depending on the power of luminosity you assign to him with the slider. To make it so that the character possesses the power to illuminate the tombstones, you attach a light to him. You perform this work in the CMyApplication::UpdateScene() function. Here's the code:

```
void CMyApplication::UpdateScene(float fTimeScale)
{
        // Get the character's position
        D3DXVECTOR3 vecPos =GetWorld()
                        ->GetEntity(L"Character")->GetPos();
        // Set up the torch light (above the character)
        m_pGraphics->SetPointLight(0, D3DCOLOR_XRGB(128, 128, 128),
                                        m_fIntensity,
                                        D3DXVECTOR3(vecPos.x, 1.25, vecPos.z));
        // Lines left out. . .
}
```

After the opening brace, you first declare a D3DXVECTOR3 structure (vecPos) so that you can obtain a copy of the character's original position. To accomplish this, you call a series of cascaded functions, the last of which, GetPos(), retrieves the values that identify the position of the character. These values you assign to the vecPos structure. Having stored the character's original position, you then call CGraphics::SetPointLight() to set the position of the light.

The SetPointLight() function requires a number of parameters. The first parameter identifies the number of the light, which is 0. This is the point light suspended above the character. The second parameter sets the color of the light (gray). The third parameter you obtain from the intensity slider, and this you set with the m_fIntensity variable. The final argument is a D3DXVECTOR3 structure, which represents the position of the light in world space. To set the values for the x and z elements of the D3DXVECTOR3 structure, you insert those that the vecPos vector provides in its x and z elements. For the y component, which controls how high the light appears above the character, you use 1.25, which places it just above the character's head.

Conclusion

In this chapter, you have examined a large number of topics that range from the basic psychological reasons that justify the use of special effects to the specific DirectX objects you use to create such effects as fog and shadows. Along the way, you have examined the notion of iconic logic, which is a logic that emerges from the complex of constraints you introduce to a given context of events. Modeling and mapping events effectively requires understanding that you must introduce to the events you model or map a set of constraints that allows the logic that characterizes the model or map to emerge interactively. If you try to explain things beforehand how one event in a setting causes another to occur, you completely nullify the purpose of simulation.

Simulation involves creating a context of events from which an experience arises. Given this conceptual beginning, you worked through the construction of an application that used fog to create a world in which the horizons of awareness the character in the world experienced became relative to the vision the fog allowed the character to have of his surroundings. Fog serves as a medium for making familiar things seem strange. It provides a way that you can introduce mystery and suspense into the worlds you create.

In conjunction with fog, you also worked with shadows. Like fog, shadows increase the visual intensity of the world you create. They give to objects an element of realism. The realism stems in part from the way that shadows tend to lace objects into a world, so that their dependency on each other increases. In the instance of a scene that a point light illuminates, lights cast shadows relative to the position of the light.

When a point light becomes associated with a character, so that the character's world tends to become relative to the range of the light, then the enormous potentials light, fog, and shadows offer you as you seek different ways to constrain the events in your event model become evident. You can program a character to move through a world, so that the world becomes visible in a limited way, one that is relative to the range of the character's vision as mediated by the light. Such an approach to revealing reality shows that you are under no obligation to explicitly explain anything. Your simulation or game can communicate with its users by other means. Reason becomes iconic, a function or outgrowth of the system of interaction you bring together through simulation.

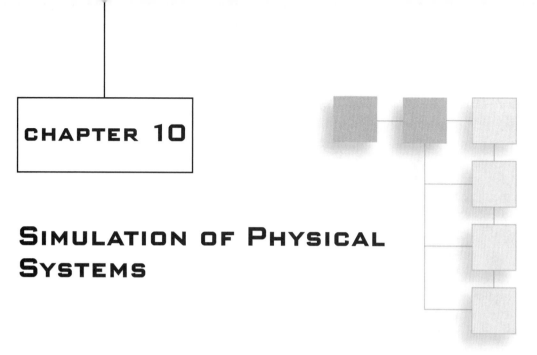

CHAPTER 10

SIMULATION OF PHYSICAL SYSTEMS

One of the key activities performed by developers who work with simulations involves creating applications that embody models of physical systems. A physical system consists of a collection of events that you can view as interrelated. A model explains the interrelations. When you possess a model that allows you to understand how events relate to each other, you can create a software simulation that allows you to adjust the significance of the events relative to each other. By adjusting the significance of events, you put yourself in a position to refine your understanding of your model. In this chapter, you construct a model of a forest fire and include in your model, among many other factors, a complex of events generated by the effects moisture has on trees exposed to fire. When trees possess less moisture, you might find that they resist combustion or burn faster when they do combust. One event relates to another. You model maps of events, and maps allow you to tell stories or to propose hypotheses. Your power to tell stories or propose hypotheses increases as you increase the sophistication of your model. In this chapter, you start with a rudimentary model of a forest fire and then scrutinize and revise it to increase its sophistication. Here are a few of the topics you cover as you engage in this project:

- Conceptualizing physical systems
- Creating a systems context
- Creating trees
- Simple approaches to modeling behavior
- Creating a forest as a system
- Growing and destroying forests
- Understanding event models and controls
- Using system events to change behaviors
- Developing a complex interface

Systems as Physical Systems

People have been creating models of the physical universe at least since the beginning of recorded history. The drawings Paleolithic people made on the walls of caves in Lascaux and Lortet in France represent models. The drawings often feature animals. The animals—often deer and bison—were a source of food, but then they were also aesthetically important for the artists. When the artists spent their time creating their artwork, they gave expression to a system of interaction. It may have been that the artists defined themselves as hunters, and yet they might have been showing that they viewed themselves as dependent on or hunted by the animals. The art of the cave provides a simulation of the model, and the model embodies a form of understanding.

Simulations and event models that address purely physical systems characterize and dominate our understanding of the world we live in. They are so pervasive that in many instances recalling that they are not the things modeled proves difficult. A model provides a formal way to *hypothetically* explain how events relate to each other. As was discussed in Chapter 1, "What Is Simulation?," this is easy to forget. People usually prefer meaning over chaos. Models are the primary means by which people bring meaning into their lives. A model might be simplistic and even silly, but because it has the power (some call it *magic*) to create order where chaos once reigned, it can tend to entrance those who use it.

A model that you cannot improve with time is likely to be a fraud. Consider, for example, the classical model of the solar system. This model incorporates physical laws respecting the force of gravity and the Earth's rotation around the sun. The model draws upon the work of such people as Kepler, Copernicus, Galileo, Newton, and many other renowned physicists, mathematicians, and astronomers. It joins assumptions about gravity, the Earth's rotation, the position of the sun, and the paths planets travel as they move through space. The model takes on a reality of its own when it enables those who learn it to understand the solar system. Still, over time, with the development of general relativity, ways to improve it have been introduced. A good model is like a good tool. Using the tool allows those who use it to discover ways to improve it.

note

Ian Tattersall noted that in the caves of the Ice Age you find a historical record of the work of the artists. Over time, rather than erasing the work of their predecessors, artists tended to find clear walls deeper in the cave on which they reworked the work of their predecessors. One model led to another. (See Ian Tattersall, *The Human Odyssey: Four Million Years of Human Evolution* [New York: Prentice Hall, 1993].)

Conceptualizing Systems

Simulation extends models in powerful ways. Scientists might develop a model in purely mathematical terms and then create a simulation that allows them to experiment with the model so that they can elaborate or refine it. Success in this undertaking depends on interacting with the model. A model consists of data and rules that apply to the data. When brought together into a whole, the whole creates a context in which the rules can be refined using that data and the data can be refined using the rules. This dynamic explains why, as they work with a given model of natural events, scientists tend to perfect their understanding as they perfect their models.

note

Software that cannot be maintained or improved seldom passes as a safe investment. Some software engineers go so far as to contend that such software always amounts to a liability. Models, art, and the theories of science follow the same pattern. A model that you cannot change proves nearly worthless. A work of art that does not move those who behold it to create their own art tends to be little more than a sterile artifact. And at the basis of all science lies the rule that when you conduct an experiment you must do so in a way that makes it possible for others to verify, refute, or improve your findings.

Figure 10.1 illustrates how conceptual models usually help those who develop them to better understand physical systems. Those who develop a systematic explanation of a given phenomena create a model. The model allows them to isolate specific events within the model. When they can isolate specific events within the model, they can also develop ways to control these events. When they can control events, they can begin to map the relative significance of events within the system. By focusing on specific (or reductive) aspects of the system, they can tremendously improve their understanding of the forces that are at work in the system. When they improve their understanding, they are in a position to improve their model.

A conceptual model lays the foundation of an experiment. An experiment is a context of interaction with the physical word in which someone wishing to learn about the physical world can repeatedly observe a limited number of events that can be controlled to some extent in a formal way. From this perspective, a simulation becomes an experiment that you can repeatedly perform.

Modeling Physical Events

In the sections that follow, you construct an application that simulates a forest fire. A forest fire is a physical system, and a system is ultimately a collection of related events. The events you concentrate on as you develop the simulation of the forest fire involve such things as the direction the wind blows, the moisture content of the trees, and the size and shape of the forest.

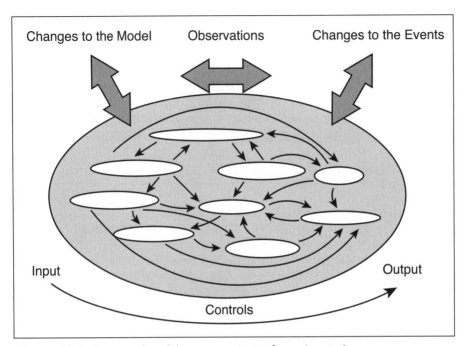

Figure 10.1 Conceptual models create contexts of experimentation.

While the simplicity of this model makes it unsuitable for real-world use, working with the model still provides a way for you to explore how you can use a model of a physical system to create a software simulation. Figure 10.2 illustrates a few of the key elements involved in developing such simulations.

A simulation serves as a means by which those who develop models can refine their models. Likewise, a simulation serves as a means by which those who possess a given understanding of events can refine their understanding. Refinement begins in many places. As Figure 10.2 illustrates, how you define data proves to be an essential part of model building.

How you define data determines how you control it. How you control data determines the descriptions of the events that result. A control serves as a way to influence an event. When you influence different events in different ways, you discover the many ways in which events relate to each other. Events exist as manifestations of contexts of interaction. One event exists in association with others, and in some cases, you can discern that one event causes another. Through the development of a simulation, you can explore these inter-actions through many iterations and continuously change the influences you exert upon the system so that you can explore the validity of your generalizations about the system.

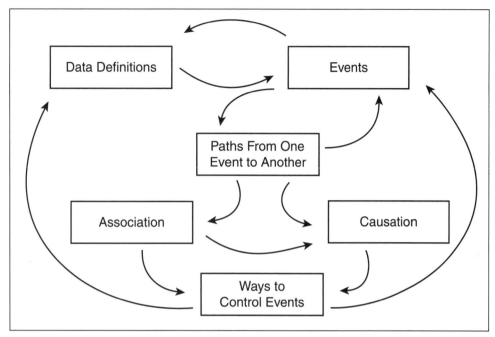

Figure 10.2 Event models grow with interaction.

Creating the Context: Trees and Forest

As a first stage in the creation of a simulation of a forest fire, you can use the application framework to create some trees and distribute them as isolated entities across a field of green. Beginning the construction of a simulation in this way allows you to arrive at a sense of the difference between dissociated and associated events. The trees in isolation do not comprise a system, nor do they give expression to a model. Only when you bring them together through events do you begin to create a systems context. When you create such a context, you also create the possibility of replicating and refining the interactions of the entities the context brings together. This is one of the primary purposes of simulation.

To see how this works, access Listing10_01 and compile the project. When the application first starts, you witness a scattering of trees (see Figure 10.3). The trees appear as bright growths on the field of view and then darken until they disappear. A model allows you to know what the event of changing color means. The simulation brings the trees and the events that characterize their existence together within the conceptual framework a model provides. The model allows you to map the events and to exert control over them to deepen your understanding of them.

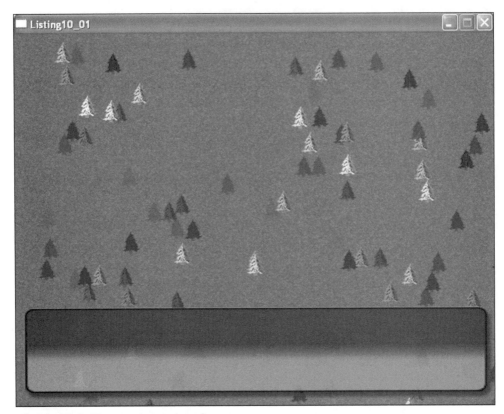

Figure 10.3 You see a scattering of trees.

Sprite Preparation

You developed functionality that supports sprites in Chapter 4, "Implementing the Framework." Now you can employ a sprite to represent a tree. A sprite consists of a simple, flat image. What image you use depends on a multitude of cultural, cognitive, and practical factors. Graphical artists given the task of providing a software developer with a "tree" usually have questions. In this context, the image of a pine tree suffices.

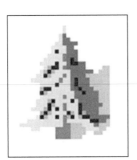

You transform sprites in two primary ways. You change their positions, and you change their colors. With respect to position, you replicate them to appear in different locations in the client area of the application. With respect to color, for this application, you want them to first appear as green, change to red, and then disappear. To implement the functionality that supports these transformations, you alter the CSprite class. Changing the position and color of the sprites centers on a new, overloaded, Draw() function. Here is the code for this function:

```
void CSprite::Draw(int x, int y, DWORD dwColor)
{
    // Transform by the identity matrix by default
    D3DXMATRIX matIdentity;
    D3DXMatrixIdentity(&matIdentity);
    m_pSprite->SetTransform(&matIdentity);
    // Generate a vector with the sprite's position
    D3DXVECTOR3 vecPos((FLOAT)x, (FLOAT)y, 0);
    // Draw the sprite
    m_pSprite->Begin(D3DXSPRITE_ALPHABLEND);
    m_pSprite->Draw(m_pTexture,          //tree image
                    &m_rcSource, NULL,
                    &vecPos, dwColor);
    m_pSprite->End();
}
```

The first two parameters of the Draw() function designate the x and y coordinates that you use to position the sprite. The third parameter furnishes you with the ability to set the color of the sprite. Given this start, you declare an identifier (matIdentity) of the D3DMATRIX matrix type to define the transformations of the sprite. Following this declaration, you call the D3DXMatrixIdentity() function to set the data in the matrix. The lone argument to the D3DXMatrixIdentity() function consists of a reference to matIdentity. You reset the elements of the matrix so that you do not accidentally transform the sprite when you copy its values in subsequent operations.

After declaring and setting the matrix, you create a D3DXVECTOR3 object (vecPos) to control the position of the sprite along the x and y axes. To supply arguments for the first two parameters of this object (those that correspond to the x and y axes), you use the x and y parameters of the Draw() function. The last parameter of the object constructor sets the position of the sprite along the z axis. Since a sprite is a 2D object, you set this parameter to zero.

After attending to the position of the sprite, you render it. To render the sprite, you call the D3DXSPRITE::Begin() function. This function takes a single parameter, which is a flag or combination of flags that sets the rendering state for the sprite. In this instance, you employ the D3DXSPRITE_ALPHABLEND flag to enable alpha blending. Alpha blending enables you to render objects transparent.

Having set the render state, you call the D3DXSPRITE::Draw() function to draw the sprite. This function requires five parameters. The first parameter supplies the texture of the sprite. The second parameter furnishes a source rectangle for the sprite. You employ the third parameter to represent the center of the sprite, but in this case, since you require no center, you set this parameter to NULL. For the fourth parameter, you retrieve the D3DXVECTOR3 matrix, vecPos, which tells the function where to place the sprite. As the final parameter, you provide the color you want to apply to the sprite. You obtain the color from the Draw() function's parameter list (dwColor). Given that you have set all these parameters, you then call the CSprite::End() function to restore the state of the Direct3D device to what it was before the call to Begin().

Creating the Tree Class

After making it so that you can change the position and color of the images you paint using the CSprite class, you make use of the CSprite class to create a new class, CTree. This class encapsulates the functionality of CSprite and allows you to create tree entities and control their behavior. In later sections, you enhance this class. For now, it suffices to implement the functionality that attends to drawing and coloring these entities.

Tree States

To accommodate drawing and coloring of tree entities, you provide the CTree class with a few basic attributes. Here is the code from CTree.h that creates the attributes:

```
// The sprite for the tree
static class CSprite *m_sprTree;
// Reference count for the tree objects, so you can
// determine when to delete the tree sprite
static int m_iReferenceCount;
// The burn factor of the tree. 1 = burned away, 0 = fully alive
float m_fBurnFactor;
// X and Y position for the tree
int m_iPosX,
    m_iPosY;
```

The first of the five attributes that you see in the class declaration of CTree allows you to create a static CSprite pointer (m_sprTree). This attribute stores the image you invoke to draw a tree. You declare it as static because you need only one copy to accommodate all trees. Using the CSprite pointer in this way saves memory and helps improve load time, since you render the sprite file only once during initialization.

The second attribute of the CTree class (m_iReferenceCount) tracks whether you need to delete the static CSprite pointer. To use this attribute, you increment it each time you call the CTree constructor, and you decrement it with each call to the destructor. When the destructor causes m_iReferenceCount to equal zero, you unload the sprite file and free the memory it uses. This ensures that no memory leaks if your application continues to execute and create more sprites.

The third attribute of the `CTree` class consists of a floating-point variable, `m_fBurnFactor`, which you employ to store the burn state of a tree. When you assign a value to this attribute, you set the color of the tree. If you set the value to 0, then the color of the tree is green, signifying that the tree has not yet burned. If you set the value to 1.0, then the tree becomes transparent, signifying that it has burned completely away.

The last two attributes of the `CTree` class, `m_iPosX` and `m_iPosY`, determine the position in which you draw a tree. As you see later on, the `Draw()` function employs these attributes extensively.

Tree Behaviors

As the program increases in complexity, the functions that attend to behaviors of the `CTree` class increase in number. For now, you concentrate on three basic behaviors: creating, locating, and coloring. To attend to the first of these activities, creating trees, you use the constructor. The code for the constructor appears in the CTree.cpp file. Here is the code:

```
CTree::CTree()
{
// If the tree sprite hasn't been loaded,
// do this now
    if(!m_sprTree)
    {
        m_sprTree = new CSprite();
        m_sprTree->Load(L"Tree.png");
    }
    // Increment the reference count
    m_iReferenceCount++;
    // For now, pick a random burn factor for the tree
    m_fBurnFactor = (float)rand()/(float)RAND_MAX;
}
```

The constructor for `CTree` requires no parameters, but it allows you to perform three essential tasks. First, you load the sprite associated with the tree. Next you increment the reference counter to account for the new tree instance. Finally, you set the initial color of the tree.

After the opening brace, you determine whether you need to create a first instance of a `CSprite` object. The `if` selection statement determines whether an instance of `CSprite` already exists. If it already exists, the class attribute `m_sprTree` holds a value other than `NULL`. If `m_sprTree` holds a `NULL` value, you are creating the first tree, so you call the `CSprite` constructor and dynamically create a `CSprite` object, which you assign to `m_sprTree`. Having created the `CSprite` object, you then call the `CSprite::Load()` function to associate a sprite file ("Tree.png") with it. Since these actions take care of the needs of all trees that follow, they occur only once.

When you count references, you create the referenced object only once. From then on you count references to the object. You take care of this bit of work when you increment m_iReferenceCount (which is a static integer). This attribute serves as a reference counter. Each time you call the class constructor, you add one to the reference counter. Given the reference count, you can know when to destroy the m_sprTree object (which occurs when m_iReferenceCount hits zero).

After creating it and appropriately incrementing the reference count to reflect its creation, you color the tree entity. Coloration allows you to simulate the states of a tree as it burns. By the time you have finished developing the program, you will have made it so that all trees begin in a lush, healthy condition. At this point, to test the program, you limit activities to varying initial colors from green to black so that you can test your program. You perform this task by altering the value you assign a class attribute, m_fBurnFactor. To alter values, you call the C library rand() function and divide its returned value by the C library RAND_MAX constant.

Destroying Tree Entities

When you create trees, you continuously use sprites. When you remove a tree, you remove a sprite. When you remove a sprite, you decrement the count of the reference counter that tracks sprites. When the reference count reaches zero, you destroy the sprite object. To perform this work, you implement a constructor for CTree that can track sprite reference counts. Here is the code from CTree.h that shows you the work the destructor performs:

```
CTree::~CTree()
{
    // Decrement the reference count
    m_iReferenceCount--;
    // If the count reaches zero, delete the sprite
    if(m_iReferenceCount == 0)
        SAFEDELETE(m_sprTree);
}
```

The first order of business you attend to in the destructor involves using the unary decrement operator to reduce the tree count stored in m_iReferenceCount. As you recall from the discussion of the constructor, you increase the value this attribute stores each time you create a tree entity. Now, with the destruction of the entity, you decrease the count. Following the reduction of the reference count, you check whether the count has reached zero. If the count has reached zero, no more tree objects exist, and you can use the SAFEDELETE macro to delete the m_sprTree object.

Coloring Trees

Creation and deletion provides a starting lifeline for the behavior of a tree entity, but within this lifeline, the tree passes through different states. Colors characterize these states. For example, a tree begins as a bright green image and takes on a charred color before disappearing. The CTree::ComputeColor() function allows you to set the color of the tree to reflect its different states. Here's the code for this function as shown in CTree.cpp:

```
DWORD CTree::ComputeColor()
{
    // Generate color constants
    const D3DXCOLOR colWhite(D3DCOLOR_XRGB(255, 255, 255));
    const D3DXCOLOR colRed(D3DCOLOR_XRGB(255, 0, 0));
    const D3DXCOLOR colTransparent(D3DCOLOR_ARGB(0, 255, 0, 0));
    // The resulting color
    D3DXCOLOR colResult;
    // If the burn factor is <= 0.5, interpolate between
    // white and green, otherwise make the tree disappear
    if(m_fBurnFactor <= 0.5)
    {
        D3DXColorLerp(&colResult,
                    &colWhite,
                    &colRed,
                    m_fBurnFactor * 2);
    }
    else{
        D3DXColorLerp(&colResult,
                    &colRed,
                    &colTransparent,
                    (m_fBurnFactor - 0.5) * 2);
    }
    return(colResult);
}
```

The ComputeColor() function requires no parameter values, and it returns a DWORD value that you use to set color values. To create the value that the function returns, you first declare three constants of the D3DXCOLOR type. The first of these constants, colWhite, stores a value corresponding to white (255, 255, 255). You create this color using the D3DCOLOR_XRGB() macro. The second constant, colRed, stores the value corresponding to red, and you again generate this value using the D3DCOLOR_XRGB() macro. The third constant, colTransparent, also stores a value corresponding to red, but in this case, you call D3DCOLOR_ARGB() macro to create the color. This macro differs from the D3DCOLOR_XRGB() macro because it possesses a fourth parameter, one that allows you to assign an alpha value to a color definition. When you set the alpha channel to zero, the resulting value makes any object to which it is applied transparent.

After declaring a D3DXCOLOR identifier (colResult) to receive the color value the ComputeColor() function returns, you then set up an if…else selection statement to calculate the color. You calculate the color so that you can indicate the state of the tree's combustion. The decisive value in this undertaking is 0.5. This value establishes that if the tree is in the first half of its life (below 0.5), it fades from green to red. On the other hand, if it is in the second half (above 0.5), its opacity begins to approach zero, causing it to fade away.

The selection statement makes use of the D3DXColorLerp() function. The name of this function is a mnemonic for "linear interpolation," an activity that involves taking two colors (the second and third parameters of the function) and interpolating them according to a value you assign for interpolation (the fourth value). The result of this activity is a color value that you store in the first parameter of the function (colResult).

The if statement determines if the burn factor (m_fBurnFactor) is below or equal to 0.5. If it is, you call the D3DXColorLerp() function and supply colWhite and colRed as its second and third arguments. To arrive at the interpolation value, you multiply the value stored in m_fBurnFactor by 2, which translates the burn factor so that it lies in the range of zero to one. If the if statement returns false, you invoke the else clause. Here, again, you call the D3DXColorLerp() function. In this instance, you supply colRed and colTransparent as its arguments and subtract 0.5 from m_fBurnFactor before doubling it to put the resulting color value in the range of zero to one.

As a final point, note the return statement. The returned value is of the type D3DXCOLOR. The defined return value for the ComputeColor() function differs from this, for it is of the DWORD type. No compiler error results because the type used for the return value (D3DXCOLOR) automatically converts to a DWORD value.

Positioning Trees

Before drawing a tree entity, you position it. To position a tree entity, you create the CTree::SetPos() function. Here is the code for this function from the CTree.cpp file:

```
void CTree::SetPos(int x, int y)
{
    m_iPosX = x;
    m_iPosY = y;
}
```

The SetPos() function requires two parameters, integers that set the x and y coordinates that establish the upper left corner of the tree entity. To set these coordinates, you assign the parameter values to the m_iPosX and m_iPosY class attributes.

Drawing Trees

After you have created, colored, and positioned a tree, you draw it, and the function that accomplishes this task is the CTree::Draw() function. Here is the code for this function from CTree.cpp:

```
void CTree::Draw()
{
    // Temporarily cycle the burn factor
    m_fBurnFactor += 0.005;
    if(m_fBurnFactor >= 1.0){m_fBurnFactor = 0;}
    m_sprTree->Draw(m_iPosX, m_iPosY, ComputeColor());
}
```

So that you can test draw different colors, you slightly increase the value of m_fBurnFactor each time you call the function. After increasing the burn factor value, you determine if the burn factor equals or exceeds 1.0. If this is so, then you reset the burn factor to zero. In this way, you ensure that the program cycles through the color range as it draws the tree. After setting m_fBurnFactor, you then call the CSprite::Draw() function and draw the sprite for the entity. To accomplish this, you set the first two parameters of the CSprite::Draw() function with the values you have stored in the m_iPosX and m_iPosY class attributes. To assign a color to the tree, you call the CSprite::Draw() function. You then assign the value that the ComputeColor() function returns to the third parameter of this function.

At this point, you are ready to draw trees. Now you make a few changes to the application class so that it can render trees.

Adding Trees and Grass

To alter the application so that it can invoke the functionality the CTree class embodies, you alter the CMyApplication class. The changes involve adding a few attributes and altering the Load(), Cleanup(), and Render() functions. The next few sections review these additions and changes in detail.

Tree and Grass States

Although the focus of the work you are engaged in at this point centers on creating trees, you can improve the appearance of the trees if you provide them with a background. To

complete this parcel of work, you preface your work with trees by adding an attribute to
CMyApplication.h that allows you to define a sprite for a grass background. Here is the
attribute list for CMyApplication from CMyApplication.h:

```
// The background sprite
class CSprite *m_sprBack;
// The number of trees for the test
static const int NUM_TREES = 100;
// An array of 100 trees to test the tree class
class CTree *m_pTrees[NUM_TREES];
```

You use the first CSprite attribute (m_sprBack) to load a texture for the grass background.
In addition to adding a background, you also add attributes that allow you to create a
multitude of trees. Toward this end, you declare a constant to establish the number of
trees your application creates. If you set this value to 100, enough tree entities result to
evenly populate the application's client area. To hold the tree entities, as a final attribute,
you declare an array that can contain CTree pointers (m_pTrees).

Initializing Trees and Grass

Given that you have put in place the functionality that creates trees and grass, your next
step involves initializing the entities you now have at hand. To initialize the grass and tree
entities, you make a few changes to the CMyApplication::Initialize() function. Here is the
code for this function as shown in CMyApplication.cpp:

```
void CMyApplication::Initialize()
{
    // Disable physics for this demo
    GetWorld()->SetPhysicsEnabled(false);
    // Load the grass bitmap
    m_sprBack = new CSprite();
    m_sprBack->Load(L"Grass.png");
    // Create the trees
    for(int itr=0; itr < NUM_TREES; itr++)
    {
        m_pTrees[itr] = new CTree();
        m_pTrees[itr]->SetPos(rand() % m_pGraphics->GetWidth(),
                              rand() % m_pGraphics->GetHeight());
    }
    // Initialize the application using the parent call
    CApplication::Initialize();
}
```

The Initialize() function requires no parameters. It does its work using class attributes. Before it performs any work on the tree and grass entities, it first disables the ODE physics functions that might affect these entities in unwanted ways. The results are the same as those described in Chapter 9, "Environments of Simulation." Basically, when you supply the false value to the parameter of the function, you tell your application not to invoke the ODE functions that apply to the world or the entities you place in the world.

Having disabled the physics functions, you call the constructor for the CSprite class to instantiate a sprite entity for the background, which you assign to the m_sprBack class attribute. Following the creation of the sprite instance, you call the CSprite::Load() function to affiliate the "Grass.png" file with the sprite.

After creating a sprite for the background, you then turn to trees. The work of creating trees involves a for loop that the NUM_TREES value controls. In this instance, the loop iterates up to a hundred times, and for each iteration, you call the CTree constructor and assign the resulting reference to the m_pTrees array. To position the trees you have created, you call the CTree::SetPos() function. To set the values for this function, you use the C library random() function in conjunction with the modulus operator and the CGraphics::GetWidth() and CGraphics::GetHeight() functions. Using this combination of functions, you create random x and y positions for each tree.

After placing the grass and trees on the screen, your only remaining action involves calling the CApplication::Initialize() function. This function communicates the initialization activities to the parent class.

Cleaning Up

When you work with C++, you always have a responsibility to clean up after yourself. When you employ the new operator to dynamically allocate memory, you must then call the delete operator to release the memory. For this reason, you need to follow up your grass and tree creation cycle with a grass and tree destruction cycle. You accomplish this work in the CMyApplication::Cleanup() function. Here is the code for this function from CMyApplication.cpp:

```
void CMyApplication::Cleanup()
{
     SAFEDELETE(m_sprBack);
     for(int itr=0; itr < NUM_TREES; itr++)
     {
          SAFEDELETE(m_pTrees[itr]);
     }
     // Lines left out. . .
}
```

The Cleanup() function serves as a machine for deleting grass and tree objects. The work of cleaning up requires that you call SAFEDELETE() macro to destroy the background sprite, m_sprBack. Next, you employ a for loop to iterate through each m_pTrees array and release the memory of the objects assigned to it. When you delete the last tree, the system also releases the static sprite member variable of the CTree class. If you look at the utils.h file, you can see the definition of the call SAFEDELETE() macro. This macro calls the DirectX Release() function. If you access the definition of this function, you can see that it calls the delete operator for the object you supply to it.

Rendering

In case you were wondering, an end does exist to all this activity of creating grass and trees. The end occurs in the Render() function, where the grass and tree objects you have worked so hard to create, paint, and position are at last given a visible presence in your application's client area. The work of rendering grass and trees involves making use of the m_sprBack and m_pTrees attributes. This activity occurs in the CMyApplication::Render() function. Here is the code from the CApplication.cpp file that shows how you accomplish this work:

```
void CMyApplication::Render()
{
    // Lines left out. . .
    // Draw the background
    m_sprBack->Draw(0, 0, m_pGraphics->GetWidth(),
                            m_pGraphics->GetHeight());
    // Draw the trees at random positions
    for(int itr = 0; itr < NUM_TREES; itr++)
    {
        m_pTrees[itr]->Draw();
    }
    // Lines left out. . .
}
```

To render the grass, you call one of the two CSprite::Draw() functions. (For the definition of this version of the function, see Chapter 4, "Implementing the Framework.") The parameters you supply to this Draw() function consist, first, of the x and y coordinates that establish the upper left corner of the sprite. Positioned with zero values for these coordinates (0, 0), the upper left corner of the sprite is tucked into the upper left corner of the client area. The last two coordinates you set using the CGraphics::GetWidth() and CGraphics::GetHeight() functions. These two functions return values that stretch the grass sprite so that its lower right corner corresponds to the lower right corner of the client area.

After rendering the grass sprite, you render the trees. To render the trees, you make use of the NUM_TREES attribute to cap the number of trees you create. You use a for loop and iterative calls to the CTree::Draw() function to render the trees. Since you have already set the position and color of the trees, the rendering operation does nothing more at this point than call the trees into visibility.

With this activity, your basic work of setting up a simulation comes to an end. Now, however, more involved work begins. At this point, you begin creating functionality for larger contexts of activity, such as those you encounter when you consider the dynamics of a forest system.

A Forest as a System of Trees

In the last section, your work involved creating grass and tree entities and rendering them to the client area as individual entities. When you create a model, however, you must transcend the presentation of singular entities on a random basis and seek a specific order of rendering that reflects the behavior of the system you want to model. In this instance, the system is a forest. To see the beginnings of a forest model, open Listing10_01 and compile the project. Figure 10.4 shows you the result. Use the sliders to adjust the width and height of the forest.

The forest provides a context in which trees can exist. A forest furnishes a system in which you see many trees come into and go out of existence. Like most systems, a forest is not necessarily the sum of its parts. Rather, a forest results from the interaction of the parts, which create a dynamic whole. In this section see how this can happen when you create a forest entity, which represents a collection of tree entities. In the context that the forest provides, trees take on new dimensions. For example, they can be of different sizes and colors, and their existence becomes relative to each other and to the shape and size of the forest.

Trees That Talk

Before you create a forest, you must perform a bit of preliminary work on the trees to make them suitable for inclusion in a forest. To attend to this work, you must make some changes to the CTree class. Specifically, you add two functions, CTree::GetWidth() and CTree::GetHeight(). These two functions allow you to obtain information about the trees that you can use to position them in the forest relative to each other. The forest depends on the trees, for when you create the forest, you do so using information from the trees. Here is the code from CTree.cpp that creates these two functions:

```
int CTree::GetWidth()
{
     if(m_sprTree){ return(m_sprTree->GetWidth()); }
```

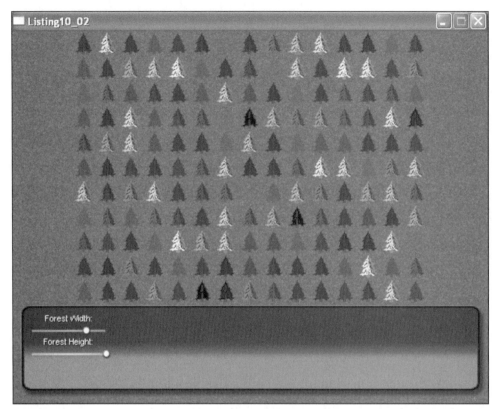

Figure 10.4 A forest provides a system in which trees have a context of existence.

```
        else { return(0); }
}
int CTree::GetHeight()
{
        if(m_sprTree) { return(m_sprTree->GetHeight()); }
        else { return(0); }
}
```

In both cases, you obtain information about trees by encapsulating functions from the CSprite class. In both cases, you first use an if selection statement to verify the existence of the tree. Given the existence of the tree, you then return its current width or height. If no tree exists, then you return zero.

A Forest from Trees

Having equipped your tree entities with functionality that allows them to provide information about their widths and heights as individual entities, you can now concentrate on creating a forest. To accomplish this, you first establish the attributes of a forest. To set the size of the forest, you make use of trees. To see how this is so, consider the declaration of the attributes for the CForest class in CForest.h:

```
int m_iWidth; // Width of the forest
int m_iHeight;  // Height of the forest
class CTree ***m_pTrees; // 2D array of pointers
```

The m_iWidth attribute tracks the width of the forest using the number of trees. You set the value of this attribute when you construct the forest, and controls allow you to alter it dynamically. The m_iHeight attribute tracks the height of the forest, again using the number of trees. As before, you set the value of this attribute when you construct the forest, and controls allow you to alter it.

The final attribute of the CForest class (***m_pTrees) might appear a little strange. It is a triple pointer. You use a triple pointer so that you can create a two-dimensional array of CTree pointers. How you accomplish this is covered in the discussion of the forest constructor. In the constructor you allocate memory for the trees and assign the result to the pointer array.

Growing a Forest

The forest class consists of a limited set of functions that resemble those of the tree class. You construct, destruct, draw, and obtain the height and width of the forest. On the other hand, you also need to consider how the forest accommodates the addition of new trees. To add trees, among other activities, you create a function that allows you to locate the center of the forest.

First things first, however. To grow a forest, you require a constructor for the CForest forest class. The primary work of the constructor entails initializing an array of trees. Here is the code from CForest.cpp that shows the work of the constructor:

```
CForest::CForest(int width, int height)
{
        // Set the width and height
        m_iWidth = width;
        m_iHeight = height;
        // Create the array for the rows
        m_pTrees = new CTree **[height];
        // Create the rows
        for(int y = 0; y < height; y++)
        {
                // Create the row
                m_pTrees[y] = new CTree *[width];
                // Create the actual trees in the row
                for(int x = 0; x < width; x++)
```

```
        {
                m_pTrees[y][x] = new CTree();
        }
    }
}
```

The two parameters the constructor employs allow you to set the width and height of the forest. After the opening brace you store the width and height values in the class attributes, m_iWidth and m_iHeight. Next, you use the new operator in combination with the CTree constructor to create a two-dimensional array for tree entities. The two-dimensional array allows you to store different rows and columns of trees. The m_pTrees attribute alone points to the start of this array. Using index operators, you access the rows and columns.

The for loop that follows shows you how to set the row and columns. It consists of two for loops, one (the outer) that populates the rows, and the other (the inner) that populates the columns. To accomplish this work, in the outer loop you make use of the height value to generate a series of y values and create an array of CTree pointers for each row. Then, in the inner loop, you make use of the width value to create a series of x values. Each of the values designates a CTree object. The two loops together place a tree at all x and y locations the two-dimensional array provides.

Removing Trees from the Forest

As has been stressed throughout this book, when you use C++, you must make certain that when you call the new operator to dynamically create an object, you then call the destructor to destroy the object. Toward this end, you use the same outer-inner loop manipulation you saw at work in the CForest constructor to attend to de-allocating the memory acquired for the forest trees. Here's the code for the destructor from CForest.cpp:

```
CForest::~CForest()
{
        for(int y = 0; y < m_iHeight; y++)
        {
                for(int x = 0; x < m_iWidth; x++)
                {
                        // Delete the tree at x, y
                        SAFEDELETE(m_pTrees[y][x]);
                }
                // Delete the row
                SAFEDELETE_ARRAY(m_pTrees[y]);
        }
        // Delete the allocated 2D array
        SAFEDELETE_ARRAY(m_pTrees);
}
```

You stored the height and width values that characterize the forest in the class attributes m_iHeight and m_iWidth. Now you make use of these stored values. The value you have stored in the m_iHeight attribute allows you to visit each row of the forest. The value you have stored in the m_iWidth attribute allows you to visit each column of the forest. As you move through the grid, you call the SAFEDELETE() macro to delete the CTree objects at each x position for each row. After you have deleted all the CTree objects the rows contains, you call the SAFEDELETE_ARRAY() macro to delete the array that contains the row (m_pTrees[y]). When you have deleted all the rows, you call the SAFEDELETE_ARRAY() macro to delete the initial column of pointers stored in m_pTrees.

Drawing the Forest

To draw a forest, you create the CForest::Draw() function. The function takes two integer arguments, xPos and yPos, which determine the position of the top left corner of the forest. Here is the code for this function as it appears in CForest.cpp:

```
void CForest::Draw(int xPos, int yPos)
{
    for(int yTree = 0; yTree < m_iHeight; yTree++)
    {
        for(int xTree = 0; xTree < m_iWidth; xTree++)
        {
            // Get a pointer to the correct tree
            CTree *pTree = m_pTrees[yTree][xTree];
            // Set the position of the tree based on x, y
            pTree->SetPos(xPos + xTree * CTree::GetWidth(),
                          yPos + yTree * CTree::GetHeight());
            // Finally, draw the tree
            pTree->Draw();
        }
    }
}
```

After the opening brace, you create two for loops. The for loops iterate through each x and y position in the m_pTrees array. For each position, you assign a CTree pointer to the pTree variable. In this way, you represent each tree's existence with a set of x and y coordinates. Next, you call to the CTree::SetPos() function, which positions each tree in the client area of the window. To calculate the x position, you retrieve the x index of the tree in the tree array (xTree) and multiply it by the width of the tree sprite, which you obtain by calling the CTree::GetWidth() function. This value you then add to the value you retrieve from xPos. The value stored in xPos represents the horizontal offset of the forest in the client area.

To calculate the y position, you perform a set of operations similar to those used for the x position. This time you use the y index of the tree in the tree array (yTree), which you multiply by the height of the tree sprite. The CTree::GetHeight() returns the height. To establish the vertical offset, you retrieve the value passed to the Draw() function through the yPos parameter. Given that you have identified the positions at which the trees are to be drawn, you then call the CTree::Draw() function to render the trees.

The Forest's Center

Ultimately, when you create a forest, your objective becomes one of varying the way the forest comes into view. You want to avoid, for example, always having the forest begin to grow from the upper left of the client area. To make possible variation in growth patterns, you can create a function that sets the start of the forest's growth at the center of the client area. The DrawCentered() function accomplishes this work. Here is the code for this function from CForest.cpp:

```
void CForest::DrawCentered(int x, int y)
{
       // Calculate half the width and height of
       // the forest in pixels
       int iOffsetX = (m_iWidth * CTree::GetWidth()) / 2;
       int iOffsetY = (m_iHeight * CTree::GetHeight()) / 2;
       // Draw the forest, but offset the position
       Draw(x - iOffsetX, y - iOffsetY);
}
```

The DrawCentered() function takes two parameters. These parameters allow you to set the x and y positions that define the middle of the forest you want to create. To position the forest using these values, you first determine half the width and half the height of the forest in pixels. To accomplish this, you first deal with the width of the forest. To calculate the offset of the width, you retrieve the width of the individual trees in the forest using the CTree::GetWidth() function, which you multiply by the number of trees in the row (m_iWidth). You then divide the resulting value by two and assign it to the iOffsetX identifier.

To obtain the offset of the height, you obtain the height of the individual trees in the forest using the CTree::GetHeight() function, which you multiply by the number of trees in the forest column. You then divide the product by two and assign the result to the iOffsetY identifier.

Having calculated the offset values for the x and y dimensions of the forest, you then call the Draw() function. The Draw() function sets the position of the forest, and to make it so that it draws the forest centered in the client area, you make use of the offset values and the DrawCentered() parameter values. To set the first, x, parameter of the Draw() function, you subtract the value stored in iOffSetX from the Draw() x parameter value. To set the second, y, parameter of the Draw() function, you subtract the value stored in the iOffSetY from the Draw() y parameter. The result is that the x position from which you draw the forest is half the width of the forest, and the y position from which you draw the forest is half the height of the forest.

Accessing Forest Information

As the previous discussions have shown, when positioning and drawing the forest, you make frequent use of a couple of accessor functions, CForest::GetWidth() and CForest::GetHeight(). The CForest class also contains functions for returning the width and height of the forest in trees. Here is the code for these functions as shown in CForest.cpp:

```
int CForest::GetWidth()
{
    return m_iWidth;
}
int CForest::GetHeight()
{
    return m_iHeight;
}
```

With these two functions, you have in place all the elements you require to create a forest and position it at the client area's center. Now you face the tasks of creating the forest object in your application and creating controls that allow you to resize it.

Rendering the Forest

To render the forest, you modify the CMyApplication class. Your modifications begin with the addition of an attribute to the class. This is in the form of a pointer to a CForest object. Here is the code as it appears in CMyApplication.h:

```
// The forest object, which manages the trees
class CForest *m_pForest;
```

Following the declaration of the CForest attribute, you can then turn to creating an instance of CForest and assigning it to the attribute. To reach this goal, you add a few lines to the CMyApplication::Initialize() function:

```
void CMyApplication::Initialize()
{
    // Lines left out. . .
    // Create a new forest
```

```
    m_pForest = new CForest(8, 8);
    // Lines left out. . .
}
```

The constructor for CForest allows you to designate values for the width and height of the forest. In this instance, you set the initial size of the forest to be eight trees wide and eight tress high.

Given that you have initialized a forest object, you can then render it. To accomplish this, you add a few lines to the CMyApplication::Render() function. Here is the code that accomplishes the work:

```
void CMyApplication::Render()
{
    // Lines left out. . .
    // Draw the forest
    m_pForest->DrawCentered(m_pGraphics->GetWidth()/2,
                (m_pGraphics->GetHeight() -
                 m_sprConsole->GetHeight()) / 2);
    // Lines left out. . .
}
```

To implement the Render() function, you provide one, somewhat involved line of code. The line is involved because you call CForest::DrawCentered() to center the forest in the client area. To center the forest, you attend to the two parameters of the DrawCentered() function. For the first parameter, you calculate half of the width of the graphics device. For the second parameter, you first subtract the height of the console sprite (m_sprConsole->GetHeight()) from the client area height. You then divide by two to establish the middle point of this distance.

Controlling the Forest's Size

To control the forest's size, you create two sliders, which you position in the console area of the application. Creation of the sliders involves, first, adding some new attributes to the CMyApplication class. These attributes serve to identify the sliders and the messages associated with them. Here are the lines of code that add these attributes in CMyApplication.h:

```
    // Width and height sliders
    static const int IDC_WIDTH = 0;
    static const int IDC_HEIGHT = 1;
    static const int IDC_WIDTHLABEL = 2;
    static const int IDC_HEIGHTLABEL = 3;
```

Sliders and Labels

Having added these attributes, you then attend to adding the controls that correspond to them. This you accomplish in the CMyApplication::InitGUI() function. Here is the function as it appears in CMyApplication.cpp:

```
void CMyApplication::InitGUI()
{
    //Lines left out. . .
    // Create the width slider
    m_GUI.AddStatic(IDC_WIDTHLABEL, L"Forest Width:",
                    25, m_iConsoleY + 10, 100, 18);
    m_GUI.AddSlider(IDC_WIDTH, 25, m_iConsoleY + 25,
                    100, 20, 1, 20, 8);
    // Create the height slider
    m_GUI.AddStatic(IDC_HEIGHTLABEL, L"Forest Height:",
                    25, m_iConsoleY + 40, 100, 18);
    m_GUI.AddSlider(IDC_HEIGHT, 25, m_iConsoleY + 55, 100,
                    20, 1, 11, 8);
}
```

As you have seen many times previously, so the parameters you are concerned with understanding involve the messages. In this regard, the first call to the AddStatic() function makes use of the static class attribute IDC_WIDTHLABEL to assign a unique identifier to a label for the first slider. The text the label displays reads, "Forest Width." The coordinates establish that this label appears in the top-left corner of the console. Following the creation of the label, you call the CDXUTDialog::AddSlider() function to create the slider that controls the width of the forest. To assign a unique identifier to the slider, you use the static class attribute IDC_WIDTH. You position the slider below the label. You assign the slider a minimum value of one, a maximum value of twenty, and a default value of eight.

Having set up the label and slider to control the width of the forest, you then attend to setting up a label and a slider for the height of the forest. To accomplish this, you again call the AddStatic() function, which you assign the IDC_HEIGHTLABEL attribute as a unique identifier. You then again call the CDXUTDialog::AddSlider() function to create the height slider. To set the unique identifier for the slider, you employ the IDC_HEIGHT attribute. You set the scale of the slider so that it extends from one to eleven and starts out with a value of eight.

Processing Messages

To process the messages that the sliders issue, you make changes to the CMyApplication::OnGUIEvent() function. Here is the code for the function from CMyApplication.cpp:

```
void CMyApplication::OnGUIEvent(UINT nEvent, int nControlID,
                                CDXUTControl *pControl)
{
    if(nControlID == IDC_WIDTH)
    {
        // Get a pointer to the slider control
        CDXUTSlider *pSlider = (CDXUTSlider *)pControl;
        // Get the new width and height values
        int iWidth = pSlider->GetValue();
        int iHeight = m_pForest->GetHeight();
        // Re-create the forest
        SAFEDELETE(m_pForest);
        m_pForest = new CForest(iWidth, iHeight);
    }
    else if(nControlID == IDC_HEIGHT)
    {
        // Get a pointer to the slider control
        CDXUTSlider *pSlider = (CDXUTSlider *)pControl;
        // Get the new width and height values
        int iWidth = m_pForest->GetWidth();
        int iHeight = pSlider->GetValue();
        // Re-create the forest
        SAFEDELETE(m_pForest);
        m_pForest = new CForest(iWidth, iHeight);
    }
}
```

Since you have seen the parameters of the `OnGUIEvent()` function before, you can focus in this context on the selection statements that process the messages. The `if` statement checks whether the `nControlID` value is equal to the identifier for the width control (`IDC_WIDTH`). If this is so, then you cast the function parameter that identifies the control as a pointer to a `CDXUTSlider` object and assign it to a local `CDXUTSlider` pointer (`pSlider`). You then employ the `pSlider` pointer to call the `CDXUTSlider::GetValue()` function to retrieve the width of the forest and the `CForest::GetHeight()` function to retrieve the height of the forest. Given that you have these two values, you can then call the `SAFEDELETE()` macro to delete any existing forest and, in the next line, using a new operator, you can construct a new forest with the values you have just obtained.

You use the `else` selection statement to determine if the `OnGUIEvent()` function has received a message from the `IDC_HEIGHT` control. To process the message, you perform the same set of operations you perform for the width control with the exception that you call the `CDXUTSlider::GetValue()` function to retrieve the height of the forest and the `CForest::GetWidth()` function to retrieve the width.

When you have implemented these message-processing capabilities, you can then compile your application and make use of the controls to dynamically reshape the forest. As you do so, you see that the trees change in various ways in accord with the dynamic way that you create them and the dimensions you have set for the forest. The appearance of the whole determines the appearance of the part, but the appearance of the part also determines the appearance of the whole.

Starting the Fire

Having developed functionality that allows you to create a forest populated with trees that can cycle through a series of transformations that simulate burning, you are now in a position to begin to simulate a forest fire. In previous sections, you dealt with trees that burned either alone or randomly. Now you develop an algorithm that causes the trees to burn systematically, as a forest. To see the forest burning, access Listing10_03 and compile the project. Figure 10.5 illustrates the resulting application. To use the application, first set the size of the forest. Then click the Start Fire button to start a fire. When you click the Start Fire button, the program selects trees randomly to ignite.

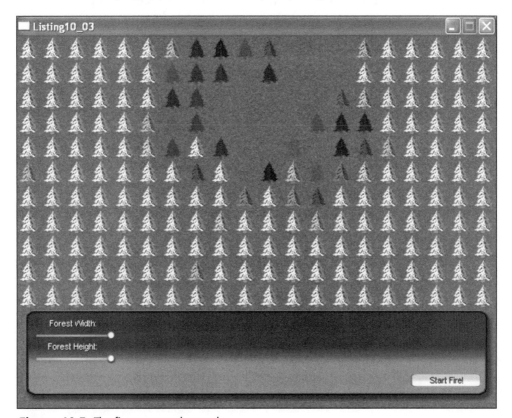

Figure 10.5 The fire starts and spreads.

At first, when the fire starts, the conflagration spreads at a constant rate from its point of origin, and you do nothing more than start it. As you progress, you modify this scheme so that you can input information to the program that alters where the fire starts and how it spreads.

Burn States

Creating a forest fire that spreads at a constant rate from a random point of origin requires that you first make some changes to the CTree class. For starters, you add an attribute to the class that allows you to store information about the state of tree entities. Here is the line that you add to CTree.h:

```
// Is the tree currently burning?
bool m_bBurning;
```

The m_bBurning attribute controls whether a tree burns. As you saw in the previous section, a tree begins in a healthy, green state and then automatically begins to turn dark. Eventually, it disappears. The m_bBurning flag allows you to delay or completely halt this process. To process information about the burn state of the tree, you set up three accessor functions. Here is the code for these functions as displayed in CTree.cpp:

```
void CTree::SetBurning(bool bBurning)
{
     m_bBurning = bBurning;
}
bool CTree::IsBurning()
{
     return m_bBurning;
}
float CTree::GetBurnFactor()
{
     return m_fBurnFactor;
}
```

These three functions work primarily in a utility capacity within the CTree class. SetBurning() allows you to assign start (true) or stop (false) values to the m_bBurning attribute, and this controls whether the tree continues on its path from bright green to oblivion. The IsBurning() function returns the current burn status of the tree. The GetBurnFactor() function returns the value stored in m_fBurnFactor, which is either 0 or 1. The value of m_fBurnFactor indicates whether a tree is still new and green or has been completely consumed by fire.

Controlling Burns

To regulate the way that the forest burns, you regulate the burn rate of individual trees. To accomplish this, you add an Update() function to the CTree class. The function requires one parameter, a floating decimal value (fTimeScale) that regulates the rate at which the tree is updated. You call the Update() function once each frame. Here is the code for the Update() function from CTree.cpp:

```
void CTree::Update(float fTimeScale)
{
    // If the tree is fully burned, return
    if(m_fBurnFactor >= 1.0)
    {
        m_bBurning = false;
        return;
    }
    // Increase the burn factor if the tree is on fire
    if(m_bBurning)
    {
        m_fBurnFactor += (0.01 * fTimeScale);
        //Below the threshold, give it a chance to die out
        if(m_fBurnFactor <= 0.50)
        {
            float fBurnoutChance = 0.05 * fTimeScale;
            float fRand = (float)rand() / (float)RAND_MAX;
            // If below the threshold, stop the burning
            if(fRand <= fBurnoutChance){m_bBurning = false;}
        }
    }
}
```

After the opening brace of Update(), you check whether the value of m_fBurnFactor equals or exceeds one. If this proves true, then you set m_bBurning to false, signaling that the tree has burned completely, and exit the function. On the other hand, if the tree has not completely burned, the value stored in m_bBurning is true, and you increase the burn factor. To increase the burn factor, you increment the value of m_fBurnFactor. To obtain the value to use to increment the burn factor, you multiply the value stored in fTimeScale by a constant (0.01). In this way, you ensure that the calculations are independent of the framerate of the application.

Having set up the burn rate, you then add code that allows the fire to die out in some circumstances. You use an if statement to determine whether the value of m_fBurnFactor is less than 0.5. If this is so, then you give the tree a chance to survive. To represent chance, you create a variable (fBurnoutChance) to which you assign the product of a constant (0.05) and the value stored in fTimeScale. You compare this value with another that you create using the rand() function (fRand). The value you assign to fRand lies between 0 and 1. If the randomly generated number is less than or equal to the chance that the tree will burn out, then you set the m_bBurning flag to false and the tree stops burning.

Designating Ignition Candidates

Having modified the trees so that their behavior as they burn varies in a way that allows some of them to survive, you next turn to the task of assembling trees into a forest and creating a forest fire. To accomplish this task, you add a new function, CheckForBurn(), to the CForest class. Here is the code for this function from CForest.cpp:

```cpp
bool CForest::CheckForBurn(int x, int y, float fTimeScale)
{
    // Eight burning neighbors, 20% chance this one will ignite
    const float fTreeConst = 1.0 / 40.0;
    float fBurnChance = 0.0;
    // Probability that the current tree will light up
    for(int yTree = y - 1; yTree <= y + 1; yTree++)
    {
        // Don't process out of bounds trees
        if(yTree < 0 || yTree >= m_iHeight){ continue; }
        for(int xTree = x - 1; xTree <= x + 1; xTree++)
        {
            // Don't process out of bounds trees
            if(xTree < 0 || xTree >= m_iWidth){ continue; }

            // Don't process the current tree
            if(xTree == x && yTree == y){ continue; }

            // Add to the burn chance if this tree is on fire
            if(m_pTrees[yTree][xTree]->GetBurnFactor() >= 0.25 &&
               m_pTrees[yTree][xTree]->GetBurnFactor() <= 0.50)
            {
            fBurnChance += fTreeConst;
            }
        }//end inner for
    }//end outer for
    // Multiply by the time scale
    fBurnChance *= fTimeScale;
    // Get a random number between 0 and 1
    float fRand = (float)rand() / (float)RAND_MAX;
```

```
    // Return true or false depending on the value
    return(fRand < fBurnChance);
}
```

The CheckForBurn() function takes in three parameters. The first two parameters indicate the x and y coordinates that identify the tree you want to evaluate for combustibility. The third parameter provides the timescale you use to regulate the rate of the simulation.

After the opening brace, your first bit of work involves declaring two identifiers. The first of these is a constant identifier (fTreeConst) that allows you to establish the extent to which the tree you have chosen for evaluation is likely to catch fire from the burning trees that surround it. In this case, you determine that if eight burning trees surround a target tree, then a ten percent chance exists that the target tree will ignite. Along the same lines, if four burning trees surround a target tree, then a five percent chance exists that the target tree will ignite. The second identifier, fBurnChance, allows you to record the chance that the target tree will catch on fire.

After you declare the fTreeConst and fBurnChance identifiers, you then use outer and inner for loops to iterate through the trees immediately surrounding your target tree to determine if they possess enough heat to cause the target tree to ignite. To initiate this activity, you use the x and y parameters of the CheckForBurn() parameter list to identify the tree you want to evaluate. The for loops start at the tree above and to the left of the tree you want to evaluate and conclude at the tree below and to the right. Along the way, the burn factors of the surrounding trees are evaluated. You use if statements to avoid going out of bounds (of the forest array) and to skip over the tree you have chosen to evaluate.

To determine if the current tree (m_pTrees[yTree][xTree]) is to be ignited, you check for burn factors in the range of 0.25 and 0.50. If the tree possesses a burn factor less than 0.25, it resists burning; if it possesses a burn factor greater than 0.50, then fire has already consumed it. Each time you find a tree that possesses a burn factor in the range of 0.25 to 0.50, you slightly increase the burn factor of your target tree. To accomplish this, you increase the value of fBurnChance by the value you have stored in fTreeConst. To retrieve the burn factor for these calculations, you call the GetBurnFactor() function for the trees you are evaluating.

Following the two for loops, you are in a position to determine whether the tree you have elected to evaluate should ignite. To make this decision, you first take the value of fBurnChance and multiply it by the value stored in fTimeScale. This multiplication ensures that the chance that a tree will ignite does not increase with the framerate alone. Next, you create a random floating-point variable between 0 and 1 and store it in the fRand variable. Then, you compare the two values. If fRand is less than fBurnChance, the statement is true, and the target tree (x, y) ignites; otherwise, it remains unchanged.

Updating for the Forest

If you can tell whether a given tree is ready to burn, you can apply this knowledge to all the trees in the forest. To accomplish this, you call the CheckForBurn() function in the scope of the CForest::Update() function. The procedure you employ involves iterating through all the trees in the forest and calling the CheckForBurn() function for each tree to determine whether it is ready to burn. If the CheckForBurn() function determines that a tree is ready to burn, then you call the SetBurning() function to set the tree ablaze. Here is the code for the CForest::Update() function in CForest.cpp:

```
void CForest::Update(float fTimeScale)
{
    // First update each tree
    for(int y=0; y < m_iHeight; y++)
    {
        for(int x=0; x < m_iWidth; x++)
        {
            m_pTrees[y][x]->Update(fTimeScale);
            if(CheckForBurn(x, y, fTimeScale))
            {
                m_pTrees[y][x]->SetBurning(true);
            }
        }
    }
}
```

While most of the activity the CForest::Update() function performs might appear fairly straightforward, note that you call the CTree::Update() function when you process information for individual trees. To call the CTree::Update() function, you employ the fTimeScale parameter of the CForest::Update() function. Passing the time scale value ensures that changes in the forest and the trees remain consistent.

Ignition

As ready as you might be to trace a fire, you still face the task of starting the fire. To accomplish this, you add a function to the CForest class. This is the StartRandomFire() function. Here is the code for it as shown in CForest.cpp:

```
void CForest::StartRandomFire()
{
    // Pick a random tree
    int iRandomX = rand()%m_iWidth;
    int iRandomY = rand()%m_iHeight;
```

```
    // Set the tree's burning flag to true
    m_pTrees[iRandomY][iRandomX]->SetBurning(true);
}
```

To implement the StartRandomFire() function, you attend to two chores. First, you call the rand() function and use it in conjunction with the modulus operator (%) and the class attributes for width and height to generate x (iRandomX) and y (iRandomY) coordinates to position the start of the fire. Next, you make use of this set of coordinates to designate a starter tree in the m_pTrees array. Having designated the first tree, you call CTree::SetBurning(), which ignites it.

Spreading the Fire

To spread the fire, you modify the CMyApplication::UpdateScene() function. Your modification consists of a single call to the CForest::Update() function. To regulate the rate of the fire's spread, you supply the Update() function with the fTimeScale parameter of UpdateScene(). Here is the code from CMyApplication.cpp that accomplishes this work:

```
void CMyApplication::UpdateScene(float fTimeScale)
{
    m_pForest->Update(fTimeScale);
    // Lines left out. . .
}
```

Controls and Messages

To allow you to control the events you have set up, you add a button to the application. When you click the button, you start a fire at a random location in your forest. To implement the button, you add code to the CMyApplication::InitGUI() function. Here is the code from CMyApplication.cpp:

```
void CMyApplication::InitGUI()
{
    // Lines left out. . .
    // Create the start button
    m_GUI.AddButton(IDC_START, L"Start Fire!",
                        525, m_iConsoleY + 85, 100, 20);
}
```

To add the button, you call the CDXUTDialog::AddButton() function. You employ a constant attribute of the CMyApplication class (IDC_START) as the first parameter of the function. For the second parameter, you supply the text that you want to appear on the button ("Start Fire!"). The third and fourth parameters position the button in the application client area. The final two parameters determine the size of the button.

Message Handling

To handle the message the Start Fire! button issues, you alter the `CMyApplication::OnGUIEvent()` function. Here is the code for this function from CMyApplication.cpp:

```
void CMyApplication::OnGUIEvent(UINT nEvent, int nControlID,
                               CDXUTControl *pControl)
{
    if(nControlID == IDC_START)
    {
        // Start a random fire in the forest
        m_pForest->StartRandomFire();
    }
    // Lines left out. . .
}
```

Since you already have investigated the parameters of `OnGUIEvent()` in previous sections, you can focus on the message the function processes. You use the `if` selection statement to confirm that the value of the `nControlID` parameter corresponds to the constant value stored in `IDC_START`. If this proves true, then you call `CForest::StartRandomFire()`, which starts the fire.

Creating a Model

When you create a model, you begin with a set of assumptions about how a number of entities interact to form a system. The system embodies the entities, and the entities interact according to a dynamic that their relations with each other create. Event mappings characterize the relations.

Using controls you can create an interactive application that incorporates a simulation of a forest fire. The simulation unfolds according to a mapping of events. The mapping of events creates the basis of a project that might become, with research and refinement, a valuable tool for analyzing the behavior of forest fires. Table 10.1 lays out event contexts that might be included in a model of a forest fire. While professional foresters might create a much longer list, this one at least serves as a beginning for a limited modeling exercise.

When you bring the event contexts Table 10.1 provides into a system that models a physical phenomena like a forest fire, you create a map of events that allows events to combine in different ways and result in different outcomes. Figure 10.6 provides an interaction diagram that explores a few of the possible relationships:

Table 10.1 Forest Fire Event Mapping

Event Context	Description
Horizontal forest extent	The growth of the forest horizontally across the client area. The shape of the forest plays a part in the burn patterns if factors such as wind and threshold come into play.
Vertical forest extent	The growth of the forest vertically across the client area. Again, the shape of the forest proves an important factor if wind and other influences come into play.
Density	The number of trees per square unit of measure. Density of tree growth proves an important factor in a number of ways. Trees that grow densely can exert a particularly lethal effect on each other.
Moisture content	The amount of moisture a tree holds. A tree that contains more moisture burns more slowly and is more likely to escape complete combustion.
Low threshold	The lower boundary of a range of temperatures that defines a tree's capacity to set fire to other trees. If a tree burns so slowly or with low enough intensity that it does not radiate heat to other trees, then it is not likely that it will cause other trees to begin burning.
High threshold	The upper boundary of a range of temperatures that defines a tree's capacity to set fire to other trees. A tree can combust so violently that its heat dissipates before it has a chance to set other trees ablaze. Forest fire fighters sometimes refer to such trees as "roman candles." Their heat explodes upward, not outward.
Burn rate	How quickly a tree burns after it catches fire. The rate at which trees burn can vary depending on a number of factors, such as moisture, wind, and threshold.
Burnout rate	The likelihood that a tree will discontinue burning after it has ignited. This might be related to any number of factors, such as moisture content and wind.
Direction of wind	The direction in which the wind blows flames. Wind exerts a number of influences on the burning forest. Among key factors are the intensity of the burn and the direction in which the fire moves.
Forest re-growth	The replenishment of the forest serves as a convenience measure that allows the user of the application to repeatedly conduct experiments involving different combinations of factors.

A forest fire as a natural system provides a fascinating topic to explore. Scientists who model forest fires use a wide variety of modeling tools that usually incorporate involved mathematical frameworks. Chaos theory is brought to bear on the data, along with such statistical tools as Monte Carlo simulations. Developing such models can involve years of work and the participation of many individuals.

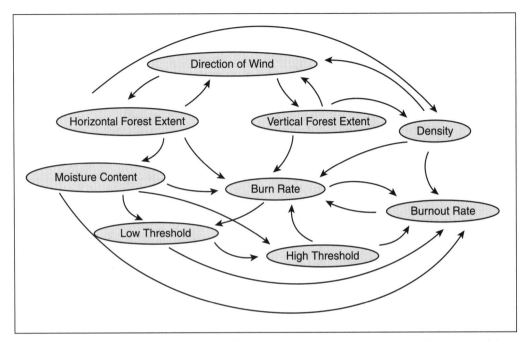

Figure 10.6 An interaction diagram reveals various event contexts and the overall mapping of the system the forest fire represents.

In the current discussion, the project of modeling a forest fire assumes much more humble dimensions. The goal here encompasses only laying out an application that allows you to see how you might develop a simple simulation of a forest fire. Key elements include a few controls that enable you to adjust variables that correspond to those Table 10.1 lists. As elementary as this approach might seem, it furnishes you with a way to understand how event models create systems that possess their own dynamics.

The Importance of Interaction

As the discussion earlier in this chapter emphasized, creating differences lies at the basis of much scientific exploration. Scientists create models so that they can vary the significance of selected variables. Controls allow them to accomplish this task. When scientists can change the significance of a given variable or event, then they place themselves in a position to be able to observe how the entire system might also change relative to a given variable or event. In this way, they create a way to establish formal correlations, for they can precisely state how much they have changed the significance of a given variable or event. Given this start, scientists can create hypotheses and then return again and again to the model to formally test them. See Figure 10.7.

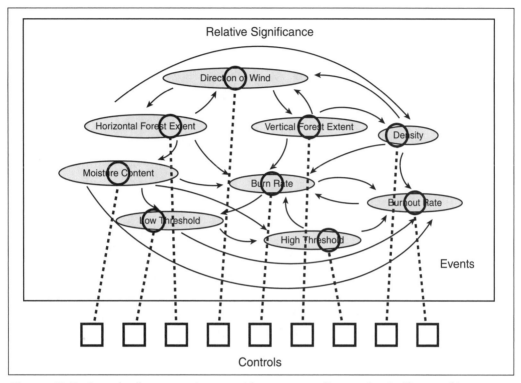

Figure 10.7 Controls allow you to interact with a system to discover the significance of its constituent events, entities, and interactions.

Use of controls for scientific modeling does not tell the whole story, however. For purposes of entertainment and education, the model implies a context of experience. Interacting with the context of experience through controls allows the participant to explore the context of experience in a variety of ways, individualizing, extending, and intensifying the experience. From this perspective, the goal of interaction becomes, not scientific formalization but rather the extension of experience through participation. When participants can assign selective events within a system of interaction different levels of significance, the meaning they derive from the experience changes.

A View of the Model

Access Listing 10_04 and compile the project. Figure 10.8 illustrates the result. To work the simulation, adjust the controls to your satisfaction and click the Start Fire! button. You can refer to Table 10.1 for information about the events to which the controls apply. To repeat your experiments, click the Regrow Forest button, adjust the controls, and once again click the Start Fire! button.

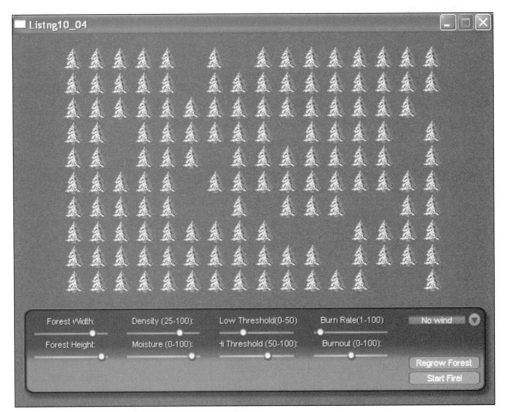

Figure 10.8 The model promotes interaction.

As simple as the application might be, it serves to show you all the most fundamental properties of a physical event model. It provides you with the ability to control selective events within a system so that you can observe the relative significance of the events. This underlies all scientific experimentation. On the other hand, on a level of experiential interaction, when you apply different settings to the controls, your actions immediately result in a transformation of experience that enables you to sense that your experience has changed as a result of your interaction with a given system. This fundamental relationship establishes an operational approach to defining the meaning of "significance."

The sections that follow dwell in detail on how to implement the simulation Figure 10.8 illustrates. To implement the events that correspond to the controls, you make changes to the CTree and CForest classes. To process the events, you alter the CMyApplication class.

Variables Instead of Constants

When you implement an application that models a physical system, as much as possible you must strive to interpret the events the system comprises quantitatively. Toward this end, you convert any values you might have inserted in your program into variables you can alter using controls.

Variables Relating to Trees

As a start in this direction, you can revisit the code for the declaration of the `CTree` class and replace the constants used in the last section with two static class attributes. As later sections of this chapter discuss, these attributes allow you to use controls to input information into the system you are modeling. Here are the new attributes as they appear in CTree.h:

```
// Variables to determine the behavior of all trees
static float BURNOUT_THRESHOLD;
static float BURN_SPEED;
```

The two attributes allow you to alter the behavior and effects of a burning tree. The `BURNOUT_THRESHOLD` attribute stores information that allows you to vary the extent to which a given tree can resist complete combustion. (See Table 10.1 for a summary of the events the system encompasses.) Generally, when the burn factor crosses the burnout threshold, no hope remains for the tree. The `BURN_SPEED` attribute stores information that allows you to vary the rate at which the burn factor increases. You can grasp the significance of a tree's burn speed if you consider that the slower the burn, the better the chance that the tree will spread its fire to other trees.

To see how the two attributes come into play in the application, you can examine the code for the `CTree::Update()` function:

```
void CTree::Update(float fTimeScale)
{
     // Lines left out. . .
     if(m_bBurning)
     {
          m_fBurnFactor += BURN_SPEED/10.0 * fTimeScale;
          //If the burn factor is below a certain threshold
          //give it a chance to die out
          if(m_fBurnFactor <= (BURNOUT_THRESHOLD))
          {
               // Lines left out. . .
          }
     }
}
```

If you glance at the discussion under "Controlling Burns" earlier in this chapter, you can see that previously literal values occupied the positions now assumed by BURNOUT_THRESHOLD and BURN_SPEED. The change prepares your application to begin treating these two events as variable in a general model of forest fires. On a more practical level, note that you divide the value stored in BURN_SPEED by 10 to prevent the animation of the burn event from occurring so quickly that you find it difficult to observe it.

Variables Relating to the Forest

As you converted constant values to variables so that you could begin modeling the behavior of trees, you convert constant values to variables so that you can begin modeling the forest. Toward this end, you add a number of new attributes to the CForest class. Here is the code in CForest.h that accomplishes this work:

```
// Moisture of the trees
float m_fMoisture;
// Density of the trees
float m_fDensity;
// Minimum and maximum spread threshold
float m_fMinSpread,
      m_fMaxSpread;
// X and Y direction of the wind
int m_iWindX,
    m_iWindY;
// Moisture of the trees
float m_fMoisture;
```

The m_fMoisture attribute tracks the moisture the trees contain. The values you supply this attribute range from 0 to 1. If you set the value to 0, you indicate that the tree is dry and will combust easily. If you set the value to 1, you indicate that the tree is saturated and will combust with difficulty. The m_fDensity attribute tracks the density of the forest. The forest array allows you to create trees in a grid that distributes the trees over the client area of your application. Using this attribute, you can determine how many trees you want to distribute over the grid. If you set the density to 1, each position in the grid contains a tree, and this represents the greatest density. If you set the density to 2, the grid contains one tree for every two positions. The forest thus becomes less dense.

When fire spreads, it does so because the burning trees possess enough heat that they can cause other trees to begin burning. You add the m_fMinSpread and m_fMaxSpread attributes to capture this event. The two attributes store minimum and maximum values and establish a temperature range in which a burning tree can cause other trees to catch fire.

To store values that allow you to account for the influence of wind on a forest fire, you create the m_iWindX and m_iWindY attributes. If you set m_iWindX to 0 and m_iWindY to -1, then the wind blows to the north. If you set m_iWindX to 1 and m_iWindY to 0, then the wind blows to the west.

System Behaviors

Having converted constant values to class attributes, you now face the task of setting up accessor and mutator functions that allow you to alter the values you store in these attributes so that you can shape the behavior of the system.

Simple Mutator Functions

In some cases, you can establish the significance of different events by directly assigning values to attributes using mutator functions. Here is the code from CForest.cpp that implements the simple mutator functions for the CForest class:

```
void CForest::SetWind(int iWindX, int iWindY)
{
    m_iWindX = iWindX;
    m_iWindY = iWindY;
}
void CForest::SetMoisture(float fMoisture)
{
    m_fMoisture = fMoisture;
}
void CForest::SetDensity(float fDensity)
{
    m_fDensity = fDensity;
}
void CForest::SetLowThreshold(float fLow)
{
    m_fMinSpread = fLow;
}
void CForest::SetHighThreshold(float fHigh)
{
    m_fMaxSpread = fHigh;
}
```

Forest Growth

As the previous section showed, setting the values of attributes can sometimes involve simple insertions of data. In other situations, you perform calculations to arrive at the values you want to assign to attributes. This more complex approach characterizes implementation of the Regrow() function, which sets the size of the forest. When you set the size of the forest, you determine the area the forest covers and the density of the trees in the forest. Here is the code for the Regrow() function from CForest.cpp:

```
void CForest::Regrow(int iWidth, int iHeight)
{
        if(iWidth == -1){iWidth = m_iWidth;}
        if(iHeight == -1){iHeight = m_iHeight;}
        // Delete the old tree array
        DeleteArray();
        // Set up the new width/height
        m_iWidth = iWidth;
        m_iHeight = iHeight;
        // Create the array for the rows
        m_pTrees = new CTree **[m_iHeight];
        // Create the rows
        for(int y = 0; y < m_iHeight; y++)
        {
                // Create the row
                m_pTrees[y] = new CTree *[m_iWidth];
                // Create the actual trees in the row
                for(int x = 0; x < m_iWidth; x++)
                {
                        // determine if you should create a tree here
                        float fRand = (float)rand()/(float)RAND_MAX;
                        // Create a tree if within the density probability
                        if(fRand <= m_fDensity)
                        {
                                m_pTrees[y][x] = new CTree();
                        }
                        else
                        {
                                m_pTrees[y][x] = NULL;
                        }//end if. . . else
                }//end for m_iWidth
        }//end for m_iHeight
}
```

You call the Regrow() function to initiate new simulations. In many instances, you want to reset the size of the forest. In other instances, you want to leave the size of the forest alone so that you can repeatedly observe the same simulation. To make it possible to either leave the size of the forest alone or change it, you employ two selection statements immediately after the opening brace of the function. If these statements determine that the value of either function parameter (iWidth or iHeight) equals -1, you accept the values for height and width that you have already stored in the class attributes (m_iWidth and m_iHeight) and calculate the size of the forest using them. If these statements detect values other than -1, then you recalculate the size of the forest using the new values.

In the event that you need to reset the size of the forest, you call the DeleteArray() function to destroy the previously existing forest array (m_pTrees). Having destroyed the old forest array, you can create another one. To accomplish this, you implement two for loops. The outer for loop creates tree rows using the m_iWidth value as a control. The inner for loop creates tree columns using the m_ iHeight value as a control.

To determine the density of trees, you iterate through the tree array (a grid) and selectively assign trees to positions within it. To determine when to place a tree in the grid, you compare two numbers. One of these numbers you obtain using the C/C++ library rand() function, which generates a random floating-point number between 0 and 1 that you assign to fRand. The other number you obtain from the class attribute m_fDensity.

When you compare the numbers, if the value of fRand is less than or equal to the value of m_fDensity, you use the new operator with the CTree constructor to dynamically allocate memory for a tree object. You assign this object to the appropriate place in the tree grid (m_pTrees[y][x]). In cases in which the values of m_fDensity and fRand do not justify the creation of a new tree, you assign a value of NULL to the place in the tree grid a tree reference might have occupied.

Clearing Forests

The CForest::DeleteArray() function destroys tree grids, and as you saw in the discussion of the Redraw() function, allows you to create new ones. As becomes evident if you revisit the discussion earlier in the chapter of the CForest destructor, the code that comprises DeleteArray() consists of code drawn from the destructor. The technical term for moving around code in this way is *refactoring*. Given that destroying the forest constitutes an event that occurs frequently during the life of the application and when execution of the application ends, you have reason to create a specialized function (*refactor* the code) that takes care of this business. Now, both the Redraw() and the DeleteArray() functions call DeleteArray(). Here is the code for the DeleteArray() function as shown in CForest.cpp:

```
void CForest::DeleteArray()
{
    if(!m_pTrees){ return; }
    for(int y = 0; y < m_iHeight; y++)
    {
        for(int x = 0; x < m_iWidth; x++)
        {
            // Delete the tree at location x, y
```

```
            SAFEDELETE(m_pTrees[y][x]);
        }
        // Delete the row
        SAFEDELETE_ARRAY(m_pTrees[y]);
    }

    // Delete the 2D array
    SAFEDELETE_ARRAY(m_pTrees);
}
```

Starting a Fire Randomly

Now that you can grow a forest and set its density and size, you might as well attend to setting it ablaze. To make igniting the forest more interesting, you randomly designate the ignition point. Such an action is not unprecedented. Consider, for example, what happens when a bolt of lightning strikes a tree. Toward this end, you implement the StartRandomFire() function. You already have seen a version of this code in an earlier section of the chapter. Now you update the existing code to pick a tree at random. Here's the updated code from CForest.cpp:

```
void CForest::StartRandomFire()
{
    // Try no more than 100 times to find a tree
    int iNumTries = 0;
    int iRandomX, iRandomY;
    do      // Pick a random tree
    {
        iRandomX = rand() % m_iWidth;
        iRandomY = rand() % m_iHeight;
        // Set the tree's burning flag to true
        if(m_pTrees[iRandomY][iRandomX])
        {
            m_pTrees[iRandomY][iRandomX]->SetBurning(true);
        }
         // Increase number of tries
        iNumTries++;
    }while(iNumTries < 100 && !m_pTrees[iRandomY][iRandomX]);
}
```

Discussions in previous sections of this chapter introduced the code for the StartRandomFire() function, which ignited a tree in the same location each time it was called. To randomize the work of the function, you now place the original code inside a do…while loop. The loop iterates up to one hundred times, and with each iteration you use the rand() function limited by the width and height of the forest to generate random positions that a tree might occupy. If you find a tree, then you call the `CTree::SetBurning()` burning function and set its flag to `true`. In this way, you are likely to see the forest fire start in a different location each time you click the Start Fire! button. In some instances, however, you might find that the fire does not start at all.

Customizing Combustion Phenomena

Customizing combustion phenomena adds complexity to your event model in significant ways. As illustrated in Figure 10.7, if you add controls to an application that enables you to change the significance of different events in a simulation, you tremendously enhance the scientific and entertainment potentials of your application. By rewriting the `CForest::CheckForBurn()` function, you can lay the groundwork for implementation of the controls. Toward this end, you add code to the function that allows you to alter the values you associate with the density, burn intensity (or threshold), wind direction, and moisture that characterize the combustion of a tree. Here's the code for the function from CForest.cpp:

```
bool CForest::CheckForBurn(int x, int y, float fTimeScale)
{
    const float fTreeConst = 1.0/40.0;
    float fBurnChance = 0.0;
    // Check each tree around this one. If it
    // is on fire, add to the probability that the
    // current tree will light up
    //Outer for. . .
    for(int yTree = y-1; yTree <= y+1; yTree++)
    {
        // Don't process out of bounds trees
        if(yTree < 0 || yTree >= m_iHeight){continue;}
        //Inner for. . .
        for(int xTree = x-1; xTree <= x+1; xTree++)
        {
            // Observe forest boundaries
            if(xTree < 0 || xTree >= m_iWidth){continue;}
            // Skip the current tree
            if(xTree == x && yTree == y){continue;}
            //Verify the existence of the tree -- DENSITY
            if(!m_pTrees[yTree][xTree]){continue;}

            // Augment burn chance if this tree is on fire
            if(m_pTrees[yTree][xTree]->GetBurnFactor() >=
                m_fMinSpread &&      //NON-CONSTANT THRESHOLD
                m_pTrees[yTree][xTree]->GetBurnFactor() <=
```

```
            m_fMaxSpread)          //NON-CONSTANT THRESHOLD
        {
            fBurnChance += fTreeConst;
            // Double the burn chance if it is in
            // the direction of the WIND
            if(yTree-y == m_iWindY || xTree-x == m_iWindX)
            {
                    fBurnChance *= 2;
            }
            // Decrease the burn chance due to MOISTURE
             fBurnChance *= (1.0 - (m_fMoisture/5.0));
        }//end if
    }//end inner for
}//end outer for
}
```

You have seen this function in previous sections, but the current implementation of the function differs from the previous implementation, first, because it adds sensitivity to the *density* of the forest. To account for the density of the forest, which creates a situation in which trees might not exist at every possible location in the forest, you add an if statement at the top of the inner for loop. This statement verifies that a tree exists at the current location. If no tree exists, then a continue statement moves the loop forward another iteration.

In addition to altering the function to accommodate density, you also equip it to account for non-constant values for m_fMinSpread and m_fMaxSpread, which establish the *intensity* or *threshold* of the fire. Use of the non-constant values ensures that the intensity to which one tree's heat affects other trees varies, so the pattern you see as the fire spreads becomes less predictable.

Along with the density and the intensity with which one tree's heat affects other trees, you also add code that brings *wind* into the picture. You add an if selection statement that allows you to determine the direction of the wind. After determining the direction of the wind, you then add code that doubles the chance that a neighboring tree will catch fire if it lies downwind from a burning tree. The result is that the fire is more likely to spread in the direction of the wind.

The final lines of the revised CheckForBurn() function allow you to add the *moisture* content of the tree to its combustion characteristics. Depending on the moisture the tree retains, the if statement can lower the burn chance. The higher the moisture content, the lower the chance that the tree will ignite. You divide the value of the moisture content (m_fMoisture) by 5 to adjust it to a range that extends from zero to one.

Fine Tuning

The need to conserve space makes it necessary to leave out a detailed discussion of changes you make to the CForest Draw() and Update() functions. Still, it remains important to note that you update these functions so that they can recognize positions in the forest array occupied by NULL values. The technique you use to recognize these positions has been shown in the code example for the CheckForBurn() function. You create inner and outer loops and then iterate through all positions in the array to check for NULL values. If you find a NULL value, you employ the continue keyword to exit from further actions. Here is a snippet that illustrates this activity:

```
int x, y;  //starting values
for(int yTree = y - 1; yTree <= y + 1; yTree++)
//Outer for . . .
{
    //Inner for
    for(int xTree = x - 1; xTree <= x + 1; xTree++)
    {
        if(!m_pTrees[yTree][xTree]){ continue; }
    }//end inner for
}//end outer for
```

Interface and Messaging

As Figure 10.8 illustrates, the interface for the forest fire simulation reduces to a minimum your interaction with the events the fire model includes. Table 10.2 provides a brief analysis of the controls the application offers.

Table 10.2 Control Event Mapping

Control	Number	Description
Slider	8	Provides a range of values for the user. Invites continuous and varied interaction. Invites relative adjustments. The user gains a sense of the dynamic of the system. It is hard to isolate one event from another.
Button	2	Provides a decisive moment of interaction. The user resets the forest. The user starts a new fire. These actions mark beginning and end points of interaction.
Drop-Down (Combo)	1	Allows the user to choose from one among a limited set of options. The wind blows in one of the cardinal directions, or it does not blow at all. The user makes a relative choice, but the choice is still decisive.

Control and Message Identifiers

Prior to discussing how you implement controls, it is worthwhile to give some attention to the attributes you add to the CMyApplication class to accommodate the identification of the controls and the messages they issue. In each instance, you declare integer values that are both static and constant. Here is the list of attributes you find in CMyApplication.h:

```
static const int IDC_WIDTH = 0;
static const int IDC_HEIGHT = 1;
static const int IDC_WIDTHLABEL = 2;
static const int IDC_HEIGHTLABEL = 3;
static const int IDC_START = 4;
static const int IDC_DENSITY = 5;
static const int IDC_DENSITYLABEL = 6;
static const int IDC_MOISTURE = 7;
static const int IDC_MOISTURELABEL = 8;
static const int IDC_SPREADLOW = 9;
static const int IDC_SPREADLOWLABEL = 10;
static const int IDC_SPREADHIGH = 11;
static const int IDC_SPREADHIGHLABEL = 12;
static const int IDC_BURNOUTLABEL = 13;
static const int IDC_BURNOUT = 14;
static const int IDC_BURNRATELABEL = 15;
static const int IDC_BURNRATE = 16;
static const int IDC_WIND = 17;
static const int IDC_REGROW = 18;
```

If you refer back to Table 10.1, you can see that the event model the forest fire introduces creates the need for two sets of identifiers. You identify the labels for the controls. You also identify the controls and the messages they issue. To make the identifiers easier to use, notice that you name them as literally as possible and prefix to them a tag (IDC) that allows you to recognize them as control and message identifiers.

Control Implementation

Implementation of the controls in this context does not differ from what you have seen in previous sections. For the sliders, you employ the CDXUTDialog::AddSlider() function. For each of the sliders you implement, you draw from the identifier list. A label accompanies each slider. You position the label directly above the slider. Here is a snippet of code from the CMyApplication::InitGUI() function that implements a slider and its accompanying label:

```
// Density slider
m_GUI.AddStatic(IDC_DENSITYLABEL,
                L"Density (25-100):", 150,
                m_iConsoleY + 10, 100, 18);
```

```
//Density slider label
m_GUI.AddSlider(IDC_DENSITY, 150, m_iConsoleY + 25,
                100, 20, 25, 100, 75);
```

Implementation of a combo box involves more work than implementation of a slider or a button. For the combo box, you employ the `CDXUTDialog::AddComboBox()`, `CDXUTComboBox::AddItem()`, and, `CDXUTComboBox::SetDropHeigh()` functions. Here is the code from the `CMyApplication::InitGUI()` function that implements the combo box for the wind values:

```
m_GUI.AddComboBox(IDC_WIND, 525, m_iConsoleY + 10, 100, 20);
m_GUI.GetComboBox(IDC_WIND)->AddItem(L"No wind",
                                     (void *)0);
m_GUI.GetComboBox(IDC_WIND)->AddItem(L"North wind",
                                     (void *)1);
m_GUI.GetComboBox(IDC_WIND)->AddItem(L"East wind",
                                     (void *)2);
m_GUI.GetComboBox(IDC_WIND)->AddItem(L"South wind",
                                     (void *)3);
m_GUI.GetComboBox(IDC_WIND)->AddItem(L"West wind",
                                     (void *)4);
m_GUI.GetComboBox(IDC_WIND)->SetDropHeight(75);
```

Implementation of buttons is an activity you have seen many times before. The current version of the application calls for two buttons. Here is the code from the `CMyApplication::InitGUI()` function that implements the Regrow button:

```
// Create the Regrow button
m_GUI.AddButton(IDC_REGROW, L"Regrow Forest",
                525, m_iConsoleY + 65, 1s00, 20);
```

Processing Messages

As with implementing controls, creating message-processing capabilities constitutes an activity you have seen many times before. For this reason, discussion can be confined to a brief review. First, as you know, the `CMyApplication::OnGUIEvent()` handles all of the events. To handle events, you create an extended set of if…else if statements. Each statement evaluates the message parameter of the `OnGUIEvent()` function to determine the control to which it relates. For example, here is the handler code for the slider that controls forest density:

```
if(nControlID == IDC_DENSITY)
{
    // Set the density
    CDXUTSlider *pSlider = (CDXUTSlider *)pControl;
```

```
        float fDensity=(float)pSlider->GetValue()/100.0f;
        m_pForest->SetDensity(fDensity);
    }
```

As you have learned in previous discussions of sliders, you cast the `pControl` parameter of the `OnGUIEvent()` function to a `CDXUTSlider` pointer and then assign the result to a local pointer identifier (`pSlider`). Using this pointer, you then call the `CDXUTSlider::GetValue()` function to retrieve the value the slider generates. For the density slider, this is a floating-point value between 0 and 1. Given that you have retrieved the floating-point value the slider has generated, you can then call `CForest::SetDensity()` to set the density. When you click the Regrow button, the application adjusts the density of the forest to accord with this value.

To process messages that the combo box issues, following selection for the control message identifier (`IDC_WIND`), you implement a secondary `if…else` structure to select the action that accords with the index value the control has issued. As with other controls, to retrieve the specific value the control has issued, you first cast the `pControl` parameter of the `OnGUIEvent()` function to a pointer that corresponds to the control you are working with. In this case, the type of the pointer is `CDXUTComboBox`. You then use the pointer to call a function that retrieves the data the control has issued. In this case, you call `CDXUTComboBox::GetSelectedData()`, which retrieves the value of the index you have selected from the drop-down box. You assign the index value to a local identifier (`idxSelected`). Fed to the secondary selection structure, you can then use the index value to determine how to set the direction of the wind. Here is the code from the `OnGUIEvent()` function in CMyApplication.cpp that processes messages from the combo box that allow you to select the direction of the wind:

```
    else if(nControlID == IDC_REGROW)
    {
        CDXUTComboBox *pCombo = (CDXUTComboBox *)pControl;
        int idxSelected = (int)pCombo->GetSelectedData();
        // Set wind to either none, north, east, south,
        // or west, in that order, depending on the value
        // of idxSelected
        if(idxSelected == 0)
            m_pForest->SetWind(0, 0);
        else if(idxSelected == 1)
            m_pForest->SetWind(0, -1);
        else if(idxSelected == 2)
            m_pForest->SetWind(1, 0);
        else if(idxSelected == 3)
            m_pForest->SetWind(0, 1);
```

```
        else if(idxSelected == 4)
            m_pForest->SetWind(-1, 0);


    }
```

The implementation of the handler for the buttons requires only the briefest of reviews. Here is the code from the OnGUIEvent() function that processes the message issued by the Regrow button:

```
else if(nControlID == IDC_REGROW)
{
    // Re-grow the forest
    m_pForest->Regrow();
}
```

To process the message, you first use the selection statement to determine whether it corresponds to the value of IDC_REGROW. If it does, then you call the CForest::Regrow() function.

Conclusion

Simulation of physical systems begins with the creation of a mode. When you interact with the model through the simulation, you discover details about its constituent events that allow you to increase your understanding of the model. The system you developed in this chapter centered on a forest fire. While the model you developed for this system was simple and ultimately requires much improvement before you can effectively employ it to simulate real-world events, it nevertheless serves as a solid framework with which to explore the primary activities involved in exploring and mapping models and developing simulations of physical systems.

Working with a physical system first involves conceptually framing the tasks you have set for yourself. At the center of this activity lies the work of understanding that an effective simulation liberates knowledge about its underlying model. Effective liberation of knowledge involves analyzing events to discover effective ways to control the significance they possess in the context the model provides. Identifying events in this way allows you to explore how events map to each other and how participants in simulations can easily manipulate inputs to the system so that specific events can be precisely controlled.

To implement a simulation based on a model of a forest fire, you first modified an existing class, CSprite, so that you could use coloration as a way to trace the life of a tree. Following your work with CSprite, you created two new classes, CTree and CForest. CTree allowed you to create isolated entities that behaved independently of each other. Your work with CForest allowed you to bring these events into relations with each other and to generate a system and allow you to begin examining your model through interactions with this system.

During each phase of development, you created new events and controls. The events increased the sophistication of your system. The controls enabled you to interact with the entities and events composing your system. Among the events you incorporated into your system were the horizontal and vertical sizing of the forest, the density of the tree growth, the moisture content of trees, the lower and upper thresholds of combustion for trees, the burnout rates of trees, the impact of wind on burning trees, and the re-growth of forests. You created sliders, buttons, and combo boxes so you could easily interact with these events.

A successful simulation of a physical system enables its users to increase both their knowledge of a system and their understanding of how to interact with the simulation. Interaction in such situations is characterized by a growing awareness of how to increase knowledge about the system. In conjunction with the analysis of events the model enables its users to conduct, controls provide users with tools to increase the overall satisfaction with the simulation. That a simulation possesses elements of realism remains important. More important, however, is the extent to which the simulation allows its participants to broaden their capacity to experience (to interact with) a given set of phenomena.

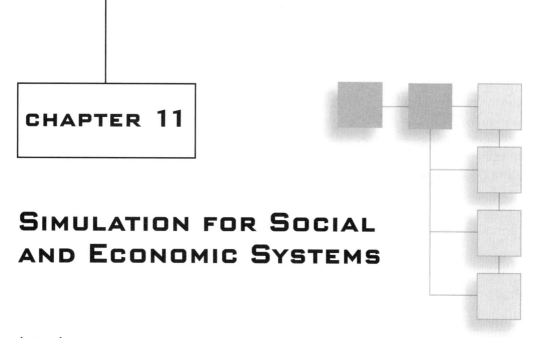

CHAPTER 11

SIMULATION FOR SOCIAL AND ECONOMIC SYSTEMS

T his chapter discusses how to develop a model and implement the code for a simulation that represents a socioeconomic system. The system represented does not strive to provide anything beyond a starter project. Still, you can grasp from the project how to structure a simulation. Key aspects of this work encompass determining what type of understanding you wish to develop through your model. A simulation of a socioeconomic model, like any other simulation, provides a valuable tool for assessing the strengths and weaknesses of the model. With this in mind, you benefit if you take time to carefully isolate and define the variables you deal with and the interpretations and calculations you apply to the variables. Such preparation allows you to rework the model after its initial development to refine its accuracy and to introduce additional variables to it. You cover the following topics, among others, as you undertake this effort:

- Conceptualizing economic and social systems
- Simulations and policies
- Revolution and the ledger
- Revolution and the spreadsheet
- Developing a class for buildings
- Developing a class for towns
- Implementing controls

Social and Economic Perspectives

When you develop a socioeconomic model and use a simulation to present or test it, you often work with a body of data that you acquire from published reports, and your efforts are guided by the desire to persuade an audience that your interpretation of the data possesses merit over others.

Several decades ago, the social sciences strove to achieve the level of empirical discipline standardized by the physical sciences. The result of this effort was short of what its advocates sought. While introducing solid practices that required sociologists, anthropologists, economists, and political scientists to formalize their findings in a fashion common to experimental scientists, it remained that a rift still separated studies relating to human culture from those relating to physical nature.

Of course, the studies of economics and the social sciences remain scientifically grounded if those who practice them observe the fundamental tenants of scientific methodology. Key among these is that every hypothesis should be evaluated experimentally and verified repeatedly by critical observers.

Practical Applications

Simulations that relate to the social sciences and economics have a vast number of applications in governmental, banking, investment, and business contexts. Those engaged in such activities usually begin from a position defined by selective policies. Models represent policies. The models created by representatives of governments often show what results from the implementation of policies, and in many instances, they create their models so that that they reveal only the desirable results of their policies. The same applies to other realms. Banking, investment, and business experts seek to maximize returns, and as they do so, they follow policies.

When banks and investment institutions finance projects that involve clearing large swathes of rain forest, using radar to increase catches over large areas of oceans so that the fishery is reduced to a minimum, increasing the production of automobiles that burn fossil fuels, or drilling for oil in environmentally delicate regions, many critics contend that they do so because the models that guide their actions selectively interpret data to promote the importance of high profits over other, equally valid, objectives. The models they create reflect their policies, and their policies stipulate that they should not follow the suggestions of environmentalists or others who advocate using ethical criteria other than economic growth as the basis of investment decisions.

Differences of policy do not render invalid simulations and event models that relate to fiscal or economic issues. In fact, the case is the opposite. Because they are so much subject to policy, simulations and event models increase in importance as vehicles for implementing policies.

Social and economic simulations provide enormous persuasive powers to those who use them. Some people might hear a newscast or read a newspaper, and they might be better informed about the world as a result, but hearing or reading an account of a given event lacks force when compared to the immediate, direct experience a simulation provides. A simulation possesses the power to transform your understanding of an event because it induces you to participate in the event.

Historical Precedents

Programs that can create simulations based on collections of data have been a standard feature of software history almost from the beginning, but one of the most significant advances occurred with the development of the spreadsheet. A discussion of the spreadsheet proves worthwhile because it provides a perspective on how technology interactively enhances and simplifies tasks involving interpreting and presenting data within the context a model provides.

Another innovation, the financial ledger, emerged in history many centuries before the spreadsheet. Like the spreadsheet, it provides a worthy topic of discussion because it so clearly embodies many of the qualities that characterize simulation. Together, the ledger and the spreadsheet reveal how technology enhances presentation through simulation. In recent decades the capacity of software to support participatory simulations created an opportunity for the powers embodied in ledgers and spreadsheets to be extended more than ever.

Ledgers

At least as far back as ancient Babylon, scribes entered columnar accounts on clay tablets. Several millennia later, Renaissance merchants in Venice performed column-based accounting using ledgers. The ledger consisted of large, stiff sheets of paper divided into rows and columns. The merchants used the ledger to track business activities. Tracking involved writing the cost of a given item in one column, the price the merchants asked or commanded in another, and the profit in a third.

The ledger served as a practical device for tracking accounts. It provided a way to simplify large bodies of data. It provided a way to present data in a standard format. It was portable, relatively inexpensive to maintain, and the data it provided could be updated over time.

Most significantly, the ledger provided a tool that merchants could use to present and simulate proposals for trade ventures. While Venetian merchants maintained ledgers that accounted for entire shiploads of greatly diversified merchandise, they also could use them to plan, simplify, model, and simulate. Capturing their activities in this way, they created a vehicle that allowed them to refine their practices. As a simulation serves as a way that scientists can refine their models of natural events, merchants used the ledger as a way to refine their models of economic transactions. See Figure 11.1.

Merchants could use ledgers to gain a clear view of trading enterprises that might require months or years to complete and encompass thousands of transactions. Merchants could grasp the big picture at any time by glancing at the summary view the ledger provided. When bankers of the Medici family looked at ledgers, they had in hand a more than adequate picture of a planned adventure, and they made the loans that allowed the economic adventurers who prepared the ledgers to embark on the trading journeys that caused the Western world to emerge from the Dark Ages.

Figure 11.1 An adventurous trader could use a ledger to persuade Renaissance bankers that a venture would render profits.

European commerce was transformed. Where the same type of accounting emerged in other parts of the word, such as China and India, similar results occurred. The ledger allowed those involved in commerce to understand a vast set of specific data through a technology that involved columnar presentations of data and convenient transfers of information. It became a tool for presentation and simulation when its users realized they could employ it to model events and simulate the outcome of prospective enterprises.

Spreadsheets

Emerging centuries after the Medici family saw its great days, the spreadsheet offers an approach to creating visions of financial adventures that followed the paradigm the ledger established. It addresses the need those involved in economic and business planning have to collect, simplify, model, and simulate data relating to their enterprises. Like its leather-bound, stiff-paged predecessor, the spreadsheet offered a magnificent way to fold enormous stores of information into a single presentation.

The names of the inventors of the ledger have been lost to history, but the names of the inventors of the spreadsheet are ready at hand. For example, during the late 1960s Rene Pardo and Remy Landauby created a program cumbersomely named LANguage for Programming Arrays at Random (LANPAR). They performed this work for Bell Canada. Their work resulted in a system that allowed telephone companies and automakers (General Motors, most significantly) to use digital computers and spreadsheets to simulate large economic and physical events. See Figure 11.2.

The early spreadsheets ran on mainframes, but a few decades later things changed. Concurrent with the development of the personal computer, Dan Bricklin and Robert Franston created Visicalc, a spreadsheet application designed to work on personal computers. This was followed by the efforts of Mitch Kapor, who created Lotus 1-2-3. With the release of Microsoft Excel (1987), the work of the earlier inventors became embodied in a tool that is used almost universally.

From the first, investment bankers and others interested in quickly modeling mergers and acquisitions purchased spreadsheets. The spreadsheet possessed great value because it made it possible for those involved in business and economics to easily accomplish a task they were only previously able to accomplish with great difficulty. This was to model complex transactions using several different scenarios. Prior to the spreadsheet, creating a model and inserting data into it were arduous, time-consuming tasks, and it was a back-breaking reversal if a commission, banker, or corporate executive wanted a model reworked, adjusted, or simulated using an alternate set of data.

Figure 11.2 The ledger becomes a spreadsheet and once again transforms the world.

Using a spreadsheet, modelers could create a model and then be at liberty to change the data applied to it with relative ease. Likewise, they could change the model while not having to rework their data. The result was the capacity to generate a multitude of simulations in quick successions.

The change in modeling and simulation technologies resulted in a revolution that was as significant as the revolution that the use of the ledger by the bankers of Venice created. When executives decided they wanted to investigate the prospects of a merger or a new business enterprise, planners could immediately develop a number of different proposals. Days, not weeks, months, or years, began to character the rapidity with which business mergers, bank loans, and a variety of large economic undertakings could be developed, proposed, and approved.

By the mid-1990s, the spreadsheet had become a part of every activity from scheduling little league tournaments to estimating World Bank and United Nations loan programs for industrial development. In the world today, the activities of every business or governmental agency of any importance at all are likely to be planned and audited using electronic spreadsheets.

note

Stephen Wolfram, the inventor of Mathematica, has written that if you develop computer applications that address complex processes, you soon come to understand that "The same forms of behavior recur over and over again almost independently of underlying behavior." (Stephen Wolfram, *A New Kind of Science* [Champaign, IL: Wolfram Media, 2002], page 4.)

Economic Protections

In political spheres for the last several hundred years, policy makers have often asserted that an economic activity that creates a profit is bound to be more ethically acceptable than activity that does not. This notion often goes under the heading of *laissez faire*, a term popularized by French Physiocrat writers during the late 1700s. For its earlier developers, limitations pertained to this notion. One such notion was that profits must occur within the bounds that common trading practices prescribe.

The Physiocrats maintained a few policies that in the centuries following the prominence of their school came to be strongly rejected by their followers. Among these policies was the stipulation that nations should follow protectionist economic practices. The Physiocrats viewed domestic agricultural labor as the most essential source of a nation's wealth. For this reason, they believed that nations should give priority to domestic workers rather than sacrificing the interests of domestic workers by turning to cheaper labor markets the international market made available. In this respect, they opposed mercantilism, which involved heavy government sponsorship of international trading ventures.

In contemporary discussions, proponents of *laissez faire* policies sometimes assert that the free market should be the sole criteria on which any ethical decision should be based. They have given up any stipulations that tariffs or other protections should be used to protect domestic labor markets. If it makes a higher profit than alternatives, they contend, it must be the preferable course of action, regardless of what it does to domestic labor, and regardless of what destruction might result socially or environmentally.

Such turns and twists in the history of economic thought have strong bearing on many of the debates that concern contemporary society. The debate over whether local economies should be protected from larger economies still rages. One debate involves the extent to which a community should try to protect its local businesses from encroachments by large national or international chain stores. Should the citizens of a small city or rural community exert a policy of local control when a retail corporation proposes to build a large store in their vicinity?

Thousands of accounts exist at this point in history of how large retail stores have moved into small cities, towns, or rural areas and driven the small businesses for miles around out of business. After a large chain store has settled into place in a rural setting, it is frequently the case that where once a rich diversity of small businesses existed, one large store now prevails. Opponents of the large stores argue that jobs are lost, local culture is smothered by corporate norms, the social fabric of the community is destroyed, and the economic potentials of the community are stifled because it loses the initiative to innovate.

Proponents argue that even if they do have tendencies to drive local business into bankruptcy and homogenize local cultures, such stores bring reduced priced goods that possess consistent quality to their customers. Further, they normalize business practices.

You can go anywhere in the world to a given chain of stores and receive the same services in the same way. Such stores encourage conformity among employees to corporate culture, purchase the products they market in container quantities at rock-bottom prices, and process merchandise with extreme efficiency.

It is often difficult to find a cozy, conclusive argument on either side. Corporations often tend to be mean, anti-union, exploitative, and insensitive to local cultures. Small businesses are often run in inefficient ways. Goods that do not sell remain on the shelves for months and even years. Small businesses cannot buy in container quantities, so their prices tend to be inflated. As for the economies and the social fabric of small communities, everyone familiar with *Main Street* or *Babbit* knows that small communities can be characterized by any number of ills.

Simulating a Scenario

The simulation you develop in this chapter allows you to investigate one side of the local control debate. The simulation you develop possesses clear and resounding biases, and in this respect, is probably more presentable as a learning tool than many of the simulations that you find that are offered in the public realm.

In this instance, the model shows a tension of large interests. A small community features a single factory that employs nearly half its workers. At first the community also possesses a thriving group of small businesses. While the factory produces goods that the owners of the factory market to the world at large, the small businesses cater to the needs of local residents. Among the small businesses are a cafe, an auto supply dealer, a gas station, a hair salon, a grocery, a sporting goods store, a florist, and a pottery shop.

One day an executive from a large retail chain store approaches the members of the city council and proposes that the chain store buy a large plot of ground at the edge of the community and construct a store on it. This information reaches the community at large through the local newspaper. A furious debate erupts in the weeks that follow. Several local business owners oppose the store, but a smattering favor it. Likewise, the community at large displays mixed feelings. Generally, however, opposition tends to fade.

Votes are taken, the construction is approved, and the large retail store soon appears on the outskirts of the community. Within a year, most of the small businesses have disappeared. The community suffers a thirty percent reduction in the total number of jobs available to its citizens. A partial exodus of its citizens occurs. School teachers lose their jobs, the number of day-care centers drops from two to one. Due to a substantial tax break the city awarded to the chain store, tax revenues are reduced, and the city lays off a few city workers and a few members of the police force.

Other changes accompany those that are most visible. The florist bought flowers from local farms, as did the two local groceries, and suddenly these markets are gone. The auto supply dealership patronized the local junk yard for used parts, and when the parts dealership closed its door, the junkyard owner suddenly found himself without a valuable source of revenue. With the loss of children, the community finds that its funding from the state government decreases, so it has to drop some of its sports programs, its science lab, and library services it provides to the community.

While telling the story provides one way to relate how a large retail store can impact a small community, the creation of a simulation provides another. The simulation provides a much more forceful presentation of the message because it immediately involves you in the event. Telling the story provides you with an account of the events. Participating in a simulation allows you to immediately experience them.

Modeling the Events

To model an event, you face the challenge of selecting the events and entities that will constitute your model. When you create event models for simulations of social or economic events, your choice of data depends on your objectives. You cannot create a model without filtering data. Some data must be left out, and the data you include is bound to be shaped by the model you create to contain it.

Entities

In the model developed here, the categories tend to be limited. Here are the main entities that the model accounts for:

- **Houses.** If you use images of houses in a model, it is easier to convey the growth or death of a community without having to attend to the details of depicting individual persons.

- **The local population.** Houses can represent groups of people, either families or large groups, such as tens, hundreds, or thousands.

- **A factory.** A simple image serves to remind people that a factory plays a significant role in the life of the community.

- **A larger department store.** You can depict the department store with a single large image. If viewers see large images of the factory and the retail store, then they can infer that these are the two prevailing economic entities in the community.

- **Small businesses.** When you depict the neighborhood, you can use several small icons to depict small businesses. The model you create traces the fate of small businesses.

- **Jobs.** How the presence of the retail store impacts jobs should be clearly shown in some way. You can darken houses to show that people move away. You can also display numbers.

Events

The relationships the model traces tend to be selective. Generally, relationships can exist between almost any two elements, but you must select from the possibilities to establish those that you can most readily model and that demonstrate the points you want to demonstrate in the clearest possible way. Here are a few possibilities:

- The retail store has a number of departments. For several of the departments, small businesses offer the same products and services. The Outdoor department, for example, competes directly with Cid's Sports Arena on Main Street.

- The number of employees of the retail store tends to be a fixed number. The retail chain prefers not to hire full-time employees. In fact, less than ten percent of the retail employees work full-time. It also tends to pay low wages. The small businesses in town tend to employee four people each, on average, and fifty percent of the people who work for small businesses have full-time positions.

- The retail store generates less in pay for its employees, on average, than do the small businesses.

- Each department in the retail store employs two people. Each department that drives a small business out of business costs the community four jobs. Two of these are full-time. Two are part-time. The retail store has no departments that employee people full-time. Only store managers work full-time.

- Declines in the total number of employed people immediately impact on the community. Fewer employed people means less revenue for the city government and the businesses that survive against the retail store.

Setting Up the Community

To begin the task of implementing the simulation, you attend first to setting up a graphical representation of the community the ShopMart impacts. Setting up the community involves creating sprites that represent houses and small businesses. As you create the functionality for the event model, you control the numbers and appearances of these sprites. Since the ShopMart and the factory provide stationary themes in the simulation, you can present them as graphical constants.

Figure 11.3 shows you the initial view of the application as it represents the community. To see the representation, execute the project in Listing11_1. The structures with the peaked roofs are residential dwellings, and those with flat roofs are small businesses. The factory is the large dark structure on the left that spouts smoke through its two smoke-stacks. The Shop Mart building bears a sign above the door.

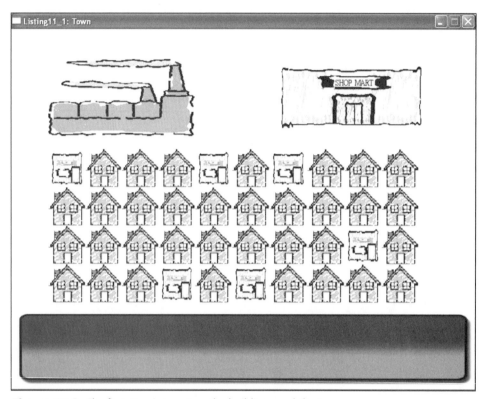

Figure 11.3 The first step is to set up the buildings and the town.

Community Structures

To represent the houses and businesses that the community comprises, you create a class called CBuilding. This class contains an array of sprites. The array of sprites enables you to give different appearances to the structures that you position in the community. Some structures are businesses, others are residences. Additionally, the CBuilding class tracks the number of people in the community, the number of people with jobs, and the number of children. Among other things, it also allows you to indicate, using a color scheme, whether a family has lost its house due to unemployment or a business has gone into bankruptcy due to competitive pressures.

Building States

You can characterize the community as a collection of people, houses, job opportunities, and businesses. A community could consist of many more characteristics, of course, but for purposes of simplification, they remain at a minimum in this context. Along similar lines, it is easiest to visually characterize the community as a collection of structures—businesses and houses. The CBuilding class accommodates the creation of all these structures. To make it possible to create the different structures, you set up a number of attributes in the declaration of the CBuilding class. Here are the attributes as you declare them in CBuilding.h:

```
class CBuilding
{
        private:
        // Constants for each building type
        static const int HOUSE = 0;
        static const int FACTORY = 1;
        static const int BUSINESS = 2;
        static const int SHOPMART = 3;
        static const int NUM_BUILDINGS = 4;
        // Sprites for each building type
        static class CSprite *m_sprBuildings[NUM_BUILDINGS];
        // Reference count
        static int m_iRefCount;

        // The type of building
        int m_iType;
        // X and Y position
        int m_iPosX, m_iPosY;
         //Lines left out . . .
};
```

The community displays four types of buildings. To identify each type of building, you create attributes that are static and constant (HOUSE, FACTORY, and so on). The reason you make these attributes static is that you must use them in other classes to identify building types.

To make it so that you can easily iterate through the building types when you perform operations, you assign sequential integer values to them (0, 1, and so on). To have at hand an attribute from which you can obtain the total number of building types you use, you add the NUM_BUILDINGS constant.

To accommodate the sprites (which are the images for the different types of buildings), you create a pointer array of the type CSprite (m_sprBuildings). The CSprite array stores reference to CSprite objects, and the CSprite objects—to repeat—are primarily the images for your buildings. The array holds sprites for all the building types. When you create the first building, you load these sprites. In this way, you avoid wasting memory by loading a multitude of images.

To track the number of buildings of all types that you create as you operate the simulation, you declare a static integer attribute, m_iRefCount. You increment the value of the m_iRefCount attribute whenever you create a building.

note

If you are interested in learning about the code in this project, one project might be to create an abstract base class, CBuilding, with a concrete subclass. Generally, experts in object-oriented design tell you that when you have a type change based on a variable, you should create an inheritance structure. You would still have a collection of CBuilding objects, but now you could use something like a Factory pattern to create buildings. A good book to explore in this respect is Erich Gamma and others, *Design Patterns, Elements of Reusable Object-Oriented Software* (Reading, Massachusetts: Addison-Wesley, 1995).

All structures in the community use sprites. When you create the first building, regardless of its building type, you load the sprites for all the building types into memory. These images remain in memory, used as needed, until you destroy the last building. At that moment, you destroy all the sprites. The reference counter (m_iRefCount) makes it possible to know when to load and unload the sprites.

In addition to loading sprites for buildings, you also track the type of sprite each building uses. You do this for a number of reasons, one of which is to be able to identify the building type when you create a town. To identify the building type, you add the m_iType attribute.

Along with the type of the building, you also track its positions. Since the dimensionality of the simulation is 2D, you require only two attributes for this purpose, m_IposX and m_IposY. These two attributes allow you to uniquely position each building on x and y coordinates that define the application's client area.

Building Events

For now, the events that apply to buildings consist only of those that allow them to come into existence and assume a location in the community. (In the next development iteration, you can add many other behaviors.)

Constructing Buildings

The first step in creating a building involves constructing it. Here is the code for the constructor for the CBuilding class from CBuilding.cpp:

```
CBuilding::CBuilding(int iType, int x, int y)
{
        // Load the sprite if the reference count is zero
        if(m_iRefCount == 0)
        {
                // Create the sprite objects
                for(int itr=0; itr < NUM_BUILDINGS; itr++)
                {
                        m_sprBuildings[itr] = new CSprite();
                }

                // Load the images
                m_sprBuildings[HOUSE]->Load(L"House.png");
                m_sprBuildings[FACTORY]->Load(L"Factory.png");
                m_sprBuildings[SHOPMART]->Load(L"ShopMart.png");
                m_sprBuildings[BUSINESS]->Load(L"SmallBusiness.png");
        }

        // Increment the reference count
        m_iRefCount++;
        // Set the type of building
        m_iType = iType;
        // Set the x/y position
        m_iPosX = x;
        m_iPosY = y;
}
```

The constructor for the CBuilding class takes three parameters. The first parameter (iType) allows you to set the type of the building. The values you assign to this parameter consist of values you retrieve from the building attributes in the class declaration (CBuilding::HOUSE, for example). The two parameters that follow (x and y) allow you to set the location of the building. In the last few lines of the constructor, you set the m_iType class attribute using the value of iType and the coordinate attributes (m_iPosX and m_iPosY) using the values supplied by x and y. The m_iType attribute receives use in the Draw() function, which is discussed later on.

Prior to other activities, however, you first attend to the reference count. Just after the opening brace of the constructor, you implement a selection statement that ascertains whether any sprites have been created. If no sprites have been created (m_iRefCount == 0), then you load all the sprites you require to identify the buildings in your community.

The approach you use to set up the sprites involves a for loop. The for loop makes use of the NUM_BUILDINGS attribute, which identifies the number of building types your community accommodates. Using this number to determine how many times to do so, you then repeatedly call the constructor for the CSprite class, employing the C++ new operator each time you do so to assign a reference to a CSprite object to the m_sprBuildings array.

When you exit the for loop, the m_sprBuildings array contains a pointer to enough sprites to cover all the building types you need to identify (there are four of them). You can then proceed to load images for the sprites. To accomplish this task, you use the sequence of attributes you have set up in the class declaration (HOUSE, FACTORY, and so on). The values you have assigned to these attributes sequentially identify building types. They also indicate CSprite references in the m_sprBuildings array. Given this preparation, you can call the CSprite::Load() function to load an image file for each of the CSprite objects.

As mentioned before, the constructor allows you to store the identity of the specific building type in the m_iType attribute and to set the location of the specific sprite using the m_iPosX and m_iPosY attributes. Prior to attending to these settings, you increment the reference count for CBuilding objects. As mentioned previously, you increment the reference count for each CBuilding object. When the reference count reaches zero, you then destroy the sprites you have created to identify the types of buildings your community contains.

Destroying Buildings

To attend to removing buildings, you implement a destructor for the CBuilding class. Here is the code from CBuilding.cpp:

```
CBuilding::~CBuilding()
{
     // Decrement the reference count for CBuilding objects
     m_iRefCount--;
     // If this is the last building, free the sprites
     if(m_iRefCount == 0)
     {
          for(int itr = 0; itr < NUM_BUILDINGS; itr++)
          {
               SAFEDELETE(m_sprBuildings[itr]);
          }
     }
}
```

The work of destroying a building first involves decrementing the m_iRefCount attribute to indicate that you are deleting a CBuilding object. Having decremented the count, you then perform the opposite of the operation you perform in the constructor of the CBuilding class.

In this case, you employ an `if` selection statement check to see whether the operations of the class have reduced the reference count to zero. If this is so, then you need to remove the sprites that support the identification of the building types.

To delete the sprites, you use a `for` loop with the `NUM_BUILDINGS` attribute as a control. You iterate through the `m_sprBuildings` array the number of times the value of the `NUM_BUILDINGS` attribute allows. For each iteration, you call the `SAFEDELETE()` macro to remove the sprite. In this way, all sprites supporting the `CBuilding` objects are removed.

Drawing Buildings

To draw a building, you use the `CBuilding::Draw()` function, which wraps the `CSprite::Draw()` function. Here is the code from CBuilding.cpp that implements the `CBuilding::Draw()` function:

```
void CBuilding::Draw()
{
    m_sprBuildings[m_iType]->Draw(m_iPosX,m_iPosY);
}
```

The value you store in the `CBuilding::m_iType` attribute when you call the constructor determines which sprite to draw.

Communities and Towns

After attending to constructing, drawing, and destroying buildings, your next task involves creating a community. To create a community, you must create buildings of different types and distribute them around the area you have designated to hold the community. To accomplish this, you create a second class, `CTown`.

Town States

Another name for a community is a town. A town might be said to formalize a community through incorporation or some other means. In this case, formalization amounts to creating a class called `CTown` and then adding attributes to it that allow you to assign a specific area to the town and then to populate this area with houses and businesses. Here is the code in CTown.h that accomplishes this work:

```
class CTown {
    private:
    // Width of the town
    int m_iWidth;
    // Height of the town
    int m_iHeight;
    // A list of all the buildings
```

```
    vector<CBuilding *> m_lstBuildings;
      //Lines left out . . .
};
```

The first two attributes, m_iWidth and m_iHeight, determine the size of the town as it appears in the client area. To attend to structures in the town, you create a vector (m_lstBuildings). The vector stores pointers to CBuilding objects, and these represent all the structures in the town.

Town Events

The CTown class at this point in the development effort closely resembles the CBuilding class. The events you attend to involve constructing, drawing, and destroying the class object.

Constructing the Town

The constructor for CTown accomplishes five tasks:

- It sets the size of the town. To do this, you set the size attributes.
- It sets up a factory. To do this, you create a CBuilding object and add it to the town array.
- It sets up the retail store, ShopMart. To do this, you create a CBuilding object and add it to the town array.
- It creates local businesses. To do this, you create a set of CBuilding objects and add them to the town array.
- It creates residential dwellings. To do this, you create a set of CBuilding objects and add them to the town array.

Attending to these tasks involves only a few operations. Here is the code from CTown.cpp that implements the constructor for the CTown class:

```
CTown::CTown(int iWidth, int iHeight)
{
      m_iWidth = iWidth;        // Set width and height
      m_iHeight = iHeight;
      // Create the factory in the top middle
      CBuilding *pFactory = new CBuilding(CBuilding::FACTORY,
                                          64, 50);
      m_lstBuildings.push_back(pFactory);   //add to vector
      // Create the ShopMart
      CBuilding *pShopMart = new CBuilding(CBuilding::SHOPMART,
                                           iWidth-340, 50);
      m_lstBuildings.push_back(pShopMart);   //add to vector
```

```
// Create houses and businesses
for(int x = 64; x <= iWidth - 128;  x+= 64)
{
        for(int y=200; y < iHeight; y+=64)
        {
                float fRand = (float)rand()/(float)RAND_MAX;
                CBuilding *pBuilding = NULL;
                if(fRand < 0.1)  /* 10% chance - small business*/
                {
                        pBuilding = new CBuilding(CBuilding::BUSINESS,
                                                        x, y);
                }
                else
                {
                        pBuilding = new CBuilding(CBuilding::HOUSE,
                                                        x, y);
                }

                // Add the building to the list
                m_lstBuildings.push_back(pBuilding); //add to vector
        }
    }
}
```

Setting the size of the town involves using the iWidth and iHeight variables from the parameter list of the CTown constructor. You assign their values to m_iWidth and m_iHeight attributes of the CTown class. These values are then available when you create the grid in which you position the structures the town comprises.

Setting up a factory for the town involves declaring a pointer of the type CBuilding (pFactory) and then using the C++ new operator and the CBuilding constructor to create a reference that you assign to the pointer. To construct the factory, you retrieve the static value that identifies the building type (CBuilding::FACTORY), which you pass to the first parameter of the constructor. To position the factory in the upper left of the client area, you assign just enough pixels to the second parameter to move it in slightly from the edge of the client area (64). After constructing the factory building, you then call the vector::push_back() function to add it to the m_lstBuildings vector.

Setting up the retail store requires the same set of operations involved in creating the factory. First, you declare a pointer (pShopMart). Then you use the C++ new operator in conjunction with the CBuilding constructor to create a reference that you assign to the pointer. In this case, for the first parameter of the constructor, you retrieve the value that identifies the retail store (`CBuilding::SHOPMART`). To position the retail store in the upper left of the client area, you access the width of the town (`iWidth`) and subtract the width of the retail store sprite (340). Having constructed the retail store building, you then call the `vector::push_back()` function to add it to the `m_lstBuildings` vector.

Creating local businesses and residential dwellings takes a little more work but involves the same set of operations. To begin with, you set up two `for` loops. These two loops employ the `iWidth` and `iHeight` values you pass to the `CTown` constructor to create a grid. The grid designates the locations of all the buildings in the town save those of the factory and the retail store. The top edge of the grid runs just below the factory and ShopMart buildings. The lower edge runs just above the console.

When you create the town grid, you establish blocks within the grid that measure 64 by 64 pixels. You use the `for` loops to randomly place the buildings in the blocks. On the first line inside the inner `for` loop, you call to the `rand()` function to create a random floating-point variable in the range of 0 to 1. This value you store in a local variable, `fRand`. Next, you declare a pointer to a `CBuilding` object (`pBuilding`) and assign a `NULL` value to it as a precaution.

You then determine whether to create a residential dwelling or a local business. To accomplish this, you make use of the value you have stored in `fRand`. If this value is less than 0.1, you create a small business building and place it at the position that the current x and y values designate. To instruct the `CBuilding` constructor to use the local business sprite object, you retrieve the value stored in `CBuilding::BUSINESS`, which you use for the constructor's first parameter value.

If the value of `fRand` is greater than 0.1, you create a residential dwelling building. As with the business building, you place the residential building at the position that the current x and y values designate. To instruct the `CBuilding` constructor to use a house sprite to create a building object, you retrieve the value stored in `CBuilding::HOUSE`.

In either instance, having created the `CBuilding` object, you then call the `vector::push_back()` function to add it to the `m_lstBuildings` vector. Given that the range of random values you use to designate business buildings falls between 0 and 0.1 and the range of random values you use to designate residential dwellings falls between 0.1 and 1.0, one in ten structures is likely to be a local business.

Destroying the Town

When you destroy the `CTown` object, you invoke the destructor and delete all the `CBuilding` pointers you have stored in the `m_lstBuildings` vector. Here is the code from CTown.cpp for the destructor:

```
CTown::~CTown()
{
     for(int itr = 0; itr < m_lstBuildings.size(); itr++)
     {
          SAFEDELETE(m_lstBuildings[itr]);
     }
}
```

To destroy the CBuilding objects, you loop through the m_lstBuildings vector and call the SAFEDELETE macro for each CBuilding object. The vector.size() function returns the number of items the vector contains.

Drawing the Town

To draw a building, you use the CTown::Draw() function, which wraps the CBuilding::Draw() function. Here is the code from CTown.cpp that implements the CTown::Draw() function:

```
void CTown::Draw()
{
     for(int itr=0; itr < m_lstBuildings.size(); itr++)
     {
          m_lstBuildings[itr]->Draw();
     }
}
```

The CTown::Draw() function uses a for loop to iterate through each of the buildings in the m_lstBuildings vector. For each object in the vector, it calls CBuilding::Draw().

Rendering the Town

Having implemented the CBuilding and CTown classes, you can now attend to rendering the town to the client area. To render the town, you make a few changes to the CMyApplication class. These changes consist of the addition of an attribute and modifications of the Initialize(), Render(), and Cleanup() functions.

With respect to the addition of the attribute, you add a pointer to a CTown object. Here are the lines in CMyApplication.h that add the attribute:

```
// The town object
class CTown *m_pTown;
```

After adding an attribute to the class declaration, you then turn to the implementation of the class. Specifically, you make changes, first, to the CMyApplication::Initialize() function. Here's the code for this function from CMyApplication.cpp:

```
void CMyApplication::Initialize()
{
      // Code left out. . .
      // Create the town
      m_pTown = new CTown(m_pGraphics->GetWidth(),
                          m_pGraphics->GetHeight() -
                          m_sprConsole->GetHeight() - 64);
}
```

After the opening brace, you make use of the attribute you just declared to create an instance of a CTown object. To accomplish this, you use the C++ new operator in conjunction with the CTown constructor. For the parameter values of the constructor, you call to the height and width values that the CGraphics class provides for the client area and the CSprite class provides for the console. The town takes up the width of the client area (m_pGraphics->GetWidth()) and descends to the top of the console area (m_sprConsole->GetHeight() - 64).

note

As a reminder, you create identifiers for the client area and the console in the declaration of the CApplication class (see CApplication.h).

Cleaning Up

When you finish using the application, it is necessary to delete the CTown object. You attend to this duty in the CApplication::Cleanup() function:

```
void CMyApplication::Cleanup()
{
      SAFEDELETE(m_pTown);
      // Clean up using the parent call
      CApplication::Cleanup();
}
```

To delete the CTown object, you call the SAFEDELETE() macro. This invokes the destructor for the CTown object, which in turns cleans up the sprites used by the buildings in the town.

Rendering the Town

To render the town to the client area, you use the CMyApplication::Render() function. Here's the code for this function from CMyApplication.cpp:

```
void CMyApplication::Render()
{
      // Lines left out. . .
      // Clear the background
```

```
        m_pGraphics->Clear(D3DCOLOR_XRGB(255, 255, 255));
        // Draw the town
        m_pTown->Draw();
        // Lines left out. . .
}
```

The significant points about the Render() function consist of setting the background color and calling the CTown::Draw() function. In this instance, you create a white background (255, 255, 255), which heightens the visibility of the images painted to the canvas. As for the call to the CTown:Draw() function, you again make use of the CTown attribute you declared (m_pTown). This causes the town to be drawn.

At this point, if you compile the application, you can see the features Figure 11.3 illustrates. The application does nothing more at this point than display the town and its four types of structures. In the next section, you add functionality to the application that enables you to simulate the effects the retail store has on the town's economy.

Implementing the Simulation

Access the folder for Listing11_02 and compile the project file. Figure 11.4 illustrates the results. The console area now displays a variety of data, and two sliders allow you to set levels of unemployment and the influence the retail store has on the local economy.

To use the simulation, perform the following actions:

1. Set the Unemployment Rate slider at roughly a fourth of the way from the right. This indicates that unemployment exists in the community, but the rate remains low.

2. Set the ShopMart Influence slider at roughly halfway. This indicates that while the ShopMart will have an impact on the community, when people lose their jobs because of it, they may be able to compensate by doing such things as commuting to other towns to obtain employment.

3. Click Reset. At this point, you can see the economic condition that prevails when the ShopMart opens for business. (Figure 11.4 illustrates the initial state.)

4. Click Next Month six times to indicate that you want to see the state of affairs after six months. As you click Next Month, the images representing the local stores turn red, as do the houses that people abandon or sell as they lose their jobs. Figure 11.5 illustrates the situation.

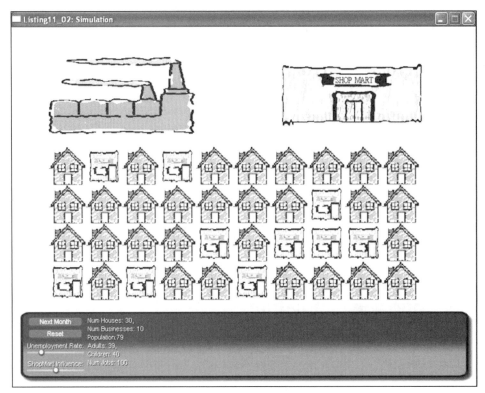

Figure 11.4 Use the sliders to set the initial condition.

If you examine the fields in the console, you see the following data items:

- **Number of Houses.** The starting values for this number extend from 29 to 37. To find a specific number, click a few times. When a house becomes vacant, the image representing it turns brown.

- **Number of Businesses.** The starting values for this number extend from 1 to 11. To find a specific number, click a few times. When a business goes bankrupt, the image representing it turns red.

- **Total Population.** The highest starting population of the community is around 100, and the lowest is around 68. Again, to find a specific number, click a few times.

- **Number of Adults.** Usually, around half of the community consists of adults.

- **Number of Children.** Roughly half the community consists of children.

- **Number of Jobs.** The number of jobs varies. It can go as high as one job per adult. It can also diminish substantially.

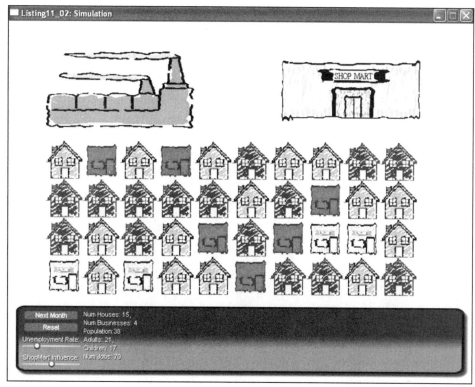

Figure 11.5 Clicks of Next Month show changes in the local economy.

Altering the Building States

The event model you use for this simulation centers on houses. Each house in the community houses, on the average, two adults and two children. When both adults lose their jobs, then the house must be vacated. To enhance the CBuilding class so that you can account for such transformation, you add a number of new attributes. To account for the behavior of the new attributes, you add a number of new functions and alter a few old ones.

The new state of information you add to the CBuilding class allows you to account for a number of factors. Table 11.1 provides a summary of the new attributes and the information they track. Here is the code that you offer to the CBuilding class definition in CBuilding.h to cover the new information:

```
int m_iNumPeople;   // Number of people in this building
int m_iNumAdults;      // Number of adults
int m_iNumChildren;      // Number of children
float m_fRent;      // Monthly rent of this building
float m_fMoney;      // How household income/savings?
float m_fIncome;      // Monthly Income
```

Table 11.1 Building State Information

Name	Description
int m_iNumPeople	The number of residents, children and adults, in a building. Each building houses at least one adult. Usually, you find two adults and two children.
int m_iNumAdults	The number of adults. This attribute allows you to specifically identify the number of adults in the household. An employed adult contributes income to the household. When unemployed, an adult increases the cost of a household.
int m_iNumChildren	The number of children. This attribute allows you to specifically identify the number of children in the household. Each child increases the cost of maintaining a household. The child does not contribute income to the household.
float m_fRent	The rent or mortgage payment a residence or business requires of its residents or owners. Rent or mortgage payments for a residence are subtracted from the total income of the adults living in the residence.
float m_fMoney	The funds that each adult has in reserve after taking care of expenses. This can be viewed as money in a bank account. The presence of this reserve makes it possible for residents of a dwelling to remain in the dwelling even after they have lost their jobs.
float m_fIncome	The monthly income of all residents of a dwelling.

Building and Population Behaviors

To enable you to manipulate data according to the model you are using to evaluate the effects of the retail store's presence in the community, you add a substantial amount of functionality to the CBuilding class. This functionality begins with the addition of accessor functions. The most extensive additions are to the constructer. You add an additional functionality to the Draw() function. You also add a wholly new function, ProcessMonth(), to track the impact of the economic changes over time.

Accessing Information

To attend to changes that characterize the community, you must obtain population and housing type information. To attend to this work, you add a few accessor functions to the CBuilding class. The following code, taken from CBuilding.cpp, shows you the new functions:

```
int CBuilding::GetType()
{
     return m_iType;
}
int CBuilding::GetNumPeople()
{
     return m_iNumPeople;
}
```

```
int CBuilding::GetNumAdults()
{
      return m_iNumAdults;
}
```

House and Business Construction

You make changes to the CBuilding constructor to attend to four basic tasks. These tasks are as follows:

- Calculate the cost of maintenance (rent or mortgage) for a house or business.
- Calculate the amount of money residents have in reserve in bank accounts.
- For a house, determine the number of occupants. Determine whether they are children or adults. Calculate the monthly income.
- For a business, determine the expense of maintenance and the number of owners or employees.
- For buildings that might fall outside those set up for businesses or homes, establish income realities, ownership, and maintenance costs.

Here is the code you add to implement this functionality in the constructor for the CBuilding class in CBuilding.cpp:

```
CBuilding:CBuilding:(int iType, int x, int y)
{
      // Lines attend to the sprites and positioning left out . . .
      // Calculate monthly expenses of maintenance
      float fRand = (float)rand()/(float)RAND_MAX;
      m_fRent = (400 + fRand*100);
      // Calculate the money deposited in the bank
      fRand = (float)rand()/(float)RAND_MAX;
      m_fMoney = 300 * fRand;
      // Set up households, businesses, or other entities
      if(iType == HOUSE)
      {
             // 1 to 4 people in each house (1 adult, 0-2 kids)
             m_iNumPeople = rand()%4 + 1;
             // Get the number of adults in the house
             m_iNumAdults = max(1, m_iNumPeople - 2);
             m_iNumChildren = m_iNumPeople - m_iNumAdults;
             // Generate a random number
             fRand = (float)rand()/(float)RAND_MAX;
             // Calculate a monthly income
             m_fIncome = m_iNumAdults * (600 + fRand*1000);
```

```
        }
        else if(iType == BUSINESS)
        {
                // Assume a 0% profit to start
                m_fIncome = m_fRent;
                m_iNumPeople = 1;
                m_iNumAdults = 1;
                m_iNumChildren = 0;
        }
        else
        {
                // Defaults for other types of buildings
                m_iNumPeople = 1;
                m_iNumAdults = 1;
                m_iNumChildren = 0;
        }
}
```

Maintenance

To calculate the cost of maintenance for the structures in the community, you use the rand() function to generate a random value that you divide by the value of RAND_MAX. You assign this to a local variable, fRand, which you then use to calculate the cost. The calculation involves multiplying the value stored in fRand by 100, and adding 400 to the product.

To calculate the money that residents can deposit in the bank, you once again use the rand() function. After dividing the returned value of the rand() function by RAND_MAX, you assign the result to fRand. You then multiply the value stored in fRand by 300 and assign the product to m_fMoney.

Mortgages and Rents

Having calculated the values to assign to rents, mortgages, and bank deposits, you then begin to profile residential dwellings, businesses, and other buildings. To accomplish this, you first create an if...else if selection structure. For the first selection, you determine whether the CBuilding object you are dealing with is of the HOUSE type. Recall that you decide the type of the building when you construct it.

Residential Dwellings

If the type of the building is CBuilding::HOUSE, you call the rand() function to generate a random number to represent the number of people living in the house. This ranges from 1 to 4. You assign the resulting value to the m_iNumPeople attribute.

To calculate the number of adults residing in a specific home, you call the C/C++ max() function. The max() function takes two values as its parameters and returns the value of the larger one. (If the values equal each other, it returns this value.) The first parameter of the max() function number establishes the minimum number of adults, which must be one. For the second parameter value, you subtract 2 from the number of people you have randomly generated and assigned to the m_iNumPeople attribute. The result is either one or a number greater than one.

To calculate the number of children (m_iNumChildren), you subtract the number of adults (m_iNumAdults) from the number of people (m_iNumPeople) in the household. To then determine the amount of income to attribute the household, you once again generate a number and assign it to fRand. You then multiply fRand by 1000 and add 600 to the product. The result you then multiply by the number of adults (m_iNumAdults) in the household. You assign the final result to m_fIncome.

Small Businesses

If the selection statement determines that you are dealing with a BUSINESS building, then you assume no profit at the start and simply assign the value of m_fRent to m_fIncome. For the number of residents, you assign a constant of 1 to the m_iNumPeople and m_iNumAdults attributes. Assuming that most small businesses are run by a single person tends to limit the scope of the model, but it still provides a beginning. As for children, the assumption is that none of the small businesses involve children as owners or employees (m_iNumChildren = 0).

Others

For other buildings, you assume one owner and no children. It provides not definable incomes or expenses beyond what have been established generally. Such a building does not require more definition, at least for the present purposes.

Showing Losses

As people lose their incomes, their capacity to pay mortgages and rents declines. When they reach the end of their resources, they must vacate the houses they inhabit. To show the vacancies, you change the color of the buildings. You accomplish this change of color in the CBuilding::Draw() function. Here is the code for this function from CBuilding.cpp:

```
void CBuilding::Draw()
{
    // White color by default
    DWORD dwColor = D3DCOLOR_XRGB(255,255,255);
    // Red color if nobody is there
    if(m_iNumPeople == 0)
    {
```

```
            dwColor = D3DCOLOR_ARGB(192, 255, 0, 0);
        }
    m_sprBuildings[m_iType]->Draw(m_iPosX, m_iPosY, dwColor);
}
```

If the number of people (m_iNumPeople) in a house reaches zero, you change the color of the dwelling to red. To create the color you apply to the dwelling you first employ the D3DCOLOR_XRGB() macro to create a value for white. You use this as a normal value, and you assign this value to the local DWORD variable dwColor. If the house is not empty, then you can assign this value to the sprite and not change it.

You use an if selection statement to determine whether the house is empty. If the house is empty, then you call the D3DCOLOR_ARGB() macro to create a solid red value.

Given the creation of the right color, you then use the index of the m_sprBuildings array that corresponds to the type of the current building to call the CSprite::Draw() function. This function uses the attribute values for the position of the current object to designate which object to draw. You assign the dwColor variable to the third parameter to determine the color to use for drawing.

Calculating Monthly Changes

To determine changes that occur in income, employment, and residential and business occupancy from month to month, you implement the CBuilding::ProcessMonth() function. Here's the code for this function from CBuilding.cpp:

```
void CBuilding::ProcessMonth(float fPopulation, float fUnemployment)
{
    if(m_iType == HOUSE || m_iType == BUSINESS)
    {
        // Increase the amount of money by the income
        m_fMoney += m_fIncome;
        // Decrease money by rent
        m_fMoney -= m_fRent;
        // Decrease money by # children
        m_fMoney -= (m_iNumChildren * 100);
        // Decrease number of people to 0
        if(m_fMoney <= 0){ m_iNumPeople = 0; }
        float fRand = (float)rand()/(float)RAND_MAX;
        if(fRand < fUnemployment) { m_fIncome = 0; }
    }
    if(m_iType == BUSINESS)
    {
        // Re-calculate income
```

```
m_fIncome = m_fRent * (1.1 * fPopulation);
// Random chance of going out of business due to
// lowered population/people moving to shop-mart, etc
float fRand = (float)rand()/(float)RAND_MAX;
if(fRand <= CTown::SHOPMART_INFLUENCE/10.0)
   {
        m_iNumPeople = 0;
   }
   }
}
```

The `ProcessMonth()` function takes two arguments. The first parameter, `fPopulation`, represents the current population of the town as a percentage of what it started at. The second parameter, `fUnemployment`, represents the unemployment rate for the town.

To implement the function, you create an `if` selection statement. You use this statement to determine if the type of the current structure (`m_iType`) is a house (`CBuilding::HOUSE`) or a local business (`CBuilding::BUSINESS()`). If it is either of these types, you perform a number of operations to determine how much in financial reserves (`m_fMoney`) is available to the residents or owners of the building and whether this amount allows them to continue to reside in or own the building.

To accomplish this task, you begin by augmenting the value of `m_fMoney` by the monthly income of the residents or owners (`m_fIncome`). Next, you consider the costs of rents or mortgages by decreasing the value of `m_fMoney` by the amount the owners or residents must pay each month for their mortgage or rent (`m_fRent`). In addition to subtracting rent, if the structure is a residence and children dwell in it, then you subtract the cost of each child (a bare 100 units per month) from the financial reserves.

In the end, if you find that the financial reserves are less than or equal to zero, you force the tenants or owners out.

The calculations thus far have assumed a constant rate of employment for the community. It happens, however, that regardless of the role of the ShopMart store, people still lose their jobs for any number of reasons. The factory might discontinue a given brand of product or have a temporary slowdown. To accommodate this factor, you generate a random variable (`fRand`) using the C/C++ `rand()` function. The values range from 0 to 1. You check this value against the unemployment rate. If the value of `fRand` is less than the value of the unemployment rate (`fUnemployment`), you set the income (`m_fIncome`) to zero.

In addition to calculating values that apply to both residences and businesses, you also calculate values that pertain to businesses alone. To attend to this chore, you first use an `if` selection statement to verify that you are dealing with a building of the BUSINESS type. Having confirmed the type, you then calculate the value to assign to the income of the business (m_fIncome) based on the rent and the current population. To scale the influence of the population on revenues, you apply the value of 1.1, which designates a 10% profit with 100% of the population.

To determine whether a business is holding its own against the competition that the ShopMart store exerts, you generate a random value and assign it to fRand. This value represents the chance that customers will purchase a given type of merchandise from ShopMart. To determine the outcome of the chance, you check the random value against the value of CTown::SHOPMART_INFLUENCE. If the random value is less than or equal to the value of SHOPMART_INFLUENCE, ShopMart has won the sale.

If the local business goes bankrupt, then more people face unemployment. To show the increase in unemployment, you set the value of m_iNumPeople to zero. Given this setting, the color of the business structure is changed to red, and in this way you simulate how ShopMart runs local businesses out of business.

Changes to the Town

The changes you make to the CTown class allow you to add controls to the slider. These controls alter the unemployment rate and influence you want to assign to the ShopMart store. They also allow you to reset all the values of the simulation or to make it so that values accumulate on a monthly scale. Additionally, you add a field to display the way the data that relates to the economic and social definition of the town changes over time under the influence of the ShopMart store.

The States of the Town

To store data relating to unemployment, population, and the influence of the ShopMart store, you add attributes to the CTown class declaration. Here is the code from CTown.h that shows these additions:

```
// Unemployment rate
float m_fUnemploymentRate;
// Starting population
 int m_iStartingPop;
 // Base unemployment rate
static float BASE_UNEMPLOYMENT;
// Influence of the ShopMart on other businesses
static float SHOPMART_INFLUENCE;
```

You use the first attribute (m_fUnemploymentRate) to store the current unemployment rate of the town. You use the second attribute (m_iStartingPop) to save the starting population of the town for future reference. The two static attributes represent the base unemployment rate of the town (BASE_UNEMPLOYMENT) and the influence the ShopMart store has on the local economy (SHOPMART_INFLUENCE).

Changing the Town's Behavior

Given the declaration of the new attributes for the CTown class, the number of variables you work with increases to a sizeable set. Some of these variables you derive from the CBuilding class. It remains, however, that when you seek to monitor all data as a manifestation of changes that take place in the town's economy, you must retrieve the data from the CTown class object. To accomplish this, you create a number of accessor methods for the CTown class. Here are their prototypes:

```
// Gets the population of the town
int GetPopulation();
// Calculates the number of jobs available
int GetNumJobs();
// Get the number of houses
int GetNumHouses();
// Get the number of adults
int GetNumAdults();
// Get the number of children
int GetNumChildren();
// Get the number of businesses
int GetNumBusinesses();
// Get the unemployment rate
float GetUnemployment();
```

If you examine the implementation of the accessor functions as shown in CTown.cpp, you'll find that they either return the values stored in the corresponding attributes of the CTown class or call the corresponding attributes or accessor functions from the CBuilding class.

Monthly Changes to the Town

Given that you have ready access to the data that allows you to change the state of the town's economy, you can then proceed to implement the functionality that effects the changes of state. You accomplish this by adding a new function to the CTown class. This is the ProcessMonth() function. Its purpose is to generalize the changes of individual buildings to create events that pertain to the entire town. Here's the code for this function as shown in CTown.cpp:

```
void CTown::ProcessMonth()
{
    // Calculate the unemployment rate
    float fRatio = (float)GetNumJobs()/(float)GetPopulation();
    m_fUnemploymentRate = max(0, (1.0 - fRatio) * 0.5);
    m_fUnemploymentRate += BASE_UNEMPLOYMENT;
    // Get the current population ratio
    float fPopRatio = (float)GetPopulation()/(float)m_iStartingPop;
```

```
    for(int itr=0; itr < m_lstBuildings.size(); itr++)
    {
        m_lstBuildings[itr]->ProcessMonth(fPopRatio,
                                        m_fUnemploymentRate);
    }
}
```

Your first task after the opening brace involves calculating the ratio of the number of jobs (the value returned by the GetNumJobs() function) to the number of people in the town (the value returned by the GetPopulation() function). You assign the ratio to a local variable, fRatio.

After calculating the basic ratio of the number of jobs to the population, you adjust the ratio to account for the unemployment rate. To accomplish this, you subtract the ratio from 1.0 and multiply the difference by 0.5. You use the C/C++ max() function to filter the resulting number so that it is either zero or a number greater than zero. You assign the outcome to the m_fUnemploymentRate attribute.

Following the calculations for determining the raw unemployment, you further adjust the rate by adding the value stored in the BASE_UNEMPLOYMENT attribute. This provides you with a rate you can use for the simulation.

Having dealt with the unemployment rate, you then calculate a population ratio that you assign to a local variable, fPopRatio. To arrive at this number, you divide the current population (retrieved with the GetPopulation() function) by the starting population value (m_iStartingPop). (Recall that you set the starting population value when you call the CTown constructor.)

To cap the activities you attend to in the CTown::ProcessMonth() function, you use the values you have calculated thus far to change the values assigned to the CBuilding objects stored in the m_lstBuildings array. To accomplish this, you create a for loop and iterate through all of the objects stored in the array. As you do so, you call the CBuilding::ProcessMonth() function for each CBuilding object. The CBuilding::ProcessMonth() function takes as its parameters the values stored in fPopRatio and m_fUnemploymentRate.

Controlling Influences

To set up the controls for the panel, you make changes to the CMyApplication::InitGUI() function. The controls you create consist of buttons, sliders, and static text displays. To process messages relating to the controls, you declare a set of attributes for the CMyApplication class that uniquely identify the controls and their messages. Here is the code from CMyApplication.h that accomplishes this work:

```
static const int IDC_PROCESS = 0;
static const int IDC_RESET = 1;
static const int IDC_UNEMPLOYMENT = 2;
static const int IDC_INFO = 3;
static const int IDC_UNEMPLABEL = 4;
static const int IDC_SHOPMARTLABEL = 5;
static const int IDC_SHOPMART = 6;
```

Given the declaration of the control identifiers, you can then proceed to add code to the CMyApplication::InitGUI() function that implements the controls. Here is the code in CMyApplication.cpp that you use to create the controls for the four primary values that apply to the ShopMart simulation:

```
void CMyApplication::InitGUI()
{
    // Call parent initialize
    CApplication::InitGUI();
    // Add a button to process a month
    m_GUI.AddButton(IDC_PROCESS, L"Next Month",
                        25, m_iConsoleY + 10,100, 18);
    //Add a button to reset values
     m_GUI.AddButton(IDC_RESET, L"Reset",
                        25, m_iConsoleY + 30, 100, 18);
    // Add the unemployment rate label and slider
    m_GUI.AddStatic(IDC_UNEMPLABEL, L"Unemployment Rate:",
                        25, m_iConsoleY + 50, 100, 18);
    m_GUI.AddSlider(IDC_UNEMPLOYMENT,
                        25, m_iConsoleY + 60, 100, 20, 0, 100, 0);
    // Add the ShopMart influence label and slider
    m_GUI.AddStatic(IDC_SHOPMARTLABEL, L"ShopMart Influence:",
                        25, m_iConsoleY + 80, 100, 18);
    m_GUI.AddSlider(IDC_SHOPMART,
                        25, m_iConsoleY + 90, 100, 20, 0, 100, 50);
    // Add the info to the textbox
    m_GUI.AddStatic(IDC_INFO, L"Info",
                        130, m_iConsoleY + 10, 400, 128);
    m_GUI.GetStatic(IDC_INFO)->GetElement(0)-> dwTextFormat
                                    = DT_LEFT | DT_TOP;
}
```

For the most part, if you examine Figure 11.4, you can see that the arrangement of controls the code presents reflects the arrangement you see on the control panel. Here is a list that reviews the controls according to their message identifiers:

- **IDC_PROCESS.** This is a button. You use it to alter the values so that the simulation shows changes as they accumulate over time. Each click of the button pushes the history of the town along by a month.
- **IDC_RESET.** This is a button. You use it to reset all values so that a new simulation begins.
- **IDC_UNEMPLABEL.** This is the label for the unemployment rate slider.
- **IDC_UNEMPLOYMENT.** This is the unemployment rate slider. When you use it, you can increase or decrease the level of unemployment you want to apply to the town as a background value.
- **IDC_SHOPMARTLABEL.** This is the label for the slider that sets the influence of the ShopMart.
- **IDC_SHOPMART.** This is the slider that controls the value you want to assign for the influence of the ShopMart store.
- **IDC_INFO.** This is a label that displays all the values that change as your simulation progresses.

Updating the Display of Data

To update the display of data, you alter the `CMyApplication::UpdateScene()` function. To alter the function, you use the C/C++ `wprintf()` function to create a long string of the wide character type. To feed data to the string, you make a series of calls to the accessor functions for the `CTown` object. The string is displayed by the `IDC_INFO` control. Here's the code in the `UpdateScene()` function in CMyApplication.cpp that accomplishes this work:

```
void CMyApplication::UpdateScene(float fTimeScale)
{
    // Update the info text
    TCHAR buf[1024];
    wsprintf(buf, L"Num Houses: %d, \
                \nNum Businesses: %d \
                \nPopulation: %d, \
                \nAdults: %d, \
                \nChildren: %d \
                \nNum Jobs: %d",
                m_pTown->GetNumHouses(),
                m_pTown->GetNumBusinesses(),
            m_pTown->GetPopulation(),
                m_pTown->GetNumAdults(),
                m_pTown->GetNumChildren(),
            m_pTown->GetNumJobs());
```

```
      m_GUI.GetStatic(IDC_INFO)->SetText(buf);
  // Lines left out. . .
}
```

After forming the string using the wsprintf() function, you store it in the buf array. You are then in a position to call the CDXUTStatic::SetText() function, which displays the text.

Handling Messages

To process the messages that pertain to the controls, you implement event handlers for the messages you issue from the control panel using the sliders and buttons. Here is the code from the CMyApplication::OnGUIEvent() function in CMyApplication.cpp that implements the event handlers:

```
void CMyApplication::OnGUIEvent(UINT nEvent, int nControlID,
                                        CDXUTControl *pControl)
{
    if(nControlID == IDC_PROCESS)
    {
        m_pTown->ProcessMonth();
    }
    else if(nControlID == IDC_RESET)
    {
        SAFEDELETE(m_pTown);
        // Create the town
        m_pTown = new CTown(m_pGraphics->GetWidth(),
                        m_pGraphics->GetHeight() -
                            m_sprConsole->GetHeight() - 64);
    }
    else if(nControlID == IDC_UNEMPLOYMENT)
    {
        CDXUTSlider *pSlider = (CDXUTSlider *)pControl;
        float fValue = (float)pSlider->GetValue()/100.0;
        CTown::BASE_UNEMPLOYMENT = fValue;
    }
    else if(nControlID == IDC_SHOPMART)
    {
        CDXUTSlider *pSlider = (CDXUTSlider *)pControl;
        float fValue = (float)pSlider->GetValue()/100.0;
        CTown::SHOPMART_INFLUENCE = fValue;
    }
}
```

You employ an if…else if selection structure to process the messages. Taking the messages sequentially, the first you process is IDC_PROCESS. This message allows you to accumulate information over time. Each time you click the Next Month button, you call the CTown::ProcessMonth() function, which updates the data of your simulation using as a baseline the data generated with the last click of the Next Month button. In this way, you see the history of your town's economy unfold a month at a time.

The second message you process is IDC_RESET, which allows you to wipe out existing values and start over. The CTown class constructor resets the number of houses and local business and arranges them randomly in the town grid. Prior to calling the constructor, you invoke the SAFEDELETE() macro, which clears away objects that might occasion memory leaks.

To process the third message, IDC_UNEMPLOYMENT, you recast the value stored in the pControl parameter as a pointer to a CDXUTSlider object. This allows you to call the CDXUTSlider::GetValue() function to retrieve the value you have set with the slider. This value you then assign to the BASE_UNEMPLOYMENT class attribute. The BASE_UNEMPLOYMENT class attribute stores the value you want to use as the background unemployment level for your simulation.

To process the fourth message, IDC_SHOPMART, you again recast the value stored in the pControl parameter as a pointer to a CDXUTSlider object. As before, the cast allows you to call the CDXUTSlider::GetValue() function. This time, you retrieve the value that pertains to the level of influence you want the ShopMart store to have on the local economy. This value you assign to the SHOPMART_INFLUENCE class attribute.

Given the processing of the four key messages, you are in a position to proceed with multiple simulations. As you perform the simulations, you immerse yourself in a context of events that enables you to immediately grasp how the ShopMart store changes the dynamics of the town's economy.

Conclusion

In this chapter, you created a simulation for an event model that involves social and economic factors centering on a small town impacted by the construction of a large retail store. The simulation incorporated a relatively crude event model, but the purpose of the simulation was not to show sophistication in the use of social or economic models but to demonstrate how such a model can be transformed into a simulation.

The exercise demonstrates that you can employ a few basic icons to create a sophisticated simulation. To a great extent, the fewer the icons, the better. At least with respect to social and economic issues, simulations are likely to reflect the policies and consequent biases of those who create them. This reality does not excuse you from developing simulations in a responsible, testable way, but it does serve as a reminder that the efficacy of a simulation is often based on its ability to involve its participants or observers in a basic set of events that allows them to understand how your view of the world unfolds. Delving into minute details can be self-defeating.

Through a discussion of the role of the ledger in the development of Renaissance trading practices and, later, the use of the spreadsheet in modern economic planning ventures, it became possible to observe that simple applications of simulation technologies possess enormous potentials. In light of these potentials, developing an application that uses a few controls and graphical changes to simulate how a community changes under the influence of a large retail store proves worthwhile. Among other things, it demonstrates just how much even a simple simulation can serve as a powerful tool for teaching and spreading ideas.

Specific implementation tasks in this chapter included the development of the `CBuilding` and `CTree` classes. Work with these classes reveals how you can encapsulate fairly complex processes in one class and then use another class to draw this complexity into a more generalized context. In this case, you created a class that allowed you to identify specific buildings within a town. You then collected the buildings into a large grouping that represented the economy of a town.

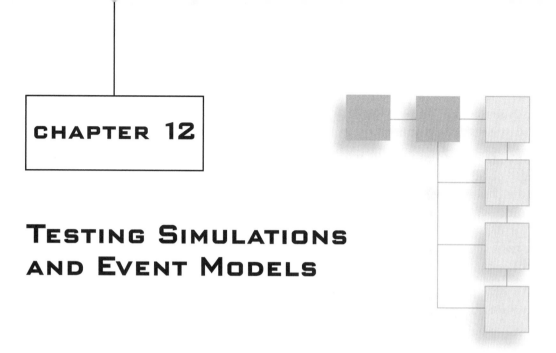

CHAPTER 12

TESTING SIMULATIONS AND EVENT MODELS

This chapter centers on a few techniques and tools you can employ to test simulations and event models. Testing begins with establishing approaches to depicting the cognitive characteristics of a simulation. Toward this end, you can use an approach to diagram the interactions that constitute a simulation. To accomplish this, you picture the simulation as consisting of nodes, transitions, event contexts, and pathways of interaction. To assess how completely you have employed the functionality you have developed as you have implemented your simulation, you use the notion of "cognitive saturation." To illustrate how to apply a cognitively oriented approach to testing, this chapter offers you a basic simulation testing application, *Inspect*. Using a game developed in an earlier chapter (now named *Gold Finder*), you generate test data. You then employ the test application to assess the effectiveness of the simulation. The topics covered include the following, among others:

- Conceptual foundations of testing simulation and event models
- Approaches to evaluating systems, contexts, and interactions
- Context influence
- Path transitions
- Using *Insight* to process data from *Gold Finder*
- System Cognitive Saturation Index

The Effectiveness of Simulation

As Chapter 1, "What is Simulation?" emphasized, an event model determines the extent to which your simulation can regenerate experiences. When you develop an event model, your options vary according to the description of the project you are involved with. Simulation can be characterized as having both subjective and objective aspects. A subjective approach to simulation emphasizes experiences that are not easily repeated or summarized. An objective approach to simulation emphasizes experiences that can be repeated and summarized.

In addition to classifying them according to subjective and objective descriptions, it is also possible to regard simulations as static and dynamic. This approach to classifying simulations originates in part with designer Suguru Ishizaki, who proposed that computer application design efforts can proceed from two basic starting points. One starting point is based on traditional views embodied in print and film media. Think of a framed picture that you manipulate within a frame. You do not change the frame, only the features you see framed. Such a view of design is static.

A dynamic approach to design involves thinking of a framed picture that can change both its frame and what it depicts. This constitutes a dynamic approach to design. This approach to design views an application as a context of elements that continuously changes.

If you work in an industrial setting in which your job entails creating simulations for games, you are likely to start with a static set of specifications for the application you want to create and work toward satisfying these specifications. While a great deal of exploration might characterize such a development effort, in the end, you face what can be described as a standard design for the game. You implement the game according to the standard design. What applies to game development also applies to other computer applications, such as those used for training.

Another type of project places much less emphasis on the use of a standard template. In this case, a dynamic design applies, for the template changes with use. Suguru Ishizaki refers to such design efforts as "improvisational." With respect to simulation, improvisational design encompasses several of the ideas discussed in this book. Your development efforts involve much more of the creation of contexts in which the constraints you introduce afford those who use your application, not a static path of interaction that leads to a determined end, but rather a fairly unlimited set of alternative paths to a multiplicity of ends.

Cognitive Saturation

In this chapter, you work with a software tool that measures a quality called *cognitive saturation*. Cognitive saturation addresses both static and dynamic design activities. It describes the interactive potentials of an application, and it is based on an assessment of the extent to which given contexts of interaction possess potentials to lead application users to discover other contexts of interaction. To calculate the cognitive saturation of a system of interaction, you combine measurements of the potentials each node of interaction possesses and the significance of the transitions and pathways that connect the nodes.

To grasp cognitive saturation on a tactile level, consider a situation in which you have a set of marbles. You place the marbles on the floor and begin playing with them. The play constitutes a game. By the time you finish playing the game, you might have used all the marbles or only a few. If your play involves all the marbles and leads you to make many innovations, then the game possesses a high degree of cognitive saturation. The available marbles and the actions you take toward them represent the cognitive structure of the game. The more marbles you use and the more ways you find to interact with them, the more you realize the cognitive structure the game offers. Realization of the cognitive structure can be viewed as saturation.

Cognitive saturation measures satisfaction. If you use only a few marbles and make few innovations as you play, then the degree of cognitive saturation remains low. You see a number of marbles lying dormant and untouched after the play ends, and you do not feel a great degree of satisfaction with the actions you have taken as you have played the game.

What applies to a game involving marbles applies to software. If you develop an application that offers a hundred functional contexts and you find that, on the average, those who use your application visit only ten, then the design of your application lacks conceptual balance. It is likely that the lack of balance will become especially evident when you consider the experiences the users report. If the users make use of only ten of one hundred options and perhaps understand the application only in terms of these ten options, they are not likely to express a high level of satisfaction. Much of your design and development effort will have been wasted.

If cognitive saturation measures the effectiveness to which users actually use functionality, it also measures the extent to which a system induces its users to investigate potentials. When users investigate potentials, they find different pathways through the functionality the system offers. The pathways of interaction present users with interesting challenges that result in rich, new experiences. Such experiences alter their understanding of the significance of the events the system maps.

Systems Significance

A system interaction provides significant experiences when it in some way allows its users to change their understanding of a given set of events. As has been discussed in previous chapters, understanding possesses subjective and objective characteristics. Understanding also possesses characteristics that relate to logic. You can understand a group of events in one way, using one set of rules and one path of reasoning to arrive at your understanding. You can refer to this type of logic as *mono-modal*. On the other hand, you can understand a group of events in a multitude of ways, using many sets of rules and following paths of reasoning that vary with the feelings and perspectives you encounter as you experience the events that constitute a given context of interaction.

You can associate *subjective* understanding with multi-modal reasoning and *objective* understanding with mono-modal reasoning, but it is unlikely that any given analysis falls into one or the other category. Testing systems of interaction using both perspectives is the best approach, for you then have a way to adjust your tests so that you achieve useful results. You might use tests that are objective and mono-modal to evaluate a control that allows users to control a standard feature of a game; you might use tests that are subjective and multi-modal to evaluate options concerning the appearance and position of the control.

Testing and interaction induce you to discover new ways to understand the system as you work with it. You can use the concept of *iconic logic* to guide your activities in this respect. When you evaluate a system using a logic that you find implicit in the system, then you follow an iconic approach to logic, and your reasoning is multi-modal. On the other hand, if you undertake this activity in an experimentally controlled manner, then your activity takes on an objective description.

From an objective perspective, a simulation can originate with an explicitly defined model. The model embodies understanding, but this type of understanding consists of rules and events you have carefully described. When you participate in the simulation, you discover facts about the model that allow you to improve on the model. In this respect, a simulation brings the model to life in a dynamic way, so that you can critically evaluate the model and improve it. See Figure 12.1.

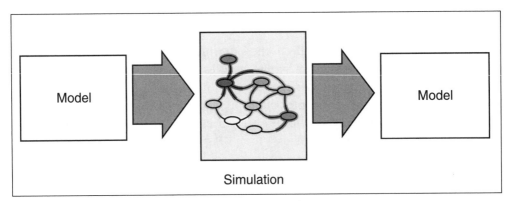

Figure 12.1 Significance arises from explicit understanding.

From a subjective perspective, what applies to a model applies to subjective understanding. The type of understanding consists of rules and events, but the rules and events are purposely left in a complex, largely undefined condition. When you participate in such a simulation, you transform and extend your understanding as an undifferentiated vehicle for mediating experience. See Figure 12.2.

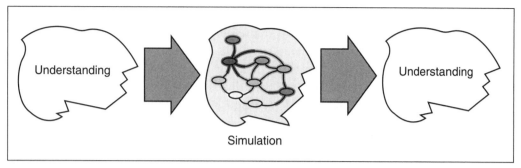

Figure 12.2 Significance arises through implicit understanding.

The Significance of Interaction

Significance depends on interaction. If you cannot interact with a system, your lack of interaction restricts you to the role of an observer or spectator. Whether you view the use of your product as a participant or a spectator heavily impacts the ways you conceptualize, design, and test your product. Clearly, participatory simulations must be evaluated in terms of the interactions they foster. Still, for many analysts, interaction constitutes a relative term. The term is relative because its meaning depends on the analytical tools the analyst applies. When you assess a system, among other things, you begin with certain assumptions about how the elements that constitute the system (nodes and transitions, for example) should be defined, measured, and tested. Ultimately, how you test for significance depends on the approach you develop to measure how interaction can be significant.

Approaches to Diagrammatic Systems Evaluation

When you assess interactive systems using multi-modal logic, you can quantitatively analyze the significance of event contexts (nodes) and scenario mappings (pathways) without heavily encroaching on the integrity of someone who is interacting with the system. At the same time, you are in a position to impose fairly high objective standards on your testing.

When you interact with a system, what you find significant depends on what you bring to the experience of interacting with the system. When you design a system, however, you face the problem of instilling in the system the play potentials that lead to rich experiences for its users. Play potentials depend to a great extent on the cognitive complexity of the application you develop. As mentioned previously, cognitive complexity relates to whether the user of the system discovers its domain of potentials. You can characterize a domain of potentials as the number of possible interactions the system makes available to its players. Alone, however, a count of the possible interactions does not reveal the significance of the experience the interactions create.

Interactions imply mappings of events, and event mappings relate to system transitions, system event contexts, and the scenarios that emerge as you follow pathways of interactions. The sections that follow provide extensive discussion of a model derived from systems theory that you can use to assess the levels of cognitive saturation a system of interaction supports. A software application, *Inspect*, embodies functionality that allows you to put this model to use to test *Gold Finder*, which you explored in Chapter 9.

Nodes

Nodes are elements within a system. As the discussion in Chapter 2 emphasized, any discernable entity or control can serve as a node of interaction. What creates a node is whether the entity interacts with other entities or allows you to interact, as the user, with it. To fairly assess the potentials the element offers for interaction involves avoiding assumptions that it does or does not possess only a specific set of interactive potentials. The case is likely to be that while the element possesses the potentials designers have designed it to possess, it possesses many others as well.

To test interactive potentials, you assign the discernable elements of a system a tentative node status. Then, to avoid testing only for assumed potentials, you can begin your examination of the nodes of a system by first isolating them from each other. You isolate them so that you can inductively establish that they do, in fact, possess properties that allow you to associate them. Figure 12.3 illustrates a collection of elements viewed in this way. The dotted line surrounding the collection signifies the tentative standing of the system of interactions that join the elements together (properly transforming them into nodes).

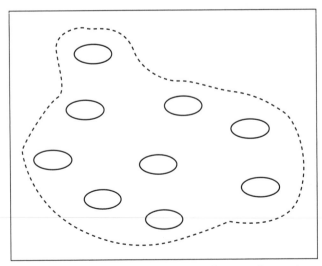

Figure 12.3 A system begins as a collection of tentative nodes.

In Figure 12.3, the nodes appear as a collection bounded by a dotted line. The dotted line is the *system boundary*. System boundaries usually represent arbitrary designations that systems analysts propose for establishing a *domain* of actions. Setting the scope of the domain usually involves designating the level of significance you wish to assign to relationships. Ecologists contend that all living processes on Earth relate to each other, so the scope of an ecological system could be extremely broad.

System boundaries represent arbitrary designations of a domain. They emerge from an *existential* definition of the *scope* of the system. In other words, you acknowledge from the start that your definition of the domain is conditional and arbitrary. To establish the validity of an existential definition, your main obligation to your audience involves stating your assumptions. In this case, the assumptions involve establishing a context in which a limited number of nodes using a limited number of interactions create a context in which levels of cognitive saturation can be quantitatively assessed.

Naming Nodes

When you designate an element as a node, it is important to create a naming system that does not immediately imply relationships. One approach is to use the number of nodes and apply a combinatorial algorithm to create an array of random names. In Figure 12.4, for example, if you consider that the interaction network consists of nine nodes, then you can take the square root of nine to determine the minimum number of letters required to generate unique names beginning with the same letter. If you generate a complete matrix that encompasses all possible names, you have 27 to work with.

Having developed a set of names, you can then apply the names to the prospective nodes. Again, for purposes of objective analysis, you should randomize the application of names as much as possible. Numbers and letters used with periods or other punctuation immediately imply an order. Generally, if you select names from a table of the type Figure 12.4 illustrates, then you are likely to be able to name nodes without at the same time assigning an implied order to them. Figure 12.5 illustrates the appearance of the collection of prospective nodes after names have been applied.

Identifiers Without Implied Order		
r r r	x x x	o o o
r r o	x x o	o o r
r o r	x o x	o x o
r o o	x o o	o x x
r o x	x r r	o o x
r x o	x r o	o r r
r x x	x r r	o x r
r x r	x r x	o r x
r r x	x x r	o r o

Figure 12.4 Name nodes so that you imply no order.

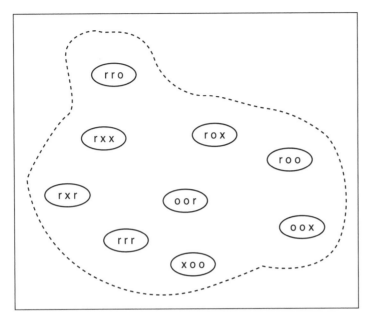

Figure 12.5 Apply random names to identify prospective nodes.

Transitions

Transitions represent relationships between nodes. To speak generally about transitions, you can call them connectors. Connectors and transitions are analogous to elements and nodes. A connector lacks directionality. Directionality designates that the connector occasions the movement of information from one node to another.

The construction of a system results from the application of transitions to the nodes. In the system Figure 12.6 illustrates, transitions relate nodes to each other. Each transition represents a flow of information, and to determine whether a transition exists between two nodes, you ask whether one node receives information from or transmits information to another node. Nodes transmit and receive information according to the boundary, or scope, of interactions that existentially characterize the system.

You can use a number of symbols to represent connectors and transitions. Curved lines without arrows designate *connectors*. Curved lines with arrows designate transitions. See Figure 12.7.

The Focus of Awareness

A transition indicates that information flows between two nodes, but this is only part of the picture. When information flows between two nodes, the node toward which the arrow points indicates the direction of information flow and the movement of the focus of awareness that accompanies the flow of information. The focus of awareness refers to the focal point of *cognitive awareness*—awareness as established by the structure of interaction the system sustains.

Consider what happens if you use a pencil to examine the transitions in the diagram. Using the pencil, you trace the paths of arrows from node to node. (See Figure 12.8.) When you trace the paths of the arrows in this way, your activity creates a *focal point of interaction*. The tip of the pencil at any given point represents the focal point of cognitive awareness that you sustain as you trace the path of the transitions.

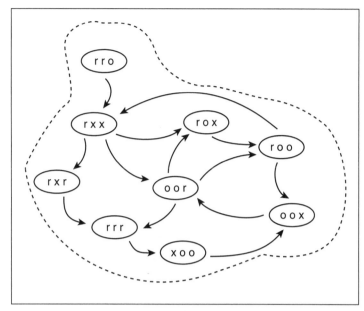

Figure 12.6 A system consists of transitions and nodes.

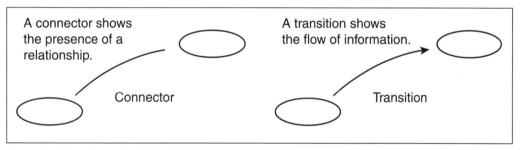

Figure 12.7 A transition differs from a connector because a transition indicates directionality.

The movement of the pencil provides a way to understand the directionality of the arrows. You carry information from one node to the next, and the significance of the information you carry is relative to the position you occupy in the system. As you move through the system from node to node, the information you gather allows you to make decisions about the directions you take. With each decision, your awareness grows.

Figure 12.9 illustrates that the transition from node oor to node roo shows that node oor contributes information to node roo. If you are tracing this path, when you reach roo, you are aware that you have passed through oor and you are aware of the potentials oor holds with respect to roo.

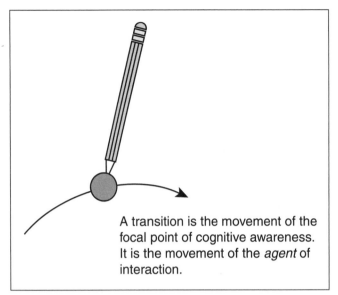

A transition is the movement of the focal point of cognitive awareness. It is the movement of the *agent* of interaction.

Figure 12.8 The context of cognitive awareness moves as you trace the path of the transitions.

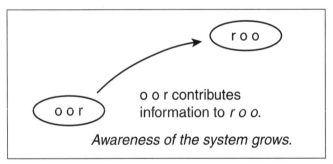

o o r contributes information to *r o o*.

Awareness of the system grows.

Figure 12.9 Transitions represent increased awareness.

If you consider that the transition from one node to the next represents a growth in your awareness of the system, then you also have a way to understand that the direction of the arrow represents, not the solicitation of information, but the growth or transformation of understanding. The nodes are not in themselves agents of intelligence. They represent moments in which decisions can be made about how information is to continue to flow.

A transition implies that an agent acquires and transforms information as he or she moves from one node to another. From the standpoint of information theory, this acquisition and transformation of information is accompanied by an *acknowledgment* of some type. You can view acknowledgement as a focus of awareness accented by a moment of new understanding.

Abstracting and Diagramming Acknowledgment

As becomes evident in the discussion a little later in the chapter, you can diagram an acknowledgement if you picture it as an event context. You can picture an event context as a combination of several factors. Consider, for example, what happens if you stand on the peak of a hill. You can turn on your heel and see a varied set of views. A simple turn on your heal gives a different view, but each view differs according to how you think about it. If in one direction you see a park, you might begin planning an outing for a picnic. If you see a river in a second direction, you might think about kayaking. If you see houses in a third direction, you might start planning a move or a construction project.

What you see is not simply a result of having turned on your heel. You might see a park as an opportunity for a picnic, but you might also remember that you were once mugged in a park. Again, you might remember a time when you played a softball game in a park. In other respects, you might see a valley you think a wonderful spot for a house, but you might also be thinking about the opportunities afforded by a raise or a new job. To assess the significance of your interaction with the settings you see as you turn on your heel atop the hill, you must consider the significance of memories, what you see, your sense of your abilities in the future, and among many other things, the general set of chance views your turns on your heels offer you.

How you account for your thoughts as you turn atop the hill is analogous to what happens when you analyze a transition. Each factor that you include in your analysis represents an abstraction of acknowledgement. As Figure 12.10 illustrates, you use the curved arrow to represent a moment that almost inevitably consists of a complex exchange of information and complex form of acknowledgement.

Contexts of Interaction

You can begin to see nodes as giving shape to a system when you see the nodes as contexts of interaction. Contexts of interaction emerge from the ways that nodes relate to each other to provide information, foster the growth of awareness, and set occasions for decisions. (See Figure 12.11.) They do so as a system, and the shape the system assumes depends

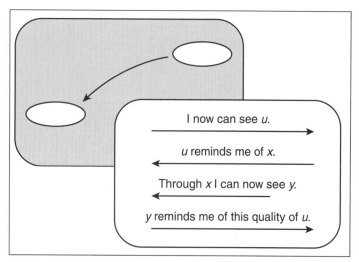

Figure 12.10 Transitions imply acknowledgements.

on the ways that the contexts of interaction relate to each other. The great benefit you derive from this view of the system consists of understanding how the parts and the whole relate. As the elements of the system (the parts) join to create the system (the whole), the system subordinates the elements to the scope of activity that the system existentially represents.

At first, your view of the whole system might lead you to concentrate specifically on the connections between specific nodes, so that you resist allowing the elements to merge into the whole. There is a benefit to be derived from this view. The tension you feel as you view the whole and in relation to the parts allows you to discern how your awareness of the system changes depending on the point of focus.

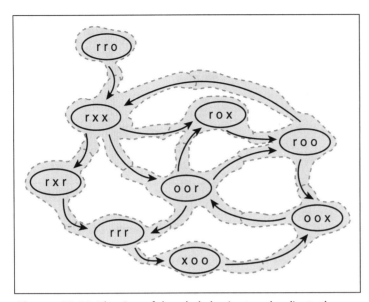

Figure 12.11 The view of the whole begins to subordinate the elements.

In Figure 12.12, the double circles represent moments of transition. A moment of transition constitutes what might be viewed as a testing or confirmation of understanding. Imagine moving the pencil tip from rox to roo. The awareness you possess as you make this movement can vary according to the path you follow. Your most recent transition might have been from rxx to rox. Or it might have been from oor to rox. What you find significant as you reach roo depends on the path leading to it. With each new movement, the center of focus for the system changes, and with this change comes a new view of the system, a new awareness of the reality it creates for someone who participates in it.

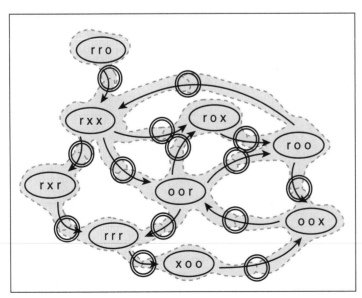

Figure 12.12 Junctions of interaction might draw your attention as you first examine a system.

As your awareness of the whole increases, so does your awareness of the parts. The awareness consists of acknowledgements given to contexts of interaction. Contexts of interaction represent nodal clusters of transitions. These clusters are dynamic and their significance takes shape according to the paths that create them. Figure 12.13 illustrates the emergence of nodes as dynamic contexts of interaction.

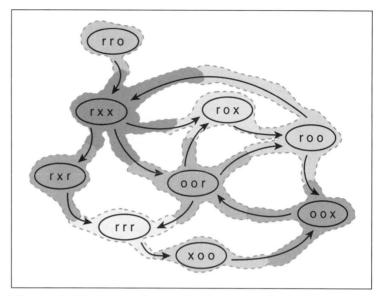

Figure 12.13 The significance of nodes emerges from system interactions.

Determining Significance

You can determine the significance of each context of interaction if you first isolate it from other contexts of interaction. In Figure 12.14, for example, node rxx now appears in the foreground. When positioned in the foreground, node rxx has a distinct form, one that abstractly represents its potentials for dynamically interacting with other nodes.

One way to picture the situation that now emerges involves considering for a moment the concept of a hologram. A hologram is a photograph, but it differs from other photographs because each part of a hologram possesses the information you require to re-create the image of the whole. Normally, photographs consist of a set of dots colored to provide a single image. A hologram is different. Imagine, for instance, that you have a holographic picture of an apple. If you cut the hologram into pieces and then illuminate any one of the pieces using a laser, you will see that each piece creates a whole image of the apple. The part re-creates the whole because each part of a hologram possesses the information you require to re-create the whole.

Figure 12.14 is not a hologram. Still, node rxx possesses the shape it possesses because it interacts with the other nodes in the system in a specific way. In one sense, the shape of the whole depends on the shape of the part. On the other hand, the shapes of the parts depend on the shape of the whole. Transitions converge in node rxx in a specific way. Transitions converge in all the other nodes in specific ways. From these convergences—these contexts of interaction—arise the distinctive character of the system as a whole.

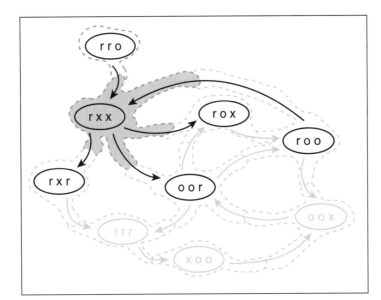

note

A gateway node is a node that has only one connector and that you do not need to depict as receiving feedback. Node rro is a gateway node. Such nodes provide ways to define open systems without at the same time making evaluations of the system impossible.

Figure 12.14 Isolating a context of interaction allows you to explore its significance.

Context Influence

A node can be described as a context of interaction. You can begin to evaluate the significance of a given context of interaction by considering both how it influences other contexts of interaction and how other contexts of interaction influence it. This type of relatedness constitutes the general connectivity of the node (NC). Influence flows in two directions. Movement from the node consists of an output (NO). Connectivity can also be viewed as reception of information (NR). The number of connectors that tie a context of interaction to other contexts of interaction provides a quantitative assessment of this connectivity. The value you arrive at when you assess connectivity in this way gives you the context influence (CI) of the node you are examining.

$$CI = NR \; x \; NO \; x \; NC,$$

where NR, NO, or NC = 1 if NR, NO, or NC = 0.

This formula indicates that the product of the number of node receptors (NR), the number of node outputs (NO), and the number of node connectors (NC) provides the influence of the context of interaction (CI). Figure 12.15 illustrates an event context and the factors involved in determining its influence. Table 12.1 provides a summary view of the values involved and how they can be used to determine the context influence of a given event context.

In Figure 12.15 and Table 12.1, the formula used to determine the influence of the context of interaction (CI) contains an indexed value. For example, notice that CI(rxx)[1] has an index of 1. The 1 indicates the *order* of the analysis. Order is something akin to the internal scope or boundary of analysis. The order is the degree of analysis that you conduct to establish a given value. In this case, as Figure 12.15 shows, you evaluate the node only to discover its significance relative to the

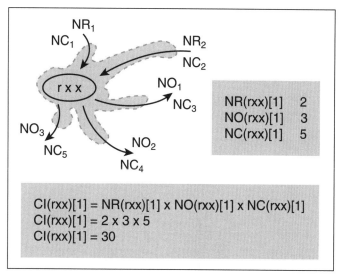

$$CI(rxx)[1] = NR(rxx)[1] \times NO(rxx)[1] \times NC(rxx)[1]$$
$$CI(rxx)[1] = 2 \times 3 \times 5$$
$$CI(rxx)[1] = 30$$

Figure 12.15 The influence of a context of interactions can be discovered by considering its connectors.

nodes with which it is most immediately connected. This is the first order of nodes.

If you wanted to take the analysis to a second order, you could assess the significance of each of the transitions of each of the nodes with which rxx is connected. This order of evaluation lies beyond the scope of this discussion.

Table 12.1 Terms for Influence and Significance

Term	Abbreviation	Discussion
Context Influence	CI(node)[order]	Context Influence for a given node relative to a given order of evaluation. CI = NR x NO x NC, where NR, NO, or NC = 1 if NR, NO, or NC = 0.
Node Reception	NR(node)	The number or transitions that show a node receiving information.
Node Output	NO(node)	The number of transitions that show a node supplying information to another node.
Node Connectivity	NC(node)	The total number of connectors for a given node.
Context Significance Influence	SI(node)[order]	The product of the contexts of influence that contribute a given context of interaction. $S = CI_1 \times \ldots \times CI_n$

Systems Significance

Using the information that you gain from the quantitative influence of given contexts of interaction, you can move on to assess the influence the overall system possesses. The influence of the overall system consists of the sum of the influences of the nodes that constitute the system. Figure 12.16 provides a summary view of event contexts and the influences that characterize them.

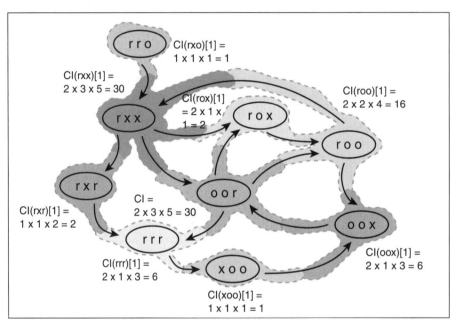

Figure 12.16 Cognitive saturation (SI) for cognition is the sum of the influences of the constituent event contexts.

Path Transitions

Evaluating the significance of a system involves evaluating both its nodes and its transitions. Just as the influence of individual contexts of interactions can be summed to obtain a view of the overall influence of the system, the values of transitions can be combined to evaluate the significance of different paths. A path consists of the set of transitions a given scenario includes. Figure 12.17 depicts a scenario. The scenario encompasses a series of sequentially numbered transitions. The subscripts indicate the order in which the focus of attention approaches the transitions. For the segments T_5 and T_9, you see that path uses the same transitions.

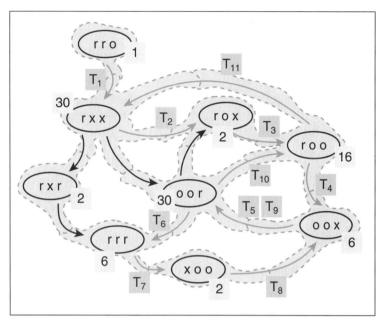

Figure 12.17 Path values are calculated using context significance.

Table 12.2 summarizes the terms that apply to the assessment of transitions and paths. The values for the individual transitions (T) are combined to determine the path value (PV). The path value represents only the paths of a given scenario. Total path value for the system (TPV) represents all the transitions that constitute the system.

Table 12.2 shows you that several types of paths can be characterized in special ways. For example, some paths allow you to move through the transitions a system offers without redundancy. You can refer to such paths as *progressive*. The path shown in Figure 12.17 falls into a second category, that of a *constrained* path. Such a path allows you to repeat transitions up to twice each, and it generally moves forward in a fairly efficient way from start to terminal point.

After constrained paths come *regenerative* paths. Such paths can repeat a given transition a large number of times. The limiting number is a number that allows you to complete a path the system provides. (Picture turning right three times to complete the circuit of a square or seven times to complete the circuit of an octagon.)

A final path is identified as *degenerative*. This form of path is not necessarily doomed to failure, but it allows you to repeat single transitions a number of times far in excess of the number of transitions that characterize the system. The number can even go to infinity.

Table 12.2 Types of Paths

Term	Abbreviation	Discussion
Progressive Path		The order is CI1 -> C12 -> ... ->CIn, and no path (transition) is repeated more than once (TC <= 1 >)
Constrained Path		The order is CI1 -> C12 -> ... ->CIn, and no path (transition) is repeated more than twice (TC <= 2>)
Regenerative Path		The order is CI1 -> C12 -> ... ->CIn, and no path (transition) is repeated more than the context count (CC) for the system (TC < = CC>)
Degenerative Path		The order is CI1 -> C12 -> ... ->CIn, and one path (transition) becomes infinite (Tn = Infinity>)
Transition Value	(TV)	The value is the sum of the two contributing contexts. TV = CIn + CIn+1.
Path Value	(PV)	The sum of the path transition values that constitute a given scenario. PV = Sn{TV1 + TV2 +...+ TVn}.
Total Path Value	(TPV)	The square of the sum of the smallest transition value added to the largest transition divided by 2. TPV = (TVmin + TVmad / 2)2

Calculating the Relative Path Value

Drawing from the information Table 12.2 provides, you can determine the total path value the system provides. To accomplish this, calculate a value you can use to represent the sum of all possible paths in the system. This requires that you find a reasonable limitation to the number of paths you consider. Toward this end, you can sum the minimum and maximum transition values, divide this sum by two, and then square the result. This results in the *total path value* for the system (TPV):

$$\text{Total Path Value} = \left(\frac{\text{Minimum Transition Value} + \text{Maximum Transition Value}}{2} \right)^2$$

You can also calculate the *traversed path value* (PV) of a path a scenario designates. Again, drawing from the information that Table 12.2 provides, to accomplish this, you need only to add up the values you find for each transition (T) in the path you have taken. Here is the formula:

$$\text{Traversed Path Value} = T_1 + \ldots + T_n$$

To find the *relative path value* (RPV) of the path taken, you need only to find the ratio of the traversed path value to the total path value:

Figure 12.18 shows the result of the calcula-tions for the system depicted thus far in this chapter. The relative path value is 0.4156378.

$$\text{Relative Path Value} = \frac{\text{Traversed Path Value}}{\text{Total Path Value}}$$

The large number of decimal places can be reduced to accord with your needs. In more complex systems such as the one that you deal with a little later on in this chapter, you require a large number of decimal places because your interaction scenario represents a small fraction of the total path value.

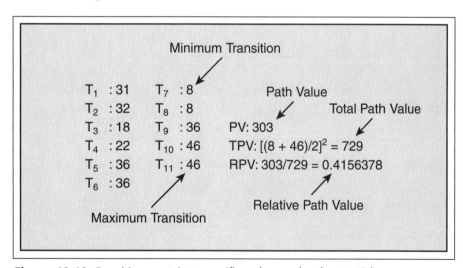

Figure 12.18 Transitions pertain to specific and general path potentials.

Calculating the Relative Context Value

The relative context value is the ratio of the nodes included in a given scenario to the nodes that comprise the entire system. To obtain the relative context value (or signifi-cance) of the session, you take the number of contexts the traversed path includes and find the ratio of this value to the number of contexts the system includes:

Total Context Count = 9
Actual Context Count = 8
Relative Context Value = 8/9 = .888

The system Figure 12.13 depicts features 9 event contexts. Since 8 of the event contexts lie in the path the scenario designates, the ration is 8/9, or 0.888.

Calculating the Cognitive Saturation Value

If you know the relative context value and the relative path value, you can then calculate the level of cognitive saturation that characterizes a given user session. The cognitive saturation level is the average of the sum of the relative context value and the relative path value.

$$\frac{\text{Relative Context Value} + \text{Relative Path Value}}{2} = \text{Cognitive Saturation}$$

Given the figures used so far, when you apply this formula you arrive at a saturation of approximately 0.651.

$$\frac{.415 + .888}{2} = \text{Cognitive Saturation}$$

A Trial Run of Inspect

To place the discussion provided thus far in a context that allows you to arrive at a more concrete, tactile grasp of the meaning of cognitive saturation, access the Inspect_Sample folder in the Chapter12_Code folder. In this folder is another, called Inspect_Sample. Open this folder and the Inspect.exe file. Figure 12.19 displays the result.

Inspect is a C# application. You can find the source code and a Microsoft Studio .Net project for *Inspect* in the Inspect folder in the SimulationSrc directory for Chapter 12. Due to limitations of space, this chapter does not provide a discussion of how to implement the code for the application. Instead, the focus is on how to use *Inspect* in conjunction with a game to derive data that you can use to assess the cognitive saturation of the game.

The data that *Inspect* displays consists of five types. Here is a breakdown:

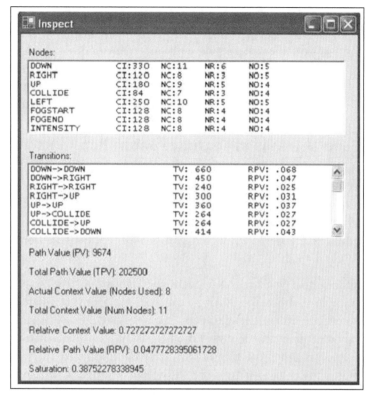

Figure 12.19 *Inspect* provides you with a view of data you can use to assess application performance.

- **Node data.** Each node provides a context of interaction. Nodes communicate with other nodes by passing information to them (NO). They also receive information (NR). They have a general context weight based on their role as connectors (NC). Using the formulas shown in Table 12.2, you can assess the interactive context influence (CI).

- **Path data.** Each path possesses significance on the basis of the two nodes it connects (PV) and overall path to which it contributes (RPV).

- **Summary node data.** Each node offers a point at which you can make a decision regarding what to do next. It is not enough to say that a node offers only an opportunity to make a decision. Nodes can differ in significance depending on the number of choices they offer and the significance of the paths to which the choices lead.

- **Summary path data.** The total path value of the system describes what might be considered the maximum potential that a system offers to extend pathways. Picture this in terms of the number of kilometers of trails a park might offer. After a time, you begin hiking the same trails, even if you do so in differing orders.

- **Cognitive saturation.** The way that nodes and paths merge to shape the interactive potential of a game can be assessed using cognitive saturation. If you finish a user session after interacting with only a few nodes and pathways, then the cognitive saturation of the application is probably fairly low. On the other hand, if you end up exploring many of the nodes and paths available to you during your session of interaction, then the cognitive saturation of the application is probably fairly high.

General Trends in Cognitive Saturation

Figure 12.19 represents data drawn from a single session of play involving *Gold Finder*, which is a slightly altered version of the game you developed in Chapter 9. This session results in a cognitive saturation reading of around 0.39. This figure gains significance when you assess its value relative to data collected from a number of play sessions. Consider Figure 12.20, which graphically represents a trend you might observe if you collect data about multiple sessions.

Assume that you acquire a game and over time have different experiences with it. For example, if at first you abruptly conclude the game after starting to play it, you are likely to experience little satisfaction, and the level of cognitive saturation that characterizes your play session is close to zero. Given this start, consider what happens if you again play the game, this time exploring more options and learning more about its features. You make more choices and follow more paths. The cognitive saturation moves into the middle area of the curve. Chances are that you experience greater satisfaction.

If you practice a few more times, you might find that you discover a multitude of features and paths of interactions. Your level of satisfaction increases, as does the level of cognitive saturation that characterized your session of interaction.

Running Inspect

Now that you have had a chance to examine how cognitive saturation can be pictured on an abstract level, you are ready to engage in some practical exercises. These exercises allow you to accomplish two primary tasks. First, you alter the application you developed in Chapter 9 so that it can write data to a file. The data you write to a file allows you to track your interactions with the application. Second, you alter the application so that it automatically opens *Inspect* to analyze the data you have generated. To begin this activity, access the SimulationSrc folder in the Chapter12_Code folder, and then look in the Listing12_01 folder for the project (*.sln) file. Compile the project. Figure 12.21 illustrates a view of *Gold Finder*, which you last saw in Chapter 9.

To begin generating data, you can follow a test scenario. Software testers employ use case to map test scenarios. Figure 12.22 illustrates a test scenario to follow as you play *Gold Finder*. While you can set up a use case to help you maintain a complex set of interactions during testing, you can also employ the use case as a tool to help you assess the data that you obtain through *Inspect*.

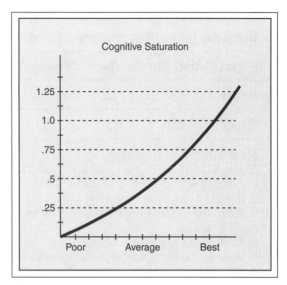

Figure 12.20 Cognitive saturation gauges interaction and satisfaction.

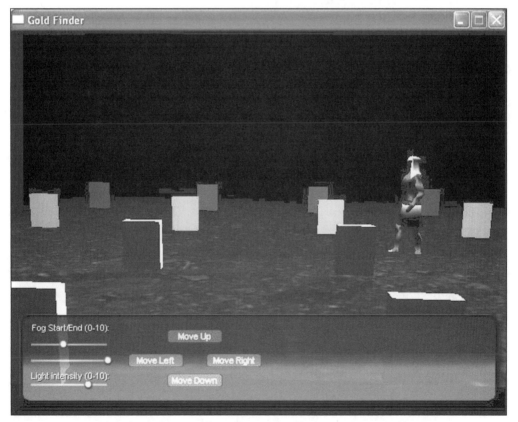

Figure 12.21 The Gold Finder game from Chapter 9 makes a reappearance for testing.

Use Case Name: Play scenario for cognitive saturation testing

Player (Actor) Context (Role): Player

Precondition(s): Game up, ready to play.

Trigger(s): Start of game.

Main Course of Action:
1. Adjust start fog to the middle of the slider.
2. Adjust the end fog to the start of the slider.
3. Set the Light Intensity to high.
4. Move the camera on the z axis until you see six rows down and six across.
5. Walk to the last row, turn right.
6. Walk to the far right row, turn right (so you're facing forward).
7. Walk forward two rows, turn left.
8. Walk all the way across the cemetary, turn right.
9. Walk to the last row, turn right.
10. Walk to the center row, turn right.
11. Walk forward until you are even with the gold stone, turn left.
12. Walk until you collide with the stone.

Alternate Course(s) of Action:
1–12. If you need to correct actions, do so. But keep to the plan.

Exceptional Course(s) of Action: n/a

Figure 12.22 A test scenario for playing *Gold Finder*.

If you follow the test scenario Figure 12.22 provides, when you perform step 12, which involves guiding the character to the golden tombstone, the game displays a message box. The message box informs you the data from your user session has been collected and can be displayed. Figure 12.23 illustrates the message box.

You might have to move other windows on your desktop around before you can see it, but the *Inspect* window appears as soon as the game ends. The game ends when you collide with the gold stone, and the message box informs you that *Inspect* has executed to show you the data your session has generated. To close the message box, click OK. This leaves you with the *Inspect* data window. Figure 12.24 illustrates the *Inspect* data window that results if you follow the use case Figure 12.22 illustrates.

The upper data pane displays data on the nodes or event contexts that *Gold Finder* encompasses. The lower data pane displays data on the transitions that characterize your interactions with the game. At the very bottom, the *Inspect* window displays the data used to calculate the level of cognitive saturation that applies to your use of the application.

Figure 12.23 A message box informs you that the application has generated data and invoked *Inspect*.

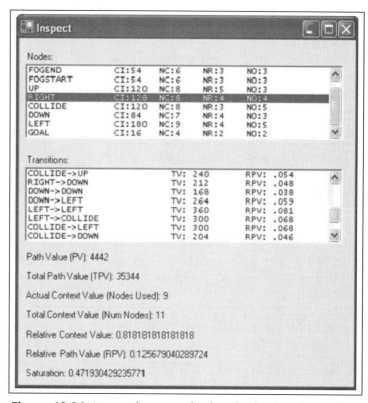

Figure 12.24 Inspect shows you the data that has been logged for your user session with *Gold Finder*.

Assessing Messages

As the earlier sections of this chapter have discussed, to a great extent you can assess interaction in terms of event contexts (nodes) and pathways (transitions). *Gold Finder* provides several contexts of interaction. You can identify the contexts of interaction if you assess the messages the application can process. As is shown in greater detail a little later on in this chapter, the application class for *Gold Finder* features eleven messages. Each of these messages can be the basis of an event context. To fully identify the context, however, you must assess how one event leads to another. As Figures 12.14 through 12.16 illustrate, the significance of an event context depends on the transitions it maintains with other nodes and the complexity of the nodes with which it communicates.

As Figure 12.25 shows, UP, RIGHT, LEFT, and GOAL events display the greatest potentials. INTENSITY and FOG tend to be less complex, as is the game's end (goal) event. Event contexts that tend to character actions frequently performed tend to have greater overall significance than other actions. In this respect, it might be said that frequently performed actions should have greater significance than other actions. Certainly where design of an application is concerned, you work hard to ensure that the users of your application find that the actions they frequently perform are logical and laden with cognitive significance.

Node/Event Context Data				
INTENSITY	CI: 30	NC: 5	NR: 2	NO: 3
FOGEND	CI: 54	NC: 6	NR: 3	NO: 3
FOGSTART	CI: 54	NC: 6	NR: 3	NO: 3
UP	CI: 120	NC: 8	NR: 5	NO: 3
RIGHT	CI: 128	NC: 8	NR: 4	NO: 4
COLLIDE	CI: 120	NC: 8	NR: 3	NO: 5
DOWN	CI: 84	NC: 7	NR: 4	NO: 3
LEFT	CI: 180	NC: 9	NR: 4	NO: 5
GOAL	CI: 16	NC: 4	NR: 2	NO: 2

Figure 12.25 Event contexts reveal trends of significance.

In addition to event contexts, the interactive potentials of your application depend on the transitions between event contexts. As Figure 12.26 illustrates, transitions establish paths, and paths have significance according to the value of the nodes they connect. Paths also have significance with respect to the extent to which they account for the total number of possible paths that a system offers.

As Figure 12.26 illustrates, *Inspect* tracks the actual path you follow as you interact with *Gold Finder*. If you examine this data in detail, you can see that it accounts for not only the movement of the arrow keys but also the settings you apply to the lights.

In each case, the records that *Insight* generates relate transitions as passages between event contexts. *Inspect* employs the algorithms discussed earlier in the chapter to arrive at the values of transitions. Transitions that lead to collisions often show high significance. Turns tend to have values that fall into the middle range. Adjustments to the lighting tend to have the lowest significance.

Transition/Path Data		
INTENSITY –> INTENSITY	TV: 60	RPV: .014
INTENSITY –> FOGEND	TV: 84	RPV: .019
FOGEND –> FOGEND	TV: 108	RPV: .024
FOGEND –> FOGSTART	TV: 108	RPV: .024
FOGSTART –> FOGSTART	TV: 108	RPV: .024
FOGSTART –> UP	TV: 174	RPV: .039
UP –> UP	TV: 240	RPV: .054
UP –> RIGHT	TV: 248	RPV: .056
RIGHT –> DOWN	TV: 212	RPV: .048
DOWN –> DOWN	TV: 168	RPV: .038
DOWN –> LEFT	TV: 264	RPV: .059
LEFT –> LEFT	TV: 360	RPV: .081
LEFT –> COLLIDE	TV: 300	RPV: .068
COLLIDE –> LEFT	TV: 300	RPV: .068
COLLIDE –> DOWN	TV: 204	RPV: .046
LEFT –> UP	TV: 300	RPV: .068
LEFT –> GOAL	TV: 196	RPV: .044
GOAL –> null	TV: 16	RPV: .004

Figure 12.26 Messages can be used to track paths.

Code Implementation for Testing

To test the *Gold Finder* game, you add a few lines of code to it to generate test data. The lines of code you add complement existing code. Your work begins with the message processing capabilities you created when you developed the game in Chapter 9. After attending to message generation, you add a few lines of code to invoke *Insight*. You do not need to perform any work to create Insight. The executable already resides in the Bin directory for the code for this chapter.

Identifying Messages

As discussions in previous chapters have emphasized, you create attributes in the CMyApplication class that enable you to track messages. When you create class attributes to track messages, you also have a way to log each message your application processes. You can log messages because upon declaration you associate each attribute with a unique number. Here is the attribute list for the CMyApplication class, which you find in CMyApplication.h:

```
static const int IDC_START = 0;
static const int IDC_END = 1;
static const int IDC_STATIC = 2;
static const int IDC_INTENSITY = 3;
static const int IDC_STATIC2 = 4;
static const int IDC_UP = 5;
static const int IDC_RIGHT = 6;
static const int IDC_DOWN = 7;
static const int IDC_LEFT = 8;
static const int IDC_GOAL = 9;
static const int IDC_COLLIDE = 10;
```

Logging Messages

Whenever you play *Gold Finder*, the actions you take are logged to a file. Logging your actions to a file requires that you perform three tasks. First, you set up a log file. Second, you create a function that writes numbers to the file that identifies your actions. Last, you create a function that signals the termination of a game and invokes *Inspect* so that the data you have logged can be processed and displayed to you.

Setting Up a Log File

To set up a log file, you make a small addition to the CMyApplication class. This addition consists of the declaration of FILE attribute. The attribute identifies a file stream—an identifier that holds a pointer to which you can write data. Here is the code for the attribute in CMyApplication.h:

```
// Output file
FILE *m_fpOutput;
```

note

> As a note for C++ buffs, to include file i/o, you can adopt the newer convention of including C header files using the names they have been assigned under the latest ANSI C++ specification. In this respect, stdio.h becomes cstdio. Since these header files are now in the std namespace, you no longer append *.h to identify them.

To use the file handle, you must first associate it with a file. You perform this work in the CMyApplication::Initialize() function. You use the C language fopen() function to accomplish this. This function requires two parameters and returns a pointer to a file stream, which you assign to m_fpOutput. The first parameter of fopen() identifies the file to which you want to write data. The second identifies the mode in which you want to use the file. The typical modes are read ("r"), write ("w"), and append ("a"). You can also use "t" and "b" in conjunction with the basic file mode specification to indicate whether you want to write in text or binary mode. In this instance, you use "wt", for "write text":

```
// Open the output file
m_fpOutput = fopen("data.txt","wt");
```

Writing Data to the File

Having designated a stream that you can write to, you can then begin to write data to it. To accomplish this task, you make use of the C language fprintf() function, which you call in the scope of the CMyApplication::OnGUIEvent() function. The procedure is fairly simple. Each time you invoke the OnGUIEvent() function—which is every time you issue a message—you call fprintf() to write to the file. Here is a snippet of code to illustrate this activity:

```
void CMyApplication::OnGUIEvent(UINT nEvent, int nControlID,
                                CDXUTControl *pControl)
{
      // Log the message
      if(m_fpOutput)
      {
            fprintf(m_fpOutput, "%d\n", nControlID);
            fflush(m_fpOutput);
      }

//. . . lines left out
}
```

The fprintf() function requires two parameters, but it is a function that takes a variable number of arguments. The first identifies the file stream. The second is a character string, possibly containing escape sequences describing the types required for succeeding arguments. In this case, "%d" designates a signed or decimal integer. All parameters after the second provide the types specified in the second argument in the correct order to fill in the string.

The data you write consists of the unique identifiers for each of the messages you process when you play the game. The nControlID parameter of the OnGUIEvent() function provides these identifiers. Each time you issue a message, you call fprintf() to write data to the file. After writing the data to the file, you call the C language fflush() function to clear the stream for the next message.

If you access Inspect_Sample and open the data.txt file, you can view the result of this activity. The information you log consists of the integers that uniquely identify the messages. Figure 12.27 provides a small sampling of the data.

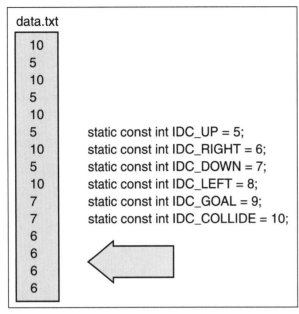

data.txt

```
10
5
10
5
10
5
10
5
10
7
7
6
6
6
6
```

static const int IDC_UP = 5;
static const int IDC_RIGHT = 6;
static const int IDC_DOWN = 7;
static const int IDC_LEFT = 8;
static const int IDC_GOAL = 9;
static const int IDC_COLLIDE = 10;

Figure 12.27 The program writes message identifiers sequentially.

Processing Messages

To process messages, you add a set of selection statements to the OnGUIEvent() function. The selection statements filter messages and process them accordingly. For most of the section statements, Chapter 9, "Environments of Simulation," discusses the actions you perform to implement message processing. In this context, however, you implement a few statements in special ways. For example, consider how you process messages relating to the end of the game. Here is a snippet of code from the OnGUIEvent() function that accomplishes this work:

```
//. . . Lines left out
        else if(GetWorld()->IsCollision(L"Gold", vecNewPos))
        {
                // Log the message for a collision
                if(m_fpOutput)
                {
                        fprintf(m_fpOutput, "%d\n", IDC_GOAL);\
                        fclose(m_fpOutput);
                }
                //../../Bin
                // Run Inspect.exe
                ShellExecute(NULL, L"open", L".\\Inspect.exe",
                                NULL, NULL, SW_HIDE);
                // Open up the inspect application
                  MessageBox(NULL, L"You found the gold! \
                                Press OK when finished viewing \
                                data.", L"Winner!", MB_OK);
                pEntity->SetPos(D3DXVECTOR3(0, 0, 0));
```

```
                CreateStones();
                // Re-open the file
                if(m_fpOutput)
                        fclose(m_fpOutput);
                        m_fpOutput = fopen("data2.txt", "wt");
        }
        else
        {
                pEntity->SetPos(vecNewPos);
        }
    }
    m_pGraphics->SetFog(D3DCOLOR_XRGB(0,0,0), m_fFogStart, m_fFogEnd);
}
```

Unlike other messages, the message that signals the end of the game has a special standing. It occurs only once, and when it occurs, you face a couple of tasks. First, you must announce that the game has ended. Next, given that you want to evaluate the play session using data you have extracted from it, you want to open *Inspect* so that you can process and view the data.

To log the final event of the game, you call the fprintf() function one final time to write the IDC_GOAL message to the file. In most cases, the game logs this message last, but in some cases, if you do not clear the file, you might see it displayed several times. (The numerical value of the message is 9.) After writing the GOAL message, you call the C library fclose() function. The sole parameter for this function is the file stream (m_fpOutput).

Calling Inspect

To open *Inspect*, you call a special function that the Win API library includes. This is the ShellExecute() function. This function allows you to open one application from another. It provides a handy, safe, and simple approach to opening external executables.

The ShellExecute() function requires six parameters. Table 12.3 provides a breakdown of the parameters. Here is the prototype for the function:

```
HINSTANCE ShellExecute( HWND hwnd,
                        LPCTSTR lpOperation,
                        LPCTSTR lpFile,
                        LPCTSTR lpParameters,
                        LPCTSTR lpDirectory,
                        INT nShowCmd
);
```

Table 12.3 ShellExecute Parameters

Parameter	Discussion
hwnd	Designates the parent window. In this case, *Inspect* has no parent window, so you assign NULL.
lpOperation	You assign any of a number of string values to this parameter. Among these are open, find, print, and explore. Each of these strings indicates a task. In this instance, you open *Inspect*.
lpFile	Designates the file or executable you want to open. In this case, the file is the executable for *Gold Finder*.
lpParameters	Designates any values you want to pass to the executable.
lpDirectory	Designates the path to the executable.
nShowCmd	You can control how the application you open first displays. Among the options are SW_HIDE, SW_MAXIMIZE, SW_MINIMIZE, and SW_RESTORE. The initial value is set to SW_MAXIMIZE. You might want to change this to SW_HIDE.

Inspect is a C# application that you can compile and modify as you wish. Describing how to work with C# and *Inspect* on a programming level lies beyond the scope of this book. However, it might be beneficial to point out that you can find the project for *Inspect* in the SimulationSrc/*Inspect* folder. The project file is named Inspect.sln. If you execute the project file, you can find the algorithms for the calculations in NodeList.cs. Although the code is in C#, you can readily work with it if you know C or C++.

The Message Box

After using the ShellExectute() function to call *Inspect*, you call the MessageBox() function to display a message box. The message box serves as a transition from one application to another. If you intend to engage in frequent testing, you can comment out the message box code. *Inspect* grabs the data it requires when it opens, so you do not have to worry about loss of data.

Following your call to the MessageBox() function, your last task involves cleaning up. To clean up, you call the C library fclose() function. This function requires only one parameter, which identifies the file stream you have opened (m_fpOutput). This closes the file but does not destroy the data in it. Following the call to the fclose() function, you include a call to the fopen() function. This call to fopen() serves to clean up after one session of play and prepare for the next. At this point, the data file is blank.

Conclusion

In this chapter, you have examined a few of the topics that might be associated with testing simulations. This chapter has emphasized a model for simulation that includes event nodes and transitions. Each event node consists of a collection of decisions that establish relationships with other nodes, so you can consider any given node to be an event context. Using a little basic math and some systems diagrams, you can formulate approaches to assigning numerical values to nodes. Given this approach to modeling, it becomes evident that different nodes possess different levels of significance within the context of the system.

Just as nodes possess significance relative to their relationships with other nodes, the relationships between nodes gain significance relative to the values of the nodes they connect. You can refer to the relationships between nodes as transitions. While a transition from one node to another constitutes a simple path, paths within the logical system of a game usually consist of a number of sequentially connected transitions.

The collection of all the nodes in a system constitutes the total node significance of a system. If you compare the number of nodes you navigate through during a given scenario of play to the total number of nodes the system provides, you can determine the relative context value of your session of play. On the other hand, if you consider the paths you navigate during a session of play and compare the value of these paths with the value that represents all the paths the system provides, then you can determine the relative path value of a session of play.

Taken together, relative context value and relative path value allow you to determine the cognitive saturation of a session of play. Measuring the level of cognitive saturation provides you with a way to evaluate how much of the functionality of an application you use during a session of play. No strict standards apply to levels of cognitive saturation, but one general observation to begin with involves considering that if during repeated sessions of play you use only a low percentage of the functionality the system provides, then it might be worthwhile to alter the way you have laid out your game or simulation. You might want to add a few features that induce the user of the game or simulation to more comprehensively explore the features of the game.

This chapter includes a discussion of *Inspect*, an application that processes data generated from *Gold Finder*, the sample game developed in Chapter 9. Using *Inspect* to process data based on the messages generated during a session of play, you can see how levels of cognitive saturation change from session to session. Given a number of sessions of interaction, you can begin to assess whether an application adequately engages its users.

The following books address some of the topics discussed in this chapter:

Virginia Anderson and Lauren Johnson. *Systems Thinking Basics: From Concepts to Causal Loops* (Waltham, Massachusetts: Pegasus Communications, Inc., 1997).

Mat Buckland. *AI Techniques for Game Programming.* (Indianapolis, IN: Premier Press, 2002).

Alistair Cockburn. *Agile Software Development* (Boston: Addison-Wesley, 2002).

Jamshid Gharajedaghi. *Systems Thinking: Managing Chaos and Complexity* (Boston: Butterworth Heinemann, 1999).

Neal Hallford with Jana Hallford. *Swords and Circuitry: A Designer's Guide to Computer Role-Playing Games* (Indianapolis, IN: Premier Press, 2001).

Suguru Ishizaki. *Improvisational Design: Continuous, Responsive Digital Communication.* (Cambridge, Massachusetts: MIT Press, 2003).

Sun-Joo Shin. *The Iconic Logic of Peirce's Graphs* (Cambridge, Massachusetts: MIT Press, 2002).

INDEX

Gamedev.net

The most comprehensive game development resource

- The latest news in game development
- The most active forums and chatrooms anywhere, with insights and tips from experienced game developers
- Links to thousands of additional game development resources
- Thorough book and product reviews
- Over 1,000 game development articles!
  Game design
  Graphics
  DirectX
  OpenGL
  AI
  Art
  Music
  Physics
  Source Code
  Sound
  Assembly
  And More!

Gamedev.net